The Confederate Carpetbaggers

Daniel E. Sutherland

The Confederate
Carpetbaggers

Louisiana State University Press
Baton Rouge and London

Copyright © 1988 by Louisiana State University Press
All rights reserved
Manufactured in the United States of America

10   9   8   7   6   5   4   3   2   1

Designer: Laura Roubique Gleason
Typeface: Sabon
Typesetter: The Composing Room of Michigan
Printer: Thomson-Shore, Inc.
Binder: John H. Dekker & Sons, Inc.

Library of Congress Cataloging-in-Publication Data
Sutherland, Daniel E.
   The Confederate carpetbaggers / Daniel E. Sutherland.
      p.   cm.
   Bibliography: p.
   Includes index.
   ISBN 0-8071-1393-X. ISBN 0-8071-1470-7 (pbk.)
      1. Reconstruction. 2. Migration, Internal—United States—
History—19th century. 3. Southern States—Social conditions.
4. Southern States—History—1865–1877. I. Title. II. Title:
Carpetbaggers.
E668.S96   1988
975'.041—dc19

The author is grateful for permission to reproduce several passages that have appeared
in a somewhat different form in the following publications under the following titles:
"Virginia's Expatriate Artists: A Post–Civil War Odyssey," *Virginia Magazine of
History and Biography*, XCI (April, 1983), 131–60; "The Kentuckians in New York,"
Filson Club History Quarterly, LVII (October, 1983), 345–64; "Exiles, Emigrants, and
Sojourners: The Post–Civil War Confederate Exodus in Perspective," *Civil War
History*, XXXI (September, 1985), 237–56; "Southern Fraternal Organizations in the
North," *Journal of Southern History*, LIII (November, 1987).

To my parents and grandparents

Contents

Illustrations

Acknowledgments

One can accumulate a remarkable number of debts of gratitude after working on a project for ten years. Numerous scholars and friends have contributed advice, recommended sources, and supplied encouragement during those years. Grady McWhiney, always a courteous critic, wise counselor, and staunch friend, has done the most to shape my ideas about the Civil War, Reconstruction, and American history generally; but other people, if less influential, have been no less helpful. Thanks especially to the late Wayne Andrews, Fred A. Bailey, Barbara L. Bellows, Richard E. Beringer, Gary L. Browne, Joseph G. Dawson III, Joseph George, Jr., Herman Hattaway, Perry D. Jamieson, Ruth Currie McDaniel, Forrest McDonald, Penelope K. Majeske, George C. Rable, the late Jack Scroggs, and Goldwin Smith.

My colleagues at McNeese State University have not only proved exceedingly tolerant of my obsession over the past several years, they have also given timely assistance and valuable ideas. Thanks go to Carolyn E. DeLatte, Thomas Fox, and Thomas D. Watson. Joe Gray Taylor deserves special credit for patiently reading various drafts of the manuscript. Thanks also to Lisa Roberts for many hours spent counting numbers, drawing maps, and reading biographical sketches. Cindy Fontenot deserves thanks for her fine typing.

I want also to thank the many descendants of Confederate carpetbaggers and those twentieth-century southern emigrants to the North who have submitted to personal interviews or otherwise supplied me with invaluable information about themselves or their kin. Especially gracious were Russell Bailey, Louis Burford, John S. Chapman, Virginius Dabney, Walter G. Dunnington, Jr., Henry Field, William H. Fulkerson, Sadler Hayes, H. Harding Isaacson, Ashbel Green, Frederick O. McKenzie, Maynard H. Mires, Joseph J. O'Donohue IV, William C.

Read, Jr., James Lawrence Sprunt, Kerwin B. Stallings, K. Dwaine Williams, Orme Wilson, Jr., and Robert K. Young. I extend special thanks to Ursula Harrison Baird and Sally Harrison Dieke, grand-daughters of Burton and Constance Harrison, and to Mary Baird Gilbert, a great-granddaughter.

Innumerable librarians, archivists, and historical enthusiasts deserve thanks for their aid. They are far too numerous to mention by name. Suffice it to say that I have used materials from more than sixty institutions in twenty-three states and the District of Columbia, approximately two-thirds of them being manuscript depositories listed on the following page of abbreviations. I greatly appreciate the labor performed on my behalf by the people associated with these institutions. Additionally, I feel compelled to acknowledge six people, five of whom I have never met, who generously supplied me with rare sources of information. Thanks to Horace Fraser Rudisill for material about Esther B. Cheesborough; Hugh Buckner Johnston, Jr., and J. Robert Boykin III for material about Charles Force Deems; Ben Ritter for material about Charles Rouss; Richard T. Lemal and H. Harding Isaacson (once more) for information about the New York Southern Society; and Marjorie Dintelmann for material about Confederate carpetbaggers in Illinois.

I also appreciate the diligence and sharp eye of Trudie Calvert, my copy editor for Louisiana State University Press.

Finally, I would be inexcusably remiss if I failed to acknowledge the financial support given to me by the National Endowment for the Humanities, the American Association for State and Local History, and McNeese State University. And thanks to Kim for trying to handle Christopher while I was away on all those research trips.

Abbreviations

LC   Library of Congress, Washington, D.C.

LSU Department of Archives and History, Louisiana State
     University, Baton Rouge

MHS Maryland Historical Society, Baltimore

MOHS Missouri Historical Society, St. Louis

MSA Mississippi Department of Archives and History, Jackson

NCA North Carolina Department of Archives and History,
     Raleigh

NYHS New York Historical Society, New York City

NYPL New York Public Library, New York City

OHS Ohio Historical Society, Columbus

SCHS South Carolina Historical Society, Charleston

SCL South Caroliniana Library, University of South Carolina,
     Columbia

SHC Southern Historical Collection, University of North
     Carolina at Chapel Hill

TL   Tennessee State Library and Archives, Nashville

TU   Howard-Tilton Memorial Library, Tulane University, New
     Orleans, Louisiana

UA   William Stanley Hook Special Collections Library,
     University of Alabama, Tuscaloosa

UF   Yonge Library of Florida History, University of Florida,
     Gainesville

UG   University of Georgia Library, Athens

UK   King Library, University of Kentucky, Lexington

UT   Barker Texas History Center, University of Texas, Austin

UV   Alderman Library, University of Virginia, Charlottesville

VHS Virginia Historical Society, Richmond

VL   Virginia State Library, Richmond

VM   Valentine Museum, Richmond

VU   Vanderbilt University Library, Nashville, Tennessee

WHS Winchester-Frederick County Historical Society, Winchester, Virginia

WK Kentucky Library, Western Kentucky University, Bowling Green

YU Sterling Library, Yale University, New Haven, Connecticut

The Confederate Carpetbaggers

Prologue

Waiting for Something to Turn Up

I was struck several years ago by a remark made to me by an elderly southern lady. "Any southerner with ambition," she said sadly but knowingly, "will leave the South." This woman was not a student of history. She had not been analyzing demographic curves or trends in population shifts. She had simply stated a fact of southern life that has been accepted as common wisdom since before the Civil War. Southerners have been leaving the South for generations, moving west and north in search of what they vaguely conceive to be a better life. Americans as a whole are famous for their restlessness, their mobility. Alexis de Tocqueville recognized the passion; Horace Greeley sanctified it. Millions of Americans each decade desert the states and regions of their birth, but southern Americans seem always to have led the way. In no other part of the country is the habit rooted so firmly in tradition or considered so necessary by young people who wish to make something of themselves. Education, culture, wealth, excitement, fame: southerners have associated all of these with northern residence. An antebellum southern mother urged her son, a promising young engineer, to move to a free state. Virginia, she sighed regretfully, was "a good place to hail from but a bad place to live." Wilbur J. Cash, that brilliant if erratic dissector of the southern mind, lamented the vitality of this tradition into the mid-twentieth century. Since Reconstruction, observed Cash, the South's rush to the West and North had drained the region of its "most energetic and intelligent elements," its "strength and brains."[1]

1. U.S. Bureau of the Census, *The Statistical History of the United States from Colonial Times to the Present* (New York, 1976), Ser. Cl-14; James H. Justus, "On the Restlessness of Southerners," *Southern Review*, XI (1975), 65–83; Jack Temple Kirby, "The Southern Exodus, 1910–1960: A Primer for Historians," *Journal of Southern History*, XLIX (1983), 585–600; L. Minor Blackford, *Mine Eyes Have Seen the Glory: The Story of a Virginia Lady, Mary Berkeley Minor Blackford, 1802–1896* (Cambridge, Mass., 1954), 104; Wilbur J. Cash, *The Mind of the South* (New York, 1941), 277, 319–21.

Given this penchant for escape, there would seem to be nothing re-markable about the flight of any particular generation of southerners. Yet the exodus of the South's Civil War generation, its Confederate generation, holds elements of drama, irony, and tragedy not found in other southern migrations. No other generation had more reason to escape the South, yet no other generation presumably had so little chance of success in the larger world. Civil wars are terrible things. They poison a nation; they leave physical and psychological scars. It is hard to forgive a bitter foe the murder of husbands, brothers, fathers, and friends. True, many Americans, North and South, had grown weary of war by 1865. They welcomed peace, if not immediate reconciliation. But who could have predicted what happened next. Some astute ob-server may have anticipated a rush of Yankee speculators to the South, but no one foresaw a migration from south to north. What audacity, what foolhardiness; what courage, what impertinence; what boldness, what naiveté. Confederate generals and congressmen walking the streets of New York and Chicago only weeks after Lee's surrender? Impossible. Former slaveowners seeking jobs, loans, and investment opportunities in towns and cities across the North? Fantastic. Yet thou-sands of Confederates—no one knows for sure how many—burst the bonds of constrained expectations to join the northward trek.

About sixteen thousand southerners settled in Yankeedom between 1860 and 1870, and several thousand more joined them during the next decade. It is impossible to say what portion of these emigrants had fought for southern independence. Census takers, who tabulated the numbers, identify people according to their place of birth, not their political sympathies, and a good number of Unionists—southerners who opposed secession, slavery, and the war—moved north during and after the conflict. This book, however, is about Confederates, and one senses that they formed at least half of the postwar migration. I have been able to identify 1,068 Confederates who moved north between 1861 and 1880. I have based my conclusions about Confederate emi-gration to the North on their lives. Of these 1,068, I have accumulated enough biographical information about 571 people—referred to here-after as the "core group"—to draw a fairly complete statistical portrait of the typical Confederate carpetbagger (see Appendix).[2]

2. U.S. Bureau of the Census, *Population of the United States in 1860* (Washington, D.C., 1864), 41, 104, 130, 156, 207, 227, 248, 262, 310, 319, 346, 398, 439, 445, 498, 544, *Ninth Census of the United States: Population* (Washington, D.C., 1872), I, 328–42, *Tenth Census of the United States: Population* (Washington, D.C., 1883), I, 480–95.

The appellation *Confederate carpetbagger* may cause some scholars to blanch. The term *carpetbagger,* long applied with unflattering connotation to Yankees who moved South after the Civil War, has acquired a very narrow meaning. Most scholars now accept Richard N. Current's "nonevaluational" definition of a carpetbagger as a white northerner who went South after 1860 and became involved in southern politics as a Republican before the end of Reconstruction. Professor Current justifies his political definition by showing that postwar southerners defined carpetbaggers in this manner. He also insists that many carpetbaggers, contrary to the historical image of profiteers, villains, thieves, and scoundrels affixed to them by generations of southerners, were honest, well-intentioned men, not bent on destroying or punishing the South. This is a useful definition and a desirable modification of the term's pejorative meaning.[3]

Yet by adhering religiously to this political definition, we sacrifice other equally valid meanings of the word. By permitting lifeless definitions to obscure real people, we sadly dilute the spirit of adventure, the mad dash in search of the "big chance" that inspired so many northerners to go south and that must remain central to understanding the motives of any carpetbagger. Adelbert Ames, the New England–born Reconstruction governor of Mississippi, recognized a number of nonpolitical implications of the term *carpetbagger,* which he used to designate "men whose experiences during the war taught them they could by changing their locations better their conditions." Confederates moved north for the same reason. Ames also found a universality in the word that transcends the confines of southern political history. "What an audacious, pushing crowd carpet-baggers are," he confided to his wife in describing how a band of local wheeler-dealers seized control of the race track at Mississippi's annual fair. "From the day Columbus imposed upon the simple Indians of this continent to this act of capturing a State Fair they have not permitted quiet folk, or any other as far as that matter, to have a moment's peace." As will be seen, Confederates in the North sometimes referred to each other as carpetbaggers, and northerners, including Ames, did not fail to dub them such on occasion.[4]

Perhaps a more important criterion than political involvement in

3. Richard N. Current, "Carpetbaggers Reconsidered," in David H. Pinkney and Theodore Ropp (eds.), *A Festschrift for Frederick B. Artz* (Durham, 1964), 139–57.

4. *House Reports,* 42nd Cong., 2nd Sess., No. 22, pp. 743, 1097, 1710; Blanche Butler Ames (comp.), *Chronicles from the Nineteenth Century: Family Letters of Blanche Butler and Adelbert Ames* (2 vols.; Clinton, Mass., 1957), I, 253–54, 258, 386, II, 46–47.

defining a carpetbagger should be continued loyalty to one's native section, whether that loyalty be expressed in cherished political "principles" or nonpolitical sectional values and traditions. The majority of Confederates who moved north did not become active in party politics. Yet insofar as these people sought to improve their social and financial fortunes while remaining loyal to their native South, the term *carpetbagger* seems eminently descriptive. Insofar as most emigrants remained proud of their Confederate heritage and continued to believe in the rightness of the Confederate cause, they can only be regarded as Confederate carpetbaggers.

To relate the unfamiliar to the familiar, it may be useful to think of the southern-bred species of carpetbagger as a close cousin of a fictional character well known to students of southern history and literature: Ashley Wilkes. In *Gone with the Wind,* indisputably the most famous stereotypical account of the Old South and the southern condition during Reconstruction, Ashley Wilkes, *beau ideal* of southern manhood, contemplates moving to New York City after the war. "Yes," he tells Scarlett O'Hara, "I've decided to go North. An old friend who made the Grand Tour with me before the war has offered me a position in his father's bank." This episode occurs when Scarlett, still hopeful of inflaming our hero's passion and claiming him for her lover, seeks to persuade Ashley to help her operate a lumber mill in Atlanta. She succeeds ultimately in doing so, and Ashley remains in Georgia.[5]

Had Ashley gone north, he would have been a fairly typical Confederate carpetbagger. Though a planter by inheritance, he was far from being one by vocation. Ashley felt more inclined toward the business or professional world. More important, Ashley Wilkes intended to rebuild the South as an *American* rather than as a partisan southerner. Likewise, he realized, in the tradition of true Confederate carpetbagging, that the North offered opportunities for effecting this rebuilding that, for the moment, had been stifled in the South. Ashley was a realist, a man with a vision but with a sober view of how best to achieve that vision. Ashley never denounced the Confederacy or regretted his defense of southern honor. He laid down his sword willingly but not in shame. He simply understood that, whatever its merits, the Confederate cause had died at Appomattox. As Ashley's creator wrote of him to a literary critic, "I have become somewhat weary of reading reviews which call Ashley 'weak,' 'idealistic,' 'a dreamer,' 'a coward,' *et cetera.* I never thought of

5. Margaret Mitchell, *Gone with the Wind* (New York, 1938), 725.

him in this way and always considered him the greatest realist in the book because his eyes, like those of Rhett, were always open." Ashley understood what resources the South required to survive the rigors of Reconstruction and what individual southerners must do to survive in the New South and a new nation.[6]

Ashley's reason for wanting to go north was characteristic, too. "I want to stand on my own feet for what I'm worth," he tells Scarlett. "What have I done with my life, up till now? It's time I made something of myself—or went down through my own fault."

"But I don't understand!" Scarlett cries in protest. "If it's work you want, why won't Atlanta do as well as New York?"

"No Scarlett," he replies. "This is my last chance. I'll go North. If I go to Atlanta and work for you, I'm lost forever."

Ashley's plan distresses Scarlett: "The words 'lost—lost—lost' dinged frighteningly in her heart like a death bell sounding. Her eyes went quickly to his but they were wide and crystal gray and they were looking through her and beyond her at some fate she could not see, could not understand."

Ashley Wilkes, then, like those real-life southerners who did go north, feared being "lost," buried in a postwar South threatened by Yankee carpetbaggers, scalawags, freedmen, Scarlett O'Haras, and all else they regarded as unholy, unwholesome, and unpredictable. Few men could have survived a plague like Scarlett, and, though it tests the imagination, some circumstances of southern life in the years after the war made even Scarlett seem like a minor irritation.[7]

Before all else, one must appreciate the confusion that followed Confederate defeat. An angry pause descended upon the land. The stillness of history struck different people at different times, in different places, depending on when the news of surrender overcame them and when they decided that this gloomy report, unlike so many previous ones, was not rumor but the harshest of truths. The effect, momentarily gut-wrenching, paralyzed, immobilized them. For some people, the moment lasted only a few hours. For others, it dragged on over the course of days, weeks, years, lifetimes. Some people, in their response, resembled cresting waves. They rose silently, majestically, in breathless, tantalizing

6. Richard Harwell (ed.), *Margaret Mitchell's "Gone with the Wind" Letters, 1936–1949* (New York, 1976), 120–21.

7. Mitchell, *Gone with the Wind*, 725–26; Daniel E. Sutherland, "Southern Carpetbaggers in the North; or, Ashley Wilkes, Where Are You Now?" *McNeese Review*, XXIV (1977–78), 9, 16–17.

pause before crashing violently on the rocks in determined action. Less resolute people slid slowly back into reality, not as waves crashing on rocks but as leaves ripped forcibly from branches by a ferocious gale. Suspended for an instant in midair, they did not plummet to earth. Rather, they floated, swirled, and weaved in syncopated patterns that deposited each soul in a different spot at a different moment, some right side up, some upside down, some caught in crevices of rocks, some blown unpredictably across the landscape until the storm subsided.

Determined, relentless folk, the crashers on rocks were likely devotees of Sir Walter Scott. Scott, who has often been credited with helping to shape the antebellum southern mind, would appeal to them. Honor, chivalry, inbred traits of character that required no thought or contemplation, only action, would decide their response to defeat. They made immediate decisions about the future. They would stand by the South; they would sell their property and move north; they would flee to Mexico. Whatever their choice, these people did not stick at trifles. They decided soon after the war what course to set, which path to follow.

Most former Confederates floated and drifted. However much political and economic circumstances may have required flight, however forlorn the hope of prospering or even living peacefully in the South, people could not lightly desert family and friends, the buried bones of parents and grandparents, the familiar hills and meadows of childhood, the suffering comrades and sacred soil for which they had risked their lives. Ashley Wilkes hung "in a state of suspended animation" for several months after the war, a floater and drifter of the highest order. Other Confederates paused too. They dallied, they inquired, they contemplated past, present, and future as few people ever do.[8]

Perhaps they read, not Walter Scott but Charles Dickens. Certainly southerners had more than a passing acquaintance with Dickens' serial episodes of *David Copperfield*. Wilkens Micawber, not Ivanhoe, haunted the postwar South. Dickens' grand procrastinator—his grand survivor—served as guide, counsel, and inspiration for many depressed Confederates. Micawber's eternal prediction that something would soon "turn up" resonated through the land. "I am at a loss what to do, in fact there is nothing left for me to do, but to wait quietly here until something turns up," fretted a Missouri Confederate in May, 1865. "I have delayed writing," confessed a Georgian to his father, "hoping that something would turn up." "I hope something will turn up for both of us

8. Mitchell, *Gone with the Wind*, 725–26.

soon," wrote a Texan who admitted that his "Macauber spirit" was "well nigh exhausted." "So you see, my friend," explained an Alabamian, "like most of my neighbors I have no very settled plans for the future but live in a Micauber-like state of expectancy of what may 'turn-up' in this Congress-ridden land."[9]

What would turn up, when, how, or where it would turn up, no one knew; but most people hesitated to move, to make any decision, without first seeing how the winds of fortune might blow. Like Micawber, southerners in the previous four years had spent more lavishly—in both human and monetary terms—than they could afford. The interest rates of war are uncompromising. Now they must pay the human and physical debts of a conquered people. Yet, again like Micawber, they refused to surrender totally to their grief and anxiety. If the past held sorrow and smashed dreams, the future meant sunny hopes. Despite doubts about the future, southerners dared to hope, all the while keeping an eye to events and anticipating what their response should be.

9. William M. McPheeters Diary, May 26, 1865 (MS in William B. McPheeters Papers, MOHS); Valerius Wynne to Alfred R. Wynne, October 8, 1866, in Wynne Family Papers, TL; Wash L. Hill to Stevenson Archer, February 22, 1869, in Archer Family Letters, MHS; T. W. Hall to Burton N. Harrison, March 19, 1867, in Burton Norvell Harrison Family Papers, LC.

1

Looking for a Home

It is spring, 1865. The southern Confederacy shudders in its death throes. Most of its armies have disbanded. "You will go home now," a kindly Virginia woman reminds a bedraggled Mississippi soldier, still numbed by the finality of defeat. "Home!" he chokes out, his voice cracking, his eyes glistening; "home—alas! Mother earth is my only couch and the canopy of the heavens my covering. What was once a home is now a monumental ruin. I have no home, unless it be in the hearts of kind and generous friends."[1]

The precise scene is probably apocryphal, but its spirit was universal. Confederate soldiers wandering homeward after Appomattox entered a new world. Everything had changed; they themselves had changed. Lads of twenty returned witnesses to death and carnage unimaginable in a normal lifetime. Missing limbs and bandaged wounds bore silent testament to their combat, yet veterans betrayed the deepest scars, the ones etched on their souls, by vacant expressions in haunted eyes. They stared at houses and barns gutted, gardens and fields grown wild, fences and sheds flattened or spent for firewood. Even people whose houses had not been physically destroyed sensed the loss of something equally precious: the happiness and security that define a home, the emotional and spiritual roots that anchor it, the sense of community that nourishes it.

Imagination, pushed to extremes by fear of the unknown, distorted the future. The Confederacy had been a military state; war was its profession. Rebel soldiers and civilians had borne wartime casualties, destruction, and misery with a spirit of sacrifice. The war had been a nightmare, but with the accompanying sense that the ugliness and car-

1. *Metropolitan Record and New York Vindicator,* June 30, 1867, p. 4.

nage of war would seem slight once the dream had passed. To find that one nightmare only led to another, different vision of horror became too much to bear. With no money to rebuild and scant food to nourish the rebuilders, former Confederates despaired of their ability to control the South's destiny. Tens of thousands of dispirited people chose exile over defeat and humiliation. They fled north to Canada, east to Europe, south to Latin America, west to California. Their exodus, like patches in a quilt, assumed different patterns and sported varied colors, but all the pieces fit neatly together. To appreciate the brilliantly colored and ingeniously patterned patch of carpetbagger settlement in the northern states, one would do well first to examine the entire fabric.

It is not easy to think simultaneously of what might have been and what will be. One or the other must win out, and so it came to pass that former Confederates, in their season of uncertainty, became alert to the possibility of mass exodus. They seemed possessed, driven, victims of some dread fever that mounted through 1865 and reached epidemic proportions by 1866. People spoke of "Texas fever," "Mexico fever," "Brazilian fever." A frenzy not witnessed since "gold fever" had sent Americans streaming to Sutter's Fort in 1849 swept through the South. Excitement and restlessness pervaded the air. The correspondence of bruised, broken, and bewildered Confederates overflowed with speculation and inquiries about the prospects for emigration. People who were not themselves thinking of leaving knew someone who was. "Does anybody in your country have the Mexico fever?" a Georgia woman asked her sister in Tennessee. Another Georgian inquired of his friend: "Have you any authentic news from Honduras? What of it and what have you determined on? How would California do? We are now receiving direct intelligence from our friends in Brazil all doing well and highly pleased." A Virginian claimed that one hundred to one thousand families in the vicinity of Lynchburg were eager to go to Brazil. A South Carolinian estimated that five thousand people in his state spoke of exodus. People not inclined to emigrate marveled as the "expatriation mania" seized "many of the most intelligent, spirited, and useful of the Southern people."[2]

2. Carrie Stakely to Martha Hall, January 25, 1866, in Hall-Stakely Family Papers, KPL; J. T. Magruder to William W. Fergusson, January 7, 1868, in Fergusson Family Papers, TL; Valerius Wynne to Alfred R. Wynne, October 8, 1868, in Wynne Family Papers, TL; Douglass A. Grier, "Confederate Emigration to Brazil, 1865–1870" (Ph.D. dissertation, University of Michigan, 1968), 23; *Metropolitan Record and New York Vindicator*, February 3, 1866, p. 3.

So rampant, so contagious did this fever become that people rushed blindly for distant shores. Even organized groups of colonists seldom followed logical plans in proceeding or knew what to expect once they reached their destinations. People followed impulse, gut reaction. Their instincts said "flee"—flee the gloating Yankees, flee the uppity freedmen, flee devasted lands, flee everything that reminded them of their lost world and shattered dreams. In the earliest exodus, that to Mexico, Confederate soldiers who had been stationed in the Southwest plunged across the Rio Grande without even visiting their old southern homes. Consequently, one Virginian en route to Mexico with a group led by General John G. Walker admitted that his plans remained "indefinite & inchoate." "Everybody seems to vacillate now," he confided to his diary in describing the general attitude. "No one seems to have any decided plan of action." Later emigrants, if not so totally at sixes and sevens, would nonetheless frequently regret their precipitous flight.[3]

Some people predicted disaster, for they understood the deeper significance of the exodus. Cautious souls feared nothing less than the extinction of southern civilization, southern identity, perhaps even the southern people. "What do you think will become of the Southern States?" asked a Missourian of a friend. "That is one thing that causes me considerable reflection." "The men are all talking about going to Mexico and Brazil," fretted a Georgia girl just a fortnight after Robert E. Lee's surrender; "if all emigrate who say they are going to, we shall have a nation made up of women, negroes, and Yankees." One old gentleman, saddened, disheartened, and totally disillusioned by Confederate defeat, shuddered to think of the South's fate. "It is difficult to determine," he lamented, "what is to become of our poor Southern people. I much fear they will scatter and become merged & lost among the various nations among whom they may settle." He could not bear to think what the ultimate consequences of exodus might be. "It is deplorable to contemplate," he concluded, "this wiping out of the South as a people."[4]

3. Douglas French Forrest, *Odyssey in Gray: A Diary of Confederate Service, 1863–1865*, ed. William N. Still, Jr. (Richmond, 1979), 310, 317, entries of May 21, June 4, 1865; Joseph O. Shelby to R. J. Lawrence, February 2, 1866, in Civil War Papers, MOHS; Whitelaw Reid, *After the War: A Southern Tour, May 1, 1865 to May 1, 1866* (New York, 1866), 211, 374.

4. Eliza Frances Andrews, *War-Time Journal of a Georgia Girl, 1864–1865*, ed. Spencer Bidwell King, Jr. (Macon, 1960), 184, entry of April 25, 1865; Claude Baxley to Matthew F. Maury, September 1, 1865, in Matthew Fontaine Maury Papers, LC; J. W. Wilson to John F. Snyder, December 7, 1866, in John F. Snyder Papers, IHL.

Much of the South's civilian population had entered this homeless condition four years earlier. Noncombatants had been set in motion by the first threat of northern invasion, and by war's end tens of thousands of southern women, children, and old men formed a new social class: the refugees. Seeking to escape advancing Union forces, these southerners became more mobile than some Confederate armies. They wandered aimlessly through the South and sometimes fled to foreign shores. "Half the world is refugeeing," testified a Georgia girl, and so it must have seemed. Wartime refugees returned to their homes in the spring of 1865—all, that is, who could return. Many people were delayed. Roads became clogged, not only with homesick refugees but with Union occupation forces, returning Confederate veterans, and roaming freedmen. Some people lacked the means, either financial or physical, to return home immediately. Still others, anticipating dangers, simply hesitated until the future became more certain. Refugees who returned home hoped to recapture the sense of community denied them by the war, but not a few people were disappointed. "This homeless existence," explained a weary sojourner who found his plantation house in ashes, "is worse than refugeeing, for then we had excitement attendant to war, and hope of a glorious future to sustain us. Now the present is dreary and comfortless, we can but mourn our dear lost cause, and sicken at the remembrance of the sea of blood shed in vain." These dejected folk often continued to wander.[5]

Yet the necessity of finding new homes became only an expression and a focus of more far-reaching discontent. Confederates who feared imprisonment and possibly execution as "traitors" believed exile to be literally a matter of life and death. Confederate cabinet members Judah P. Benjamin and Robert Toombs escaped imprisonment by fleeing to Europe. General Edmund Kirby Smith resolved, in his words, "to place the Rio Grande between myself & harm." Former Louisiana governor Henry Watkins Allen intended to stay in Mexico until assured of a pardon or "guarantee" that he would not be "cast into prison or otherwise persecuted." An obscure young naval officer, upon learning that Raphael Semmes, legendary commander of the Confederate raider *Alabama,* had been arrested for piracy, feared the same treatment. He roamed the world for one and a half years before returning to the United States. Two Kentuckians who had served as Confederate agents in Can-

5. Daniel E. Sutherland, "Looking for a Home: Louisiana Emigrants During the Civil War and Reconstruction," *Louisiana History,* XXI (1980), 341–46; Mary Elizabeth Massey, *Refugee Life in the Confederacy* (Baton Rouge, 1964), 4, 11–47, 263–67, 270–71.

ada decided that "in view of the summary hanging of people" in their state they would head west and seek employment "under assumed names." "Our family has taken too prominent a part in our struggle to be allowed to remain here even if they did not prefer to expatriate themselves rather than be ruled by Yankees," explained a Texan. One family member, already in Cuba, would probably move on to Europe. Two others had settled in Mexico, and a fourth intended flight to France or Italy.[6]

Relatively few Confederates actually feared for their lives, but many believed southern pride and honor dictated exodus. Unreconstructed rebels, even if their lives or freedom were not in jeopardy, could not tolerate the thought of living under Yankee rule. "We are turning our eyes to the little Confederate colonies of Mexico as future homes for exiles from the oppression of the Yankees," wrote an Alabamian. A Virginian who had served in both the Confederate army and navy declared, "There is *no* reason why I should put myself in the hands of the loathed Yankees." He headed for Mexico. John Slidell, Confederate commissioner to France, remained in Europe after the war with no thought of returning "home." "Nothing could induce me ever to become a citizen of the U.S.," he wrote to his counterpart in England, James Mason, "nor will any of my children, I trust, ever establish themselves there." Slidell advised no one to return to the United States who had means or connections to live elsewhere. Jacob Thompson, resident in Canada, declared: "To be ruled by Negroes is bad enough, but to be ruled by vile abolitionists is intolerable." "I think it would be best for us all to move to Texas," concluded a disheartened soul "—perhaps we might find a quiet home in South America. I cannot live in peace under Yankee rule." "This is no place for me," agreed another Virginian after surveying his native state. "I would rather earn a scanty livelihood elsewhere indeed anywhere else than make a fortune here. Already I can scarcely stand the Yankees who surround me on every side."[7]

6. Robert Douthat Meade, *Judah P. Benjamin: Confederate Statesman* (New York, 1943), 331; William Y. Thompson, *Robert Toombs of Georgia* (Baton Rouge, 1966), 219–25; Joseph Howard Parks, *General Edmund Kirby Smith, C.S.A.* (Baton Rouge, 1954), 481; Henry W. Allen to A Friend, February 10, 1866, in Sarah A. Dorsey, *Recollections of Henry Watkins Allen* (New York, 1866), 357–58; John Grimball to John B. Grimball, January 3, 27, 1866, both in John Berkley Grimball Papers, DU; John W. Headley, *Confederate Operations in Canada and New York City* (New York, 1906), 449; Fanny Baylor to Virginia L. King, June 7, 1865, Thomas Butler King Papers, SHC.

7. Joseph Hodgson to Richard L. Maury, February 18, 1866, in Maury Papers; Forrest, *Odyssey in Gray*, 3–7, 322, entries of June 4, 24, 1865; John Slidell to James M. Mason,

Belligerence and bitterness marked the countenances of these Confederates. Some men in flight to Mexico even flirted with the idea of reforming Confederate armies and launching an invasion of the United States from Mexico or the Southwest. An especially large number of Confederate generals fled to Mexico. Rumors said that at least one of these officers, Sterling Price, had been commissioned by the puppet regime of Archduke Ferdinand Maximilian to raise an army of 100,000 Confederates to face Philip Sheridan's force along the Rio Grande. Edmund Kirby Smith stood ready to lead ten thousand men into Mexico if the emperor would accept their services. John Bankhead Magruder told his troops that he would rather live with the Comanches than "bow the knee to Yankeedom." He hinted that French military aid might be made available to Confederates through the Mexican government. Jubal Early rushed to Mexico hoping "there might be war with the U.S." A Virginian thought Mexico a good place to make a modest living and "bide the time" until he might again meet the South's enemies in battle. "I hate the infernal Yankee worse than I ever did," he admitted.[8]

Disgust with their own people further embittered some diehards. A popular guidebook encouraging emigration to Brazil declared that the Confederacy had been betrayed by its own politicians, and its author accused many of those same men of ingratiating themselves with the postwar federal regime. Other people expressed anger at the refusal of fellow rebels to continue their fight against the hated Yankee. "What a shame on this country," wrote a Louisiana planter, "eight million of people, whipped, subdued, thoroughly subjugated in four years of war! I disown this cowardly people. I will leave the country as soon as this side caves in; I am bound for Brazil." Jubal Early, who spent time in Mexico and Cuba before ending up in Canada, informed his brother,

October 7, 1866, in Louis Martin Sears, *John Slidell* (Durham, 1925), 231; Grier, "Confederate Emigration to Brazil," 93–94; Jacob Thompson to James M. Howry, October 8, 1867, in Percy L. Rainwater (ed.), "Letters to and from Jacob Thompson," *Journal of Southern History,* XI (1940), 107; George W. Munford to Elizabeth Munford, May 9, 1865, Munford-Ellis Family Papers, DU.

8. Forrest, *Odyssey in Gray,* 312–13, entry of May 24, 1865; *Senate Executive Documents,* 39th Cong., 1st Sess., No. 8, p. 34; Robert E. Shalhope, *Sterling Price: Portrait of a Southerner* (Columbia, Mo., 1971), 281–90; Parks, *General Edmund Kirby Smith,* 458; *Metropolitan Record and New York Vindicator,* May 27, 1865, pp. 3, 9; Jubal A. Early to T. L. Rosser, May 10, 1866, in William D. Hoyt, Jr. (ed.), "New Light on General Jubal A. Early After Appomattox," *Journal of Southern History,* IX (1943), 115; Richard Maury to Matthew F. Maury, June 18, 1865, in Maury Papers.

"The rebels that go home are treated well by the Yankee soldiers but badly by *Union men.*" "I cannot but be disgusted," Early grumbled on another occasion, "at the self-abasement of some of our public men." Emigration to Venezuela appealed to an old gentleman who believed southerners had "lost all pride of state" and were "pandering" to the new political regime. "Oh! that I were young and buoyant again," he cried; "I would adopt a new land to transfer all my fond affections."[9]

Confederate veterans who hailed from Unionist strongholds in East Tennessee, West Virginia, Missouri, and Kentucky received icy receptions from the home folk. "When I went home," recalled one Tennessean, "the people who had been in the Union army were so bitter that I had to leave home. I went first to Ga. Then to Texas and stayed until the bitter feeling had passed away to some extent." Other Tennesseans experienced the same treatment. One man told of whippings and murders by Unionist bushwhackers. "It was very unsafe," he claimed; "nearly all the Rebels in our neighborhood had to leave for protection." A Kentuckian complained that "a bitter feeling between neighbors" still prevailed in many regions of the state. Fear of reprisals spread through Confederate ranks in West Virginia, where Unionist newspapers warned Confederate veterans that they returned home at their own risk.[10]

Other people, equally anxious to leave, did not fear or despise the Yankee as conqueror, but they were pessimistic about the South's future. Most apprehensions stemmed not so much from the South's political plight as from its economic and social predicament. Southerners voiced the same fears immediately after the war, when the nature of the federal government's Reconstruction program was still undecided, as they did in 1867, after the Reconstruction Acts had become law. "I am thoroughly impoverished like all who stood faithful to our cause," wrote a Tennessean in 1865 to a friend who had already fled to Mexico, "and like them I have no fortune—disfranchised, an object of constant suspicion, I am an exile and a stranger at my own home." "Knowing our

9. Ballard S. Dunn, *Brazil, the Home for Southerners* (New York, 1866), iii–iv; Louis A. Bringier to wife, May 11, 1865, in Louis A. Bringier and Family Papers, LSU; Jubal A. Early to Samuel H. Early, June 1, 1865, August 21, 1866, in Jubal A. Early Papers, LC; J. T. Magruder to William M. Fergusson, August 15, 1867, in Fergusson Family Papers.

10. Augustus Henry Gothard and Franklin Sevier Leonard, in Civil War Questionnaires (Confederate), TL; Alden B. Pearson, Jr., "A Middle-Class, Border-State Family During the Civil War," *Civil War History,* XXII (1970), 335; Headley, *Confederate Operations in Canada and New York,* 440; Penelope K. Majeske, "Virginia After Appomattox: The United States Army and the Formation of Presidential Reconstruction Policy," *West Virginia History,* XLII (1982), 100–101.

situation and the condition of the country," wrote a Louisianian in 1867, "you will not be surprised to hear that the Genl and the rest of us have begun to turn our eyes towards Brazil—the Land of Promise." "I left, as you know," wrote an Alabamian from San Domingo in 1869, "because of anarchy, which I expected to prevail—of the poverty that was already at our doors and the demoralization which I thought and still believe will surely cover the land." The principal cause of Confederate exodus to Venezuela seems to have been widespread despair with the "new order." A Virginia lawyer headed for Texas because he could not bear the destruction and gloom of his home state.[11]

How to make a living, how to eat, were the problems facing returning veterans. Investment opportunities, cheap farmland, jobs, work of any kind became magnets for emigrants. A young naval officer stranded in France heard much talk about the financial field awaiting Confederates in Mexico. "That appears to offer the best chance for a man to settle and become rich," he decided in June, 1865, "for now that I have lost my country, I must have something to occupy my ambition as well as to give me a position in life." "This country is completely broken down," lamented a Texan; "no money in it and no business done. Every thing at a stand still. . . . Every prospect is that things will get worse." "I am very anxious to leave this country," confessed a young Canada-bound Virginian, "and get something to do at once . . . and contribute to the support of our family." A number of Virginia lawyers went west because test oaths and the abridgment of civil rights prohibited them from practicing their profession in the South.[12]

A North Carolinian summed up the situation. In a long letter to his

11. James D. Porter, Jr. to Thomas K. Porter, August 20, 1865, in George Bibb Edmondson Papers—Porter Family Correspondence, AA; Moses I. Liddell to J. Andrew Liddell, May 28, 1867, in Liddell Family Papers, LSU; John W. Keyes to Colonel Hawthorne, November 16, 1969, in Julia Louisa (Hentz) Keyes Diary (MS in AA), 95–96; Alfred Jackson Hanna and Kathryn Abbey Hanna, *Confederate Exiles in Venezuela* (Tuscaloosa, 1960), 13–14; Edmund P. Turner to Edward C. Wharton, September 9, 1865, in Edward Clifton Wharton and Family Papers, LSU.

12. C. V. Berrien to George Barnsley, January 17, 1866, George Barnsley to George S. Barnsley, April 9, 1868, both in Barnsley Family Papers, TL; Maggie N. Tucker to Maggie and Sallie Munford, October 9, 1865, in Munford-Ellis Family Papers; Thomas K. Porter to Mrs. Alexander Hall, June 16, 1865, Edmondson Papers; Steven Archer to Hannah Archer, September 11, 1867, in Archer Family Papers, MHS; Beverley D. Tucker to Charles Ellis, August 20, 1865, in Munford-Ellis Family Papers; A. Fred Fleet to mother, January 29, 1867, in Betsy Fleet (ed.), *Green Mount After the War: The Correspondence of Maria Louisa Wacker Fleet and Her Family, 1865–1900* (Charlottesville, 1978), 24.

brother, a blockade runner who found sanctuary in England, he described the deplorable state of business in their state. Stay in England, he urged, until business prospects took more definite shape. Many local merchants spoke of commencing business, but they built their plans more on hope and desperation than on solid expectations. Yankee merchants and speculators were already pouring into the state, and they would doubtless capture a large share of the retail and investment markets. "The self-expatriated Americans in Europe need sympathy from all true and noble hearts and no doubt they have that sympathy to an eminent degree, no country, no homes, exiles and wanderers upon the face of the earth, their fate is indeed to be commiserated," concluded the North Carolinian, "but still how much better off they are than we, here, in our once happy sunny South, *once happy,* but now the present and future to us is any thing but pleasant, crushed and ground down by an over-whelming military despotism." What exile would dare think of returning home in the face of such a report?[13]

A closely associated and age-old cause of emigration also spurred Confederate flight: adventure. One might suppose that four years of war would have dampened the appetite of even the most hearty spirits for further excitement, but it was not so. The hope of rallying Confederate forces west of the Mississippi justified strategic retreat for many veterans. The alluring image of romantic, tropical paradises in Latin America—rich in gold said some reports—transfixed others. Opportunities for speculation in real estate, mining, and business ventures in the West and Europe seemed more promising than life in Virginia or Georgia. A Louisianian reported hordes of southerners streaming into San Francisco. Most of these refugees were distinguished, he remarked sarcastically, by the "true characteristics of southerners, generous, kind, and consequently poor." He added, however, that opportunistic people, "sordid and selfish enough to put to shame the veriest Yankee peddlar," had made fortunes. People in less settled regions compared their experiences with those of their pioneer ancestors on the early American frontier. A South Carolinian sensed the spirit of these daring and adventurous types. They were, he said, behaving as Americans, "a migratory people," had always behaved. They felt compelled to be in motion, in action, "and while not unmindful of the question of profit, they sometimes dash into a venture for the venture's sake, even though it may fail

13. Armand L. DeRosset to Louis H. DeRosset, August 9, 1865, in DeRosset Family Papers, SHC.

to pay!" An Alabamian, in private ruminations from Brazil, explained the emigration fever by observing that "only thus could restless spirits be made quiet."[14]

Foreign governments, colonization agents, and emigration enthusiasts exploited these numerous tendencies to emigrate and became themselves important contributors to exodus. By planting seeds of restlessness in the minds of discontented yet undecided Confederates, they convinced people who leaned toward emigration that it was sound policy. Latin American governments, by selling lands at bargain prices—sometimes giving them free—and promising jobs to prominent settlers, proved especially active in luring southerners. Most governments did not beckon southerners alone. They encouraged "American" emigration in hopes that American settlers would infuse their countries with sorely needed economic vitality and political stability. Americans, northerners and southerners alike, had been casting greedy, expansionist eyes on Mexico, Honduras, Cuba, Brazil, and Venezuela since the 1840s. The Confederate government had sought to establish a commercial presence in Mexico and Cuba during the war. Both sections joined the postwar rush for cheap lands in tropical havens, but southerners, always the more enthusiastic advocates of Latin American expansion, formed the dominant element and driving force in the most successful emigration schemes.[15]

14. W. B. Prichard to grandmother, August 17, 1866, in Lewis Texada and Family Papers, LSU; Lawrence F. Hill, "The Confederate Exodus to South America," *Southwestern Historical Quarterly*, XXXIX (1936), 179; Keyes Diary, 21–22, 1; Charles A. Pilsbury, "Southern Emigration—Brazil and British Honduras," *DeBow's Review*, n.s., IV (December, 1867), 544; John Hammond Moore (ed.), *The Juhl Letters to the Charleston Courier: A View of the South, 1865–1871* (Athens, Ga., 1974), 81, letter of March 8, 1866.

15. Grier, "Confederate Emigration to Brazil," 93–94; *Metropolitan Record and New York Vindicator*, May 13, 1865, p. 7, May 20, 1865, p. 5, August 19, 1865, p. 5; Frank J. Merli (ed.), "Alternative to Appomattox: A Virginian's Vision of an Anglo-Confederate Colony on the Amazon, May 1865," *Virginia Magazine of History and Biography*, XCIV (1986), 210–19; Peter C. Thomas, "Matthew Fontaine Maury and the Problem of Virginia's Identity, 1865–1873," *Virginia Magazine of History and Biography*, XC (1982), 214–16; Samuel Bernard Thompson, *Confederate Purchasing Operations Abroad* (Chapel Hill, 1935), 103–27; Thomas David Schoonover, *Dollars Over Dominion: The Triumph of Liberalism in Mexican–United States Relations, 1861–1867* (Baton Rouge, 1978), 25–47. In addition to Schoonover, see the descriptions of antebellum interest in Latin America in Robert E. May, *The Southern Dream of a Caribbean Empire, 1854–1861* (Baton Rouge, 1973), and Charles H. Brown, *Agents of Manifest Destiny: The Life and Times of the Filibusters* (Chapel Hill, 1980).

The decisions of friends and neighbors persuaded other people to emigrate. Many Confederates soon realized that home meant more than a house or a particular place; it included the people who lived in a neighborhood. A South Carolina woman deftly explained their perspective. "The business in our neighborhood is so completely broken up," she confided to her aunt, "that really no one knows what to do, all think it quite impossible that a planter any where about here, will ever again be what he was. . . . Of course we should feel very sad at leaving our dear old home, but if it would benefit in any way, we would all be willing to make the sacrifice and go." Then the woman hit upon a significant point that largely explains the apparent ease with which many people fled the South. "I feel quite loath to leave this section of the country," she admitted, "and yet when I think of it, it is not so much the attachment to this particular State, or portion of the State, but the people I've grown up among. When they are taken away, my local attachments are not very strong." She would ever venerate her old home, "but still I think if all the friends I've been brought up among and accustomed to associate with should leave this part of the country, I too should be willing to go." Her view adds interest to the assertion of one scholar that extensive family and business connections, sometimes stretching back to the 1840s, inspired formation of several Brazilian settlements.[16]

The prospects of living alongside free blacks sent Confederates scurrying in all directions. Emigrants who lamented their lost civilization invariably grumbled about their lost labor force. Latin America earned its popularity as a refuge for planters largely because of "the Negro problem." Either lacking confidence in free black labor or unwilling to experiment with it, planters knew that Brazil was one of the last countries in the hemisphere to countenance slavery. Slavery was illegal in Mexico, but hopeful talk about cheap peon labor or a system of indentured servitude promised the next best thing to the South's peculiar institution. Equally important, the abolition of slavery had deprived southerners of the only reliable means of controlling a potentially dangerous portion of their society. Without slavery to keep blacks in place and give structure to race and class relations, southern society, people predicted with proper inflections of horror, would differ little, if at all, from northern society. The thought of living alongside former slaves as

16. Sarah Tennent to [Hattie Taylor], October 27, 1865, in Edward Smith Tennent Papers, SCL; Laura J. Pang, "Confederate Migration to Brazil: A Socioeconomic Profile," paper presented at Annual Meeting of the Southern Historical Association, November, 1984.

political and social equals angered and terrified southerners, who saw flight as their only salvation. The Yankees were not content with military victory, charged one Texan. They now sought to promote social and financial chaos in the South by turning loose "thousands of idle, thieving & impudent niggers among us with a standing army over us to protect their pets." He was bound for Mexico. "When it comes to sitting in juries with negroes, voting with them and being sworn against by them," protested another man, "I for one will leave the country." Venezuela appealed to an old Georgian, horrified by examples he had already witnessed of whites and blacks mingling socially—drinking together and engaging in "a little miscegenation."[17]

Confederates fleeing to California, Canada, and Europe likewise voiced their desire to escape the freedman. The war had cost Joseph LeConte, South Carolina's nationally renowned scientist, severe financial losses, but it had not disheartened him. Indeed, he found social life in postwar Columbia, where he taught at the state university, to be "really gay, the necessary result of the rebound from the agony and repression of the war." LeConte's attitude changed dramatically in 1867, however, with the installation of a carpetbagger-scalawag-freedman government in South Carolina. The new regime threatened not only to introduce black students to the university but to replace some white professors with blacks. It was too much for LeConte, who resigned his secure professorial post. Having earlier considered emigration to Mexico, he headed for California. Another discontented soul concluded that California's "climate, fertility, and freedom from the everlasting negro" made that state "more desirable" than any other place he could imagine. More than a few Confederates headed for England, where, as one southerner expressed it, blacks did not "offend your nostrils as in these USA." Paris appealed to this gentleman for the same reason.[18]

17. Francis Leigh Williams, *Matthew Fontaine Maury: Scientist of the Sea* (New Brunswick, N.J., 1963), 432–33; Daniel E. Sutherland, "Exiles, Emigrants, and Sojourners: The Post–Civil War Confederate Exodus in Perspective," *Civil War History,* XXXI (1985), 239–41; Stevenson Archer to Hannah Archer, September 9, 1867, in Archer Family Papers; John R. Baylor to Louise Wharton, January 11, 1866, in Wharton and Family Papers; J. T. Magruder to William W. Fergusson, August 15, 1867, in Fergusson Family Papers.

18. Joseph LeConte, *The Autobiography of Joseph LeConte,* ed. William D. Armes (New York, 1903), 229–32, 236–40; Lester D. Stephens, *Joseph LeConte: Gentle Prophet of Evolution* (Baton Rouge, 1982), 93–94, 104–108; Grier, "Confederate Emigration to Brazil," 12; G. S. Crafts to William P. Miles, April 13, 1867, in William Porcher Miles Papers, SHC.

Even southerners who welcomed the end of slavery sought havens from free blacks. The destination did not matter. Escape became the only goal. One man, typical of many, had no use for slavery, but he despaired of living amiably with free blacks. He intended, as soon as he could sell his lands, to expatriate himself. "I have not determined yet when I will go," he admitted, "but either to Central, South America, or to New Mexico any place to get away from here." John F. Pickett, former Confederate commissioner to Mexico, believed that not even Brazil would suffice. Brazilians, Pickett warned a friend, lacked the racial prejudices against blacks felt by most Americans. "Now, I take it," he explained, "*we* were fighting rather for the supremacy of our race—the maintenance of caste, etc than for slavery *per se*. True, we may endure free negro equality in other lands, though how we shall ever be able to brook its assertion from our late slaves is a question I do not care to speculate upon at present." Pickett planned to return to Mexico. Few Negroes lived there, and he felt "no prejudices of race against the redskins."[19]

The reasons for flight thus present a jumbled picture. The only patterns appear to have been fashioned by perceptions of how long the South's uncertain political status and dismal financial state might continue. The key to understanding individual flight became the destination, not the impulse, and the key to selecting a destination was the length of time emigrants intended to be away. People with little or no hope for the South sought permanent exile, generally in Latin America or some place in the United States outside the South. More optimistic folk sought temporary refuge, most often in Canada, Europe, and sometimes Mexico. Other factors directed people, too. Friends, relatives, or business associates residing at the point of arrival influenced decisions; so did the economic status, age, and occupation of individual emigrants. Farmers, for instance, would more likely move to Mexico than to Paris; merchants and lawyers would find brighter prospects in San Francisco than in Honduras. But all other things being equal, length of intended residence became the determining factor.[20]

Considering all the hoopla it created, emigration fever proved a short-lived epidemic. As months and years passed, more and more people who had spoken enthusiastically of emigration accommodated themselves to Yankee rule. For every exile, emigrant, and sojourner, scores of other

19. John R. Baylor to Louise Wharton, September 9, 1868, in Wharton and Family Papers; John F. Pickett to William C. P. Breckinridge, August 2, 1865, in Breckinridge Family Papers, LC.
20. Sutherland, "Exiles, Emigrants, and Sojourners," 250–55.

southerners only spoke of flight. Some people realized they could not afford to emigrate; they had the "inclination," wrote a Mississippi woman, but "not the means." Some people had family or business ties that forbade their leaving. Others stumbled into promising circumstances that made life under Yankee rule bearable. Still others grew ashamed of their original intention to desert the South in perhaps its hour of most severe need; they spoke of their "duty" to the South. Southerners also became aware of the possibilities of reprisals, as the federal government actively discouraged emigration by forbidding entrance of U.S. citizens into Mexico and closing emigration offices in the South. A Georgian who had contemplated emigration to California, Honduras, Brazil, and Venezuela became convinced by the summer of 1868 that his own state was "*the* place for making money enjoying good health and a good sprinkle of pleasure when properly sought." "I did feel for a good time as if I wished to emigrate to Kamhschatka or the Desert of Sahara," admitted another veteran, "but I am getting bravely over it, and have fully determined to accept the present condition of things, support the Gov't, be a good citizen, & do the best I can under the circumstances." Luckily, emigration required time for preparation, and as time passed, so, too, did the fever.[21]

Nearly all southern newspapers and magazines advised people to stay home. "The South cannot spare any of her sons," said the Richmond-based *Southern Opinion;* "we are opposed to the exodus of our manhood. . . . Immigration is what we want, not emigration." The Charleston *Courier* acknowledged the "spirit of unrest" that had seized many southern hearts but reminded potential emigrants in September, 1867, that all of the earliest colonization projects had failed and those currently under way showed every sign of following suit. Contributors to *DeBow's Review* gave much publicity to emigration abroad but concluded that southerners had best stay at home. Every emigrant, said one writer, drained another drop of the South's "life blood." Despite the impoverishment and apparent helplessness of the South, the section

21. Elizabeth B. Waddell to Priscilla E. Bailey, January 29, 1866, in John Lancaster Bailey Papers, SHC; Sister to Jane Smyth, July 10, 1865, in Adger-Smyth-Flynn Family Papers, SCL; Amelia Mandeville to Rebecca Mandeville, January 24, 1868, in Henry D. Mandeville and Family Papers, LSU; Andrew F. Rolle, *The Lost Cause: The Confederate Exodus to Mexico* (Norman, 1965), 140–41; James L. Roark, *Masters Without Slaves: Southern Planters in the Civil War and Reconstruction* (New York, 1977), 122–23; J. T. Magruder to William W. Fergusson, June 11, 1868, in Fergusson Family Papers; W. N. Haldeman to Robert McKee, August 7, 1865, in Robert McKee Papers, AA.

could revive and protect itself if southerners would take heart. "Will not the same labor here—and labor you must in the lands to which you are going—accomplish as much as in Brazil or British Honduras?" This same writer reminded readers of the disadvantages and hardships in store for settlers in new lands with foreign tongues and customs. "In a new country you will have many obstacles to overcome, which have already been surmounted here. You begin your new homes, as the first settlers in this country began theirs, and of whose labor you are now reaping the benefit. . . . Even a despotism," he concluded, "may be preferable to a wilderness; to life in a far-off, semi-barbarous land."[22]

A rising tide of antiemigration talk by influential Confederates proved a powerful antidote to flight. Robert E. Lee and Jefferson Davis opposed emigration. Lee told proemigration friends, including Matthew Fontaine Maury and Jubal Early, that the South could ill afford to lose its most industrious sons and daughters. Davis, though spending time in Canada and Europe after his release from prison, urged friends abroad to return home. "All cannot go," Davis reasoned, "and those who must stay will need the help of all who can go away. *The night may seem long, but it is the part of fidelity to watch and wait for morning.*" Wade Hampton, after investigating the possibilities of emigration, decided against flight. "I doubt the propriety of the expatriation of so many of our best men," he explained. "The very fact that our State is passing through so terrible an ordeal as the present should cause her sons to cling the more closely to her." Hampton advised southerners to devote "their whole energies" to restoring law and order to the South and to rebuilding southern agriculture, commerce, and education.[23]

Disenchanted Confederates abroad added voices of discontent. The exodus to Mexico first betrayed the problems of expatriation. The colonizing schemes and the plans of individual settlers seldom fulfilled early hopes of wealth, comfort, and safety. The "negro problem" continued to haunt emigrants. Settlers expecting to transport Negroes to Mexican plantations found few volunteers. Freedmen who did follow former

22. New Orleans *Daily Picayune*, April 24, 1867, p. 1; *Southern Opinion*, July 27, 1867, p. 2; Moore (ed.), *Juhl Letters*, 173, letter of September 6, 1867; Pilsbury, "Southern Emigration," 544.

23. Robert E. Lee to Richard L. Maury, July 31, 1865, to Jubal A. Early, March 15, 1866, both in Robert E. Lee Papers, VHS; Jefferson Davis to Varina Davis, March 13, 1866, in Hudson Strode (ed.), *Jefferson Davis: Private Letters, 1823–1889* (New York, 1966), 239; Wade Hampton to Editor of Columbia (S.C.) *Phoenix*, July 25, 1865, in Hampton Family Papers, SCL.

masters across the border just as frequently abandoned them once in Mexico. Nor did the relatively free and elevated social position of blacks in Mexico please southerners. Poorer emigrants destined to perform their own work and looking for free government lands discovered that the first few hundred arrivals had claimed all the usable land. By the spring of 1866, the only available real estate was being sold by private citizens for thirty dollars an acre. "Since emigration commenced," spit a former Confederate in disgust, "these greaser Mexicans think their land is the best in the world." Prospective engineers and bureaucrats learned that government jobs were few in number and could be acquired only through personal contacts. Mexico was no place to bring a family, complained others, a dearth of schools and Protestant churches being the principal objections. "I was not pleased with Mexico," Jubal Early said in summarizing the situation, "and think that our people who have gone there will be disappointed. The published accounts were very much exaggerated."[24]

The final blow to Mexican settlement came from the disrupted political condition of the country. One dared to travel through Mexico only in armed groups, for desperadoes, banditos, and warring political factions preyed openly on emigrants. These dangers and the anti-American feeling among large segments of the population had not been mentioned in promotional literature. The situation worsened rapidly in the spring of 1866, when anti-imperial troops, opposed to pro-Confederate, French-backed emperor Maximilian, conducted a series of raids on American settlements in the region of Cordova. The raids, inspired largely by Napoleon III's decision to withdraw all French troops from Mexico, made kidnapping for ransom, looting of shops and houses, confiscation of livestock, and destruction of farm implements and other property almost daily episodes. Americans fled their interior settlements for the safety of inland cities and coastal ports. In May, 1867, Maximilian was captured by the Liberal troops of Benito Juárez; in June, he was executed. The influx of emigrants suddenly stopped. People already in Mexico, fearful of persecution by the Juárez regime, prepared to leave. A few stouthearted southerners stayed on, but most emigrants began looking elsewhere for new homes. Some pushed on to Central and South America; most stumbled back wearily to the United States.[25]

24. Reid, *After the War*, 454; Hill, "Confederate Exodus to South America," 318–19; Manning M. Kimmel to father, March 31, 1866, Glasgow Family Papers, MOHS; Jubal A. Early to Samuel H. Early, April 11, 1866, in Early Papers.

25. Alexander Watkins Terrell, *From Texas to Mexico and the Court of Maximilian in 1865* (Dallas, 1933), 74; Tom J. Russell, "Adventures of a Cordova Colonist," *Southern*

Most of the same problems, Confederates quickly learned, awaited them elsewhere in Latin America. Rumors spread about the dangers posed by jealous Honduran natives who desired the lands being given to southerners. Central American swampland cost five dollars an acre, and no amount of money could produce sufficient labor for large plantations. A Georgian experienced the same problems in Brazil. "The mistake that our people have made," he reported, "is, that they have expected to make a living here without personal labor or the means to buy labor with." For those able to work the land, the problem of getting agricultural goods to markets remained formidable. Most settlements were isolated and distant from principal towns. Primitive roads and infrequent access to railroads made transportation difficult. Unscrupulous colonizing agents left a bitter taste in the mouths of some settlers and dampened the enthusiasm of potential colonists. Some colonizing agents arranged settlement on picturesque but agriculturally wretched lands. Others swindled colonists out of their savings. In Brazil, as in Mexico, failure to establish a flourishing system of slavery or peonage discouraged settlers. The physical hardships of pioneer life also took their toll. Few settlers escaped bouts of hunger, exposure, fever, and sickness. They had frequently arrived at their destinations ill-prepared and inexperienced in the colonizing process. "The big forest was too much for us," explained a returning Honduras colonizer. More complex and subtle obstacles such as the language barrier or culture shock defeated still other colonists.[26]

Political events in the North produced much fluctuation in individual plans and public perceptions about the advisability of flight. Generally, Confederates seemed most anxious and most ready to flee during two periods: from the spring of 1865 to the early weeks of 1866 and then from the spring of 1867 to the end of 1868. It was during the first period,

Magazine, IV (August, 1872), 162; Rolle, *Lost Cause,* 182–86; Frank A. Knapp, Jr., "A New Source on the Confederate Exodus to Mexico: *The Two Republics," Journal of Southern History,* XIX (1953), 364–73.

26. Will Stakely to Carrie Stakely, November 8, 1867, in Hall-Stakely Family Papers; New Orleans *Daily Picayune,* September 15, 1865, p. 2; Hill, "Confederate Exodus to South America," 165–66, 170, 190, 192; Grier, "Confederate Exodus to Brazil," 35, 99; J. Carlyle Sitterson, "The McCollams: A Planter Family of the Old and New South," *Journal of Southern History,* VI (1940), 360–61; Hanna and Hanna, *Confederate Exiles in Venezuela,* 136–37; Charles Willis Simmons, "Racist Americans in a Multi-Racial Society: Confederate Exiles in Brazil," *Journal of Negro History,* XLVII (1982), 34–39; Desmond Holdridge, "Toledo: A Tropical Refugee Settlement in British Honduras," *Geographical Review,* XXX (1940), 380; William Clark Griggs, "Confederate Emigration to Brazil, 1865–1870" (Ph.D. dissertation, Texas Tech University, 1982).

a time of rumor and intrigue, that Confederates who most feared reprisals slipped out of the country. The New York *Daily News,* Democratic and prosouthern, sensed something sinister in this sudden exodus. The *Daily News* had shrugged off early reports of southern flight.
Soon, however, editor Benjamin Wood expressed concern. Between
mid-1865 and mid-1866 his paper carried at least one editorial per
month urging southerners to stay home. "The South, now more than
ever," ran a typical appeal, "needs the presence of its prominent and
influential men. It would be treachery for the few who have the means of
seeking their fortunes elsewhere, to leave the many helpless and without
guide or counsel amid the ruins." Wood had a theory to explain this
sudden "depopulation" of the South. Radical Republicans in Congress,
he claimed, were deliberately encouraging former Confederates to leave
the country so that the Republican party might seize political control of
the South. The entire congressional program—its unwillingness to compromise, its insistence on heaping "all the humiliations of conquest" on
the South—had been a "cunning" plan to drive out the "influential
classes of the South." Publicly insisting on their intention to preserve the
Union, the Radicals had actually sought "to goad, insult, and provoke
the vanquished" into flight.[27]

Then, in February and March, 1866, Andrew Johnson vetoed the
Freedmen's Bureau Bill and the Civil Rights Bill. Much to the surprise of
some Confederates, the president seemed determined to defend the
white South and defy the Radicals. "I, for one, am determined to hang
on to old Virginia still longer," wrote one woman following Johnson's
first veto, "and look to Providence to bring us out of our difficulties."
General William Preston returned to Kentucky from Canada upon
learning of "the altered circumstances and the new policy of St. Andrew." But some people still worried. A Confederate in Mexico complained that Johnson lacked the "boldness" to "lock horns" with the
Radicals and his "army chiefs." The *Daily News,* though cheering Johnson's boldness, warned that if the president failed to escalate his efforts
to protect the South "against the schemes of the revolutionists" thousands more of that section's best citizens would be driven from the
country.[28]

27. New York *Daily News,* July 21, 1865, p. 4, January 25, 1866, p. 4, March 14,
1866, p. 4.
28. Sarah Payne to Mary M. Clendenin, March 18, 1866, in Sarah P. Payne Correspondence, VHS; William Preston to I. G. Walker, December 2, 1866, in Preston Family
Papers–Davie Collection, FC; Thomas C. Reynolds to Jubal A. Early, May 10, 1866, in
Thomas C. Reynolds Papers, MOHS; New York *Daily News,* February 26, 1866, p. 4.

As Benjamin Wood feared, Johnson lost control. Congress eventually passed both of the vetoed bills. The president's coalition suffered a massive setback in the congressional elections of 1866. When the new Congress passed the first of its Reconstruction Acts, in March, 1867, panic seized the South. A Georgian observed that the acts sparked a new wave of southern resolution to escape Yankee oppression. "Those who had been returning from exile," he reported, "are talking of resuming their homes beyond the seas, while many of the colonial associations that had long since concluded to abandon the idea of emigration, are busily preparing to emigrate to Brazil, Venezuela, and other promising sections of South America." Robert Toombs, former Confederate general and cabinet member, felt a gnawing dread. Toombs had fled the country in 1865, first to Cuba, then to Europe. He returned to the United States in February, 1867, but passage of the Reconstruction Acts turned his thoughts toward Canada. "There is a great disposition among the people of the South to emigrate," he observed to John C. Breckinridge, himself tucked safely away in Canada, "and I think if the Radicals succeed in their policy, the abandonment of the country will take place to an extent that I had no idea of until I reached home. . . . I now think a sufficient emigration will take place from the South to become an important element in any government with which it may be directed." The "greatest exodus that has ever been witnessed in modern times" was about to begin, Toombs predicted. Toombs had earlier opposed "permanent emigration." He had preferred that the entire southern people should perish in defense of its "native land." Such a drastic show of loyalty seemed futile by the spring of 1867. Toombs now deemed emigration of the entire population preferable to living under Yankee tyranny.[29]

The panic did not spread as far the second time, partly because many people had already determined to make the best of a bad situation. Moreover, plans to colonize Mexico had already failed, serving as a disquieting reminder of the perils of emigration. The largest numbers of emigrants to Central and South America left the United States after the spring of 1867, but the anticipated rush did not materialize. The picture became muddled. Southerners slowly learned to accommodate themselves to the new regime. The hazards of emigration became more wide-

29. *Metropolitan Record and New York Vindicator*, June 1, 1867, p. 12; Robert A. Toombs to John C. Breckinridge, April 30, 1867, Robert Augustus Toombs Letter, UG. For the political situation generally in 1866–67 see Dan Carter, *When the War Was Over: The Failure of Self-Reconstruction in the South, 1865–1867* (Baton Rouge, 1985), 232–75.

ly publicized. People still reacted variously to events during the spring and summer of 1868. Johnson's impeachment proved the power of the Republican party, yet his acquittal was a hopeful sign. Johnson's proclamation of universal amnesty, issued in December, encouraged emigrants who had earlier feared for their lives to think seriously about returning to the United States. Ulysses S. Grant's presidential nomination and eventual election, in 1868, placed the political picture in sharper focus and reassured southerners who respected Grant as an honest fellow pledged to peaceful coexistence. Confederates who had not already fled seemed less inclined to do so, regardless of political events. By 1869, emigration for most southerners was as distant and unreal as an independent Confederacy. Judah B. Benjamin estimated that few Confederates remained in London by the early summer of 1867, and few seem to have been left on the Continent by the following summer. Most exiles had left Canada by 1870, and probably 80 percent of all Latin American refugees had returned home by the early years of that decade, most of the diehards remaining in Brazil.[30]

Ultimately, people returned because they could not find new homes to replace the old. Some people anticipated that outcome from the start and never intended permanent exile. Others realized the cold, brutal facts only after much suffering and heartache. "Exile," explained one exhausted but wiser emigrant returning from Mexico, "whether voluntary or enforced, imposes on the wanderer, in spite of himself, its crop of bitter reflections. Though the face may smile and the merry laugh ring out, the exile's heart turns instinctively to the distant home, where his loved ones are." Summarizing the myriad individual reasons for return-

30. Grier, "Confederate Emigration to Brazil," 19–20; William C. Davis, "Confederate Exiles," *American History Illustrated,* V (June, 1970), 40; Barrie Hayne, "Confederate Exiles in Canada West, 1865–68" (Typescript in VHS), 6–7; Judah P. Benjamin to James M. Mason, May 29, 1867, in Judah Philip Benjamin Collection, LC; Braxton Bragg to Joseph G. Wheeler, September 20, 1869, in Joseph G. Wheeler Papers, AA. For post-1870 conditions among Brazilian colonists see Hamilton Basso, "The Last Confederate," *New Yorker,* November 21, 1953, pp. 143–61; Frank Cunningham, "The Lost Colony of the Confederacy," *American Mercury,* XCII (July, 1961), 33–38; James E. Edmonds, "They've Gone Back Home! The Last of a Confederate Colony," *Saturday Evening Post,* January 4, 1941, pp. 30, 33, 46–47; Eugene C. Harter, *The Lost Colony of the Confederacy* (Jackson, Miss., 1985); Holdridge, "Toledo," 376–93; Mark Jefferson, "An American Colony in Brazil," *Geographical Review,* XVIII (1928), 226–31; Jose Arthur Rios, "Assimilation of Emigrants from the Old South in Brazil," *Social Forces,* XXVI (1947), 145–52; Madeline Dane Ross and Fred Kerner, "Stars and Bars Along the Amazon," *Reporter,* September 18, 1958, pp. 34–36; Bell I. Wiley, "Confederate Exiles in Brazil," *Civil War Times Illustrated,* XV (January, 1977), 22–32.

ing to the South, the Charleston *Courier* told readers in October, 1868: "Many have emigrated from this section since the war and have sought new homes in Brazil, Honduras, Mexico, Texas . . . and other places; but strange to relate, all these emigrants, with scarcely an exception, have come back again, damaged of course to the extent of the outlay and sacrifices involved in such expeditions, but greatly enriched in an experience whose sad chapters would make a gloomy volume for a rainy day." The sight of these broken, hungry, desolate people as they straggled back into a hundred communities across the South became the best argument against emigration.[31]

Yet even as the first dusty, exhausted Confederate soldiers forded the Rio Grande into Mexico, and long before the first Brazilian or Venezuelan expeditions set sail, another emigration had begun. A Charleston woman confided to her sister that she did not fancy living in "wild countries" like Brazil. If one must live abroad, surely England was the only habitable country, but why roam so far? "I would rather go to the North & live in . . . their beautiful cultivated country." A Virginian, who had no intention of leaving his home, preferred life in the North to the uncertainty of Mexico or South America. "For my part," he insisted, "if I left the South, my first thought would be to seek a home among the Yankees, either in New York City or in one of the North Western States." A Virginia woman decided that, if forced to move by a "despotic" Yankee government, she, too, would head north. "What do you think of it?" she asked a cousin. "I have no desire to try one of the *reconstructed* States. I am waiting patiently to see what will turn up."[32]

This northward migration is hard to define. The Confederates who embarked upon it were not exactly exiles; they could not be called expatriates. Yet, like the caravans of colonists to Latin America, they expected to leave their southern homeland forever. They despised the Yankee and spoke wistfully of their vanished antebellum society, yet they had no hope of reviving either the plantation system or slavery. They were as adventurous and courageous as the most reckless Honduran colonizer, yet they seemed more willing to cooperate with Yankees in reforming the United States. They exceeded in number the exodus of all

31. Terrell, *From Texas to Mexico*, 66; Moore (ed.), *Juhl Letters*, 255, letter of October 4, 1868.

32. Sister to Jane Smyth, July 10, 1865, in Adger-Smyth-Flynn Family Papers; L. Minor Blackford, *Mine Eyes Have Seen the Glory: The Story of a Virginia Lady, Mary Berkeley Minor Blackford, 1802–1896* (Cambridge, Mass., 1954), 244; Sarah P. Payne to Mary M. Clendenin, September 18, 1868, in Payne Correspondence.

but those Confederates who sought refuge in the West, yet few people protested or marveled at their flight. While the nation fixed its attention on the noisy, almost jubilant departures of Confederates seeking exile abroad, these other emigrants folded their tents and slipped quietly into the night. Without fanfare, with no large groups crowding aboard chartered ships and moving en masse, they limped away as individuals or in single families to seek new lives and new homes. These were the Confederate carpetbaggers, and it is time to tell their story.

2

The Lure of Yankeedom

Burton Norvell Harrison collapsed wearily into the chair behind his desk at No. 11 Pine Street. He felt exhausted, yet even as he sat staring with glazed eyes at the photograph on his desk of a pretty golden-haired young woman, a sense of renewed vigor pulsated through his body. He had disposed of a weighty emotional and moral obligation just hours earlier. If physically spent, he felt mentally fit, even cocky, and ready to challenge a world that for the past two years had buffeted, bruised, and used him sorely. His response to these trials had been determined, very nearly heroic. It was May, 1867. He felt ancient, even though he had not yet celebrated his twenty-ninth birthday. Men who fight wars, especially when they lose those wars, are older than their years.

As he sat trying to sort out the future, Harrison's imagination drifted back to a distant time and place, a thousand miles away and half a decade in the past. It all started as he sat lounging in his mother's parlor, at Oxford, Mississippi, reading newspaper accounts of Jefferson Davis' inauguration as president of a new nation. A telegram arrived. Colonel Lucius Q. C. Lamar, an old family friend, had recommended him to the president as a private secretary. The president trusted Lamar's judgment. Would the Yale Phi Beta Kappa consent to leave his professorial post at the university in Oxford and join the president's staff? Harrison's reply was assumed. The athletic, handsome young man had been looking for a chance to serve the Confederacy. He preferred military service, perhaps in the Washington Artillery of his native New Orleans, but service to the president would suit him equally well. Neither he nor his "Chief," as he would thereafter call Davis, ever regretted the decision. An extraordinary intimacy grew between the two men. Harrison, young enough to be the president's son, became his most valued and devoted aide. He protected Davis, comforted him, and buoyed his spirits. Even the president's volatile wife, Varina, succumbed to Harrison's charm. He became one of the few people who dared to criticize her, and she never quarreled with him.[1]

The president and his loyal secretary would be separated only when, on a stormy, melancholy night in May, 1865, somewhere in the wilderness of Georgia, federal troops captured Davis and his aides in flight to Texas. Harrison, suffering the ravages of dysentery and fever, had been extremely ill on that gloomy night. The thought still haunted him years later that had he been more alert, not so incapacitated, the Chief might have escaped. Instead, the entire entourage suffered imprisonment, Davis and the other aides being transported to Fort Delaware, New Jersey, Harrison alone sent for interrogation to the Old Capitol Prison at Washington. The parting of president and secretary was a poignant moment. It brought home to both men the realization of a cause irretrievably lost.[2]

Harrison spent nine months in prison, most of the time, as events proved, at Fort Delaware, after Davis had been transferred to Fortress Monroe. His incarceration had some unpleasant moments, particularly in Washington, where he quickly found himself in the U.S. Arsenal. This gloomy place, on the marshy banks of the Potomac, was the closest thing the authorities had to a maximum security prison, the place of confinement for the Lincoln murder conspirators. Harrison suffered total darkness, solitary confinement, no exercise. Not until his guards heard him singing and laughing to himself after five weeks of such treatment did the War Department permit outdoor exercise and a cell with a window. At the end of another month, Harrison was transferred to Fort Delaware, and his spirits soared. He remained in a solitary cell and enjoyed only limited exercise, but he felt as though he had rejoined the living. The buoyant, unflagging spirit that ensured his popularity whatever the company, the unfailing graciousness that made him the center of attention in any drawing room, reappeared. He won the respect of his

1. Hudson Strode, *Jefferson Davis* (3 vols.; New York, 1955–64), II, 203–204, III, 286; Eron Rowland, *Varina Howell: Wife of Jefferson Davis* (2 vols.; New York, 1927–31), II, 238, 361.

2. Strode, *Jefferson Davis,* III, 218–19; Burton N. Harrison, "The Capture of Jefferson Davis," *Century Magazine,* XXVII (November, 1883), 130–45. For the story of Davis' capture, see Michael B. Ballard, *A Long Shadow: Jefferson Davis and the Final Days of the Confederacy* (Jackson, Miss., 1986).

jailers as readily as he had captivated the Davises and the heart of every young woman in wartime Richmond.[3]

Harrison's guards, upon his request, brought him books. They brought him Alfred Tennyson, and Tennyson brought him salvation. By the end of his third month at Fort Delaware, Harrison treasured a library of fourteen volumes, but Tennyson became his favorite. He read and reread the Englishman, steeping his senses in Tennyson's harmonies. Tennyson's rhythms ran through his head all day, and those rhythms would echo in his memory for many years.

> My life has crept so long on a broken wing
> Thro' cells of madness, haunts of horror and fear,
> That I come to be grateful at last for a little thing.

That little thing was his sanity, the strength to cope, week by week, with the full tragedy being acted out in the country, the failure of southern nationhood, and his own dismal prospects for the future. Tennyson's words nourished him. Only sunlight and fresh air could have done more for his resolve:

> It is better to fight for good, than to rail at ill;
> I have felt with my native land, I am one with my kind,
> I embrace the purpose of God, and the doom asign'd.[4]

As his health improved, Harrison looked ahead. What should he do when released? Two years later, sitting in his New York law office, Harrison vividly recalled those weeks and months of confusion and indecision. He focused his thoughts more sharply on the pretty face framed on his desk, his fiancée, Constance Cary:

> O that 'twere possible
> After long grief and pain
> To find the arms of my true love
> Round me once again!

3. Mrs. Burton Harrison, *Recollections Grave and Gay* (New York, 1911), 228–37, 240–43; Fairfax Harrison (ed.), *Aris Sonis Focisque: Being a Memoir of an American Family, the Harrisons of Skimino* (New York, 1910), 162–66.

4. Harrison, *Recollections Grave and Gay,* 240–43; Harrison (ed.), *Aris Sonis Focisque,* 171–77, 188–89; Burton N. Harrison to Constance Cary, September 9, 1865, in Burton Norvell Harrison Family Papers, LC; Alfred, Lord Tennyson, "Maud; A Monodrama," in *The Poems and Dramatic Works of Alfred, Lord Tennyson* (Boston, 1898), 216, 217.

He recalled writing long letters, smuggled out by sympathetic guards, asking her advice about the future. Where should they go? What should they do? Should he resume his legal studies, disrupted by the war? Where should he practice? "I shall never reside again in Mississippi," he recalled telling her, "or perhaps anywhere else in the Southwest. I think that practice at the New Orleans bar would insure me a fortune, but I doubt whether all the money in Christendom could make me happy there now." He had heard wonderful tales about Australia. If he left the United States that would be his destination. If he stayed in the country, his choice would be San Francisco or Baltimore. He preferred the latter. What did Constance think? He emphasized above all else his desire to get on with life. Burton Harrison had never been one to whine or complain about life's misfortunes. He did not fancy being a "martyr" or "heroic sufferer" to any cause, not even the Lost Cause. The war was over; the cause was dead. He would willingly submit to whatever punishment he must, pay whatever price might be required, but when all the punishment and suffering had ended, he fully intended to resume his steady pace along the high road to the future. He had learned from Tennyson "that men may rise on stepping stones of their dead selves to higher things."[5]

He smiled, ever so faintly, to think of it. Funny how things worked themselves out. Australia indeed! Toward the end of his imprisonment, two former Yale classmates, transformed into Union army officers at Fort Delaware, supplied Harrison with law books. He studied diligently, preparing for his new life. He had decided, having listened to advice from northern and southern friends, that neither San Francisco nor Baltimore but New York City held the brightest prospects for an ambitious young man. "What think you?" he asked half-incredulously of an uncle living in New York, "I shall . . . perhaps become your near neighbor in business, practising at the New York bar." Harrison left prison in late January, 1866, largely because of Constance's lobbying efforts among influential mutual friends. He joined Constance and her family at Washington to celebrate and recuperate from the long ordeal. In March he traveled to Mississippi for a reunion with his mother and sister, whom he had not seen since receiving the fateful telegram nearly four years earlier. But this holiday, if such it could be called, proved short-lived. Friends soon summoned him to New Orleans to discuss a possible legal partnership in

5. Harrison (ed.), *Aris Sonis Focisque*, 176–77; Tennyson, "Maud; A Monodrama" and "In Memorium A.H.H.," in *Poems and Dramatic Works*, 214, 163.

that city. Harrison's father had enjoyed a distinguished legal career in New Orleans before his untimely death in 1841, but Burton, after discussing the offer, decided against it. Most of his friends admitted that New York was "a better field for a lawyer now."[6]

Another factor had also to be considered. The Chief again required his services. Mrs. Davis, on the president's advice, had asked Harrison to accompany her to New York and consult with attorneys who were working to free the president. "Mr. Harrison will I know do all in his power to provide for your comfort," Davis advised his wife, "and I feel great confidence both in his head and his heart. I once hoped to have been of service to him," the Chief continued, "and much regret that the reverse has been the result of his connection with me." For the next thirteen months, Davis' release from prison remained the dominant objective of Burton Harrison's life. Working with the president's principal attorneys, Charles O'Conor in New York and William B. Reed in Philadelphia, Harrison had little time to plan his own life. Even marriage, he regretfully informed Constance, must wait until the Chief was free ("Oh hard, when love and duty clash!"). Harrison functioned most effectively during the next year as a messenger between New York and Virginia, traveling south whenever important—particularly discouraging—news had to be relayed to Davis. With typical aplomb, the former private secretary would inform the Chief of another delay in his trial or explain some failure to win concessions from the government.[7]

In July, 1866, when Davis' trial was postponed until October, Harrison traveled to Europe, where he acted as the financial agent in the affairs of some friends and relatives. Bad news greeted his return to the United States. Davis' trial had been postponed yet again, this time until spring. Faced with this lull in the proceedings, Harrison, who had all the while been spending spare hours with his Blackstone and Story, accepted an invitation from Charles O'Conor (apparently urged on O'Conor by Mrs. Davis) to study law in the office of John Fullerton, a former New York judge. Fullerton proved an able tutor. Harrison was admitted to the New York bar in December. Early in the new year, he formed a

6. Harrison (ed.), *Aris Sonis Focisque*, 185–92; T. L. Bayne to Burton N. Harrison, December 19, 1865, in Harrison Family Papers, LC.

7. Strode, *Jefferson Davis*, III, 274–75, 278; Jefferson Davis to Varina Davis, March 13, 1866, in Hudson Strode (ed.), *Jefferson Davis: Private Letters, 1823–1889* (New York, 1966), 239; Burton N. Harrison to sister, May 13, 1866, to Varina Davis, June 28, 1866, to Constance Cary, July 13, 1866, all in Harrison Family Papers, LC.

partnership with Charles H. Wesson, an old Yale classmate, and together they opened chambers in Pine Street.[8]

No sooner had Harrison accomplished all this than the events of May, 1867, overwhelmed him. O'Conor hurried Harrison off to Virginia. Davis' bail bond, set at a hundred thousand dollars, had been assured; a writ of *habeas corpus* had been secured; an appeal for his release would be heard. Davis entered a Richmond courtroom. Harrison, the president's comfort and support as of old, accompanied his Chief to the prisoner's dock. He heard with Davis Judge John C. Underwood's acceptance of bail, the sound of the gavel, the order to discharge the prisoner. Pandemonium followed: rebel yells, rejoicing crowds, tears, toasts, more shouts, more tears. The strain on Davis became obvious. He leaned on the strong arm of his youthful friend, who guided him to the Spotswood Hotel and his waiting wife. There were more tears and hushed prayers. Images of those hectic hours again rushed through Harrison's mind: the decision to leave Richmond that evening via steamer for New York; the arrival at New York; the endless stream of well-wishers at the New York Hotel; the decision to transfer Davis to O'Conor's country residence, where he could rest and from whence, after a few quiet days, he could travel to see his children in Canada.[9]

Now it was over. Harrison sat exhausted but exuberant. The Chief, he trusted, was sleeping soundly at O'Conor's. Harrison's eyes and thoughts focused again on the face of Constance Cary. He reached for pen and paper. She must know what had happened. He recounted the events of the past few days. He must, Harrison explained to her, attend Mrs. Davis while she stayed in New York a day or two more, but then he—they—would be free, for the liberation of Davis meant their liberation, too. We are "released from all bonds—save one," he whispered to her. He need not say more. Mutual dreams require no embroidery. Now they could wed. She must hurry home from France, where she had been living since October. Beginning this very day, he would devote himself to his law practice and their future happiness. They would be poor at first, but they would be together. All the dreams of youth, detoured, delayed,

8. Harrison (ed.), *Aris Sonis Focisque*, 192; Strode, *Jefferson Davis*, III, 289; Burton N. Harrison to General Chesnut, January 11, 1867, in Williams-Chesnut-Manning Family Papers, SCL.

9. Strode, *Jefferson Davis*, III, 306–11; Burton N. Harrison to mother, May 18, 1867, in James Elliott Walmsley (ed.), "Some Unpublished Letters of Burton N. Harrison," Mississippi Historical Society, *Publications*, VIII (1904), 83–85; Harrison, *Recollections Grave and Gay*, 263–68.

nearly thwarted by war, would be realized. "The past is now the past," he told her, "all is now in the future." Tennyson would have approved.[10]

Constance Cary, barely twenty-four years old, read Burton's letter through tears of joy. Still a schoolgirl when the war began, she, like her sweetheart, was a product of Virginia ancestry, though of a slightly more aristocratic blend than the Harrisons. Her earliest memories were of the hills and meadows of Cumberland, Maryland, where her father edited the local Whig newspaper and practiced law. When he died in 1854, the Cary females—five in number—moved to Grandma Fairfax's homestead, Vaucluse, near Alexandria, Virginia. Constance's formal education, begun in Maryland at a young ladies' school and with a Latin tutor, continued at a Richmond boarding school and with a French governess. When the war came, the family fled Vaucluse, which was destroyed soon afterward by federal soldiers. The refugees settled at Culpeper Court House, where Mrs. Cary volunteered to nurse sick and wounded soldiers. But Culpeper was no place for an attractive young debutante, so, in the winter of 1862, Constance went to live in Richmond with relatives.[11]

In no time, graceful, willowy Constance became one of the most hotly pursued young ladies in Richmond society. With her refugee cousins Hetty and Jennie Cary and Jennie Fairfax, she brightened the city's principal social functions. She watched the rain-drenched inauguration of President Davis from the enviable and cozy vantage point of an upper-story window in the Virginia capitol, a convenience arranged by the state's chief librarian, John R. Thompson, a warm personal friend thereafter. Constance played charades at the Confederate White House, danced with Robert E. Lee, gossiped with Mary Chesnut (who declared Constance "clever" and "witty"), and starred in amateur theatricals. She even initiated a modest literary career during the war. Constance signed her short stories and poems, published in the *Southern Illustrated News, Magnolia Weekly,* and Richmond *Examiner,* "Refugitta," a name not only affixed to her favorite riding mount, owned by Fitzhugh Lee, but one aptly descriptive of her homeless wartime condition.[12]

10. Harrison, *Recollections Grave and Gay,* 265–68.

11. *Ibid.,* 3–66; Dorothy M. Scura, "Homage to Constance Cary Harrison," *Southern Humanities Review,* X (1976), 36–39; Mrs. Burton Harrison, "Virginia Scenes in '61," in Robert Underwood Johnson and Clarence Clough Buel (eds.), *Battles and Leaders of the Civil War* (4 vols.; New York, 1887), I, 160–66.

12. Harrison, *Recollections Grave and Gay,* 67–219; Mrs. Burton Harrison, "Richmond Scenes in '62," in Johnson and Buel (eds.), *Battles and Leaders of the Civil War,* II,

Hetty and Jennie introduced Constance to Burton Harrison soon after she arrived in Richmond. Constance had been prepared to dislike him. Her cousins had praised him so lavishly that Constance, who soon wearied of his name, assumed that he must be a conceited swell. She knew cousin Hetty's taste in men ("gilt-edged and with stars") and had every reason to believe that "Colonel" Harrison (for such was his title) came from that mold. She discovered, instead, a charming, unassuming fellow who put everyone immediately at ease, a true gentleman. He was strikingly handsome. Burton stood all of six feet tall, with dark brown hair, "smoky topaz" eyes, drooping mustache, broad shoulders, and erect carriage. But Constance felt instinctively that those good looks and his "fashion plate" appearance (for he maintained an immaculate yet tasteful wardrobe when everyone else went out in patched and faded garments) concealed a generous heart. Harrison fell just as swiftly under the spell of the effervescent Constance. Her reddish-blonde hair, classical Greek profile, finely modeled lips, and dancing blue eyes beguiled him. He waltzed with her. He wrote poetry to her. He proposed marriage during the siege of Richmond, and she accepted. The engagement had its pyrotechnic moments. Handsome, debonair Burton and high-spirited, fun-loving Constance were like flint and steel; sparks had to fly. But they became, without question, one of the most adored couples in Richmond.[13]

Constance Cary's life as a " 'fugee," the name given by Richmond citizens to homeless civilians in their midst, continued after the war. She had been seated in her customary pew at St. Paul's Episcopal Church, directly behind the Davises, when the end came. It was a bright, sunny morning, very different from the dreary inaugural day. She watched the president's careworn face as he read the fateful note telling him that Lee's lines had broken at Petersburg. Yankee hordes were marching on the city. Civilians and soldiers streamed out of the capital as the federals closed in. The deserted buildings, the smoke and flame of property put to the torch, reminded Constance of nothing so much as a medieval town "smitten by pestilence." She witnessed Abraham Lincoln's tri-

439–48; C. Vann Woodward (ed.), *Mary Chesnut's Civil War* (New Haven, 1981), 528, 530–38, 540, 577.

13. Harrison, *Recollections Grave and Gay,* 67–219; Woodward (ed.), *Mary Chesnut's Civil War,* 539; Harrison (ed.), *Aris Sonis Focisque,* 156–60; John S. Wise, *The End of an Era* (Boston, 1902), 401; Francis B. Harrison, "About It and About" (Typescript in Francis Burton Harrison Papers, UV), 32–34, 38.

umphal tour of the captured city but could not tolerate the occupation that followed. Shortly after Lee's surrender, Constance traveled north at the invitation of Unionist cousins living in New Jersey. Years later she still remembered the kindness shown her. Her cousins tried to cheer their "little storm-tossed, rebel visitor," taking her on shopping sprees in Philadelphia and visits to other northern relatives, but though these joys raised her spirits momentarily, the specters of Confederate defeat, a desolated South, and an imprisoned lover haunted her thoughts. Many were the nights she cried herself to sleep. Not until August, in a letter smuggled out of Fort Delaware, did she receive word from Burton or any news of his fate. With the help of her mother and a New Jersey cousin, she dedicated herself to freeing Burton, just as he, in turn, would dedicate himself to his Chief. She journeyed to Fort Delaware but was not allowed to visit the prisoner. She took up residence in Washington, to lobby among influential friends for his release. In January, 1866, her efforts were rewarded.[14]

Upon Burton's advice, Constance and her mother joined the Confederate exodus to Europe in October. They spent most of the sojourn in Paris, where Constance acquired the "finishing touches" of a lady's education and joined the "Confederate set" in France. Her social circle included not only prominent Confederate exiles John C. Breckinridge and Dudley Mann but English visitors, well-placed Parisians, and northern sympathizers vacationing in Europe. As in Richmond, Constance attended many exclusive social events: a public ball at the Tuileries (presided over by Napoleon III, music conducted by Johann Strauss), parties at private homes, ballets, operas, and, of course, the Exposition Universelle. She witnessed astonishing spectacles of luxury and culture, of "pomp and vanities" she had hitherto only fantasized. Yet she could not escape the burden of Confederate defeat. Every now and again, some reminder of the war—a military review, a chance encounter with one of the wandering children of the South—brought tears to her eyes. She was still a Confederate, still unreconstructed. Thus Burton's letter brought joy and sorrow. Reminded once more of home, her day, for a moment, turned gloomy; but as she read on, learned of the release of Davis, of her lover's unspoken plea for her return, she exulted. The past, she realized, must be left behind. She, too, looked to the future.[15]

All that spring and summer, Burton Harrison and his law partner,

14. Harrison, *Recollections Grave and Gay*, 212, 219, 238–44.
15. *Ibid.*, 244–59, 262–63, 268–71.

Wesson, worked feverishly to build a practice. Wesson, the northerner, supplied the library and northeastern clients. Harrison became responsible for attracting southern clients. He contacted old comrades and friends, particularly gentlemen at the southern bar, asking them to recommend his services to any Confederate who required legal aid in New York. He advertised his services in newspapers and magazines, both northern and southern, with large southern readerships. He need not mention his southern heritage in these advertisements; everyone knew Burton Harrison. Harrison mingled socially, too, using his wit and charm to infiltrate the higher echelons of northern society, thus meeting those people who most often required legal assistance and who could pay most handsomely for it. By March, he appeared likely to get his first big case. His opponent, of all men, was to be Judge Fullerton, his Gamaliel of a few months earlier. Burton was to defend a former Confederate official ("rich and pugnacious") being held accountable for government debts by "a set of renegade Southern men" who sought "heavy damages." It would be a "test" case, involving new points of constitutional law with few precedents, a case certain to attract widespread press coverage. Harrison waxed confident, sure he could beat Fullerton or any other New York lawyer. Even if he lost the case, Burton would attract national attention and establish his reputation. In any event he wanted a crack at those renegade southerners. "I am fiercely resolved," he told Constance, "to give their recreant backs a drubbing in the presence of all assembled Yankeedom."[16]

Burton penned word of his good fortune to his prospective mother-in-law. He admitted that success was not certain. He must compete with dozens of promising young attorneys, he warned her, most of them with valiant war records as federal soldiers. He could not yet offer Constance the comforts she deserved. Indeed, he told Mrs. Cary plainly that he could not guarantee Constance "immunity from actual discomforts" during their first year of marriage. But life without Constance had become unbearable. The Carys returned from France in early November, 1867. Before the month had ended, Burton and Constance wed at St. Ann's Episcopal Church, Morrisania, New York. They held their reception, attended by "a large assemblage of representatives of New York

16. Burton N. Harrison to Armistead Burt, January 11, 1867, in Armistead Burt Correspondence, DU; Burton Harrison to General Chesnut, January 11, 1867, in Williams-Chesnut-Manning Family Papers; William Preston Johnston to Burton N. Harrison, August 10, 22, 1867, Burton N. Harrison to Constance Cary, March 8, 1867, all in Harrison Family Papers, LC.

and Virginia families," at the Morrisania home of Constance's aunt, Patsey Jefferson Cary, who had married Gouverneur Morris, Jr., before the war. Constance, adorned in her Paris-made wedding gown, was, as tradition would have it, radiant. The groom, his usual debonaire self, withstood the jibes of old Yale classmates, including his best man, financier William C. Whitney. As their honeymoon-bound carriage left the wedding party behind, the couple laughed and waved while the lyrics of traditional Eli ditties grew fainter in their ears. Burton's favorite college song had been "Lauriger Horatius." He had introduced the air to Jennie Cary, Constance's cousin, before the war. Jennie, in turn, had fit the words of James R. Randall's "Maryland, My Maryland" to the stately music, thus producing one of the Confederacy's most memorable war songs:

> Hark to an exiled son's appeal . . .
> For life and death, for woe and weal.

The words, so familiar to Burton and Constance, held poignant reminders of who they were, where they had been, and whence they were bound. Their lives to come, like the words of the song, would entwine past, present, and future.[17]

By the time the newlyweds drove off to begin their life in a land of strangers, thousands of other former Confederates had embarked on the same adventure. The flight of southern rebels to northern climes had become an acknowledged and somewhat startling phenomenon. James D. B. DeBow, influential editor of the South's leading economic journal, announced earlier in the year that twenty thousand southerners had settled in New York City alone since the war. DeBow exaggerated. The 1870 census showed not quite nine thousand southerners living in New York and Brooklyn combined, and most of those people had lived there before the war. Barely fifteen thousand native-born white southerners populated the entire state of New York, and fewer than a thousand of those people had arrived since the war. But if DeBow erred in estimating the magnitude of rebel migration, he correctly identified the beginning of an important trend, not only in New York but across the North.[18]

That southerners should venture into the lair of Thaddeus Stevens gives rational folk reason for pause, yet on they came, and in larger

17. Burton N. Harrison to Monimia Cary, June 1, 1867, in Harrison Family Papers, LC; Harrison, *Recollections Grave and Gay,* 271–72; Harrison (ed.), *Aris Sonis Focisque,* 147–48.

18. *DeBow's Review,* n.s., II (February, 1867), 115.

numbers than before the war. Census statistics show that by 1870 the number of southerners living in the North exceeded antebellum levels for all states except Maryland, Virginia, and the Carolinas. Even when the North's southern-born population declined in the 1870s, seven southern states defied the trend. The surge of postwar emigration, as these data suggest, also came early. One-third of the core group arrived in Yankeedom before 1866; 70 percent settled in by 1870. But census numbers obscure the origins of Confederate emigration, at least as reflected by the core group. According to the census, the sharpest declines in the numbers of people moving north between 1860 and 1880 occurred in Virginia and the Carolinas. Within the core group, however, more Confederate carpetbaggers hailed from Virginia (136) than from any other state. The other top-ranked states, by birth of the refugees, are Tennessee (62), Kentucky (56), South Carolina (43), Alabama (43), and North Carolina (40). The list is altered only slightly when considering states—not always the place of birth—from which the largest numbers of carpetbaggers departed for the North. Virginia again tops the list (134), followed by Tennessee (68), Kentucky (67), Alabama (47), Georgia (43), and South Carolina (36).[19]

Curiously, census reports also suggest that southern emigration northward exceeded, in some aspects, the more famous march of northerners southward. Northern population in the former slave states dropped by nearly twenty thousand between 1860 and 1870, and the rare increases in Yankee residency appeared not in rebel strongholds such as South Carolina, Alabama, or Georgia but in Missouri, Kentucky, Maryland, and Tennessee. The first three of these states never officially joined the Confederacy and consequently did not experience the rigors of Reconstruction. Tennessee was a Confederate state, but it was the first rebel state readmitted to the Union and, with Virginia, one of the first to reestablish a conservative government. The number of northerners living in the South did not increase until the 1870s, the decade during which most former Confederate states regained home rule. True, many northerners who moved south after the war returned home before the 1870 census takers made their rounds, but the tabulation of southerners in the North is affected by the same circumstance. Northern population in the South shot up significantly in the 1870s, by

19. U.S. Bureau of the Census, *Population of the United States in 1860* (Washington, D.C., 1864), 41, 104, 130, 156, 227, 248, 262, 310, 319, 346, 398, 439, 445, 498, 544, *Ninth Census of the United States: Population* (Washington, D.C., 1872), I, 328–42; *Tenth Census of the United States: Population* (Washington, D.C., 1883), I, 480–95.

nearly fifty thousand; yet, given the North's larger white population—nearly twice as large as the South's—southern emigration northward in the fifteen years following the war seems to have been proportionately more significant than the northern emigration southward.[20]

Some commentators reveled in the spectacle of so bizarre an emigration, especially when contrasted with the postwar northern invasion of the South. The regions seemed to be exchanging populations, observed a South Carolinian. The Radicals in Congress, he warned, had better beware. Their policies, intended to subdue and harass white southerners, might boomerang. Using an analogy from war, he chuckled over the Radical attack:

> Very many of those who first drew their fire have judiciously flanked their batteries and are actually in their rear or otherwise out of range. Hence if Mr. [Thaddeus] Stevens or Mr. [Charles] Sumner have more shells to throw in this direction they should be reminded of the fact that they are more likely to blow up some of their late constituents than any of the principal "rebs." What a subject for a comic painter! Scene: Washington City; a long line of Radical batteries with guns all pointing South and manned by honorable members; in the rear, as lookers-on, crowds of former Southerners, once known as prominent "rebs," smoking and gaily commenting on the performance; in the distance the shells are seen bursting among New Englanders, freedmen, and a few poor natives "away down South in Dixie."[21]

Confederates went north for much the same reasons they dashed westward and abroad. Indeed, even in the broader context of nineteenth-century migration patterns, postwar southerners left the South for the same jumble of reasons, real and imagined, rational and irrational, that sent other emigrants scurrying across continents and oceans of the Western world. Conditions in the South forced out some people; the attractions of the North lured others. Some people responded to both impulses; others drifted without seriously considering their reasons. Some went with no firm prospects and unsure of their intentions but ready to try their luck. Not a few emigrants would have left the South anyway; the war only delayed or accelerated their departure. As in the case of emigration abroad and to the West, many more Confederates

20. U.S. Bureau of the Census, *Population of the United States in 1860*, 10, 20, 56, 76, 185, 196, 215, 272, 301, 362, 453, 470, 490, 523, *Ninth Census of the United States: Population*, I, 328–42, *Tenth Census of the United States: Population*, I, 480–95.

21. John Hammond Moore (ed.), *The Juhl Letters to the Charleston Courier: A View of the South, 1865–1871* (Athens, Ga., 1974), 127–28, letter of October 11, 1866.

than actually left the South felt the urge to emigrate. The obstacles to flight were the same, too: lack of money, ill health, family obligations, the burden of property, and so on. People who dared the journey operated on the vague notion that life in the North would provide better opportunities, a fresh chance in life, a new identity, a new home. That Confederates should be appalled by the general trend in southern affairs goes without saying, but some attention should be paid to the forces pulling people northward.[22]

The lure of Yankeedom radiated most powerfully from bustling, boisterous northern towns and cities. Urban areas monopolized business and professional opportunities, the best schools, and most of the jobs. Their vitality and prosperity appeared to southerners in the fell clutch of circumstance as "the wonder of the world." "From here to New York," exclaimed an awed Virginian in Chicago, "you are hardly ever out of sight of a town or village. Rail Roads run in every direction & seem to be more numerous than bridle paths with us. The energy and enterprise of this people have no limits. The most gigantic schemes are undertaken and carried through with a rapidity that takes ones breath away." A Texas businessman in Philadelphia expressed astonishment—not an easy thing for a Texan—at how much the North had changed in appearance since before the war. Towns and cities had replaced fields and forests. "Is it any wonder such hosts overpowered us?" he asked. "Pittsburgh and Chicago astonish us most of all," he told a friend. "I may say *hundreds* of canal boats and barges lay all along the river at Pittsburgh, each carrying a pile of barrels full of Petroleum! It is perfectly astonishing." These northerners had created a new world. And they were just beginning to flex their industrial muscles. "The energy and thrift of these people is amazing," testified another visitor to Pittsburgh. "I feel like 'Rip Van Winkle' every time I come on here."[23]

Of all northern cities, New York most often attracted ambitious young Confederates. One rebel, content to settle in Baltimore after the war, warned a brother not to follow his example. "New York is the place for you," he advised. "I often feel that it was a great mistake of my own in squatting down in this suburban city (for, indeed, all of our Atlantic

22. Daniel E. Sutherland, "Exiles, Emigrants, and Sojourners: The Post–Civil War Confederate Exodus in Perspective," *Civil War History,* XXXI (1985), 237–56; Everett S. Lee, "A Theory of Migration," *Demography,* III (1966), 47–57.

23. P.M.T. to John R. Bryan, October 4, 1867, in Bryan Family Papers, VL; Thomas Affleck to Anna Affleck, December 31, 1865, in Thomas Affleck Papers, LSU; Henry C. Yeatman to Mary Yeatman, May 6, 1868, in Yeatman-Polk Collection, TL.

cities are suburban to New York)." "I find this great city as it is, and ever shall be, the greatest city on the American continent," declared the unprejudiced correspondent of a South Carolina newspaper. "There are many magnificent cities in the United States, but New York excels them all. . . . New York is *the* city after all." A North Carolinian, evaluating Gotham's advantages as a mercantile center, agreed. "The whole world is open to this great city," he judged, "every body comes to N. York. They may go to Balt & Phila & Boston & purchase a few articles but the bulk of all goods must be bought here." Whether pursuing business, culture, education, or entertainment, most southerners held New York to be synonymous with northern urban life.[24]

Chicago became the midwestern magnet for downtrodden rebels. "There was a city worth talking about!" declared a fictional Kentuckian. "I found Chicago to far exceed all my expectations of it," confessed a real-life Kentuckian; "indeed it approximated much nearer to New York than I had imagined any city of its size could do." A Virginian on State Street declared himself "very much impressed with the size, wealth, and wonderful business prospects of that marvel of the West." A Mississippian judged it "an excellent place for a young man with business talent." Railroads made Chicago the hub of the nation in the decade after the war. Expanding railroads required any number of workers, southerners as well as northerners, to construct, maintain, and operate them. As the gleaming steel rails stretched east, south, and west, the city's wholesale houses gained vast new markets. They were among the first mercantile houses to send armies of "drummers" into the countryside. Extensive manufacturing sprang up to serve railroad, farming, and urban domestic needs. The city spent over $70 million on construction in the first five years after the war. Long before Carl Sandburg sang its praises, Chicago had become the "Hog Butcher for the World," the "Nation's Freight Handler." Chicago vibrated with promise. New streets, new houses, new shops, new schools, new churches, and new jobs made it an exciting city.[25]

24. Moses J. DeRosset to Louis H. DeRosset, November 20, 1869, in DeRosset Family Papers, SHC; Charleston *Daily News,* May 22, 1866, p. 1; James Southgate to Delia Southgate, August 14, 1867, in James Southgate Correspondence, DU.

25. Emma M. Connelly, *Under the Surface* (Philadelphia, 1873), 194; Lafayette Green to Ella Scott, September 3, 1865, in Green Collection, WK; Charles Ellis to George W. Munford, May 1, 1870, in Munford-Ellis Family Papers, DU; Josephine Rozet to Rebecca Mandeville, September 14, 1865, in Henry D. Mandeville and Family Papers, LSU; Homer Hoyt, *One Hundred Years of Land Values in Chicago: The Relationship of the*

Nearly 70 percent of the core group lived, at one time or another, in just seven cities and towns: New York, Brooklyn, Chicago, Philadelphia, Cincinnati, Evansville, and Boston. The largest number of people in the group, 93, became merchants and businessmen. The next largest number, 71 physicians, practiced their healing craft in cities and towns more often than in rural hamlets. Farmers and farm laborers ranked third on the occupational list, with 66 representatives, but they are only 12 percent of the group. Nearly all of the remaining people— lawyers, bankers, clerks, journalists, educators, clergymen, artists, railroad agents, fifty-two job categories in all—found work in towns and cities. By contrast, a whopping 184 Confederate carpetbaggers had fathers who had labored as planters, farmers, or farmhands; that is more than half of the fathers with known occupations. One-third of the core group had been students when the war started, uncommitted to any occupation or profession, adaptable, able to begin life anew. Of those people committed to occupations before the war, 65 had engaged in trade or business, and 63 had been farmers or planters. Other sizable groups included journalists and literary people (37), physicians (37), lawyers and jurists (28), and educators (12). Additionally, large numbers of people, not counted in the core group, came north with no intention of settling in Yankeedom but hopeful of securing jobs as agents in the South for northern merchants, insurance companies, and shipping firms.[26]

Businessmen and merchants found the financial opportunities in northern cities irresistible. Some of these men had enjoyed enviable reputations and profitable connections in the antebellum North, either through their own businesses or as partners in northern-based firms. The war disrupted many such arrangements, but businessmen ventured to reform their companies after the conflict. Some people contacted old partners; others began paying off old debts to reestablish their credit. At the very least, they stationed agents in northern cities to provide reliable reports on market conditions, fluctuations in interest rates, and the pulse of financial and mercantile activities. Even retail merchants not interested in moving north or dependent on northern financial conditions traveled north to replenish their inventories, thus stimulating a

Growth of Chicago to the Rise in Its Land Values, 1830–1933 (Chicago, 1933), 83–87; P.M.T. to John R. Bryan, October 4, 1867, in Bryan Family Papers.

26. Joseph P. Dobbins to John S. Dobbins, 1865–67, in John S. Dobbins Papers, EU; James Southgate to Delia Southgate, 1867, in Southgate Correspondence.

swarm of mercantile activity. Thousands of boxes, crates, and bales filled northern streets and wharves, to be inspected by southern clients. Buyers from as far away as the Carolinas, Georgia, Alabama, Louisiana, and Texas crowded the exchanges and wholesale warehouses. Likewise, sojourning Confederates appeared in New York, Chicago, and Philadelphia seeking northern financial backing for southern railroads, coal mines, plantations, harbor facilities, schools, and similar projects required for the region's physical reconstruction. Former Confederates needed "Green Backs," declared a Mississippian bitterly, "to plaster them over the fields of the dead South to make them green again."[27]

Of course, caution was demanded; these were perilous times. If southerners in general hesitated to move north, businessmen proved downright skittish. So many things had to be considered. Southerners heard glowing reports of golden economic opportunities. A successful cotton broker judged northern financiers "ready to settle on most any terms" with southerners who openly declared their financial situations and expectations. Yet even this gentleman urged friends to "take time" and carefully analyze the prospects before plunging northward. If one could only tell with some assurance what the future held. So many imponderables threatened ruination for impulsive Confederates. Would southern Negroes work? Would all Confederates have to take the loyalty oath? Would the federal government close southern ports to foreign trade? How would the new bankruptcy act affect antebellum debts? Should southerners rush to settle old accounts or wait on events? What about pride? It was one thing to talk about moving north, quite another to take the step, to enter a northern bank and plead for money. Would the Yankees help? Were the rumors of their generosity true? One Charleston factor threw up his arms in despair. "It will most likely be 18 months before we shall know our condition," he decided in late spring 1865, "or what sort of Govt. is to be established over us. What are we to do in the meantime?" "We are still receiving all sorts of contradictory & uncer-

27. Harold D. Woodman, *King Cotton and His Retainers: Financing and Marketing the Cotton Crop of the South, 1800–1925* (Lexington, Ky., 1968), 245–46; *Metropolitan Record and New York Vindicator,* September 12, 1865, p. 12, September 30, 1865, p. 3; Sam H. Corey to William Crutchfield, February 7, 1868, in Crutchfield-Fearn-Steele Papers, MSA; John Hope Franklin, *A Southern Odyssey: Travelers in the Antebellum North* (Baton Rouge, 1976), 263–83; Lawrence N. Powell, *New Masters: Northern Planters During the Civil War and Reconstruction* (New Haven, 1980), 38–39; John F. King to Lin Caperton, November 21, 1865, in Thomas Butler King Papers, SHC.

tain rumors," he reported a fortnight later, "and living in the dark as to the future, or even as to what is going on around us."[28]

The activities of H. R. Johnson and Company, cotton brokers, of Americus, Georgia, illustrate the early postwar probings conducted by many firms. Formed in 1859 by Henry R. Johnson and Uriah B. Harrold, Johnson and Company barely survived the war years. By 1866 the firm owed over thirty thousand dollars to more than a dozen northern firms. Uriah Harrold traveled to New York early in the summer of 1866 to acquire firsthand knowledge of brokers, markets, investment opportunities, and the possibilities of reestablishing the firm's northern credit. He immediately noticed a significant change in the northern financial climate. Speculative fever had grown rampant since 1860. Money had become "a drug," and so many brokers engaged in speculation that it had become impossible to judge a company's solvency and stability. Harrold quickly sought the advice of an old hand in northern business, Thomas Wood, another southerner, who had served as New York supplier for Johnson and Company before the war. Talk of a partnership began, with Harrold and Wood joining forces to pay their debts and establish offices at St. Louis and New York.[29]

Meanwhile, Uriah Harrold learned to be wary of Yankee sharpers. When shipping a consignment of flour to Georgia, he noticed that the barrels of flour being stowed aboard ship were marked "in bad order." He hurried to halt the loading but was too late. He rushed to the agent who had sold him the flour, "a very nice old gentleman" named Thomas Earl. Earl assured him the flour was fine; only a couple of barrels were discolored. Harrold expressed dissatisfaction. He insisted that the bill remain unpaid until his firm unloaded and inspected the flour at Americus. If it arrived in bad order, the bill must be reduced accordingly. The R. M. Reynolds Company, which had supplied the flour, claimed the suspect barrels had merely been mislabeled by careless shipping clerks, but it agreed to Harrold's arrangement for payment.[30]

Despite such experiences, Harrold became enthusiastic about estab-

28. Moore (ed.), *Juhl Letters,* 40, letter of September 4, 1865; A. H. Jones to Henry L. Reynolds, October 3, 1865, in Henry Lee Reynolds Papers, SHC; Henry Gourdin to Robert N. Gourdin, May 22, June 3, 1865, both in Robert Newman Gourdin Papers, EU.

29. Uriah B. Harrold to Thomas Harrold, June 24, 1866, in Harrold Brothers Papers, EU. See Woodman, *King Cotton and His Retainers,* for a broader view of H. R. Johnson and Company's antebellum and postbellum activities.

30. Uriah B. Harrold to H. R. Johnson and Company, July 11, 1866, in Harrold Brothers Papers.

lishing the firm in New York. He told his father, an associate of the company, that an agent based in New York could generate revenue from any number of sources once he had won the confidence of a few Georgia planters. Planters, Harrold observed, tended to be "a *clanish* sett." If a company acquired the consignments of one, it soon had several more, all of them swayed in their choice by the first enlistee. "The fact of it is," he explained, "all the grocery trade & dry goods too as far as that is concerned of the South is seeking new channels and if we expect to do anything with it we ought to get to work this fall." He volunteered to stay in New York and help the company rebuild. Rebuilding would be hard work. In his weeks of observation and negotiation, Harrold had "only been idle when it was hot enough to kill a Gopher or a Salmander." He had not even had time to see "the sights" or take his wife into the city. His father advised waiting another year before establishing a northern branch. The lure of Yankeedom was intoxicating, but, like the sirens' voices, dangerous. One did not dare go north unprepared.[31]

Northern schools attracted ambitious southerners who sought preparation for life's contest, but this situation was not new. Private academies, trade schools, female seminaries, colleges, medical schools, law schools, and military academies had all received their quotas of southerners before the war. The South had some good schools, but the North had more and better schools, and the war only widened the breach. Most southern schools, whether public or private, lost their financial base during the war, when educators could no longer depend on state or private funds. A formerly wealthy planter explained to the superintendent of a Louisiana seminary that he could not afford his usual annual donation. The planter was even considering sending one of his sons, who had "a mechanical turn of mind," to Cornell University, where the young man could work his way through school. "The times," he explained regretfully, "demand of us to do the best according to our means." Good teachers were at a premium, too. Some of the South's ablest antebellum teachers, tutors, and professors had been northerners who returned north when hostilities commenced. These men were hard to replace, and some of the South's ablest natives, such as the LeConte brothers, joined the postwar migration. Sidney Lanier, the Georgia poet and musician, tried to earn a living by teaching after the war, but he soon gave up. "These Southern Colleges are all so poor," he complained to a

31. Uriah B. Harrold to Thomas Harrold, July 28, 1866, in *ibid.*

friend, "that they hold out absolutely no inducement in the way of support to a Professor."[32]

The essential problem with southern education at all levels became the large number of competing schools. Schools scrambled for scarce funds and students when half as many schools could have done the job more cheaply and more efficiently. Sectionalism within the South and within states produced ridiculous duplication of facilities and diluted the quality of instruction. Northern and southern states with similar-sized populations, like Georgia and Michigan or Virginia and Massachusetts, remained fairly equal in numbers of colleges, numbers of professional schools, and student-faculty ratios. Yet gaps in quality and variety were apparent, and the largest northern states, especially New York, Pennsylvania, and Ohio, offered both a variety and quality of education impossible for any southern state to match. A young South Carolina woman who had traveled in Europe immediately after the war entered a Philadelphia school in 1872. She was older than most of her classmates, which embarrassed her, but she understood the benefits of a northern education. "From what I hear of this school," she explained to a cousin, "I hope to learn there to write better and quicker, to express myself more readily, to get a better idea of History and Geography, Latin, French, and some of the higher English branches." She believed the school would remedy her "ignorance."[33]

Southerners seeking something other than a liberal arts education often had little alternative but to follow the polar star. The North had far more commercial and technical schools than the South. Daniel A. Tompkins, one of the principal builders of an industrialized "New South," obtained his expertise at a northern school. Born and raised on a South Carolina plantation, Tompkins naturally gravitated toward

32. Franklin, *Southern Odyssey,* 53–80; Francis Butler Simpkins and Charles Pierce Rowland, *A History of the South* (4th ed.; New York, 1972), 165–75; J. Thornton Mills III, "Fiscal Policy and the Failure of Radical Reconstruction in the Lower South," in J. Morgan Kousser and James M. McPherson (eds.), *Region, Race, and Reconstruction: Essays in Honor of C. Vann Woodward* (New York, 1982), 380–83; St. John R. Liddell to David F. Boyd, July 30, 1869, in Liddell Family Papers, LSU; Sidney Lanier to Milton H. Northrup, March 15, 1869, in Charles R. Anderson, *et al.* (eds.), *The Centennial Edition of the Works of Sidney Lanier* (10 vols.; Baltimore, 1945), VIII, 9.

33. U.S. Bureau of the Census, *Ninth Census of the United States: Population,* I, 462–69; John Samuel Ezell, *The South Since 1865* (2nd ed.; Norman, 1978), 242–46, 259–64; Lee Soltow and Edward Stevens, *The Rise of Literacy and the Common Schools in the United States: A Socioeconomic Analysis to 1870* (Chicago, 1981); Minnie Adger to Jane Smyth, September 19, 1872, in Adger-Smyth-Flynn Family Papers, SL.

South Carolina College in 1867, but he soon learned his error. South Carolina College offered a fine classical education, but Tompkins had no use for Cicero and Shakespeare. He wanted to be an engineer, and so Rensselaer Polytechnic Institute, at Troy, New York, became his alma mater. Similarly, northern medical and law schools offered superior facilities and training. Few nineteenth-century medical schools, north or south, had rigid entrance requirements; few schools offered postgraduate training. They engaged in "diploma traffic," sometimes offering their sheepskins for a fee by mail. The University of Louisville and the University of Louisiana, probably the best southern medical schools, did not engage in that practice, yet even they accepted all white males who could read and write English, and they provided only minimal training. Most observers conceded that the advantages, slim as they may have been, rested with New York and Pennsylvania schools. Certainly anyone seeking advanced medical training went north or to Europe. Consequently, several Confederates who became distinguished physicians in the North, including John Allan Wyeth, William Mecklenburg Polk, and Walker Gill Wylie, moved north originally to complete their medical training.[34]

After obtaining an education, whether in the North or South, many professional people moved north to cash in on northern prosperity. Lawyers, like Burton Harrison, found the financial opportunities of a northern practice too tempting to resist and far superior to the livelihoods they anticipated earning in Charleston, Richmond, or New Orleans. The northern legal profession many have been crowded, a dog-eat-dog competitive world, but southern lawyers were accustomed to competition. Establishing a law practice in the older, more settled portions of the South had been difficult even before the war, when southerners could afford legal counsel. With the advent of hard economic times after the war, many lawyers moved northward. Physicians liked the opportunities available in New York, Pennsylvania, and Ohio. The ratio of physicians to residents in most of the South was higher than in those

34. George Tayloe Winston, *A Builder of the New South, Being the Story of the Life Work of Daniel Augustus Tompkins* (Garden City, N.Y., 1920), 22–23; Howard Bunyan Clay, "Daniel Augustus Tompkins: An American Bourbon" (Ph.D. dissertation, University of North Carolina, 1950), 3–6; Martin Kaufman, *American Medical Education: The Formative Years, 1765–1910* (Westport, Conn., 1976), 111ff.; John A. Wyeth, *With Sabre and Scalpel: The Autobiography of a Soldier and Surgeon* (New York, 1914), 320, 327–30, 247; *National Cyclopaedia of American Biography* (59 vols. and index; New York, 1898–1980), XXVI, 256–57, XXXVII, 88.

three northern states, so that life's glittering prizes seemed more easily obtainable in Yankeedom. A Kentucky physician who had contemplated emigration to Canada or Brazil made a brief visit to New York City. Observation convinced him that the competition for patients in Gotham was not nearly so intense as people supposed. He decided to move north, and he encouraged his brother-in-law, a lawyer, to do the same, assuring him, "The field here is immensely large in every vocation of life."[35]

A burgeoning mass of northern magazines and newspapers, better financed and with larger circulations than their southern rivals, offered lucrative futures to aspiring writers with facile pens. An amazing number of southern magazines established in the decade following the war made life somewhat easier for writers and poets. Dozens of literary, agricultural, religious, family, and household magazines—every conceivable type and more than had been published at any time in southern history—appealed for readers from Baltimore to Atlanta, from Louisville to New Orleans. Unfortunately, their numbers too often proved to be their most impressive feature, and not even the numbers could match northern rivals. Virginia, Mississippi, and Georgia combined produced 335 daily and periodical publications in 1870. New York, Pennsylvania, and Illinois, the northern publishing centers, produced nearly 2,000 publications, and New York alone had 835. Nearly all new southern magazines failed within a decade, most within two years. Nearly all, throughout their brief histories, teetered precariously on their bank balances, a predicament that forced them to scrimp on the quality of their publications and left them unable to pay contributors. The South, as during the war, found itself outgunned.[36]

Influential, well-established northern journals, like *Harper's Monthly* and the *Atlantic Monthly,* proved loath to punish the work of former Confederates, but new journals—*Scribner's, Lippincott's,* the *Galaxy,* the *Round Table,* and *Appleton's Journal*—published their work in

35. E. Lee Shepard, "Breaking into the Profession: Establishing a Law Practice in Antebellum Virginia," *Journal of Southern History,* XLVIII (1982), 404–10; John S. Haller, Jr., *American Medicine in Transition, 1840–1910* (Urbana, 1981), 326–31; Theophilus Steele to Robert J. Breckinridge, October 3, 1865, to William C. P. Breckinridge, October 16, 1865, both in Breckinridge Family Papers, LC.

36. U.S. Bureau of the Census, *Ninth Census of the United States: Population,* I, 482–93; Cornelia P. Spencer to Dr. Wilson, March 7, 1866, in Cornelia Phillips Spencer Papers, SHC; Jay B. Hubbell, *The South in American Literature, 1607–1900* (Durham, 1954), 716–27.

hopes of claiming a national circulation and competing with the ante-bellum giants. Similar growth in the northern metropolitan press offered jobs to southern journalists. Again, numbers tell the story. Virginia and Georgia together sponsored thirty-one daily publications in 1870. New York had eighty-seven, Pennsylvania another fifty-five. Southerners with families to feed and debts to pay realized that, much as they disliked the prospects of a northern residence, sentiment and pride had to be discarded. If northern newspapers wanted reporters, editors, literary contributors, even office boys, southerners would fill the jobs. Several southern publishers even moved their offices to Yankeedom. Best known was James D. B. DeBow, who, having printed his *Review* in New York even before the war, transferred his business office there as well in 1865. Of course, one did not have to live in the North to publish there, as any number of successful southern authors and correspondents had proved. But many aspiring writers and journalists found it advantageous to be close to the action.[37]

Even successful writers could sound glum. William Gilmore Simms, broken in spirit and pocketbook, pondered the future from Charleston. "Every thing in the social atmosphere here is miserable," he complained to a northern friend. "The people are hopeless—in despair—surrounded by Ruin & threatened, in addition of the loss of their liberties, by the immediate pressure of Famine. The whole South is in this condition, and doomed to be the Ireland of the Union—a perpetual incubus." The fate of a novelist such as Simms seemed particularly bleak. The southern people had never been noted for reading; no agricultural people ever had been, thought Simms. He tried to stay cheerful, to look for a silver, even a gilded, lining. "Have Faith . . . believe in God. Patience & shuffle the cards" became his philosophy. Micawber bent over his shoulder and whispered that he must go north, "in the hope that something come down, in the shape of quails & manna, or what may be considered their equivalents greenbacks." Yet Simms shrank from prostrating his art for a northern public that, if more widely read than his southern audience, preferred trash to literature. Northerners, Simms maintained, were "given up to a mental as well as moral debauchery." In the end, Simms resided in New York only periodically, just long enough to nego-

37. U.S. Bureau of the Census, *Ninth Census of the United States,* I, 482–93; Spencer to Wilson, March 7, 1866, in Spencer Papers; Hubbell; *South in American Literature,* 716–27. Gunther Barth, *City People: The Rise of Modern City Culture in Nineteenth-Century America* (New York, 1980), 58–109; Ottis Clark Skipper, *J. D. B. DeBow: Magazinist of the Old South* (Athens, Ga., 1958), 199–201.

tiate contracts and allow a sickly daughter to escape deadly Charleston summers. He judged the price of living as a permanent "exile" in the North to be too high.[38]

Like writers seeking publishers, clerks seeking employers, lawyers seeking clients, and businessmen seeking markets, southern artists flocked to northern cities in search of patrons. They saw little alternative. Struggling to feed and clothe themselves, southerners had little money to commission paintings, monumental sculpture, or grandiose buildings. Consequently, the national and international acclaim craved by southern painters, sculptors, and architects eluded them in their native region. How different appeared the land over the rainbow, where fame and fortune beckoned. Gilded Age northerners paid hefty commissions for paintings and sculptures that commemorated their climb up the greasy pole of success or that celebrated northern war heroes and martial triumphs. Southern artists seldom refused Yankee dollars. Even artists who abhorred the "horrors of radicalism" and urged fellow Confederates to hurl back the "foul flood" of Yankee rule in the South understood the necessity of accepting northern patronage. Robert Loftin Newman, late of the 16th Virginia Regiment, complained to a friend, "Money has been so scarce that you can readily conceive that the arts would be the first and last to feel it." Newman tried to rectify the unhappy situation in Nashville by establishing an academy of fine arts, to be sponsored by artists, businessmen, and cultural benefactors. The project failed, and Newman moved to New York.[39]

Nor could Confederate artists have better timed their arrival in Yankeedom. Tremors of artistic revolution that would convulse the country for several decades had begun. New styles of painting and architectural design made their debuts, and an avant-garde atmosphere permeated northern artistic communities. The atmosphere, wafting southward, intoxicated artists, who felt isolated in their provincial homeland. Sidney Lanier believed that an artist could never flourish south of Mason's and Dixon's line, and not just for want of money. "I moved to N.Y.," he confided to his father, "to see at once, by using the severest tests,—that is, by measuring strength with the best artists—

38. William Gilmore Simms to Evert A. Duyckinck, February 10, 1866, March 21, 1867, to William H. Ferris, March 7, 1867, to Charles E. A. Gayarré, April 12, 1867, March 13, 1868, all in Mary C. Simms Oliphant, *et al.* (eds.), *The Letters of William Gilmore Simms* (5 vols.; Columbia, S.C., 1952), IV, 537, V, 22–23, 36, 42–44, 115.

39. Robert L. Newman to William Fergusson, November 8, 1872, February 6, 1873, both in Fergusson Family Papers, TL.

whether there was any hope for me to excel greatly, either as musician or writer." Once in New York, Lanier discovered that his biggest obstacle to success must be the "*lonesomeness*" of his earlier artistic life. "I mean," he explained, "from the want of that atmosphere which is only to be found in a great city."[40]

Less vibrant folk than Lanier came north seeking lonesomeness, only they called it anonymity. To their delight, they discovered that the potential for losing oneself in the urban crowd could be rivaled for effect only by the desolateness of the Great Plains. "You forget Bessie," a Mississippian explained to her aunt, "that in such an immense City as N.Y. with its population swelled to overflowing by the thousands of people from the South who are making it their home, I am but as one drop in the mighty Ocean: my identity swallowed up in the vast sea of humanity inhabitting it." "Come North," she concluded, "and you will at once see that *I* belong only to the great 'unknown.'" "One is safe from observation in this great city," repeated a South Carolinian, "never mind what he may do or how conspicuously he does it." A Virginian believed New York was the only city where a southerner could "breathe freely." "South of the line," he explained, "he suffocates beneath the eternal flag, or is crushed by inevitable 'orders'. . . but here, rich or poor, he is lost in the crowd, and feels, at least, the value of his birth-right as a man!" The city's vastness could prove a haven not only from inquisitive northerners but as a means of avoiding friends and relatives in the South. A Mr. Pinhorn of Richmond, Virginia, found the canyons of New York a blessed sanctuary from Mrs. Pinhorn, who placed an advertisement in a New York newspaper requesting information about the whereabouts of her miscreant spouse.[41]

Knowing they must live as well as work in the North, Confederates were impressed by the sympathetic political and social climate of several important Yankee cities. Again, New York headed the list. Southerners knew that the Democratic party ruled New York. They knew that wartime mayor Fernando Wood had urged his city to secede from the Union. They knew that most of the North's illicit wartime trade with the South

40. Sidney Lanier to Robert Lanier, November 29, 1873, in Anderson, *et al.* (eds.), *Works of Sidney Lanier*, VIII, 423–24; Jane S. Gabin, *A Living Ministrelsy: The Poetry and Music of Sidney Lanier* (Macon, Ga., 1985), 37–46.

41. Carlie Mansfield to Rebecca Mandeville [1867], in Mandeville and Family Papers; DeRosset Lamar to Emily Hammond, March 20, 1877, in Hammond, Bryan, and Cumming Families Papers, SCL; *Southern Opinion*, September 9, 1867, p. 2; New York *Daily News*, September 14, 1865, p. 7.

originated in New York. They knew that influential New York news-papers—the *Daily News, World,* and *Metropolitan Record*—had sup-ported the South during the war and still sided with the South in the war's aftermath. They knew that many southerners lived in New York and that during the war they had aided and concealed Confederate agents, agitated against the government, and plotted insurrection and destruction of parts of the city with Confederates in Canada. They knew that Fort Lafayette and Fort Delaware had been filled with New Yorkers incarcerated during the war for treasonous public statements. Migrat-ing rebels found all this a most comforting situation. New York, though a Yankee city with plenty of Republican vermin, nonetheless seemed less hostile, less intimidating than many places in the South.[42]

Chicago and Philadelphia boasted congenial atmospheres, too. Both cities fostered strong Copperhead strains during the war. Philadelphia, always known for its banking and mercantile activity, was cozier and less hurried than either Chicago or New York, more southern, one might say. One scholar believes the anti-Negro, antiabolitionist, pro-southern leanings of many Philadelphians represented the typical at-titude among urban northerners and that Philadelphia's Republican party retained power during the war years only because timely federal victories on the battlefield saved its candidates in the 1863 and 1864 elections. Nothing could save them by 1868. A southern sympathizer described Philadelphia in that year as a "staid, sober, dignified commer-cial metropolis." Newly arrived southerners savored the atmosphere. Chicago, more rough and tumble than the Quaker City, had a vocal Democratic minority. Influential businessmen contacted leading Con-federate exiles in Canada. The "financial godfather to the Illinois De-mocracy," Cyrus McCormick, was one of many antebellum southerners who settled in Chicago. During the war, he spoke boldly against the northern war effort. After the war, he befriended former Confederates in the city and provided generous financial aid to the South.[43]

42. Philip S. Foner, *Business and Slavery: The New York Merchants and the Irrepress-ible Conflict* (Chapel Hill, 1941), 306–14; Ludwell H. Johnson, "Commerce Between Northeastern Ports and the Confederacy, 1861–1865," *Journal of American History,* LIV (1967), 36–37, and "Northern Profit and Profiteers: The Cotton Rings of 1864–1865," *Civil War History,* XII (1966), 101–15; Bayly Ellen Marks and Mark Norton Schatz (eds.), *Between North and South: A Maryland Journalist Views the Civil War, The Nar-rative of William Wilkins Glenn, 1861–1869* (Rutherford, N.J., 1976), 215, entry of May 16, 1865.

43. John F. King to Lin Caperton, November 10, 1865, in King Papers; William Dusinberre, *Civil War Issues in Philadelphia, 1856–1865* (Philadelphia, 1965), 134–35, 175–80, 253–58; Nicholas B. Wainwright, "The Loyal Opposition in Civil War Phila-

In other words, many southerners felt confident, particularly before the Reconstruction Acts of 1867, that northerners stood ready to treat them as erring brothers. Northerners might toss a few sharp words, a few disgusted looks at the South, but that would only be for the sake of form, a ritual hand-slapping to emphasize northern displeasure. Once formalities had been dispensed with, and provided they behaved themselves, southerners would be free to resume their lives, speak their minds, and walk in the broad sunshine of life. Ironically, many Confederates assumed they would be freer in Yankeedom than in their own militarily occupied homeland. Tennyson, in his ageless wisdom, had started Burton Harrison thinking in those terms:

> You ask me, why, though ill at ease,
> Within this region I subsist,
> Whose spirits falter in their mist,
> And languish for the purple seas.
> It is the land that freemen till,
> That sober-suited Freedom chose,
> The land where girt with friends or foes
> A man may speak the thing he will.[44]

Other parts of the North, outside the cities, attracted Confederates with the same combination of sympathetic social climate and economic opportunity. Census reports say that the largest numbers of southerners settled in midwestern farming communities of Indiana, Illinois, and Ohio, and we know that many of them were Confederates. Fictional Confederates in a novel written by a rebel veteran who moved to Indiana marveled at the Midwest's prosperity. "Everything was so different from what she had been used to," explains the narrator, "and fashioned after so grand a scale, that the expense seemed fabulous." The very atmosphere seemed different. "It is like passing forth from a blooming and fragrant forest into the track of a last year's hurricane," adds one character in describing the sensation of his return to the South. "It is more as if the sun had faded the soil and dried up the people's energies,"

---

delphia," *Pennsylvania Magazine of History and Biography,* LXXXVIII (1964), 294–315; William G. Armstrong Diaries, 1867–69 (MS in HSP); Frank L. Klement, *The Copperheads in the Middle West* (Chicago, 1960), 198–202; Frederick Francis Cook, *Bygone Days in Chicago: Recollections of the "Garden City" of the Sixties* (Chicago, 1910), 74–75, 129–30; Anna J. Sanders Journal, September 18, 1865 (MS in Papers of George N. Sanders, LC); Horace Samuel Merrill, *Bourbon Democracy of the Middle West, 1865–1896* (Baton Rouge, 1953), 37; William T. Hutchinson, *Cyrus Hall McCormick* (2 vols.; New York, 1935), II, 285–92.

44. Tennyson, "On a Mourner," in *Poems and Dramatic Works,* 60.

responded a friend. No wonder the North's broad expanse of plowed prairie and vast herds of livestock so impressed southern farmers.[45]

Like the cities, some midwestern communities had significant conclaves of southern sympathizers. Descendants of antebellum emigrants from the South, staunch Democrats, Negrophiles, and merchants and financiers with southern investments had good reason to look kindly upon states' rights, slavery, the Confederacy, and the conquered South. Confederate spies and agents prowled at will through the Midwest during the war, and scores of young midwestern men went south to bear arms for the Confederacy. Additionally, thousands of southern refugees from the border states of Virginia, Tennessee, Kentucky, and Missouri settled in the Midwest during the war. Many wartime refugees were Unionists seeking to escape conscription or retribution, but many homeless and hungry Confederates joined them. By 1864, Indiana's Republican governor, Oliver Morton, worried about the impact these disloyal refugees might have on coming elections should they decide to claim Indiana citizenship and vote Democratic. He begged the War Department "to have those people returned to their homes and to send no more into Indiana."[46]

The extent and strength of midwestern disloyalty is a controversial issue. Wartime Unionists and Republican politicians undoubtedly exaggerated the dangers, either from genuine, if ill-founded, fears or as a calculated means of arousing anti-Confederate sentiment. Still, if Copperheads did not populate the Midwest by the tens of thousands, as nervous politicians claimed, they most certainly existed, and in numbers large enough to provide a friendly atmosphere for many postwar Confederate emigrants.[47]

45. Tennyson, *Poems and Dramatic Works,* 60; Maurice Thompson, *His Second Campaign* (Boston, 1883), 67, 101–102; J. W. Wilson to John F. Snyder, October 1, 1866, in John F. Snyder Papers, IHL.

46. Arthur Charles Cole, *The Era of the Civil War, 1848–1870* (Springfield, Ill., 1919), 296–99, 330–35; Frank C. Arena, "Southern Sympathizers in Iowa During Civil War Days," *Annals of Iowa,* XXX (1951), 486–538; Emma Lou Thornbrough, *Indiana in the Civil War Era, 1850–1880* (Indianapolis, 1965), 192–97; W. Stanley Hoole (ed.), *A Rebel Spy in Yankeeland: The Thrilling Adventures of Major W. P. Gorman Who Was the Emissary of the Confederacy to the Copperheads of the North, 1861–1865* (University, Ala., 1981), 16–27; F. Metcalf, "The Illinois Confederate Company," *Confederate Veteran,* XVI (May, 1908), 224–25; Kenneth M. Stampp, *Indiana Politics During the Civil War* (Indianapolis, 1949), 250.

47. Frank L. Klement, *Dark Lanterns: Secret Political Societies, Conspiracies, and Treason Trials in the Civil War* (Baton Rouge, 1984), 1–6; Bethania Meradith Smith,

Wandering and homeless Confederates found safe havens in midwestern farming communities. "I didn't go back home [after the war]," recalled a Georgia veteran who labored as a farmhand in Ohio and Indiana for nearly a quarter of a century; "I didnt have no home [and] father was killed in the war." Another Confederate soldier, released from an Indianapolis prison camp after the war, found refuge in the home of an Indiana Copperhead, or "butternut," and did not return south for over a year. "He treated me as a son," recalled the veteran. "He paid me good wages for the little work I could do with one hand [his left hand had been wounded at Bull's Gap] which was helping his wife milk the cows." A Missouri Confederate newly settled in Iowa found the political atmosphere less oppressive in his adopted state. "I am now very thankful I did not sit down in that Radical state," he confided to a friend, referring to Missouri. "I think it would be well to abandon it to the Radicals & the Negroes & let them work it out." Even before the war ended, an Illinois conservative urged a paroled Confederate to cross over into Yankeedom. "I would be much pleased should you conclude to remove here," he assured the southerner, and he promised to help the veteran in any way possible.[48]

Tidings of sympathy and invitations to come North poured south from urban and rural regions alike. Some invitations had a clear political ring. A former Democratic congressman from New York State swore that his doors stood "open to any Southern man however prominent or obnoxious he has been or is to the wretches who are now in the ascendant." A Connecticut man predicted Democratic victory in the 1868 elections, "after which," he assured a South Carolinian, "we shall insist on our Southern friends taking possession of the North." A Pennsylvania woman wrote to a Georgia friend: "I need not (I hope) tell you how we suffered with our southern friends during the wicked war—how our hearts bled as we heard of their sorrows & privations—and how *none of us* ever said a word or did a deed which could in any way favor or help

"Civil War Subversives," *Journal of the Illinois State Historical Society,* XLV (1952), 220–40; A. J. Beitzinger, "The Father of Copperheadism in Wisconsin," *Wisconsin Magazine of History,* XXXIX (1955), 17–25; Thornbrough, *Indiana in the Civil War Era,* 119–21, 180–84, 211, 214–17; John W. Headley, *Confederate Operations in Canada and New York* (New York, 1906), 226–30, 264–83; Hubert W. Wubben, *Civil War Iowa and the Copperhead Movement* (Ames, 1980), 67–68, 120–21, 138–39, 222–25.

48. David Monroe Bannister and Franklin Sevier Leonard, in Civil War Veterans Questionnaires (Confederate), TL; S. Christy to John F. Snyder, February 2, 1866, S. S. Brooks to John F. Snyder, October 30, 1863, both in Snyder Papers.

the vile cause of the abolition Yankee." She explained how she and her husband had broken with many northern friends in preference for their southern friends and political beliefs. "We felt political bonds to be the strongest on earth, for friendship & religion were trampled in the dust." Nor were they alone in their advocacy of southern rights. Their county, York, was "a splendid Copperhead region." "Indeed," she continued, "you people dont know the friends you have in the north. . . . My great & only objection to my 'southern brethern'—& will add *sisters*—is that they are too harsh on *all* northern people—making no distinction between a low mischevous Yankee & an honest decent person from Pennsylvania." Another "congenial spirit" invited a southern friend to come north. "There are a select few," he emphasized, "who have not worshipped the Juggernaut of Abolitionism & who have been as warm supporters of the South as any among yourselves."[49]

Other offers contained no hint of political partisanship. Families divided geographically by the war, such as the Carys, were sometimes reunited when a northern cousin or aunt summoned southern relations to join them. When Sidney Lanier first went north, he found unexpected aid from several cousins he had never before met. A northerner wrote to a South Carolina relation: "We sympathize with you cordially in all your troubles. . . . Is there no hope of our seeing you here this Spring? It would give us great pleasure if you would come to our house whenever you do so." Old friends, even if political rivals, also embraced after the war. "I think you are hardly warranted in assuming that your northern classmates are estranged from you by the war," one fellow advised a Louisianian. "I have never heard any of them, even the most intensely radical, speak in anything but the kindest terms of all of the class in the south, and I believe you would be cordially welcomed." A Pennsylvanian assured a Virginian, "The war has not changed my friendship for you in the least." This gentleman had not turned Copperhead during the war, and he believed his southern friend would have thought less of him had he done so. Nevertheless, he concluded, "As the war is all over I hope we will all forget and forgive and be better friends than before."[50]

49. A. C. Niven to Howell Cobb, April 9, 1866, in Ulrich B. Phillips (ed.), *The Correspondence of Robert Toombs, Alexander H. Stephens, and Howell Cobb,* in *Annual Report of American Historical Association for the Year 1911* (2 vols.; Washington, D.C., 1913), II, 679–80; Thomas H. Seymour to Milledge L. Bonham, July 13, 1868, in Milledge Luke Bonham Papers, SCL; Rebikah B. Shunk to Mary Ann Cobb, November 6, 1866, in Howell Cobb Papers, UG; Benjamin Douglass to Thomas Smyth, January 5, 1866, in Adger-Smyth-Flynn Family Papers.

50. Aubrey Harrison Starke, *Sidney Lanier: A Biographical and Critical Study* (New York, 1964), 86; Angelina Van Buren to John L. Manning, April 4, 1868, in Williams-

At least some of these invitations produced results. Nearly 30 percent of the core group had friends or relatives who welcomed them to their new northern homes; 17 percent of these emigrants had lived in the North for varying amounts of time before the war, and 9 percent had been born in the North. Additionally, at least 12 percent of the core group had received some education in northern schools. Available information suggests that only 6 percent of the core group had no previous contact, in the form of friends, relatives, education, or antebellum residence, with the North. Were all the facts known, this percentage would undoubtedly be much larger. Still, it is probably safe to assume that approximately half of the core group enjoyed some knowledge of the North, either through friends or by personal experience. This was not an uncommon pattern among nineteenth-century emigrants.[51]

It seems curious to imagine regiments of Confederates, many of whom despised Yankees and shivered at the thought of living among them, willingly moving to Ohio and New York. Necessity partly explains their actions. Unappealing as it may have been, life in the North offered opportunities not found in the postwar South. "We left our hearts in the South," explained one woman, "but took our heads to the North." Theophilus Noel, a veteran of Sibley's Texas Brigade, spoke more bluntly. Noel arrived in Chicago with the cynical, self-seeking philosophy traditionally associated with Yankee carpetbaggers. A fellow must have compassion, allowed Noel, but never to the point that his heart governed his head. "Depend only upon what you have to carry you through, and not on the promises of anybody," he advised posterity. "Keep your money, and it will keep you from all harm. . . . 'Weep and you weep alone,' but laugh with a full pocket and a good stiff bank account, and the world will laugh with you." Experience had also taught Noel that "any man born of ordinary foxy cunning and with a gift of gab can easily become a leader of any community . . . and by resorting to cunning can . . . lead the masses of ignorant mortals who are too lazy to think, to plan and to work for themselves."[52]

Not a few Confederate carpetbaggers translated this philosophy to mean revenge. An Alabama businessman with financial interests in

Chesnut-Manning Family Papers; Edwin Corning to Henry R. Slack, August 10, 1867, in Slack Family Papers, SHC; Reginald H. Shoemaker to Joseph Bryan, November 30, 1865, in Bryan Family Papers.

51. A. Gordon Darroch, "Migrants in the Nineteenth Century: Fugitives or Families in Motion?" *Journal of Family History,* VI (1981), 257–77.

52. *Confederate Veteran,* V (November, 1897), 585; Theophilus Noel, *Autobiography and Reminiscences of Theophilus Noel* (Chicago, 1904), 51–52.

Philadelphia swore he would not "rest comfortable or easy" until his fortune and dreams had been reclaimed from northern pocketbooks, "and to this end," he asserted, "whenever I see a chance of doing so, I shall avail of it, whether that chance presents itself in benefactions, loans, bargains or business transactions—if my life is spared a little, I mean to be even with them." "I am a believer in the doctrine of retribution, and the equivalent adjustments of time," acknowledged a Virginian pursuing a business deal in Philadelphia. "When diabolical scoundrelism achieves a temporary triumph," he continued, "it is worse than idle for the vanquished victim to seek full redress whilst the flush of victory gives undue importance and fatal advantage to the villain." His motto—the same one implanted in Confederate sharpshooters a few years earlier—was "Silence—patience—deliberation—and preparation." A North Carolina veteran voted in a political contest for the first time in his life after arriving in the North, not from any interest in politics or from a sense of civic duty but, as he put it, "for the pleasure and satisfaction I should experience in knowing that I had killed one radical vote in this District."[53]

Some southerners considered revenge a challenge. Could they beat the Yankees at their own game? "I wanted to go where the Yankees were millions and fight them with brains instead of bullets," recalled a Virginia merchant who settled in New York. A Georgia lawyer at first doubted his ability to carve out a northern career. "You know this living in a strange country upon one's wits and nothing else, is a very precarious existence," he confided to a friend. He succeeded eventually in his profession, but upon returning to Georgia a decade later, during the economic depression of the mid-1870s, the Georgian claimed that he had always regarded his northern residence as temporary. "So long as the community was prosperous, and one was making money," he maintained scornfully, "one could stand the sojourn, but now when these Yankees are put to the pinch and are no longer indulging in litigation as freely as formerly, there exists no reason for living among them." A son-in-law of Matthew Fontaine Maury moved north, not because he particularly wanted to go but because it seemed a more reasonable destination than Mexico and because the notion of a northern invasion amused him.

53. W. L. Corbin to Francis R. Corbin, June 15, 1869, in Francis P. Corbin Papers, NYPL; John D. Imboden to John M. McCue, October 7, 1876, in James Blythe Anderson Papers, UK; John Grimball to John B. Grimball, September 27, 1870, in Grimball Family Papers, SHC.

The war had taught him that one sought glory in the thickest of the fighting. These Confederates and many like them seemed determined, as Henry Watterson put it, to "out-Yankee the Yankee."[54]

Whatever the attraction, whatever the forces pushing and pulling them northward, southerners followed the winds of opportunity. A hurrican force of northern armies had swept away their old lives and shattered their fragile dreams. A gentler wind now lifted them skyward like some newborn species of migratory bird. Once aloft, the magnetic power of the pole drew them to northern climes. "A migrant song-bird I," fantasized a Georgia poet:

> Out of the blue, between the sea and the sky,
> Landward blown on bright, untiring wings;
> Out of the South I fly,
> Urged by some vague, strange force of destiny. . . .
> I have sought,
> In far wild groves below the tropic line,
> To lose old memories of this land of mine;
> I have fought
> This vague, mysterious power that flings me forth
> Into the North;
> But all in vain. When flutes of April blow
> The immemorial longing lures me, and I go.
> I go, I go.[55]

54. James V. Hutton, "The Barefoot Boy of Apple Pie Ridge: Life of Charles Broadway Rouss" (MS in VHS); Charles C. Jones, Jr., to George W. Owens, April 10, 1867, in Charles Colcock Jones, Jr., Papers, DU; S. Wellford Corbin to William C. Hasbrouck, December 1, 1867, in Matthew Fontaine Maury Papers, LC; Woodman, *King Cotton and His Retainers*, 323.

55. Maurice Thompson, "Out of the South," in Edwin Anderson Alderman and Joel Chandler Harris (eds.), *Library of Southern Literature* (17 vols.; Atlanta, 1909), XII, 5260.

3

Settling In

Honeymoons are always too brief, but returning to New York seemed particularly hard for the Burton Harrisons. Rather than return "home" to begin married life, they had settled in a new land, a foreign land in many respects. They appreciated the drama of their decision. Like the gallant Greek veterans of Odysseus, they had weathered northern gales to enter a world of lotus-eaters. Having tasted the land's forbidden fruit, they had forgotten, temporarily at least, their homeward way. True, Burton had been living in the North for nearly two years. He enjoyed the advantages of a profession, friends, and social position. True, Constance was not a total stranger to northern ways. She had sojourned in the North, and she had relatives there. Yet none of these advantages could alleviate their anxiety as the Harrisons stepped from the train and summoned a porter to transport their luggage to a hotel.

Constance claimed to be not overly impressed by New York. She dubbed it an "odd, provincial, pleasant little old" town that may have been larger than Richmond or Charleston or New Orleans but lacked the charm of those southern cities. Broadway seemed to her "a long, unlovely thoroughfare." She judged New York architecture "monotonous." The "abominably paved" cobblestone streets turned a carriage drive into a test of physical endurance. New York was noisy, crowded, and dirty. Ash cans and refuse barrels standing in front of otherwise respectable-looking homes scarred the landscape. Only Central Park relieved the city's vulgarity and dreariness. Frederick Law Olmsted's oasis of trees, shrubs, ponds, and rolling slopes became a refuge for country folk unaccustomed to the din of city traffic and the crush of teeming emporiums. Yet even in the park, Constance had occasion to close her eyes to blot out the squalor of squatters' cabins and garbage dumps piled high with empty tin cans and discarded hoop skirts. Then, too, she had to steel her nerves for the beastly carriage drive along those irregularly paved thoroughfares.[1]

Constance escaped these purgatorial trials by frequent visits to her uncle at Morrisania. Never dreaming of riding in a carriage all that way, several miles even beyond Central Park, she normally walked a few blocks from her West 27th Street boardinghouse to 31st Street, where she caught a horse-drawn day coach that traveled up 4th Avenue to the Grand Central Station. A locomotive replaced the horses at the station, and the journey proceeded with relative comfort and speed. An alternative route, cheaper but less congenial, carried her along 3rd Avenue by horse-drawn car. So long as the transit company maintained a first-class "palace car" (ten-cent fare) on the 3rd Avenue line, the trip was tolerable; but the palace cars soon disappeared in response to public condemnation of such "aristocratic luxury." Thereafter, this route involved cramped accommodation in ill-ventilated cars filled with common folk bearing babies and market baskets. Elevated railroads restored some pleasure to the journey by the 1870s, but timid souls found traveling along the towering trestles unnerving.[2]

Constance had plenty of time for visiting during her first few years in New York before she had a house to keep. Probably most urban-dwelling newlywed couples began their adventure in city living by residing in a boardinghouse. The Harrisons lived in at least two such establishments during their first two years in New York. Boardinghouses spared young couples the expense of buying furniture and furnishings. They spared young brides the multiple worries of cleaning and cooking. Constance, however, chafed under the restrictions of boardinghouse life. The lack of privacy, the boredom, and the want of space became more than an adventurous young woman could bear. Then, too, a little Harrison, Fairfax by name, joined the family in March, 1869. Consequently, Constance rejoiced when Burton rented a "flat" on East 18th Street. Small and perched on the third floor of a building with too little exposure to the sun, the new home nonetheless won Constance's immediate approval. The Harrisons, of course, preferred to call it an "apartment" rather than a "flat," believing the French word sounded less vulgar than the American expression. And it stood in a perfectly tolerable neighborhood. The Stuyvesant family owned the building, and

1. Mrs. Burton Harrison, *Recollections Grave and Gay* (New York, 1911), 273, 275, 277–78.
2. *Ibid.*, 275–76.

Knickerbocker types claimed most of the suites. Constance decorated her rooms after the French fashion and soon produced a delightfully cozy salon. In comparison with what they would have found in the South, the "simple quarters" seemed like a fairy-tale palace.[3]

Still, Constance's joy at managing her own home—and she loved to manage—was muted somewhat by that deadly peril of nineteenth-century housekeeping, the servant problem. Of course, servant problems plagued southern housekeepers, too, but Constance had been too young before leaving the South to participate in the rituals of acquiring, training, and disciplining household workers. She had only observed. Her initiation came after moving to the Stuyvesant apartments. Constance at first employed two French immigrants as cook and parlor maid, hoping to replicate her mother's blissful experience with servants in France after the war. She pictured herself freed of petty household cares, able to devote her time to decorating, entertaining, and raising her family. It was a pleasant vision, but not to be. Though efficient, her high-strung French ladies resembled a pair of panthers about to inflict a bit of no good on the local critters. They soon quarreled between themselves and departed.[4]

Constance employed only "unadulterated Irish" after that. She hired two servants at first, but initial success made her overconfident. Believing three servants more befitting the status of a rising young attorney's family, she hired an additional girl. It was a mistake. "I was inventing work for them," she lamented in seeking advice from her mother, "& feeling as if they were all in mischief—besides having to sit and hear the most animated entertainments going on of squads of Hibernians in my kitchen, whom I lacked courage to go & turn out bodily." Such lack of courage, totally uncharacteristic of Constance, may be attributed to her inexperience in directing servants. When she discovered her cook stealing food, Constance decided that two servants would fill her needs and pocketbook even if it meant more "in the way of dusting & putting to rights" than any young housekeeper ought to have tolerated. Not until the birth of a second son, Francis, in 1873, and the subsequent recruitment of a tiny (4 feet 8 inches tall) nursemaid, Eliza Brady, did Constance again try to install a triumvirate. Thereafter, family servants were remembered as "emotional and untidy, but goodhearted."[5]

3. Francis B. Harrison (ed.), *A Selection of the Letters of Fairfax Harrison* (Charlottesville, 1944), 4; Harrison, *Recollections Grave and Gay,* 281–82.

4. Harrison, *Recollections Grave and Gay,* 281–84.

5. *Ibid.*; Constance Harrison to Monimia Cary, April 1, 1870, October 18, 1871, both

Still, Burton and Constance knew that without such trials one could not really appreciate Heaven. They adapted readily enough to northern life. They purchased their first house, a "cheery, sunshine-haunted" residence at 11 Lexington Avenue, just a block from fashionable Gramercy Park, shortly after the birth of Francis. Grief twice tempered joy in the new house. Constance's mother died while on a visit, and a daughter died in infancy. But the birth of a third son, Archibald, in 1876, restored momentum to the Harrisons' life. Their Gramercy Park neighbors—including John Bigelow, Peter Cooper, Cyrus Field, Abram Hewitt, George Templeton Strong, and Samuel J. Tilden—welcomed them to the neighborhood, and by the late 1870s Constance and the boys enjoyed summers at Lenox and Bar Harbor, with Burton joining them on weekends. Bar Harbor became their favorite resort. They built a cottage there, Sea Urchins, in the mid-1880s. It stood a stone's throw from the newly constructed villa of Mr. and Mrs. James G. Blaine.[6]

Burton, Constance, three boys, and a collie named Colin Clout formed a rollicking crew on Lexington Avenue. The boys spent the larger part of their youthful days trying to outwit Eliza Brady, but family evenings were more subdued. Burton read, Constance wrote, and the boys studied. Chess was the only "game" played in the evenings, not because games were taboo but because the Harrisons thought games less interesting than books. Constance sometimes employed the family in planning and rehearsing amateur theatrical productions, which had remained a passion since her first thespian ventures in wartime Richmond. The boys often badgered Burton into telling stories. They appreciated his kindly humor and delighted particularly in his "southern" stories. "His frequent laughter," recalled a son, "was infectious." Burton could be stern if the occasion warranted. He believed in "the rule of ancient Rome" that boys should be taken from the nursery at age seven and "put in the charge of men." Burton used a twelve-inch ebony ruler, known as the "scorcher," to mete out justice. He sometimes winked at boyish mischief, as when his sons played football with their mother's spare bustle, and he never disciplined them without explaining precisely why it was necessary; but Burton insisted on good manners, and he would not tolerate lying. Unlike Gilbert and Sullivan's General Stanley, Burton made no distinction between the elegant diction of an innocent

in Burton Norvell Harrison Family Papers, LC; Francis B. Harrison, "About It and About" (Typescript in Francis Burton Harrison Papers, UV), 20–21.

6. Harrison, *Recollections Grave and Gay*, 300–301, 309–14, 348–53; Harrison, "About It and About," 25–29.

fiction and a regular terrible story. The boys understood his message: they may have been born in the North, but they would be raised as southern gentlemen.[7]

When Constance began a successful literary career in the mid-1870s, many of her short stories and novels included southern characters who had moved north. These fictional creations, invariably genteel but tenacious, succeeded in the North because their inbred gentility cloaked a core of brains and resolution. Her characters had nothing on Constance. She became "all the rage" in New York within a year of her arrival, and her reputation as a gracious hostess, sparkling dinner guest, and enthusiastic patron of the arts placed her even more solidly in the graces of the community as the years passed. Of course, it was her duty as the wife of a promising young attorney to plunge into the city's social and cultural life, but she performed her role with a verve and freshness that few women could match. Whether organizing amateur concerts and theatricals at the Academy of Music or attending a charity ward full of "poor degraded creatures—sweepings of the street" at Bellevue Hospital, Constance Harrison became a visible and much-admired figure.[8]

Constance won her northern niche not with beauty, cleverness, wit, or charm, though she possessed all those qualities, but with determination. She, like so many Confederate carpetbaggers, intended to prove that life had not ended in 1865. Her determination buoyed Constance throughout her northern residence. A son recalled her "indomitable character," and one senses that he and his brothers stood more in awe of delicate Constance than of their six-foot father and his scorcher. She proved more than a match for her male publishers and editors, and she would not tolerate pretense or snobbery in any form. Taking tea with some callers one afternoon, she listened patiently while a "heavily moral" matron droned on about a young lady of good family who had lately given birth to an illegitimate child. "She's behaved like a woman of the working class!" was the caller's shocked appraisal. Constance could tolerate no more. "I believe," she drawled mildly, "that illegitimate babies are arranged for in just the same way in all classes, my dear." Her visitors exited on that note.[9]

7. Harrison, "About It and About," 5–6, 9–10, 17–21, 34–37, 41.
8. A.C.P. to Constance Harrison, March 11, 1868, Mrs. Edward C. Churchill to Constance Harrison, October 6 [1876], and Mrs. Harrison's social correspondence, all in Harrison Family Papers, LC.
9. Harrison, "About It and About," 40; Constance Harrison to Edmund C. Stedman, March 7 [1890?], in Edmund Clarence Stedman Papers, CU; Thomas Beer, *The Mauve Decade* (Garden City, N.Y., 1926), 47–48.

Burton Harrison, quietly but resolutely, like a hero in one of his wife's novels, carved a niche in the city's legal profession. A combination of bravado, confidence, and charm accounts for Burton's amazingly swift and smooth adaptation to northern ways. Whatever fate the South might suffer as a result of the war, southerners, Burton believed, had a responsibility to get ahead as best they could. If that was not possible in the South, they must go elsewhere. "I am one of those disposed to get all possible good out of the inevitable," Harrison explained in an eloquent statement of his philosophy. Far from retreating from or abandoning his convictions, Harrison professed to be merely changing fronts, to be moving forward but in a different direction. The tactic was necessary, Harrison maintained, "because my former line of march has been interrupted by an impassable barrier which I must avoid or butt my head against, very foolishly." And Burton Harrison, as anyone could tell you, was nobody's fool.[10]

In a city crowded with lawyers, Burton enjoyed at least one enormous advantage: he was a good lawyer. Steadily, month by month, season by season, he established firm footing along the treacherous cliffs leading to Gotham's legal summit. He did not anticipate "substantial plunder" from his practice, at least not in the early years. "My fees will come along after awhile, I hope," he confided to a friend, "—and if I don't starve, or fall victim to my tailor's vengeance, meantime—it will all be right yet." That was Harrison's style, always a joke, always lighthearted, no matter what the circumstances. He did not starve or fall victim to his tailor. On the contrary, he remained, as in wartime Richmond, well fed and fashionably dressed. His fortunes steadily improved. Shortly after his marriage, he moved his office around the corner from Pine Street to Nassau Street. Nassau was a narrow, busy thoroughfare, with an odd assortment of prestigious banking houses, mundane real estate agencies, dingy bookstores, and fly-by-night businesses of questionable legality. A contemporary described it as a street filled with "unrest." "In no part of the great city," he elaborated, "are you so fully impressed with the shortness and value of time." Equally to the point, struggling young lawyers clustered along Nassau by the score. They seemed to judge this street, above all others, "the road to success." Burton fulfilled his potential in the mid-1870s when he opened chambers in the grandiose Equitable Building on Broadway.[11]

10. Burton Harrison to Constance Harrison, July 13, 1866, in Harrison Family Papers, LC.

11. Burton Harrison to William G. Glenn, May 27, 1867, in Glenn Family Papers,

Burton earned increasingly more substantial fees for his wisdom, skill, and counsel, but success never spoiled him. Throughout his years of active legal practice, he daily walked the two miles to his office in all weather, so as to arrive punctually at nine o'clock. Burton helped to pioneer the field of corporate law and served for many years as counsel for the Western Union Telegraph Company and New York Telephone Company. Yet despite his familiarity with corporate structure, he steadfastly refused to join the trend toward large legal firms of associated lawyers. To the end of his career he operated alone or with a single partner. His English-born clerk, Harry, was another token of a past age. Harry used no typewriter, preferring, with Burton's approval, to copy his employer's briefs and correspondence in "the finest of legal handwriting." Similarly, Burton refused many lucrative jobs that he thought would compromise his honor and integrity. Burton was a proud man and a bit aloof. Politically reconstructed as he might be, jovial and good-natured as he appeared, Harrison could be formidable. "I will crook my back to no man."[12]

Not all Confederate carpetbaggers settled in as successfully as the Harrisons. Too often the elation of escaping the South was tempered by the need to live in Yankeedom. A different climate, strange customs, new livelihoods, the absence of friends, a faster-paced life, occasionally hostile receptions from the northern populace, plus the general wear and tear extracted by the struggle for jobs, concern for loved ones at home, and uneasiness about the future stacked the odds against a smooth transition to northern life.

Differences in climate did not disturb southerners until the arrival of winter. Northern winters could be beautiful when fleecy piles of snow formed eerie drifts, ice-covered trees glistened like crystal, and frozen waterfalls arrested the flow of mighty rivers; but southerners soon learned to scoff at the fairy-tale settings of Henry Wadsworth Longfellow and John Greenleaf Whittier. Reality struck when they had to flounder "knee-deep" in snow that covered "pavements slippery as glass." "So impracticable and impassable are the streets of this 'great metropolis' (so-called)," sputtered a Georgia journalist in New York,

MHS; James D. McCabe, Jr., *Lights and Shadows of New York Life; or the Sights and Sensations of the Great City* (Philadelphia, 1872), 426–29.

12. Harrison, "About It and About," 7; Fairfax Harrison (ed.), *Aris Sonis Focisque: Being a Memoir of an American Family, the Harrisons of Skimino* (New York, 1910), 213–14, 218–19.

"that the most important business affairs often come to a stand-still."
Even the horse cars, crowded to overflowing in such weather, slipped
and slid along the streets. It required an hour to accomplish a few
minutes' ordinary travel, and in two cases out of three the traveler found
the shop or office he wished to visit closed. And that was only half the
nightmare. Snow inevitably melts, if not from the sun by the force of
feet, hooves, and wheels mashing it into slush. Then comes another cold
spell. The slush freezes, coating streets and sidewalks with yet another
treacherous glaze. "Discontented Savannahians!" warned the journalist, sounding like a revivalist preacher, "return thanks you are not
shivering, slipping, and perhaps swearing, in the gay city of New York,
where every man's nose and ears are frozen purple."[13]

Rural southerners who wandered into northern towns and cities often
became disoriented and depressed. Cincinnati appalled a young Kentucky woman. The only "pleasant feature" of life in the Queen City, she
reported, was the opportunity to attend concerts and plays. The city
itself, which she had visited before the war, looked *blacker, smokier,
cloudier* than ever before," a far cry from the "fields and trees in Kentucky." Southern children accustomed to running through fields and
meadows considered northern cities queer, unnatural places. The "list-
less and unhappy" children of a Virginia family "found no pleasure in
walking up and down the uninteresting sidewalk of a hot, dreary street."
"Loneliness," observed their sympathetic mother, "oppressed us all."
Seeking a tonic, this same mother escorted her brood from their
Brooklyn home to Central Park. She had anticipated a pleasurable ex-
cursion to the park, a few hours' relaxation amid the trees and grass, and
a recuperative journey home. Instead, a horse-car journey to the
Brooklyn ferry, a boat ride to Manhattan, a walk up Wall Street to
Broadway, and a ride along Broadway in a "lumbering" horse-drawn
omnibus brought them to their destination (in a drenching rain) at four
o'clock. They had time only to reboard the omnibus and retrace their
route to Brooklyn. The exhausted mother, like many other southerners,
had thought of cities as compact, convenient places, easily traversed and
explored. "I had no idea of the distance," she admitted.[14]

The northern urban custom of constantly moving from one rented

13. Savannah *Daily Republican,* January 1, 1873, p. 2.
14. Kate Northcott to Bruce F. Thomas, April 24, 1874, in Northcott Collection, WK;
Sophonisba Steele to Robert J. Breckinridge, October 9, 1865, in Breckinridge Family
Papers, LC; Mrs. Roger A. Pryor, *My Day: Reminiscences of a Long Life* (New York,
1909), 312.

residence or boardinghouse to another proved equally irksome. Northern city dwellers had no sense of permanence; they put down no roots, complained southerners. A Georgian caught up in the bizarre migrations that seemingly struck New Yorkers every spring found the proceedings tedious. "It is the spirit of the age here," he reasoned, "every thing is change, change. Whether you like it or not you are liable to be [dragged] onward with the moving throng unless you are willing to be left behind everyone else. With my Southern inbred local attachments, I can scarcely appreciate this love of change." This gentleman's chief complaint—and he had many—was that Yankees always carried their notions to ridiculous extremes. They even put their plants and trees in pots, "so as to be transferrable or portable rather, and you would not believe," he warned a friend, "what an amount of foliage can be grown in this way." Irksome and ridiculous as it seemed, southerners learned that the custom could be useful. A South Carolinian, following two years of unsettled residence in one boardinghouse, joined the migration. "Cause," he explained, "—disreputable location—police court lately established not many doors off—arrival of new boarders who slaughtered the English language, & did not understand the use of a fork— lastly the woman [landlady] would insist upon addressing me as plain 'Grimball' which struck me as being a deuce sight too familiar."[15]

Most southern housekeepers experienced, like Constance Harrison, unaccustomed problems in hiring and keeping domestic servants. Although the similarities between managing black slave and white free servants outnumbered the differences, those differences could create havoc. A North Carolina "exile" adjusting to life in Ohio found her biggest burden to be the acquisition of reliable "'*help*.'" "We have no *servants*," she explained in reference to the disdain northern servants displayed toward a title they associated with forced servitude. "We have tried black and white, American and foreign . . . all alike. I came to the conclusion that the only way for a woman to get well cared for and waited upon, and to have an easy life, is to hire out." A Virginian in Chicago defined a northern "House Girl" as "one of those nuisances who waste your gas and fuel, break all your china, let their beaux into your house for purposes of burglary, expose to gossip every thing that transpires in your family, keep you in a fret from Monday morning till

15. J. Horne to Julie Kell, April 23, 1876, in John McIntosh Kell Papers, DU; John Grimball to John B. Grimball, February 18, 1872, in John Berkley Grimball Papers, DU.

Saturday night, flaunt impertinances in your face and then leave without an hour's notice."[16]

Southerners hoping to solve the problem by taking old family retainers to the North sometimes misjudged the loyalty of their servants. A Virginia servant who accompanied her mistress to New York could not bear the strain of city life. The "street cries" of rag men and fruit peddlers hawking their goods mystified her. The noise and godlessness of the place appalled her. "You know I likes you and de chilern," she told her mistress in explaining why she was returning to Virginia, "but I can't stay. I'se *feared* to stay! I can't live in no place where folks plays de piano all day Sunday. I'se bown' to get out. Somp'n gwine to happin in dis Gawd-forsaken place." A South Carolina couple brought a nurse north with them. They paid her twelve dollars a month, but Jane became dissatisfied when she learned that other nurses in the neighborhood earned sixteen to eighteen dollars. Jane demanded more money, but her mistress balked. "She is not worth it," she decided. "She is awfully slow & lazy." The woman's husband was more blunt. "She is an impudent yellow wench if there ever was one," he declared. "I always keep an eye cocked & ear peeled for impertinence." Jane left the position.[17]

Without a cook who knew how to prepare southern meals, diet could be a problem. Unmarried men were thrown upon the mercy of boardinghouse and hotel cuisine that rarely featured the staples found on southern tables. One veteran bemoaned the absence of so fundamental an item as corn bread. He recalled, with some exaggeration, that his regiment had "lived entirely" on corn bread during the war. During all of his life in the South, he could not recall a single repast without cornmeal prepared in some form. Northerners' passion for wheat bread, he insisted, accounted for their poor health and puny constitution. And if one could not acquire so simple an item as corn bread, what hope was there for such southern specialties as hopping John, jam cake, gumbo, Brunswick stew, or eggnog?[18]

16. Charles C. Jones, Jr., to Mary Jones, March 17, 1866, in Charles Colcock Jones, Jr., Collection, UG; A. D. Hepburn to Cornelia P. Spencer, April 6, 1869, in Cornelia Phillips Spencer Papers, SHC; Thomas H. Ellis to Elizabeth Munford, February 17, 1878, in Munford-Ellis Family Papers, DU.

17. Pryor, *My Day*, 314–15; Katherine H. Billings to Emily Hammond, February 5, 1899, John S. Billings to Katherine H. Billings, April 24, 1899, both in Hammond, Bryan, and Cumming Families Papers.

18. *Confederate Veteran*, XXVI (April, 1918), 139; New York *Times*, December 23, 1894, p. 5.

Southerners expressed shock at the number of thieves, crooks, and villains they encountered in the North, but they might have expected as much, given their generally low opinion of Yankees. "There is one thing I like particularly in the northern character," summarized an Alabamian, "—they are perfectly fair, in not *pretending* to have any honesty." Still, the shock of most people seems genuine. "A lady had her pocket picked in the train last night," reported a Texan traveling through the North. "In every car & hotel are notices 'Beware of thieves and pickpockets.'" A South Carolinian warned southerners going north to beware of the "confidence" men, swindlers, "friendly scoundrels, polite gamesters, pretty women in distress, cheating tradesmen, and polished and smiling liars." One gentlemen sent a special warning to a son due to join him in New York. "Have your trunk carefully marked, on the top and at the ends before leaving home," he cautioned, "& be careful to lock it. . . . N.Y. is a place of vast crowd, clamor, competition, complication, cheating & chicanery of every sort." A woman living in a New York village and her friend residing in Philadelphia agreed on "the appalling wickedness of the North."[19]

One southerner felt compelled to undertake a personal crusade against northern villainy. James Dabney McCabe, Jr., son of a Virginia clergyman, graduate of the Virginia Military Institute, and biographer of Stonewall Jackson, Albert Sidney Johnston, and Robert E. Lee, moved north in 1866 to pursue a literary career. Growing familiarity with the sights and sounds of northern cities produced in him not so much contempt as dread. New York in particular he found spellbinding, dangerously so, for among the city's undeniable pleasures lurked many perils for unsuspecting tourists and emigrants. He wrote a guidebook for these innocents entitled *Lights and Shadows of New York Life*. "Coming fresh from plainer and more practical parts of the land," wrote McCabe in explaining his purpose, "the visitor is plunged into the midst of so much beauty, magnificence, gayety, mystery, and a thousand other wonders, that he is fairly bewildered. It is hoped that the reader of these

19. Jubal A. Early to Samuel H. Early, June 19, 1867, in Jubal A. Early Papers, LC; Josiah C. Nott to Ephraim G. Squier, December 5, 1865, in Ephraim George Squier Papers, LC; James Nicholson Diary, July 21, 1866 (MS in James Nicholson Papers, UT); H. C., "The Bastinado of the Pavements: A New York Sketch," *XIX Century*, II (1870), 709–10; William G. Simms to William G. Simms, Jr., July 31, 1869, in Mary C. Simms Oliphant, *et al.* (eds.), *The Letters of William Gilmore Simms* (5 vols.; Columbia, S.C., 1952), V, 237; Harriott Middleton to Susan Middleton, January 4 [1866], in Cheves-Middleton Papers, SCHS.

pages will be by their perusal better prepared to enjoy the attractions, and to shun the dangers of New York." McCabe did not pen his guide-book solely for transplanted southerners, but he certainly hoped fellow southerners would profit by his warnings and descriptions of the North's "professional criminals," "female sharpers," "swindlers," and "social evil."[20]

Northern holidays annoyed some southerners. Most obviously, Inde-pendence Day bore heavily on Confederate hearts, reminding them of their own failure to gain independence. Amid the noisy celebration of one northern July Fourth, a Virginian's thoughts drifted into the past. He thought first of boyhood celebrations with fifes and drums on this very same holiday. Next he recalled the din of bloody battles in defense of the South. Finally he relived in memory a July Fourth ten years earlier, spent in soundless, muddy retreat from the fields of Gettysburg. Another veteran feigned bewilderment when he and "other rebs of importance" failed to receive personal invitations to a local Independence Day pa-rade. In retaliation, he silently inspected local militia units as they marched past his boardinghouse window, "with an eye to the next war you know." A Georgian in the North simply reported: "Being good Christians, we did not join in the celebration of the 4th." A Virginian resented the "ding-donged Yankee Doodle" way his northern neighbors celebrated George Washington's birthday and claimed that venerable southerner as their own hero. A local pastor marked the occasion with a solemn ceremony that struck the Virginian as "a sort of High-Church Republican meeting" highlighted by "a howling patriotic discourse on the greatness and glory of the Republic which bespoke a mind that had only imperfectly grasped the distinction between the United States of America and the Kingdom of Heaven."[21]

Not even Christmas and Easter passed without mild irritation. "The people in this part of the U.S.," complained a Kentuckian in Mas-sachusetts, "do not pay as much regard to Christmas day and week as they do in Kentucky. Consequently I do not expect to enjoy such 'lively times' as I have witnessed on the day." A Confederate in New York voiced a similar complaint. Christmas, she lamented, was "not like

20. McCabe, *Lights and Shadows of New York Life*, 14–15.
21. William R. O'Donovan to Jennie Abraham, July 4, 1873, in William Rudolf O'Donovan Correspondence, HSP; Davis Bryant to Octavia Stephens, July 13, 1866, in Stephens Collection, UF; Richard M. Cuyler to William W. Gordon, July 7, 1866, in Gordon Family Papers, GHS; John R. Thompson to George W. Bagby, February 25, 1868, in Bagby Family Papers, VHS.

home, not a fire cracker or pistol have I heard, & of course it does not seem natural." Easter offered just the opposite contrast in some parts of the North. New York's celebrated Easter Parade, for example, inevitably produced comments from pious southerners about the "moral Vanity Fair." "All day long thro' Fifth Avenue and its tributaries," marveled a South Carolinian, "streamed gay crowds in their new attire, still pretending to be on their several ways to church, long after church bells had ceased tolling, visiting, greeting, criticizing, always each other eying and otherwise decorously junketing, as at a church bazaar."[22]

A New Year's Day custom, apparently first introduced in New York, struck a Virginian as comical. "Tomorrow is the great holiday here," he explained. "It is the day of universal calls upon all the people you know or care to know. . . . I believe the whole ceremony is to go in full dress— send in a card—follow it in a moment—shake hands—wish happiness—drink a glass of wine—eat a morsel, bow oneself out & hurry to the next place and go through the same performance." Despite some initial skepticism, he made fifteen calls on the great ceremonial day and thoroughly enjoyed himself. He especially enjoyed socializing with ravishing young northern ladies, always a weakness for this dashing former cavalryman. City clocks were striking midnight when he bid adieu to his last host, but he continued the celebration in his room several hours longer, so "exhilirated" did he feel after indulging in such fine food, savory liqueurs, and fair company. "Really," he concluded in mock reproach, "I think these New Years' calls, as conducted here, are dangerous to public morals. The excitement itself is intoxicating, and the picture of life one sees is so gorgeous that it gives a new zest to the earnestness with which men seek to gratify such tastes."[23]

A more sober southerner, seeking seriously to settle into Yankee ways, tried to duplicate the New Year's receptions of her neighbors. She also intended to prove that southerners knew something about hospitality. She soon regretted her rashness. Fifty gentlemen called, far more than she or her husband had met in their brief residence. She faced each caller with a charming smile and a dainty curtsy, but she felt "mighty glad when night came." Apparently, many northern hostesses felt the same

22. Bruce F. Thomas to Kate Northcott, December 19, 1873, in Northcott Collection; Sophonisba Steele to Robert J. Breckinridge, December 25, 1865, in Breckinridge Family Papers; DeRosset Lamar to Julia Cumming, April 1, 1875, Hammond, Bryan, and Cumming Families Papers.

23. New York *Times,* January 1, 1875, p. 8; John D. Imboden to Annie H. Lockett, January 1, 3, 1871, both in John Daniel Imboden Papers, UV.

way. The custom, at least in New York, was destined to die by the end of the century because of the abuses of hospitality that too often occurred.[24]

The New Year celebrations illustrate yet another serious problem of adjustment: the crush and rush of northern life. Everyone hurried to keep appointments; they scratched and clawed to make a dollar. Yankees did not know how to relax or enjoy the finer things in life. Even their grand notion of a New Year's festivity degenerated into a race to see how many receptions a person could squeeze into the day. "I still abide in my old love of home, and its peaceful, many scenes I live over in memory," lamented a displaced Confederate, "—and though I have ceased to fret and chafe as before, I am no more reconciled to the prospect of abiding away from those dear old places than the day I landed here." "The perpetual bustle & hurry is not pleasant to me at all," decided a haggard fellow in Philadelphia. "I like ample occupation. But it seems everywhere . . . as if *business* & hurry & bustle was all there is to live for in the world." A young southerner working as a clerk in New York longed all day for "knock off time," so that he might escape the city. Riding the ferry each evening to the less calamitous and hurried environs of Jersey City, where he boarded, he lapsed into peaceful reverie as the refreshing river breeze and the heave of the ferry against the current transported his thoughts southward. "I miss 'Home' as much as ever," he confessed to his family, "and am often thinking of you all."[25]

The hurry and bustle and an accompanying lack of respect and courtesy infuriated some southerners. "If you ever see a tall man in Broadway," chuckled a northern wag, "standing stock-still, glaring about him, and swearing, you may be sure that he is a Southerner, and that some one whom he can not find has run against him." "I can't stand this any longer," shouted a Kentuckian in just such a predicament; "I can't respect myself when I am run against a dozen times a day by Irishmen, Jews, Yankees, and all kinds of busy people. . . . I detest a city where seven hundred thousand people tread on my toes, and haven't a moment's leisure to apologize." The crowds, the noise, the rush, so alien to the experiences of many southerners, could make them different people.

24. Sophonisba Steele to Robert J. Breckinridge, January 7, 1867, in Breckinridge Family Papers; Robert Underwood Johnson, *Remembered Yesterdays* (Boston, 1923), 168.

25. DeRosset Lamar to Emily Hammond, March 20, 1877, in Hammond, Bryan, and Cumming Families Papers; Thomas Affleck to Anna D. Affleck, December 31, 1865, in Thomas Affleck Papers, LSU.

"*What* a world this is:—has it any *real* meaning?" asked a Georgian pushed to the brink of despair after being closeted with his business firm's books and accountants for nearly a month. "Do we really build better than we know, or are the 'men and women in it' only bits of colored glass in a huge kaleidoscope?" "I am afraid you will find me much changed," he warned a friend after pausing to catch his breath, "very uncertain in every mood, save that of a growing bad temper."[26]

A middle-aged widower discovered to his horror that the northern business mentality could even dictate the frequency with which he ought to be seen publicly in the company of any particular woman. "The social usages of these people partaking largely of the spirit and speed of their business practices and where everything is a commercial adventure," he explained, "the gravest consequences are supposed to follow when a gentleman is seen in some lady's company, half a dozen times, or they are observed *alone* together at an *opera* (as peculiarly distinguished from a theatre)." Churches and public parks had also to be avoided. The gentleman shook his head in dismay at Yankee thinking. The thought that he must abandon "the Southern custom and prediction for enjoying ladies society, for itself," struck him as a harsh penalty to pay for a northern residence. Recalling a northern expression for slavery in vogue before the war, the gentleman grumbled about the rituals surrounding "*their* peculiar institution" of courtship and marriage.[27]

On farms and in villages as well as in cities, people simply could not shake the sensation of living in a foreign country among people with strange ways and queer ideas. A North Carolinian living in rural upstate New York felt like "an exile . . . in extremest loneliness." He had not been mistreated or abused by the Yankees, but he cherished any word, the merest note, from his Carolina friends. He fondly hoped to return to the South someday, "for, in spite of all, I still feel that my home is there." "The truth is," burst out a Georgian, "I feel most infernally out of place in this Yankee country, and am most anxious to return to my own home and people, where there is sympathy and where one is not debarred from those social privileges which constitute in great measure the chances of life." A Virginian lamented, "The people are alien to me, their ways are not my ways nor their thoughts my thoughts." "We had good humored

26. John W. DeForest, "Chivalrous and Semi-Chivalrous Southrons," *Harper's Monthly*, XXXVIII (January, 1869), 192–93; DeRosset Lamar to Julia A. Cumming, December 13, 1874, in Hammond, Bryan, and Cumming Families Papers.

27. DeRosset Lamar to Emily Hammond, March 20, 1877, in Hammond, Bryan, and Cumming Families Papers.

discussions & I was treated very kindly," confessed a southerner following an evening of conversation and drinks in a Cincinnati home. Yet the evening firmly impressed upon him the differences between North and South. The gentlemen with whom he conversed clearly represented the "better class" of northern society, yet the southerner swore he would "assimilate sooner with the Fee Gee Islanders." "They are thrifty, energetic, intelligent," he admitted, "but I never would become reconciled to their *'views* & *ideas.*' "[28]

More than a few parents worried about the influence northern schools might have on innocent, fresh-faced southern children. The ultimate danger for parents who did not themselves move north was that graduated scholars might decide to say in Yankeeland, but even returning students too often sounded, behaved, and thought like Yankees. It was more than a question of how to keep them down on the farm after they had seen New York; the real danger was of losing a soul to the devil. A Georgia physician who had been educated in Philadelphia before the war recognized the threat. He sent one of his sons north after the war. The boy profited from the experience. He returned to Georgia "much improved . . . in his education, in his manners and in his physical development." Those benefits achieved, however, the father decided to have the boy finish his education in a southern environment. Radical southern reformers advised against even brief exposure to northern teachings. Enough southerners had become "semi-northernized" before the war. The postwar goal must be "home education." Yet most critics saw little chance of stopping the flight northward. The most they could hope for was that southern emigrants might attend "conservative" schools with southern sympathies rather than schools known for their "intense Radicalism."[29]

The danger of picking up undesirable habits lurked outside the classroom, too. One southerner, enjoying a game of ninepins with some northern friends, noticed a scruffy-looking boy with a dirty face stop to watch. The youth soon offered to set pins for the bowlers. Without

28. J. M. Hubbard to Cornelia P. Spencer, April 9, 1869, in Spencer Papers; Charles C. Jones, Jr., to George S. Owen, September 9, 1868, in Charles Colcock Jones, Jr., Papers, DU; John R. Thompson to Paul H. Hayne, February 17, 1871, in Paul Hamilton Hayne Papers, DU; Henry C. Yeatman to Mary Yeatman, October 4, 1866, in Yeatman-Polk Collection, TL.

29. Robert Battey to Mary Halsey, February 3, 1867, in Robert Battey Papers, EU; *Metropolitan Record and New York Vindicator,* March 9, 1867, p. 13; *The Land We Love,* III (1868), 451–52.

asking, he obviously expected some reward for his labor. "I put my hand in my pocket with half a mind to give the boy 5 cts," claimed the southerner, but he checked himself and, saying nothing about remuneration, motioned for the boy to set the pins. The southerner's conscience began to prick him after a few rounds, for he had no intention of giving the boy any money, and he confessed as much to him. "But I am geting to be a regular yankey," lamented the southerner of his untypical niggardliness. Another young southern gentleman, after several years' residence in the North, "unlearned" the universal southern custom of standing when a lady entered the room. Feeling "ashamed" of himself for neglecting the courtesies he had practiced since childhood, he privately resolved to reform.[30]

Some southern woes were not unique to northern life, but the circumstances of living in a strange land brought them to prominence. The scramble for jobs and the daily battle for survival strained the marriages of some newly arrived southerners. One woman, who loved her husband dearly and had the utmost confidence in his ability to provide for their family, sometimes felt shut out of his life as he pursued his medical career. She understood the necessity of his labors; she knew he worked for her and their children, but she missed the early, prewar years of their marriage, when life seemed less chaotic and threatening. If her husband would only "be loving to me sometimes," she confided to her father, "I could bare all else, but he is too busy." Some marriages broke down completely. A North Carolina couple separated when, after years of labor in various northern cities and towns, the husband, a very capable physician, proved unable to support his family. His wife, "soured . . . by disappointment with the matter of money," took their child and left. After eleven years of marriage, a divorce resulted.[31]

A Tennessean complained about his inability to adapt to civilized society after four years of campaigning and camp life. Released from a northern prison camp in June, 1865, he soon realized he would have to be careful of his actions and speech, especially around ladies. "It is with great effort that I can talk even decently," he confessed to his diary. "I am

30. William B. McKoy to grandparents, October 18, 1875, in William B. McKoy Papers, SHC; Alexander D. Savage to Thomas R. Savage, December 1, 1879, in William Rutherford Savage Papers, SHC.

31. Sophonisba Steele to Robert J. Breckinridge, October 28, 1869, in Breckinridge Family Papers; John B. Grimball to John Grimball, February 26, 1873, Lewis M. Grimball to Mrs. Legge, July 26, 1873, both in Grimball Family Papers, SCHS; John Berkley Grimball Diaries, November 10, 1877 (MS in Grimball Family Papers, SHC).

continualy expecting to hear myself blurt out some indecent camp slang, when I am not thinking." The fellow would have faced the same temptation in Tennessee, but because he wanted so desperately to fit into northern society, the problem seemed magnified. He felt lonely, too. He missed his home more than he had while in the army, but that would have been the case had he settled in Texas or Georgia. The only uniquely northern problem he encountered was a sense of being on display, like some exotic animal at the circus. Attending church in a Massachusetts town, he grew uncomfortable when he realized that everyone was looking at him. "I am the first rebel ever seen in these parts," he reasoned, "so that I see a great many faces at the windows whenever I go any where."[32]

Southerners moving from farms and small towns could be intimidated by the apparent sophistication of Yankee acquaintances. A young South Carolinian newly arrived in Brooklyn felt ill at ease in the home of a northern friend. The other guests impressed him as being "much nicer" than himself. He felt awkward, uncertain, lacking in dignity. "An almost unreasonable affection" for the solitude of his boardinghouse room swept over him. A Virginian regretted his "ignorance of the conventionalities of life." He knew he was an object of ridicule, even among northerners whom he considered his intellectual inferiors. He saw their barely disguised smiles, heard their ill-stifled snickers whenever he committed a social *faux pas.* "I used my knife as a *shovel,* in eating," he confessed on one occasion. "I knew from reading it was not the thing to do, but I did it unconsciously."[33]

A southerner in Iowa, essentially rural and providing a social and intellectual milieu very like the one most carpetbaggers had left behind, encountered just the opposite problem. "My chief and only objection to this section," he explained from Glenwood, Iowa, "is the d——d narrow hearted illiterate prejudiced character of a majority of its citizens." The gentleman was a doctor by profession, and he missed the intellectual repartee, slight as it may have been, in his native Missouri. He had helped to establish a medical society in his new home, but it disbanded within a year. Lack of patients forced him to rely on farming for his

32. James M. Morey Diary, June 16, 25, 1865 (MS in James Marsh Morey Papers, TL).
33. Daniel A. Tompkins to Harriet Brigham, October 14, 1874, in Daniel Augustus Tompkins Papers, SHC; Howard Bunyan Clay, "Daniel Augustus Tompkins: An American Bourbon" (Ph.D. dissertation, University of North Carolina at Chapel Hill, 1950), 12–13; William R. O'Donovan to Jennie Abraham, February 7, 1872, in O'Donovan Correspondence.

livelihood, and the subsequent isolation only worsened his "mental deterioration and demoralization."[34]

Admittedly, differences in customs sometimes made Yankees the victims. Dueling is an example. Not since Aaron Burr and Alexander Hamilton stepped off ten paces at Weehawken had any New Yorker paid much attention to the practice. So pity the northern ninny who insulted, slighted, or otherwise infringed upon the honor of a hot-blooded rebel buck. Early in 1868, a recently arrived southern emigrant named Debelieux invited a young-man-about-town named Pemberton to accompany him to New Jersey. Pemberton, fancied Debelieux, had insulted his sister; Debelieux demanded an "affair of honor." Pemberton and his friends thought the challenge a quaint joke and fully expected that the "affair" would be settled without ever drawing pistols, let alone blood. They laughed and chuckled as their boat bobbed across the river, and they likely enjoyed a nip of spirits to ward off the morning chill. Imagine their shock, Pemberton's especially, when Debelieux's bullet split the Yankee's skull with a nasty wound.[35]

And so it went. Many Confederates could not single out any particularly noxious peculiarity in their new environment. They knew only that they were unhappy. Most settlers faced similar dilemmas, but everyone battled a slightly different predicament, under slightly different circumstances. The human element in their dramas may best be appreciated by recounting some individual tales of adaptation.

Thomas H. and Euphania Ellis arrived in Chicago from Virginia in 1870. The Ellises, in their mid-fifties, were older than the typical emigrant. Consequently, they embarked on "so radical a change" with more doubts and apprehension than younger carpetbaggers. Mrs. Ellis, especially, brooded. No European refugee had ever arrived at Castle Garden in more trepidation than that good woman as she stepped onto the railroad platform at Chicago. Her biggest potential worry, money, seemed solved. Her husband, with many years of business and mercantile experience to his credit, had formed a real estate agency with a Confederate exile from Louisiana, George H. Rozet. Ellis would earn three thousand dollars per year plus one-half of all fees, less than his income in Virginia but sufficient to begin life anew, away from the political and social calamity of Virginia.[36]

34. S. Christy to John F. Snyder, October 14, 1866, February 3, 1867, both in John F. Snyder Papers, IHL.

35. *Metropolitan Record and New York Vindicator,* January 25, 1868, p. 2.

36. Thomas H. Ellis, "Autobiography" (MS in Ellis Family Papers, VHS); Matthew F. Maury, Jr., to Matthew F. Maury, May 18, 1870, in Matthew Fontaine Maury Papers, LC.

Problems soon plagued the couple. Boardinghouse life proved an acute embarrassment for people of their age. Reduced financial circumstances meant economy of dress, and Mrs. Ellis grew extremely sensitive to criticisms and sneering remarks by fellow boarders about their patched and humble attire. The pressure of "condition and circumstance" and the need to be "exceedingly guarded in speech as well as conduct" produced additional, unaccustomed strain. Unlike Burton Harrison, Thomas Ellis could never afford to buy a house. The best he could manage after four years in Chicago was a small rented house in an undesirable neighborhood. His inability to furnish the house properly caused further humiliation. The Ellises purchased only the most essential household items. They lacked even carpets and rugs, a genuine hardship during frigid Chicago winters.[37]

By then, serious financial problems had begun to haunt the Ellises. The Chicago Fire of 1871 had spared their lives and personal possessions, but it gutted the Rozet-Ellis real estate office. Both men reluctantly agreed to cut their losses and seek individual employment. Ellis experienced trouble in his hunt for a job. Clerical work in a succession of shipping firms did not pay very much, certainly not as much as the real estate agency. With the onset of a national economic depression in the mid-1870s, Chicago became "an expensive place to live." "To compass all that we wish with my limited salary," moaned Ellis, "imposes about as hard a scuffle as we have yet experienced." Their earlier "scuffle," it must be remembered, included the privations of the war.[38]

But financial woes were not the worst of it. Social adaptability, their willingness to live alongside Yankees and accept Yankee ways, became the unconquerable barrier for the Ellises. They were amiable people. They made many friends in Chicago, among both northerners and transplanted southerners, but they never felt comfortable. "The great desire I have," confessed Thomas Ellis by 1875, "is to be restored with my family to our old home and friends, and while performing there, to the best of my ability, any duty to which I may be called, to spend the residue of my days in a manner more congenial to my taste, than it seems possible to do here." His partner in sickness and health pined even more for Virginia. Her health suffered in the northern climate, but her "distress of mind" most worried her husband. Having escaped the embarrassments of boardinghouse life, Euphania wilted under the strain of

37. Thomas H. Ellis to George W. Munford, July 4, 1873, to Charles Ellis, Jr., April 10, 1877, to Powhatan Ellis, December 16, 1877, all in Munford-Ellis Family Papers.

38. Thomas H. Ellis to Charles Ellis, Jr., April 10, 1872, to George W. Munford, July 4, 1873, both in *ibid.*

obtaining reliable servants and the burdens of housekeeping. The necessity of sending her children to racially integrated schools bore heavily on
her Virginia conscience. Separation from family and friends, whom she
never expected to see again, tore daily at her heart. Her misery grew
pitiable. She "implores me as if her existence depended upon it to take
her from Chicago," reported a distressed husband. She nourished a
"consuming desire" to escape the North. "Chicago does not grow in
favor with her," judged Ellis with marvelous understatement on another
occasion.[39]

After fourteen years in Chicago, Thomas, to his wife's immense joy,
found work in Baltimore. Eventually he and his "not fully 'reconstructed' " helpmate returned to their beloved Virginia. Toward the end of
their Chicago residence, Thomas Ellis summed up the couple's experience by observing, "It is a pity for people to have to live in a community
where they form no real attachments."[40]

Lest the Ellises' inability to adapt to northern life be attributed solely
to their age, consider the story of Thomas Ellis' real-estate partner and
his wife, only half the age of the Ellises. When New Orleans withered
before the blazing guns of Admiral David Porter's fleet in April, 1862,
George and Josephine Rozet fled the city, first to the Mississippi plantation of Mrs. Rozet's father, later, in the winter of 1863, to Philadelphia.
The Rozets had friends in the Quaker City, including George's parents;
but no amount of friendship could compensate Josephine, or Josie, as
she preferred to be called, for her forced separation from kith and kin,
particularly while her family remained exposed to the perils and suffering of war. Writing to a sister-in-law, Mrs. Rozet insisted that, despite
the well-intentioned efforts of friends to make her feel at home, Philadelphia was "still not like one's own home. I feel like a wanderer," she
moaned, "an exile banished from all the heart fondly cherishes." The
Rozets moved to Chicago in the spring of 1864 in hopes that the boom-
ing Midwest held more promising business prospects than staid old
Philadelphia. Chicago also sat within easy range of the Canadian
border, should discovery of their Confederate sympathies and George's
Confederate service make them unwelcome.[41]

It was all the same to Josie. While George slowly established himself

39. Thomas H. Ellis to Charles Ellis, Jr., March 17, 1878, June 6, 1880, to George W.
Munford, July 4, 1873, to Elizabeth Munford, August 28, 1878, all in *ibid.*
40. Thomas H. Ellis to Charles Ellis, Jr., April 6, 1875, in *ibid.*
41. Josephine Rozet to Amelia Mandeville, December 30, 1863, in Henry D. Mandeville and Family Papers, LSU.

in business, first as a real estate and loan broker, then, after the Chicago Fire, as a produce commission merchant, Josie bore two children and pined for home. She frequently made plans to visit the South and to have her father and siblings visit her, but few of the trips were consummated, none during her first decade in Chicago. A brother, hoping to find work in Chicago, joined her and Rozet in 1868, but his health could not stand the northern climate. He returned south in 1871 and died the following year. Josie knew that she and George were better off than they would have been in the South. "I wish you joy of the 'carpet-baggers' & the darkey justice-of-the-piece," she told a sister in 1869. "Oh! When will things get right in the South!" But the South's agony did not make life in Yankeedom any easier. The Chicago Fire destroyed Josie's "beautiful house & every thing in it," not to mention George's real estate business. George took the loss philosophically. He might well have thrown up his hands after this colossal stroke of ill fortune, but he braced himself and announced that he "must try again." Josie, he observed proudly, provided "infinite consolation and help" and did not "complain."[42]

Indeed she did not. Josie viewed the family's financial position realistically. She understood the necessity of living in the North, and she had every confidence in her husband's ability to provide for her and the children. "He has no money at present," Josie informed a sister following further financial setbacks in the depression year of 1874, "but you know I have infinite faith in something turning up, always." Yet, brave and determined as her words sounded, Josie shared a deep grief with Euphania Ellis. She buried her sorrow as best she could in letters to her sisters and father. A visitor to Josie's parlor would have to fathom her emotions in silent testimonials, perhaps the occasional dullness in her eyes, more likely a photograph of Robert E. Lee hanging on the wall or a canary named "Dixie." The bouts of homesickness bore far more heavily on her than the financial struggles. Dreaming of her "dear old southern home" midst the snowy depths of a Chicago winter, Josie envisioned "yellow jasmine, violets, lady beds . . . & all the other sweet things of early spring." "All my love is for the South," she admitted fifteen years after moving north, "and I get terribly home-sick for . . . quiet old Natchez."[43]

42. Josephine Rozet to Rebecca Mandeville, May 14, 1869, January 1, February 5, 1877, to Henry D. Mandeville, October 10, 1871, George Rozet to Henry D. Mandeville, January 17, 1872, all in *ibid.*

43. Josephine Rozet to Rebecca Mandeville, March 14 [1874], February 19, 1876, March 21, 1877, all in *ibid.*

Yet Josie at least enjoyed the warmth of her husband and children. Loneliness often magnified the problems of unmarried emigrants, people alone. The Rozets eventually prospered and fell into a comfortable routine of northern life. One of Josie's nieces failed this ultimate test. Carlie Oakley began her adult life by marrying in haste and repenting in prolonged and painful leisure. Carlie's dashing Confederate husband abandoned her and their unborn second child during the war. Most of Carlie's family quietly rejoiced, for they had always suspected her *beau ideal* of being a leech, a sycophant, "habitually depraved and despised" by all who knew him, a bounder who had married Carlie for her modest income. Carlie did not share this view. His desertion broke her heart. She grieved for more than a year before fleeing the maudlin looks of her family and the scenes of bitter memories. With her two babies, one newborn, the other not quite three, she traveled through the North seeking a livelihood in cities and towns as varied as New York, Philadelphia, Cleveland, Indianapolis, Springfield, and St. Louis. She refused all help from her family, which she unjustly believed felt embarrassed by her "position."[44]

Finally, late in 1866, Carlie settled in New York City. She earned a living by whatever means came to hand, including work as a "poetical contributor" to a weekly newspaper, a seamstress, and a legal copyist. Part of her earnings, necessarily, employed Irish "help" to clean her flat and assist with her youngest child, Dick, named for his father. Her daughter Mary had been left in St. Louis, evidently at a boarding school. Carlie reveled in her independence. She let her hair grow and arranged it in the latest style. She acquired a new wardrobe, noting that *"shabby folks command no respect in the North."* She impressed her independence on family members by returning a five-dollar Christmas gift sent by a kindly Mississippi aunt. She thanked her aunt for her thoughtfulness but added a kindly rebuke. "If I must gain my living," she insisted, "it must be in my own way—and wherever I think I can best prosper there I must go." "I *am* 'living comfortably,' " she assured concerned relatives; "have health, plenty to eat, and to wear. My baby is well and a treasure; soothing the old wound in my heart." Not until the snows of a fourth winter did she relinquish the remnants of her dead marriage and resume using her maiden name.[45]

---

44. George Rozet to Henry D. Mandeville, July 14, 1864, Carlie Oakley to Rebecca Mandeville, November 25, 1866, both in *ibid.*
45. Carlie Oakley to Rebecca Mandeville, November 25, 1866, [1867], both in *ibid.*

Soon, however, Carlie's confident tone began to crack. Hints of teardrops appeared between the lines of her increasingly painful letters. She admitted being unhappy and lonely. By March, 1868, while her son slowly recovered from an ulcerated throat, Carlie sublet half of her flat so she could pay the rent. She soon joined her new boarder, "a very nice refined lady" who owned a sewing machine, in sewing for a large clothier. Carlie rejoiced at the opportunity to earn a living at her fireside and "without being *over* worked, as *I* have been every winter," she revealed, "since my arrival here." The following March, Carlie confessed that life had become very hard. "Oh Bessie," she wrote to a Mississippi aunt, "I do not mean to sadden you, but it seems to *me if I could only be at home* once more, I would be at rest—& so happy." Carlie nearly died of diphtheria that summer. By the following spring, her sewing and literary work had so strained her eyes that she started to wear spectacles. Her doctor prescribed "perfect rest" for her abused eyes, "but alas!" Carlie lamented, " 'perfect rest' with *me* meant 'starvation.' " She turned thirty on April Fool's Day, 1870, and her hair was rapidly turning gray. "Oh! I get *so* homesick sometimes; if it were not for *my boy* I should indeed think that 'all the light had gone out of my life.' " The boy, named after the long-departed lover, remained her inspiration.[46]

The financial depression of the mid-1870s nearly sunk the spunky Mississippi woman. "I am *so* weary of my toilsome struggle for bread & the means of procuring an education for my boy," Carlie reported in the summer of 1872, even before the depression commenced. She abandoned sewing to lease a house and sublet the rooms to boarders. She enjoyed being a "landlady" more than any other position she had held during her seven-year "sojourn" in New York, but the boardinghouse turned into a disaster after six months. When Carlie could not pay her lease, the landlord seized her possessions and turned Carlie into the streets, "*a begger.*" Carlie swallowed her pride and turned to Mississippi for help. "Is there *nothing* in the 'old Bank' which if *sold* would give me a few dollars?" she pleaded. "There is the *Piano*—useless now—any quantity of old *silver ware,* & curious old *crape* shawls, etc., any of which disposed of would give me $50 or $100 & stave off possible starvation."[47]

Money arrived; the crisis passed; but Carlie unerringly found new

46. *Ibid.*, March 3, 1868, March 15, 1869, May 6, 1870.
47. *Ibid.*, August 26, 1872, October 14, 1873, May 1, 1874.

troubles. She suffered through the 1870s from frequent bouts of illness. After the boardinghouse fiasco, she followed Mr. Micawber's advice and grabbed any opportunity that turned up. "Aint all this funnie?" she asked Josie in thanking her for sending some old clothes, "and yet there is pathos in so much contriving to live which, even as I laugh at my words, bring tears to my eyes." Her tears flowed more easily than they might have done because Carlie, as she wrote, was trying to recover from still another smashed love affair. Shortly before her boardinghouse venture, she met a promising young lawyer. Polish by birth, French by education, the man—younger than herself—courted Carlie and proposed marriage. "He is . . . as *beautiful as the morning,* a perfect blonde, spendidly formed, & with the most lovely voice I ever listened to," Carlie gushed to an aunt. His problem was money. He was poor; he needed capital to establish a law practice. Could the family send a few hundred dollars to help him, to help them both? "Oh Bessie," she beseeched her aunt, "my heart is breaking. I *cannot* live without him & yet I cannot drag him down with me in my poverty."[48]

Carl, her lover, returned briefly to France seeking money, but he returned empty-handed, and Carlie's family could not help. Then more problems developed. Carl discovered that the law he had learned in France, based on the Napoleonic Code, was useless in New York. He talked of taking Carlie to France. They could live for half as much as in the United States, and Dick could be educated for one-third the cost. "After all, what difference would it make if I *did* end my days in France or Italy," Carlie reasoned. "I could not be more completely isolated from my family even in those far off countries than I am here in N. York. . . ." She nearly went, but something held her back. She could not bring herself to leave the United States. Carl went to France alone, but he promised to return in a few months. Whether he did is unknown, but in any case, Carlie decided marriage was impossible. "*I shall never marry,*" she vowed. She never did.[49]

Carlie's life never rebounded from the disappointments of the 1870s. In fact, the hardest blow had yet to fall. Sometime around 1880, Dick died. The cause is unclear; it may have been smallpox. Carlie tried to fill the void. She worked as a four-dollar-per-week seamstress; she clerked in a store; she labored in a factory. She only existed. She enjoyed a few

48. *Ibid.*, December 15, 1876, Carlie Oakley to Josephine Rozet, March 7, 1877, to Rebecca Mandeville, August 26, 1872, all in *ibid.*

49. Carlie Oakley to Rebecca Mandeville, January 16, June 16, October 14, 1873, all in *ibid.*

bright moments. She became very fond of a boy who, with his mother, boarded in the same house she did. She begged Josie to send her some small treat for the boy's Christmas—"old toys—old ragged picture books—an old worn jacket or over coat, or old cap or old furs"— anything that might make his little face shine as Dick's would have on Christmas morning. About 1900, Carlie's daughter reentered her life. Married and with two children, she moved east with her family to live on Long Island. Carlie lived with them and, though sixty years old by this time, insisted on contributing to the household's slender income by laboring in a factory sixteen miles away. Northern winters continued to be hard on her, but then winters were always hard, she explained, on "the 'laboring class,' to which *we* belong." Increasingly she lived among her memories, particularly memories of her beloved Dick. "Oh! God!" she beseeched her Mississippi relatives in 1902, "is there no help for me? Is there *nothing* of my Mother's I could sell you could send me?" It was the last time Carlie would have to beg.[50]

Esther B. Cheesborough—friends called her Essie—found life equally hard, but for different reasons than Carlie Oakley. Carlie blamed her unhappy northern life on circumstances, fate, the roll of the dice. She never attributed her torment to Yankees. She lamented the distance of New York from Mississippi, but she understood that, save for familiar faces, Natchez could be as formidable as Gotham. Essie Cheesborough thought otherwise. Perhaps Essie, older than Carlie by fourteen years and born and raised in Charleston, South Carolina, the seat of secession, felt more strongly about the Old South, the Confederacy, and Yankees. Carlie insisted that she had been well treated by northerners she met; Essie never forgave the North for smashing the Confederacy, sacking Charleston, and murdering her youth.

Essie Cheesborough was a writer. Indeed, before the war she had been fairly famous. In company with such literary luminaries as William Gilmore Simms, Henry Timrod, and Paul H. Hayne, Essie had helped spark a southern literary renaissance in Charleston in the 1850s. The vehicle of this renaissance had been *Russell's Magazine,* published in Charleston and edited by Hayne. Essie became the magazine's most prominent female contributor, publishing more short stories in *Russell's* than any other author. She also wrote poems, book reviews, essays, and social satires, not only for *Russell's* but for the *Southern Literary Ga-*

50. Carlie Oakley to Josephine Rozet, December 15, 1882, October 9, 1896, to Rebecca Mandeville, June 14, 1902, all in *ibid.*

zette, Charleston *Courier, Southern Episcopalian, Godey's Lady's Book,* and the prestigious *Southern Literary Messenger.*[51]

The war ended Essie's promising literary career. She had moved to Philadelphia with her widowed mother and two sisters shortly before the war, evidently to further her career. She remained there for two years after the war began to collect and distribute clothing, food, and personal items to Confederate prisoners at Fort Delaware, New Jersey, Burton Harrison's future home. Forced by federal authorities to terminate her activities in the spring of 1863, Essie returned to South Carolina, where she wrote Confederate propaganda for the state's newspapers. The war over, Essie sensed that the South, in its poverty, could not sustain her literary ambitions. She returned to Philadelphia.

But if the South could not support Essie's dreams, the North seemed reluctant to do so. Even such renowned southern authors as Simms and Hayne found Yankee publishers "absurdly exclusive" and antisouthern in the first few years after the war. Essie, believing that even with a reduced market New York offered better opportunities than Philadelphia, convinced her family to accompany her to Gotham. Early experiences did not bode well. Few New York periodicals accepted her work, but she considered this more annoying than fatal. She found plenty of work on "southern journals" published in the North and the South. The *Watchman,* a "family journal" published in New York by a transplanted North Carolinian, provided employment for a year before it folded. Essie brightened the *Watchman's* pages with a series of articles on the role of women in history. It was a good series, different from the sentimental romances and biting satires typical of her antebellum work.[52]

The Darlington *Southerner,* a South Carolina weekly newspaper to which she had contributed since 1860, provided Essie's chief support. Early in 1867, James M. Brown, publisher of the *Southerner,* hired Essie to be his "literary editress." He wanted her to make the *Southerner* a "family paper" and to elevate its "literary tone." Essie's new responsibilities required her to return to Charleston, where she resided at her family's house on Bull Street. The next year and a half proved to be a very

51. Daniel E. Sutherland, "The Rise and Fall of Esther B. Cheesborough: The Battles of a Literary Lady," *South Carolina Historical Magazine,* LXXXIV (1983), 22–30.

52. Paul H. Hayne to Jeannie A. Dickson, October 11, 1866, in Jeannie A. Dickson Correspondence, DU; Esther B. Cheesborough to Paul H. Hayne, December 24, 1866, in Hayne Papers; Daniel E. Sutherland, "Charles Force Deems and the *Watchman:* An Early Attempt at Post–Civil War Sectional Reconciliation," *North Carolina Historical Review,* LVII (1980), 422–24.

"dispirited" and apprehensive time for Essie. She devoted nearly every waking hour to the *Southerner* while becoming increasingly depressed by South Carolina's rapidly disintegrating political and social condition. She returned to New York in the autumn of 1869, still holding her post with the *Southerner,* to reside with her mother and sisters in a flat on West 19th Street.[53]

Why Cheesborough continued with the *Southerner,* unless from sheer loyalty, is hard to understand. "I do the entire work," she complained to her old friend Paul Hayne, "excepting writing the locals and book notices. . . . I do all the clipping, arranging of the columns, condensing news, write some of the editorials and letters and poems and tales etc." She did all this hundreds of miles from Darlington and for less money than the "sewing girls." She labored under these appalling conditions at first because the payment was "sure." Soon, however, even that advantage disappeared. By 1876, with the *Southerner* in financial trouble, Essie received such irregular paychecks from Brown that she had to take a second job with the New York–based *Family Journal.* She tried to handle both jobs for eight months. She labored in the *Journal* office from 8 A.M. to 6 P.M., then returned home to scrape together the next edition of the *Southerner.* Finally, having received not a penny's wages from Brown in months, Essie's loyalty wore thin. She reluctantly resigned from the *Southerner* after nine years of service.[54]

Meantime, Essie had turned fifty, a difficult age at which to find a new job or launch a new career. She lost her place with the *Family Journal* when mounting debts forced the editor to reduce his staff. She found temporary work with *Wood's Household Magazine* and *Demorest's Magazine,* but she considered neither a true literary position. Still, she had to support her aged mother and mentally deficient younger sister. "I drudge away with my pen," she complained to Paul Hayne, "and submit to having my pieces improved (?) by people who cannot write five lines of correct English, in the faith and hope that some day I will break these chains of stern necessity that bind me, and once again belong to myself." In the process, she became a hack, writing only to put food on the table. "I have written when sick in bed," she admitted, "written when I have been nursing the sick of my family, written when I have been bowed down by grief caused by death in my family, written when I have been moving, written when I have been cooking and sweeping and dusting."

53. Esther B. Cheesborough to Paul H. Hayne, November 25, 1871, in Hayne Papers.
54. *Ibid.,* September 16, 1872, July 17, 1876.

Her postwar writing embarrassed her. She had prostituted her art and forsaken her potential.[55]

Like most people who fail in their highest ambitions, Essie came to terms with her shattered reputation and reduced circumstances, but she also sought to place blame. She traced her woes to northern editors and publishers who dictated Philistine northern literary tastes and controlled the broadest avenues of literary fame. Their prejudices, she declared, stifled not only her voice but those of many promising southern writers who sought a national audience. In her private correspondence and published writings, Essie accused northerners of harboring unreasonable resentment and hatred and of using their postwar power to punish southerners who had fought for the Confederacy. From the southern shrine that served as her parlor, filled with plaster busts and framed portraits of John C. Calhoun, Jefferson Davis, and Robert E. Lee, Essie railed against her adversaries. "You would be astonished," she exclaimed to Hayne, "to see what ignorant men, utterly without literary culture or taste . . . 'run' the New York weekly story papers." Only authors low enough and stupid enough to employ their "wretched standards" could succeed. "These Yankees," she decided, "are a wretched set of humbugs, without doubt."[56]

On one occasion Essie prepared a serial short story for Frank Leslie's popular magazine, but she decided not to submit it. She had not spent enough time, she told herself, to develop the story properly. More important, she knew that she had not written the story "in a style to please the Yankee public." She had not made it sufficiently " 'Fanny Fernish,' or Gail Hamiltonish, or Beecherish, or Stowish" to compete with those leading female arbiters of northern popular literature. Cheesborough was especially contemptuous of Fanny Fern. She expressed "wonder and indignation" that northern readers clamored for Fanny's "vulgar trash." An even more personal affront to Essie's literary instincts came while she worked for *Demorest's,* where a former seamstress presided over her as an editor. "All of a sudden," marveled Essie, "she thinks herself competent to do literary work; and I write *under* this

55. *Ibid.,* September 16, 1872, August 13, 1877, November 23, 1878, June 21, 1879, November 1, 1886; Esther B. Cheesborough to Mrs. Paul H. Hayne, April 16, 1887, in *ibid.*
56. Esther B. Cheesborough, "The Female Writers of the South," *The Land We Love,* II (1867), 331–32.

woman and my articles are subject to her corrections. She is quite a success. Why?"[57]

Poor Essie could not adapt to changing times, to a world controlled by former seamstresses—Yankee seamstresses. In truth, her postwar writing did not equal her youthful efforts, but Cheesborough blamed her misfortunes on northern prejudices. The daughter of a prosperous Charleston banker, she had been raised to believe that Yankees were an inferior people. Her northern residence proved it. A writer who had earned fame in the finest southern periodicals of the day, she had always believed southern literary standards superior to northern. Her experiences confirmed that, too. By 1887, Essie was in despair. Her mother had died in 1884. Her Charleston house had been severely damaged in the great earthquake of 1886. The city's relief committee awarded her a thousand dollars for repairs, but that represented a tiny proportion of the cost of necessary renovations. She lost her job at *Demorest's* that same year, at the very moment her landlord raised the rent to such an exorbitant level that Essie and her younger sister were forced to move. She existed on a loan from a Charleston cousin. She spoke of retiring to a village. Life in the country, she fancied, would be "a rest" after so many years of "toil, and all the bustle and noise of the city." At this point, Essie Cheesborough, aged sixty, disappeared from history.[58]

The timeless echo that made the plight of Essie Cheesborough and Carlie Oakley so familiar to other weary southerners in the North was the coldness of the Yankee population, particularly the urban masses. Sidney Lanier marveled at the crush of men and women seeking livelihoods and amusements in New York's teeming thoroughfares. Equally striking, thought Lanier, was the callousness and indifference of the people. Hard-edged reality and soulessness stalked northern cities. "I have not seen here," Lanier insisted, "a single eye that knew itself to be in front of a heart:—but one, and that was a blue one, and a child owned it." One might protest that Lanier, just arrived in the city, was experiencing that shiver of dread felt by anyone set down in a throng of busy strangers; but even years later, after Lanier had spent considerable time in the North, he never reconciled himself to the inhumanity of its people.

57. Esther B. Cheesborough to Paul H. Hayne, September 16, 1872, July 17, 1876, August 13, 1877, April 2, 1885, all in Hayne Papers.

58. *Ibid.*, November 1, 1886; Esther B. Cheesborough to Mrs. Paul H. Hayne, April 16, 1887, in *ibid.*

Inevitably, some southerners attributed this coldness to the northern climate. "It even effects the nature of the people," asserted a Mississippian, "who are selfish, cold, and bad; besides being cowardly."[59]

Women seemed to be more susceptible than men to this coldness and the melancholia it bred, perhaps because nineteenth-century women were conditioned to be more emotional, but more likely because they had less opportunity for diversion. While husbands engaged in the hectic yet exciting ordeal of obtaining a livelihood, wives, especially those without children or their own houses, had much time to dwell on the past and suffer real and imagined slights. Euphania Ellis endured her toughest time in Chicago when cooped up in a boardinghouse for long hours every day. Carlie Oakley did not languish alarmingly until her son died and Carl, her last chance for married love and companionship, returned to France. Then, too, men frequently had clubs, lodges, and societies, sometimes filled with southerners and former Confederates, to ease the transition. Unless fairly well-placed socially, like Constance Harrison, women often lacked opportunities for cultural, charitable, and philanthropic work that might have sustained them. Working women, like Carlie Oakley and Essie Cheesborough, had less time to brood than Mrs. Ellis, but work could be a mixed blessing. Cheesborough insisted that southern women working in the North, generally without husbands or connections, faced particular disadvantages. "A woman has to be very brave to fight the battle of work in this region," she observed; "there is precious little sympathy or help extended, and she must tread the wine press alone."[60]

The separation grew especially heartrending for southerners who knew, like Thomas Wolfe, that they could never again return to the South they had known and loved. A Virginian, having spent several years in the North, feared to visit his old neighborhood and friends, knowing time would have wrought changes. He shrank even from thinking of the old days, so intensely did he feel the "pain & distress" of those haunting images. "It would wring my heart," he confessed, "to go to the old country again." Another man pined for the hills, brooks, and people of his native land while living in a smoggy Pennsylvania indus-

59. Sidney Lanier to Robert S. Lanier, April 16, 1887, May 4, 1869, to Virginia Hawkins, May 4, 1869, to Mary D. Lanier, October 19, 1873, all in Charles R. Anderson, *et al.* (eds.), *The Centennial Edition of the Works of Sidney Lanier* (10 vols.; Baltimore, 1945), VII, 279, VIII, 20–22, 406; John F. King to Lin Caperton, January 24, 1866, in Thomas Butler King Papers, SHC.

60. Esther B. Cheesborough to Paul H. Hayne, March 4, 1878, in Hayne Papers.

trial town. Yet each time he contemplated a visit to the South, a sense of dread struck him, a fear that he had "retained a pleasant memory of things that could no longer afford me the same pleasure they used to."[61]

All Confederate carpetbaggers complained about some aspect of northern life, but most learned to adapt, to settle in. More precisely, nothing hindered them from adapting if they wanted to. Some people settled into Yankee ways more successfully than others, some more willingly, but most who stayed learned the wisdom of Saint Ambrose: "If you are at Rome live in the Roman style." Few Confederates dared go north unless they had faith in their ability to survive among an alien, if not always hostile, people. The average Confederate's real enemy, certainly his worst enemy, in the North proved to be himself. Going north expecting to be persecuted, sneered at, or scorned, many southerners developed defensive mechanisms to ward off the slings and arrows of outrageous fortune. These people continued to feel like outsiders even when accepted into a community. Even Confederates without chips on their shoulders sometimes kept a respectable social distance from their new northern neighbors. Few former Confederates were ashamed of their war for independence, even when they accepted the reality of its failure. Moving north did not make them Yankees. They were still southerners, still rebels, and they wanted that clearly understood. The biggest danger to these diehards turned out to be not violence or rebuff at northern hands but melancholy, loneliness, and pride. Separated from home, friends, and heritage, they distanced themselves as well from northerners.

As suggested by the hardships of the Ellises and Essie Cheesborough, age could be a factor. Most Confederate carpetbaggers were younger than those three, and since most emigrants seem to have adapted readily to northern life, age cannot be discounted as a factor in their adaptation. Fifty-two members (9 percent) of the core group were under twenty years old when they moved north. The largest single age bracket, people between twenty and twenty-five, accounted for 27 percent of the core, and well over half of the group was, like the Burton Harrisons, under thirty-one. Such youth not only made the carpetbaggers better able than their parents to select occupations that would suit them for places in the North's expanding urban environment, it also allowed them to view

61. George C. Eggleston to Margaret J. Preston, December 11, 1885, in George Cary Eggleston Correspondence, ISL; Daniel A. Tompkins to Harriet Brigham, February 1, 1875, December 28, 1880, both in Tompkins Papers.

Confederate defeat and the annihilation of the Old South with less bitterness than their elders. The wreck of slavery and the ruined plantation system seemed less the end of a way of life than the end of their youth, a sad loss to be sure but a good time to begin anew. Similarly, 53 percent of the emigrants of known marital status traveled north with neither child nor spouse, a condition, too, that emphasizes their youth and accentuates their slender ties to a dead past.

Those carpetbaggers who survived, regardless of age, did so by ignoring all else save the battle for survival. They might complain about the weather, scoff at peculiarities of northern customs, and grumble about Yankee hospitality, but none of those externals really mattered. If they could find work and make a home, they generally remained. Of the core group 63 percent spent the remainder of their lives in the North, and another 9 percent stayed at least ten years. One woman who returned south after eleven years, and who had called down seven different plagues upon the Yankees during her northern residence, could still confess to a twinge of sadness at abandoning a happy home. "I have taken no root in Yankee land," she insisted, almost defiantly, "and I heartily detest Yankee character, but my own four walls have contained more happiness & contentment than one often sees under this earthly sunshine—what *domestic* woman *could* leave so pretty a little nest without direful pains and tearful forebodings?"[62]

Of course, many people required help. Not all emigrants enjoyed the income, business connections, ability, or character necessary to conquer Yankeedom alone, and even those who sauntered boldly along the road to prosperity could use some help now and then. Teamwork became necessary; infiltration seemed required. Having staggered northward singly, transplanted Confederates, to ensure survival, had to adopt new identities or band together to preserve old ones.

62. Eva Jones to aunt, February 24, 1877, in Jones Collection.

4

A Case of Identity

Burton and Constance Harrison adapted to northern life at least partly by commanding identities outside of their southern heritage and Confederate past. Their new northern identities proved essential in thwarting and disarming potential adversaries. Like all Confederate carpetbaggers, the Harrisons needed a label, a disguise, as it were, that, though not completely obscuring their gray broadcloth, at least convinced northerners that Confederate sympathies no longer dominated their lives. Some people lost themselves in new professional identities. Others chose politics, religion, or fraternal organizations. These disguises helped the Harrisons and thousands more to occupy a middle ground between North and South. They would be not wholly Confederates, yet not really Yankees. They would not have to forsake the South or repent entirely of their rebellion, yet northerners would understand that they no longer posed a threat to the Union. Smart southerners welcomed this relatively painless method of winning Yankee trust and earning Yankee dollars. They had learned the futility of frontal assaults at Gettysburg and Franklin.

Not much changed for Constance when she moved north. Her new duties as wife, mother, and housekeeper gave her a different slant on life, but many of her roles remained the same. She continued to be an active figure in society. She continued to do charity work. She continued to participate in amateur theatricals. She resumed writing, after a few years, and made literature a paying avocation. All these identities, like a series of concentric circles, swirled around her, overlapped, supported, and engulfed one another, as Constance extended herself into the community. Of course, she had to adjust some of her activities to suit northern rules and changing times, but that proved an easy task for her. She bubbled with energy. She was always up, always doing, and usually in the lead as director, manager, president, or whatever title fit the activity. Some pages of her reminiscences read like a catalog of events in postwar New York's social and cultural life. Each event, meeting, concert, session, lecture, class, rehearsal, party, ball, service, and bazaar found her merging ever more surely into the northern mainstream. It was hectic. It was exciting. She loved it.[1]

One might say that Constance waltzed her way into northern society. She adored music. She had been denied first-rate musical entertainments during the war, but once established in New York, her life became one long allegro. She took private singing lessons—from an Italian, of course—to train her "sweet soprano voice." She performed in amateur musical groups, such as the Church Musical Association choir. She directed amateur musical productions and musicales. She helped to organize a musical club, whose members discussed their favorite composers and heard recitals by promising novices and renowned professionals. She attended musical performances in every season. In fall and winter, Constance haunted the Academy of Music and feasted on its cavalcade of musical geniuses: Anton Rubinstein, Henri Vieuxtemps, Lilli Lehmann, Christine Nilsson. It seems more than chance that Constance lived within seven short blocks of the Academy of Music during her first sixteen years in New York, a time when the academy reigned as the city's principal center of orchestral and operatic performance. In spring and summer, she traveled to Central Park, where Theodore Thomas conducted his orchestra in outdoor concerts. Music enabled Constance to meet people and make friends. "The affair gave pleasure to a very critical, if small audience," she reported of one of her musicales, "and the dear people who had performed for me for love, remained afterward for a high tea with substantial dishes, at which we waited on ourselves and had royal fun." Not politics, not the war, not her Confederate past, none of these possibly volatile topics sparked the conversation. Music, glorious music, had been the theme.[2]

"We went out a great deal," recalled Constance of the Harrisons' social and cultural life. The "we" included Burton. Burton Harrison sang rather worse than a rooster, and his career as a pianist had been "nipped in the bud" at age six. According to the family story, young

1. Social correspondence of Constance Harrison in Burton Norvell Harrison Family Papers, LC; Mrs. Burton Harrison, *Recollections Grave and Gay* (New York, 1911), 218ff.

2. Francis B. Harrison, "About It and About" (Typescript in Francis Burton Harrison Papers, UV), 39; Harrison, *Recollections Grave and Gay*, 285–97.

Burton had played a piano recital for Henry Clay, who was visiting the Harrison home. The Great Compromiser listened attentively and applauded politely. Then came the blow. "Ah!" he exclaimed upon completion of Burton's performance, "a beginner I perceive." Adversity breeds character, but Burton clearly could not depend on musical talent to blur his Confederate past. Instead, he accompanied his effervescent mate to parties and other social gatherings. As in wartime Richmond, they made a sparkling duo. Burton had humor, and Constance had wit. Their combined gaiety made it impossible that any social gathering they attended should resemble a tree full of owls. Burton enjoyed New York social life, but he lacked the leisure to maintain Constance's pace and range. He joined several prominent gentlemen's clubs, including the University Dining Club, "a sort of sacred circle of wits and good talkers." Burton's own table talk was "inimitable—spontaneous, learned, witty." As a club man, Burton became "an inveterate New Yorker."[3]

Still, Burton's professional status at the bar provided his principal northern identity. The law placed Burton in company with men who judged him according to his skill and competence in jurisprudence, not his past political sympathies. Another, lesser-known Confederate reported after the war that otherwise qualified lawyers need pass only one requirement to practice at the New York bar: an oath to uphold the United States Constitution. "There is no necessity at all," he emphasized, "that a man's past history should be known to the public; Politics are here ignored, except by that portion of the Community who make a regular business of it." Having taken the oath, Burton had the initial good fortune to be sponsored at the bar by some of the city's premier lawyers and jurists, including Charles O'Conor and Judge Fullerton. Once introduced, Burton carefully nourished and expanded his connections and friendships. Not by chance did he rush, in 1870, to help establish the New York Bar Association, thereby proving himself a serious professional, concerned with improving legal and judicial standards.[4]

At the same time, Burton appreciated the political inclinations of the bar association. Many of his new legal cronies happened to be Demo-

3. Harrison, *Recollections Grave and Gay,* 284, 345; Harrison, "About It and About," 35–36, 39; Fairfax Harrison (ed.), *Aris Sonis Focisque: Being a Memoir of an American Family, the Harrisons of Skimino* (New York, 1910), 218–19.

4. J. L. Scarles to William C. P. Breckinridge, June 8, 1865, in Breckinridge Family Papers, LC; Clarence Cary, "Memorial of Burton N. Harrison," in Association of the Bar of the City of New York, *Yearbook* (New York, 1905), 126–27.

crats. Burton harbored no ambitions for a public political career, but he quickly grasped the advantages to his legal fortunes of belonging to the right political party. The legendary meeting hall of New York's Tammany Society stood adjacent to Constance's favorite haunt, the Academy of Music. Burton joined the Tammany Society shortly after settling in New York, and in the early 1870s, he fought to maintain Tammany's honor by joining the legal battle against the Tweed Ring. A grateful Democratic party rewarded Burton, in 1875, with a job he knew well: private secretary, this time serving the newly elected Democratic mayor of New York, William H. Wickham. In that same year, Wickham appointed Harrison secretary and counsel of the first Rapid Transit Commission in New York. Burton's local political career ended abruptly soon afterward. He had achieved the position of chairman of the General Committee of Tammany Hall. During a heated committee meeting, one member called Burton a liar. Harrison saw red. His usually finely tuned temper exploded. He knocked the man down, resigned his chairmanship, and left Tammany forever, although he remained on close personal terms with many members.[5]

Burton began dabbling in national politics in 1876, when he supported the presidential bid of his Gramercy Park neighbor Samuel J. Tilden. During the next twenty years, Burton campaigned for every Democratic presidential candidate and attended most Democratic national conventions. When Grover Cleveland tried to reward him for loyal party service with a diplomatic post in 1893, Burton graciously declined. He enjoyed politics, but he played the game for its own sake. His last presidential campaign, a bittersweet moment, came in 1896, when he worked to elect Republican William McKinley. Many other Confederate carpetbaggers, who disapproved of William Jennings Bryan's financial policies, followed his lead. Burton came out of political retirement only once, in 1902, to help his son Francis win election to Congress.[6]

Politics, a traditional rallying point for nineteenth-century Americans, might seem an unlikely role for Confederate carpetbaggers. Former Confederates, of all people, had little chance of influencing elections or winning political success in the North. Unlike northerners in

5. Burton N. Harrison to Judge Fullerton, January 23, 1869, in Harrison Family Papers, LC; Harrison, *Recollections Grave and Gay,* 302; Harrison, "About It and About," 138.

6. Cary, "Memorial of Burton Harrison," 129–30; Harrison (ed.), *Aris Sonis Focisque,* 209–10, 213–18; Harrison, "About It and About," 40a.

Dixie, they came as the vanquished, not the vanquishers. They had no Reconstruction Acts, no conveniently rearranged state constitutions to aid them in shaping political careers. The political climate and the circumstances of their northern residence necessarily limited their political ambitions. Indeed, not a few men were legally prohibited from political activity until passage of the Amnesty Act in 1872; some longer than that. Most southerners, at least the ones who moved north, were weary of political warfare. Politics had caused the war and disrupted their lives. They wanted nothing more to do with it. "I think we are to see far less attention given to politics all over the land & far more to human progress," predicted one southerner in the North. "Politics did well for idle men:—but idlers will be at a discount, where there is a call for so much exertion, & the reward so sure." The glory days of southern political dominance had all been "a *grand humbug*," which lived on only in "the feelings of old folks when indulging in the pleasures of Memory & looking back at their enjoyments in the days of their youth."[7]

Still, aspiring politicos could be found, most of them encouraged in their ambitions by northern—mostly Democratic—political cronies. The list of elected and appointed former Confederates who held offices is impressive. Sixty-one men in the core group held political office in the North, and dozens more became active political workers, joined political clubs, campaigned for their party, flocked to political rallies, and served as delegates at local, state, and national conventions. Most of the officeholders served in local capacities—city councilmen, postmasters, highway commissioners, school board members, and the like—but the group also included a United States congressman and several state legislators. Most of these men served after 1880, by which time animosity against Confederates had lessened considerably and new identities were not as necessary as they had been. Nonetheless, political roles served their purpose.

John R. Fellows pursued the most active political career in the North. Born at Troy, New York, Fellows had moved with his parents at age eight to Arkansas, where he grew up. He opposed secession as a young lawyer in Arkansas, but when the state seceded, he enlisted in Arkansas' first regiment of Confederate volunteers. He eventually attained the rank of

7. Paul H. Buck, *The Road to Reunion, 1865–1900* (Boston, 1937), 36, 115–16; Ruston Maury to Matthew F. Maury, October 8, 1868, in Matthew Fontaine Maury Papers, LC.

colonel and saw combat in Tennessee, Virginia, and Louisiana before being captured at Port Hudson in July, 1863. He resumed his law practice and served in the Arkansas state senate after the war, but he so impressed Horatio Seymour as a delegate to the 1868 National Democratic Convention in New York that the presidential nominee persuaded Fellows to participate in his northern campaign. Fellows never returned south. The New York Democratic party adopted him and provided him with an unbroken string of political offices. He began as an assistant district attorney in 1869 and later served as district attorney, counsel to the New York board of excise, member of Congress (1891–1893), and delegate to four national conventions.[8]

Fellows always acknowledged the influence of Thurlow Weed in securing his earliest appointments, but he soon acquired his own power base. Fellows earned a reputation as an eloquent, forceful orator with an engaging, genial personality. He became a much-sought-after campaigner and after-dinner speaker. Only once did he desert his party, and even then, in 1896, he went not to the Republicans, as did Burton Harrison, but to the National Democrats, a third party composed of old-line Democrats who opposed their party's silver platform. Upon his death, shortly after the 1896 campaign, Tammany Hall praised Fellows as "one of its most devoted and honored members." All city departments in New York closed at noon on the day of his funeral. The crowd of two thousand that pressed for admission to his funeral service could not be accommodated, and some of New York's most influential politicians, judges, and financiers bore him to his final resting place.[9]

Roger Pryor of Virginia must rank as the most prominent Confederate to win northern political laurels. No antebellum southerner better deserved the name "firebrand." An impulsive, middle-aged journalist and congressman when the war came, he had helped goad the South into secession and then served the Confederacy as soldier and congressman. Nothing could have been further from Pryor's mind after the war than a northern residence. He sailed to New York for his health at the insistence of his wife. When he arrived, in the first autumn following the war, warm perfusions of Democratic comradery enveloped him. Warmest of all was Benjamin Wood, owner of the New York *Daily News,* former

8. *National Cyclopaedia of American Biography* (59 vols. and index; New York, 1898–1980), XI, 191–92; Horatio Seymour to Samuel J. Tilden, September 24, 1868, in Manton Marble Papers, LC.

9. New York *Times,* December 8, 1896, p. 8, December 9, 1896, p. 8, December 10, 1896, p. 9.

member of Congress, and brother of New York's mayor, Fernando. Wood gave Pryor a twenty-five-dollar-a-week job writing for the *Daily News,* thus caring for the Virginian's immediate financial needs and allowing him to spend his spare time brushing up on the law. Almost on whim, Pryor sought and won admission to the New York bar. His head fairly spinning in disbelief at these developments, Pryor asked his wife, waiting patiently for his return to Virginia, if she would join him in Yankeedom. "Dare I 'then, to beard the lion in his den,' " he joked with her, " 'the Douglas in his hall!' " "I have a mind to try," he warned, and concluded his invitation with words strikingly similar to those used by Burton Harrison in writing to Constance: " 'The world is all before us where to choose.' " Early in 1866, Pryor unobtrusively announced his new profession by inserting an advertisement in the *Daily News*: "Roger A. Pryor, Counsellor at Law, #3 Tyron Row, Office 1, City Hall Sq., N.Y."[10]

Initially, Pryor conceived only of a northern legal career. He had not received a pardon by 1866, and he would not receive one until 1880. A political career during the intervening years seemed impossible. Indeed, Pryor so worried about being imprisoned for his articles in the staunchly Democratic *Daily News* that he published them anonymously. Republican newspapers referred to him as "the Rebel Pryor" when describing his legal activities, just to let him know they knew all about his antecedents and current status. Still, his party label did more good than harm. Benjamin Wood continued to head the unofficial welcoming committee by sending Pryor his first court case, a judgment that earned Pryor one thousand dollars from a grateful, superbly defended client. Thomas W. Pittman, a New York lawyer, literary figure, and Democratic loyalist, joined Pryor as a law partner. John Mullaly, editor of the Democratic *Metropolitan Record and New York Vindicator,* publicly ballyhooed the alliance of these two "scholars and gentlemen." Augustus Schell, an influential New York Democrat and future national chairman of the Democratic party, introduced Pryor as a guest at the newly established Manhattan Club and arranged for the Virginian's election to that select political group.[11]

10. Mrs. Roger A. Pryor, *My Day: Reminiscences of a Long Life* (New York, 1909), 280–82; New York *Daily News,* February 13, 1866, p. 3.

11. Pryor, *My Day,* 280–82, 292, 295, 297; Robert S. Holzman, *Adapt or Perish: The Life of General Roger A. Pryor, C.S.A.* (Hamden, Conn., 1976), 91–92; *Metropolitan Record and New York Vindicator,* June 9, 1866, p. 13; Francis Gerry Fairfield, *The Clubs of New York: With an Account of the Origins, Progress, Present Condition and Membership of the Leading Clubs* (New York, 1873), 139–40.

"On the downfall of the Confederacy," Pryor proclaimed publicly in 1867, "I renounced forever every political aspiration, and resolved henceforth to address myself to the care of my family and the pursuit of my profession." But forever is a long time, and once he had firmly established his law practice, Pryor drifted into small but active political roles. To justify himself, Pryor claimed that he had never "repudiated the obligations of good citizenship," which he believed required him to speak publicly on issues that concerned the "welfare and stability" of the government. He was especially concerned with sectional political reconciliation, and during the 1870s, he reentered the political arena to work toward that goal. Horace Greeley, nominated as the Liberal Republican and Democratic presidential candidate in 1872, asked Pryor and several other former Confederates in the North to campaign for him. Pryor declined a major role, but he made a few speeches praising Greeley's desire for sectional peace.[12]

In 1876, however, spurred to action by Greeley's defeat at the hands of Ulysses S. Grant, Pryor attended the National Democratic Convention as a delegate and campaigned heartily for Samuel J. Tilden. In 1880, he worked hard, as did Burton Harrison, for the unsuccessful presidential bid of Winfield Scott Hancock, whom Pryor had fought against on the battlefield at Antietam eight years earlier. Had Hancock won, it is likely that Pryor would have been named attorney-general of the United States. Tammany Hall had urged Pryor to run for Congress in 1880, but he declined the virtually assured seat. Pryor proved his loyalty to the party again in 1884. The Democrats, badly divided that year by the nomination of Grover Cleveland, seemed destined to lose their bid for the White House again. Pryor had opposed Cleveland's nomination; he predicted that James G. Blaine, the Republican candidate, would win the election. Yet Pryor steadfastly refused to desert the party that had treated him so generously. "I abide with the Democratic party," he informed a political friend, "from a sense of obligation which may be mistaken, but which I do not feel at liberty to disregard. If the party were likely to succeed, I might abandon it, but doomed to defeat, I feel that I should go down with it." These were the words of a true Confederate, and, in this instance a victorious Confederate, for Cleveland became the first Democrat to enter the White House in twenty-eight years. In 1890, Democratic governor David B. Hill repaid Pryor's loyalty by appointing him to a vacancy on New York's court of common pleas. The following year,

12. Pryor, *My Day*, 326–29.

Pryor won election to a full term on the court, and in 1896, he became a justice on the state supreme court. No politician/lawyer could have asked for more.[13]

James Maurice Thompson, better known as a poet and novelist, played politics for awhile. Thompson left Georgia in 1868 to settle in Crawfordsville, Indiana, about forty-five miles west of Indianapolis. The congressional Reconstruction Acts and impeachment of Andrew Johnson had convinced Maurice and his brother William that life in the North could be no worse than existing under military despotism, so they decided "to reverse the procedure of the carpetbaggers and try their luck" in Yankeedom. Maurice wasted no time settling into northern life. He found a job as a civil engineer, married his boss's daughter, began to write poetry, and started a law practice, all in three years. Thompson's law practice and engineering assignments provided him with political contacts across the state, and by 1876 he was stumping Indiana for the state's Democratic party. "I've gone everywhere," he reported wearily to a friend in Georgia, "and spoke and spoke, till I speak like a machine." Having paid his political dues, Thompson sought election to the state legislature in 1878. His smashing victory in a traditionally Republican district started Thompson thinking about a political career, with Congress his next goal. Literary plaudits distracted him, however, and, although he remained politically active and received appointments as state geologist and chief of the Bureau of Natural History, he did not seek elected office beyond his first term in the legislature.[14]

In truth, Thompson, like many Confederate carpetbaggers, lacked driving political ambition. He remained politically active after 1880 only because he needed the money provided by his patronage posts. "My keenest desire," he asserted, "is to get entirely and forever out of politics and to be able to devote my whole life to making pure and beautiful literature." Thompson always tried to take the broad view of life. Though a loyal Democrat, he did not "care a straw" about a man's political affiliation. "We don't differ about matters of culture and progress," he pointed out to a Republican acquaintance, "and politics, after all, is nothing to worry about so [long as] one acts conscientiously." As if to dramatize his point, Thompson, the lifelong Democrat, supported

13. Holzman, *Adapt or Perish*, 107–10, 129–32; Roger A. Pryor to Benjamin F. Butler, July 21, 1884, in Benjamin F. Butler Papers, LC.

14. Otis B. Wheeler, *The Literary Career of Maurice Thompson* (Baton Rouge, 1965), 22–25, 31–32, 37; James M. Thompson to Paul H. Hayne, April 2, 1876, in Paul Hamilton Hayne Papers, DU.

William McKinley in 1896 and 1900, finding it impossible, as did Harrison and Pryor, to support Democratic inflationary monetary policy.[15]

John F. Snyder, after nearly three years of Confederate service, served a term in the Illinois state legislature during the same years Thompson operated at Indianapolis. Snyder had long before learned the benefits of proper party affiliation. After being captured and paroled in 1863, he began practicing medicine in Illinois the following year. From time to time, midwestern communities in need of a physician invited him to settle with them, always promising Snyder a lucrative practice based not just on his medical skill but on his Democratic loyalties. Typical was an invitation from a town in western Illinois: "We have here five Physicians who are Radical Republicans here, while we give a democratic majority at elections. If you come here you can commence all the democratic practice besides some of the other. . . . I can insure your introduction into many of the best families here. . . . You will [find] a set of public men here that will do what they can for you."[16]

Other Confederates benefited from their political identity, and although they never influenced northern politics as much as northern carpetbaggers usurped southern political power during Reconstruction, they became forces to be reckoned with. Confederate private Brent Arnold left Kentucky after the war to settle in Cincinnati, where he enjoyed a "remarkable" business and political career. Arnold served on the city council for two years as a Democrat in a Republican ward and on the city's chamber of commerce for many years. Randolph Guggenheimer, a Virginian by birth and a lawyer by profession, served three terms as New York's commissioner of schools in the 1880s and 1890s and a single term as commissioner of the board of education, 1906–1911. More important, Guggenheimer served on the New York municipal council, including terms as its president (1897–1901). Edward Owen, major of Confederate artillery, left Louisiana to fight for the khedive of Egypt in 1870, but he moved to New York upon returning to the United States and became a "conspicuous figure . . . in the business and political organizations of the city." In the 1880s and 1890s, Owen served in the city's accounting department, first as chief clerk, later as

15. James M. Thompson to Mr. Bowen, April 21, 1888, in James Maurice Thompson Letters, YU; James M. Thompson to Mr. Dooley, April 13, 1876, in James Maurice Thompson Papers, EU.

16. N. M. Purviance to John F. Snyder, January 18, 1868, in John F. Synder Papers, IHL.

department head. Augustus J. Requier, a South Carolina lawyer, poet, and playwright, became an active member of Tammany Hall after the war and was rewarded for his skillful campaign oratory with appointments as a city counsel and assistant district attorney. W. Patrick Gorman served in the Michigan legislature in 1871–1872 after moving north from Tennessee. Thomas G. Windes, a veteran of the 4th Alabama Cavalry, labored as a streetcar driver and bookkeeper in Chicago before becoming a prominent lawyer and Democrat in Cook County. In 1892, Windes won election to the state circuit court and appointment to the court of appeals. He eventually served as chief justice of the circuit court.[17]

Even when not seeking office for themselves, southerners in the North spoke out publicly on political issues. A long list of southern newspaper editors, journalists, and commentators in the North attacked political and economic policies injurious to their party and the South. Thomas L. Snead found it difficult to give up politics entirely after service in the Confederate Congress, so he directed New York's leading Copperhead newspaper, the *Daily News,* as managing editor in 1865–1866. Thomas Jordan, concerned about national financial policy, founded the *Financial and Mining Record* in New York. Many Washington politicians recognized Jordan's journal, which he directed from 1870 to 1892 to promote the interests of free silver, as the highest authority on that complex issue. Virginius Dabney, one of the Virginia Dabneys, wrote numerous articles supporting Grover Cleveland's first presidential bid and, after Cleveland's election, his financial policies.[18]

Southern literary lions roared in places other than the editorial page.

17. George Mortimer Roe, *Cincinnati: The Queen City of the West* (Cincinnati, 1895), 43–44; Charles Theodore Greve, *Centennial History of Cincinnati and Representative Citizens* (2 vols.; Chicago, 1904), II, 224–25; John W. Leonard (ed.), *Who's Who in New York City and State* (3rd ed.; New York, 1907), 594–95; *Confederate Veteran,* III (April, 1895), 114–15; Thomas C. DeLeon, *Belles, Beaux and Brains of the Sixties* (New York, 1907), 333–34; James Grant Wilson and John Fiske (eds.), *Appleton's Cyclopedia of American Biography* (6 vols.; New York, 1891–93), V, 223; W. Stanley Hoole (ed.), *A Rebel Spy in Yankeeland: The Thrilling Adventures of Major W. P. Gorman* (University, Ala., 1981), 27; *National Cyclopaedia of American Biography,* XVII, 211; *Prominent Democrats of Illinois* (Chicago, 1899), 161–62.

18. *Dictionary of American Biography* (26 vols. and index; New York, 1928–80), X, 216, XVII, 379; William J. Marrin, "Thomas Jordan," in United States Military Academy, *27th Annual Reunion of the Association of the Graduates of the United States Military Academy at West Point, New York* (East Saginaw, Mich., 1896), 80–81; New York *Times,* June 3, 1894, p. 9.

Sidney Lanier wrote a series of poems attacking the evils of Reconstruction. Most of these poems, including "Laughter in the Senate," "Raven Days," and "Steel in Soft Hands," Lanier published before moving north. A few others, such as "Them Ku Klux" and "Those Bonds," he wrote while in the North but did not publish. One of Lanier's most biting, even bitter, denunciations of Republican policy in the South came at the very moment he sought to find a niche in northern musical and literary life. "Civil Rights" is a dialect poem, the lament of a backwoods Georgian about the rabid policies of Charles Sumner and friends. " 'I've just been over to the Squire's, a' readin of the news,' " the old fellow laments, " 'My Son, this here oncivil rights is givin' me the blues.' " Lanier's old Confederate had done his best to reconstruct himself, not an easy task for a man who had lost a son in the war, watched William T. Sherman's men burn his mill, and suffered total confiscation of his livestock and crops. Yet he had been willing to get along with the Yankees, curious people as they were. " 'They saw *ther* side as we saw *our'in,*' " he reasoned, " 'and maybe both was wrong.' " But then, by gum, just as the world began to right itself, " 'Here comes this Civil Rights and says, this fuss shan't have no end!' "

> "Hit seems as ef, jest when the water's roughest, here of late,
> Them Yanks had throwed us overboard from off the Ship of State.
> Yes, throwed us both—both black and white—into the ragin' sea,
> With but one rotten plank to hold; while they, all safe and free,
> Stands on the deck, and rams their hands into ther pockets tight,
> And laughs to see we both must drown, or live by makin' fight!"[19]

The most striking show of Confederate force in northern politics came in 1892 at the place blessed with the largest concentration of former rebels, New York City. Democrats across the country still seethed at the way fish-faced Benjamin Harrison and his vile Republicans had stolen the White House from incumbent President Cleveland in 1888. Cleveland, like Tilden in 1876, had won a majority of the popular votes, but the Republicans had controlled the electoral college. Harrison and his "Billion Dollar" Congress then proceeded to "bankrupt" the country by spending money on internal improvements, jacking up the tariff, passing the inflationary Sherman Silver Purchase Act (favored by many southerners), and increasing pensions to Union

19. Jack DeBellis, *Sidney Lanier* (New York, 1972), 48–54, 60; Charles R. Anderson *et al.* (eds.), *Centennial Edition of the Works of Sidney Lanier* (10 vols.; Baltimore, 1945), I, 14–15, 40–42, 169, 191–94, 199.

veterans. Cleveland had even lost his home state of New York in the election. New York Confederates, rallying to the sacred southern battle cries of "states' rights" and "home rule"—uttered now with an ironic twist—vowed that would not happen twice. They intended that New York should elect Cleveland and a full slate of congressional Democrats.[20]

To ensure this happy result, former rebels formed the Association of Southern Democrats (ASD) in New York. The members intended to register every one of the estimated fifteen thousand inactive southern voters in New York City and get them to the polls on election day. They intended, too, that their activism in the North should awaken southerners to the dangers of continued Republican rule. The campaign's critical issue would be a proposed Force Bill that, if passed, would give Republicans control over the electoral process in the South. Democrats called it an outrageous attempt to revive the Reconstruction Acts that would allow President Harrison to steal both the popular and electoral votes. "The South must bury the Force bill," declared Edward Owen, secretary of the ASD, "or be buried by the Force bill." Members of the association knew, like that old political fox Roscoe Conkling, that political parties are not built by deportment, ladies' magazines, or "gush." Organization and energetic party workers created and maintained political power.[21]

Two hundred men attended the association's organizational meeting, and their leadership read like a "Who's Who" of influential Confederates in the city. Journalists, financiers, merchants, not to mention politicians such as Edward Owen, leaped into the fray. They printed ten thousand copies of a pamphlet attacking the Force Bill. Energetic committee chairmen in each of New York's electoral districts worked hard to identify and register southern voters. One of the most active district chairmen was Harry W. Walker, a newspaper reporter, who located three hundred unregistered southern Democrats in his district. One of his discoveries, an old Alabamian, had lived in New York for twenty years without voting. Like many other southerners, he had lost interest in politics after moving north. Besides, he said, New York was so overwhelmingly Democratic that his vote seemed unimportant. Cleveland

20. H. Wayne Morgan, "Election of 1892," in Arthur M. Schlesinger, Jr. (ed.), *History of American Presidential Elections, 1789–1968* (4 vols.; New York, 1971), II, 1703–84; Mary R. Dearing, *Veterans in Politics: The Story of the G.A.R.* (Baton Rouge, 1952), 433–34.

21. New York *Times*, August 23, 1892, p. 5, September 18, 1892, p. 17.

and a Democratic legislative slate that included John Fellows swept New York in 1892, and though it may be an exaggeration to say that New York Democrats owed their victories to the ASD (William C. Whitney's money and organizing skill probably counted more heavily), southern activists certainly did their part. The association was revived briefly in 1894 to keep renegade Democratic elements in check for New York's state elections, but that campaign, another success, marked the end of the ASD's usefulness. Members returned to their everyday pursuits, perhaps chuckling over their belated victory against a Republican war machine.[22]

Few politicians and party operatives depended on political identities alone to disguise their Confederate past. Most, like Harrison, Pryor, Thompson, and Snyder, had professional images, too. People in nearly every occupation gained some sense of identity, if not satisfaction, from their jobs, but professional people—doctors, lawyers, bankers, writers, and the like—could submerge themselves more completely than farmers, bricklayers, and shopkeepers in their working identities. Specialized training, professional organizations, respectable public images, and shared social circles enabled professionals to mask their antecedents if they wished. Of course, competition within a profession could be keen, and newcomers to a community, whether Confederate or Union veterans, were not universally welcomed by established members of their specialties, particularly in places where competition for clients or contracts was intense. Nonetheless, southern professionals seldom suffered abuse or criticism for being southerners. If they proved competent in their fields, nobler passions reigned. Not a few men and women reached prestigious, honored places in their professions. As a Kentucky lawyer explained, "The respectable portion of the community are so busily engaged in the effort to accumulate money they never have time to enquire into a neighbor's antescedents."[23]

Josiah Clark Nott, an Alabama physician of national prominence before the war, received a hearty welcome from New York's leading medical men when he moved to the city in 1868. Nott's "skill and industry" soon justified the "goodwill of his professional brethern." "Here," Nott reported triumphantly to his sister-in-law after a year's

22. Morgan, "Election of 1892," 1728–30; New York *Times*, September 18, 1892, p. 17, October 13, 1892, p. 8, October 13, 1894, p. 2.

23. Robert S. Marx to Edward Colston, April 25, 1925, in Colston Family Papers, CS; J. L. Scarles to William C. P. Breckinridge, June 8, 1865, in Breckinridge Family Papers.

residence, "I am free and an equal with the best, and if we only had your family and a few relics of our old set in N. York, we would have nothing to wish for." Nott found his expertise in wide demand, not only by patients but by fellow physicians. Nott deemed professional intercourse vital. He had resided in Baltimore for a year before settling in New York and left in part because the city's physicians maintained no active societies and exchanged few ideas. Sounding like a nineteenth-century H. L. Mencken, Nott dismissed Baltimore by saying, "They are too moral there for me, & I could find no body to talk to about a book. They have no scientific association of any kind there & in the 12 months I never heard a man allude to a book."[24]

John R. Thompson enjoyed an enviable, well-deserved journalistic and literary reputation before the war. Thompson was in England working as a Confederate propagandist when the war ended. He dawdled in England for eighteen months before an overwhelming sense of homesickness sent him scurrying back to Richmond. It did not take Thompson long after his return to realize the difficulties of resuming his literary career in the postwar South. He began contacting editors and publishers in New York, but no one offered him a position. Indeed, Henry J. Raymond, editor of the New York *Times,* expressed surprise that the rebel should even think of requesting northern assistance. Thompson then contacted Burton Harrison, a friend before the war, to ask for help. "While I should prefer living in New York to any place in this country," he explained to Harrison, "it would be little short of madness in me to encounter the risks of success and failure there as a literary man and a journalist, without a certain reliance in a connection with some established paper. Of all avocations, nothing is so precarious as literature. A man may write ever so well, and work ever so hard, *and starve,* because he can find no market for his wares." He wanted a guaranteed income.[25]

24. William Leland Holt, "Josiah Clark Nott of Mobile: An American Prophet of Scientific Medicine," *Medical Life,* XXXV (1928), 491; Reginald Horsman, *Josiah Nott of Mobile: Southerner, Physician, and Racial Theorist* (Baton Rouge, 1987), 313–21; Josiah C. Nott to Mary [Broun], August 28, 1869, in Josiah C. Nott Papers, UA; Josiah C. Nott to Ephraim G. Squier, May 28, 1868, November 18, 1869, October 7, 1872, all in Ephraim George Squier Papers, LC.

25. John S. Patton (ed.), *Poems of John R. Thompson* (New York, 1920), xlix–l, 1; Gerald M. Garmon, *John Reuben Thompson* (Boston, 1979), 129–30; John R. Thompson to Burton N. Harrison, January 18, March 2, 1867, in Harrison Family Papers, LC.

Thompson got his guaranteed income but not before a year of struggle and heartache. Thompson could not adjust to northern life. Though befriended by numerous southerners in New York, he could not shake his longing for Virginia. "I can't get reconstructed," he confessed to a friend; "I find myself most irreligiously berating the country (represented by Congress, Boston, Wendell Phillips, etc, etc), and the heaven-born banner & the eagle-bird, to the infernal gods." He joined Lanier in forging his literary gifts into southern political tools. Thompson penned biting poems condemning Republican political excesses during Reconstruction. He announced his arrival in the North by publishing "Virginia Fuit" in the *Old Guard,* a journal with Democratic tendencies and southern sympathies. The poem is a scathing diatribe, filled with allusions to Yankee tyranny, southern honor, and the vengeance of God. Thompson clearly did not intend to grovel at the feet of his new neighbors. Others of his poems launched direct assaults on the smug piety of a people who, having concluded a humanitarian crusade against black bondage in the South, now ignored the poor starving populace of their own cities. "Miserimus" paints a gloomy portrait ("a snow cloud hung darkly 'twixt' Broadway and heaven") of New York's supposedly philanthropic classes. A wandering minstrel boy, a young Trovatore, freezes to death in the bitter winter cold for want of a little charity. Thompson taunts his fat northern readers, wrapped in furs and greatcoats, for their callousness:

> The moral, O people! I leave it with you—
> The poor ye have always; oh, think of the poor
> Who perish of hunger and cold at your door.[26]

Time, however, tempered Thompson's rage and diluted his sorrow. If never fully reconstructed, Thompson, unlike Essie Cheesborough, at least came to appreciate northern literary tastes and became an expert in Yankee likes and dislikes. About a year after his arrival, having struggled for a pair of second-rate local newspapers, Thompson got his break. Some northern and southern friends arranged an interview between Thompson and William Cullen Bryant, owner of the New York *Evening Post.* The Virginian dazzled Bryant with his literary knowledge. "He had read so variously, observed so minutely, and retained so tenaciously the results of his reading and observation," recalled Bryant, "that he was never at a loss for a topic and never failed to invest what he

26. John R. Thompson to George W. Bagby, February 25, 1868, in Bagby Family Papers, VHS; Patton (ed.), *Poems of Thompson,* 49–50, 202–205.

was speaking of with a rare and original interest. His fund of anecdote was almost inexhaustible and his ability to illustrate any subject by apt quotation no less remarkable." Bryant made Thompson his literary editor and assured him, after learning of his unreconstructed nature, that he cared nothing for Thompson's politics, only for the quality of his literary work.[27]

Thompson became a familiar figure at the Bryant household and one of the most popular men on the *Evening Post* staff. Everyone loved the frail, blue-eyed, heavily bearded little Virginian. Poor health had plagued him for years, and he would die of consumption in 1873, but Thompson's feeble constitution seldom affected his spirits. He excelled at billiards and whist. As a raconteur he was priceless. "Though not a marvel of erudition or critical genius," recalled a fellow journalist, "he was a pleasant, cultivated gentleman, and abundantly capable." "I never met a person whom I admired more for his accomplishments as a scholar and his courtesy as a gentleman," insisted another member of the *Evening Post* staff. He was "a Rebel to be loved," claimed another. Edmund C. Stedman, who had recommended Thompson to Bryant, called Thompson "the connecting link between Poe's generation and my own. He was a poet, scholar, wit, and a gentleman in the finest sense of the word," Stedman elaborated; "always a fascinating companion and a lovable, affectionate friend ever devoted to the cause of the South, but in such wise that we loved him the better for it." The word "love" appears frequently in these descriptions. Love can be a powerful force, even among hard-core professionals.[28]

Artists are known for being nonconformists and visionaries. Whatever time, country, or community they may stumble into, they are frequently at odds with prevailing behavior and values. Southern artists who moved north thus concerned themselves not so much with integration into northern life as with acceptance by the northern artistic world, which was itself at odds with traditional Yankee values. People called them "Bohemians" in the nineteenth century. Bohemianism arrived in the United States in the early 1850s, inspired by the success of Henri

27. John R. Thompson to George W. Bagby, February 25, 1869, in Bagby Family Papers; Allan Nevins, *The Evening Post: A Century of Journalism* (New York, 1922), 408; Garmon, *John Reuben Thompson*, 131–33; Patton (ed.), *Poems of Thompson*, li.

28. Patton (ed.), *Poems of Thompson*, xxxviii, xliii–xlviii, lvii; Nevins, *Evening Post*, 408–409; Garmon, *John Reuben Thompson*, 133–34; Charles Marshall Graves, "Thompson the Confederate," *The Lamp: A Review and Record of Current Literature*, XXIX (October, 1904), 181.

Murger's play *Scènes de la Vie Bohème*. New York became the home of American Bohemianism, and Charlie Pfaff's grotto bar and restaurant on Broadway at Bleecker Street became its geographic pinion. Pfaff's earliest clientele included Walt Whitman, Artemus Ward, Thomas Bailey Aldrich, Fitz-James O'Brien, and the reigning "Queen of Bohemia," southern-born Ada Clare, *née* Jane McElheney. Pfaff's glory days had passed by the time postwar southern painters, poets, musicians, and sculptors arrived in New York. Like so many originally *avant-garde* institutions, the slightly scandalous rendezous soon acquired an aura of Bohemian chic. By 1865, it had moved uptown to 24th Street and become too expensive and too respectable for a genuinely hungry artist. Some scholars believe the Bohemian craze of the 1850s subsided along with the old Pfaff's, not to be fully revived until the 1880s; but Pfaff's early spirit never died completely, and many "Confederate Bohemians" (so dubbed by a Richmond newspaper) rushed to join northern artistic life, Bohemian or not.[29]

A serious obstacle remained, however, for southerners did not take naturally to Bohemianism. Bohemianism smacked of urban eccentricities and foreign influences, against which the southern nature bristled. "The Bohemian is by nature, if not by habit, a cosmopolite," insisted Queen Ada, "with a general sympathy for the fine arts and for all things above and beyond convention." Most southerners did not fit the description. Constance Harrison believed Bohemianism had been unknown in antebellum Virginia. John R. Thompson told Burton Harrison that he refused to live in the North "as a mere Bohemian." Sidney Lanier associated Bohemianism with a philosophy of despair, which went against his strict religious upbringing. Moreover, Lanier strove for financial security as an artist, a goal genuine Bohemians scorned. Lanier wanted his own house and a "homelife," not the beer, cheese, and fried fish of Pfaff's. When he finally acquired his own house, Lanier declared almost triumphantly, "No man is a Bohemian who has to pay water rates and a street-tax."[30]

29. Albert Parry, *Garrets and Pretenders: A History of Bohemianism in America* (New York, 1933), 21–22, 56–57, 61–64; Lloyd Morris, *Incredible New York: High Life and Low Life in the Last Hundred Years* (New York, 1951), 74–75; Emily Hahn, *Romantic Rebels: An Informal History of Bohemianism in America* (Boston, 1967), 33; *Southern Opinion*, September 9, 1867, p. 2.

30. Parry, *Garrets and Pretenders*, 26; Harrison, *Recollections Grave and Gay*, 132; John R. Thompson to Burton N. Harrison, March 2, 1867, in Harrison Family Papers, LC; Aubrey Harrison Starke, *Sidney Lanier: A Biographical and Critical Study* (New York, 1964), 170–71; Sidney Lanier to Gibson Peacock, January 8, 1878, in Anderson, *et al.* (eds.), *Works of Sidney Lanier*, X, 5.

DeCourcy Plantagenet Lee, the hero of *The Bohemians,* a popular novel of the early 1870s, is a Virginian who goes north after the war to work as a cashier in a large dry goods store. The son of a planter, DeCourcy finds his work "neither interesting . . . nor . . . particularly honorable." As he struggles along in his daily grind and resides in a "vulgar boarding house," DeCourcy grows ever more pessimistic about "his prospects in life." Seeking gaiety, the impressionable young man falls in with a group of local Bohemians, young writers and painters who wear "velvet jackets, loose cravats, and slouch hats," sing songs ridiculing "staid burgesses," and drink confusion to the Philistines. DeCourcy tries desperately to be a Bohemian, but his pedigree is all wrong. He is a hanger-on, a groupie. He revels in Bohemian company because of its novelty, because he is lonely, and because he relishes associates regarded as wicked by respectable Yankee society. His tenuous attachment to Bohemianism snaps when he falls in love with a flirtatious northern debutante who scorns Bohemians. DeCourcy is drawn into northern fashionable society and, for the moment, finds his niche. Yet in time, DeCourcy becomes disgusted with the "poor pasteboard creatures" of his fiancée's circle. In total disillusionment, he commits suicide.[31]

Aspiring Bohemians frequently met tragic ends. They were forever starving, dying of consumption, or freezing in a lonely garret in real life as well as in fiction. Irwin Russell, Mississippi poet, played out his Bohemian fate to its bitter end. Russell idolized Scots bard Robert Burns, a Bohemian long before the word was invented. Like Burns, who put his verse into the language of the common folk, Russell captured in his poems the character, habits, and dialect of southern blacks. Unfortunately, Burns drank to excess, and so did Irwin Russell. Drink so harmed his constitution that, when Russell headed for New York to seek literary fame in the 1870s, he fell ill with a sickness from which he never recovered. "He was a young man of bright intellect and finished education," reported the New Orleans *Times* in its obituary notice, "but becoming enamored of a Bohemian life, set out in search of fame and fortune." Russell's illness, coupled with a bout of depression and drink stimulated by news of his father's death, destroyed his fragile health. He died penniless at age twenty-six.[32]

Virginia-born sculptor William R. O'Donovan led a long life, but he

31. Charles DeKay, *The Bohemians: A Tragedy of Modern Life* (New York, 1878), 6–9, 26, 53.
32. New Orleans *Times,* December 24, 1879, p. 5.

qualified as a Bohemian on several counts. Following service in the Staunton Artillery and a depressing year in postwar Virginia, O'Donovan went north. He lived for one year in Baltimore, a popular stopping-off point for many southern emigrants who eventually landed in Philadelphia or New York. O'Donovan chose New York, and his early, near penniless days in that city tell a story worthy of Puccini. O'Donovan arrived in America's artistic mecca with ten dollars in his pocket and not a friend in sight. He resided in the poorer quarters of New York's lower east side, a once fashionable section invaded "by what may be termed the 'Bohemian' classes." He shared his twenty-dollar-a-month studio/flat with a series of Bohemian friends, some of them writers, some painters, some sculptors. Typically, their landlord hounded the men for back rent. O'Donovan even frequented a "Bohemian restaurant," where ninety-five cents secured two hearty meals a day. The aspiring artist could have been happy nowhere else; only in New York could he capture "the first place in American Sculpture." He sought nothing less.[33]

Once a southern rebel, O'Donovan became an artistic insurgent by attacking rigid, outdated artistic standards. His rise to fame proved rapid, yet O'Donovan's early renown might better be termed notoriety. O'Donovan admitted to possessing "a considerable amount of egotism," and he soon became an outspoken and controversial exponent of a new philosophy of art. O'Donovan advocated a "realistic" style of sculpture that challenged the accepted practice of idealizing subjects. He roundly insulted those gentlemen of the press who labeled themselves "art critics" and who dared defend the old ways. They knew nothing of art, sneered O'Donovan. Equipped with a few technical phrases, they practiced the "safe principle" of abusing struggling, unknown artists and lauding the already famous. "If a second Michael Angelo were to produce a second 'Moses,'" he insisted, "and expose [it] to view in New York, unless he had a reputation there would scarcely be any notice taken of it."[34]

O'Donovan made many enemies among established northern sculptors, most of them unnecessarily. John Quincy Adams Ward, the most influential American artist of his day, became O'Donovan's foremost adversary. Ward's influence meant nothing to an Irishman on the ram-

33. William R. O'Donovan to Jennie Abraham, [February or March] 9, March 25, July 28, 1871, all in William Rudolf O'Donovan Correspondence, HSP.

34. John R. O'Donovan to Mary Bright O'Donovan, August 27, 1871, to Jennie Abraham, March 16, April 7, 1871, both in *ibid.*

page. O'Donovan dubbed Ward one the "Old fossils" who controlled the art world and killed the ambitions of younger artists. "These men 'run' the Academy [of Design]," charged O'Donovan; "they 'run' the clubs, and have formed themselves into a 'ring' for the purpose of keeping to themselves all the art patronage of the Country, and I believe I am the only young man in the City who has been bold enough to fight them." O'Donovan built his own circle of admirers and patrons. He praised in print the work of young artists who were creating "a higher and purer Art than the country has ever known," and he lambasted the work of old fuddy-duddies like Ward. "I have been compelled to persue an offencive course here, in self-defense," O'Donovan (a better sculptor than speller) explained to his sister. "There is an immense social force trying to crush me here on account of the criticisms I have lately written," he elaborated; "they have and will give me a great deal of trouble but I will beat them all in the end, and I like the opposition for my victory will be all the greater after it shall have been gained, and that will not be long."[35]

The passion of youthful rebellion cooled, however, as financial success assured O'Donovan's reputation. By 1878, after a decade in northern art circles, he even deigned to accept membership from those "miserable old charlatans" in the National Academy of Design. The piece of work that earned him admission was a bust of painter William Page, a work conceived in the very unrevolutionary style of "purest Greek Art." O'Donovan had become a good ole boy, Yankee style. He had discovered the consequences of rebellion when several patrons suddenly and unaccountably canceled commissions. He had learned the vagaries of friendship as a private circle of admirers continued to praise his work but failed to provide financial support. He began to speak more kindly of fellow artists. They were "as a class," he decided, "good fellows— kind affable people," who harbored "no less degree than any other class of intelligent and cultivated people, the vanities, jealousies, and selfish qualities incident to humanity." O'Donovan's new, more tolerant view supposedly included Ward.[36]

By 1880, O'Donovan, who was as skilled with brush and palette as

35. John R. O'Donovan to Jennie Abraham, July 28, 1871, October 26, 1872, April 7, 1881, all in *ibid.*

36. "A Sculptor's Method of Work," *Art Journal*, n.s., IV (1878), 62–63; John R. O'Donovan to Mary Bright O'Donovan, December 15, 1876, to Jennie Abraham, February 11, 1877, both in O'Donovan Correspondence.

with chisel and mallet, had become a society painter. He became a regular member of the soirée/dinner party/reception circuit, and although he often complained about the fatiguing round of fashionable events, O'Donovan also admitted that he loved the glitter. "Gay and brilliant throngs of people exilerate me," he confessed, "and there is a sort of mental stimulus and training to be gotten out of it all which is by no means to be dispised—which is indeed essential—for this is not a monastic age and one cannot be of it and work in it well unless one mingles freely with it—be of it—and beyond it if one can."[37]

O'Donovan had mellowed, but he maintained his skeptic's eye, the detachment of the outsider. There even remained about him something of the Bohemian, though admittedly, he had become an aristocratic Bohemian. In 1877, he helped found the Tile Club. Its membership, the nation's finest young painters, sculptors, and architects, claimed Bohemian lineage, but it was narrowly exclusive, almost to the point of snobbery. One wag dubbed it "the Four Hundred of New York's Bohemias." O'Donovan's membership underscored his persistent distrust of the northern establishment. He knew that wealthy northern friends sometimes ridiculed his rural upbringing and limited education. He had long since approved, no doubt, of Dr. Johnson's definition of a patron as someone who gazes unconcernedly on a drowning person only, when the swimmer has reached solid ground, to encumber him with help. O'Donovan flushed with anger when he thought how his career depended on "the contemptious patronage of fashionable fools." Yet having recognized the way of the world, he accepted it. Having accepted it, he adapted, and having adapted, he prospered.[38]

O'Donovan, never a one-dimensional character, took on a second northern identity, an ethnic one. "If you were living in New York," he reported to his brother, "you will find that much is expected of an O'Donovan! you would find as I have that the name is a *power* within itself." On another occasion, observing that artists who frequented his favorite restaurant were mostly foreigners or Americans who had studied abroad, he decided, "The American element in New York is scarcely perceptible in a general way. It has become so cosmipolitan through foreign influences as to have lost most of those distinctive parts which are supposed to characterise the 'Universal Yankee Nation.' " No other

37. John R. O'Donovan to Jennie Abraham, March 4, 1879, August 4, [1882], in O'Donovan Correspondence.
38. Parry, *Garrets and Pretenders,* 64–65; John R. O'Donovan to Jennie Abraham, February 7, 1872, August 4, [1882], both in O'Donovan Correspondence.

part of the city's foreign population stood out so prominently as the Irish. O'Donovan, a brash if polite young man, depended on an inherited talent for Irish blarney to exploit his ethnic heritage in working his way to the top of New York's fast-paced art world.[39]

O'Donovan won his first important commission, a statue of Irish patriot Daniel O'Connell, by approaching without introduction some of New York's leading Irish editors, publishers, and businessmen. He first tried to interest John Mullaly, Irish-born editor of the *Metropolitan Record and New York Vindicator*. When Mullaly sympathetically pronounced O'Donovan's scheme doubtful, the sculptor went straight to John Mitchel. Mitchel, himself an Irish patriot, more fervid even than the legendary O'Connell in his hatred of the English, had been banished from Great Britain in 1848 for incautious anti-English remarks. Coming to the United States in the early 1850s, Mitchel embraced the southern cause and during the Civil War served as editor of the Richmond *Enquirer*. He went to New York after the war to continue his campaign for Irish nationalism by founding and editing the *Irish Citizen*. Mitchel took immediate interest in O'Donovan's proposed statue. He introduced the sculptor to influential Irish politicians in New York, helped establish a committee to publicize the plan, and acquired a full-time secretary for fund-raising. O'Donovan also discussed his project with "one of the strongest powers behind the throne," businessman Maurice J. Powers. After "more wire pulling and . . . more diplomacy . . . than would have served to elect two or three presidents of the United States," O'Donovan and his new friends organized one of the most lavish Saint Patrick's Day celebrations ever seen in New York. They intended that the parade should excite Irish patriotism and inspire generous donations to fund the proposed public monument. It was a huge success.[40]

Closely associated with professional recognition and identification, even in Bohemia, came membership in clubs, societies, and fraternities. Members of the core group held a total of 416 memberships in more than two score organizations. These associations, along with individual occupations and professions, allowed former Confederates to form even

39. John R. O'Donovan to James C. O'Donovan, April 16, 1871, to Mary Bright O'Donovan, August 27, 1871, both in O'Donovan Correspondence.

40. Joseph George, Jr., "'A Catholic Family Newspaper' Views the Lincoln Administration: John Mullaly's Copperhead Weekly," *Civil War History*, XXIV (1978), 112–32; Wilson and Fiske (eds.), *Appleton's Cyclopedia*, IV, 341; John R. O'Donovan to Jennie Abraham, [February or March] 9, March 20, 1871, both in O'Donovan Correspondence; New York *Times*, March 18, 1871, p. 8.

more secure northern identities. America has been dubbed a nation of joiners, and even life in a midwestern town supported the claim to some extent during the nineteenth century. Fraternal lodges and churches most frequently provided small-town Americans with opportunities for association. These groups seldom excluded anyone from membership, their purpose, unlike clubs and lodges in larger cities, being to promote a sense of solidarity within the community. Clubs in larger towns and cities restricted their membership so as to focus and limit individual identities. The largest cities offered clubs for every taste and point of view. Political clubs, social clubs, literary clubs, racing clubs, yachting clubs, not to mention the usual array of national lodges and fraternities, such as the Freemasons and Odd Fellows, offered city dwellers endless opportunities for group affiliation.[41]

Freemasonry provided the single largest affiliation among Confederates in the North. Fourteen percent of the core group belonged to Masonic lodges. "My Masonry has been a great comfort to me here," reported a newly arrived Confederate carpetbagger. A chance meeting with local Masons opened new business doors to him and relieved his loneliness. He soon acquired the habit of visiting the lodge nearly every night. Fellow Masons invited him to their homes for meals and entertainment. "They are all very cordial and give me a hearty welcome," he rejoiced. "The war has had little or no effect upon the fraternity. Whenever one brother Mason meets another, section is not considered. Are you a Mason, that is sufficient—politics has nothing to do in our order." William Gilmore Simms provided a letter of introduction for a fellow South Carolina Mason bound for New York. He asked his northern Masonic brothers to counsel his friend and to "help his innocence amidst the snares of your wicked city." Masons in cities across the North preached reconciliation within months of the war's conclusion and organized charitable events to raise money for destitute Confederate Masons and their families. "American Masons know no north, no south, no east, no west," expounded an Ohioan, "but only one common country, undivided and indivisible."[42]

Sidney Lanier may have scorned Bohemia, but he recognized the need

41. Lewis Atherton, *Main Street on the Middle Border* (Bloomington, 1954), 181–86; Fairfield, *Clubs of New York*.

42. James Southgate to Delia Southgate, August 14, 22, 1867, both in James Southgate Correspondence, DU; William G. Simms to Henry Barton Dawson, October 2, 1865, to Robert Macoy and Daniel Sickles, January 16, 1866, both in Mary C. Simms Oliphant, *et*

to commune with kindred spirits and secure loyal patrons. Socially well-placed northern cousins gave Lanier ready access to the right people. In turn, he showed them the right stuff. He diligently maneuvered his way into northern artistic circles by attending parties, concerts, poetry readings, any function at which he might meet people who could advance his fortunes. He became especially close friends with writer Bayard Taylor and actress Charlotte Cushman. Taylor introduced him at the Century Club, clearly a giant step above Bohemia. At the Century Club, Lanier won still more friends and patrons, including Edmund C. Stedman, Samuel J. Tilden (then governor of New York), Whitelaw Reid ("with whom I was greatly struck"), John Quincy Adams Ward ("a splendid fellow"), and Richard Henry Stoddard. "Without ceremony you approach any of the groups formed," Lanier explained in describing his method of circulating in the club's "stately" smoking room. A lull in the conversation, an introduction by a friend, and you were asked to have a cigar and a drink and to join in the conversation. It was a simple formula, and Lanier made it work.[43]

Southern women in the North found fewer formal clubs open to them than did their husbands, but charitable organizations, literary circles, and amateur musical and theatrical groups helped fill the void. Constance Harrison devotes more than half of her published reminiscences of life in New York to a description of her many musical, charitable, and theatrical activities. Sarah Pryor, though not so active as the whirling Constance, joined similar charitable, philanthropic, and cultural organizations. Not by chance does novelist Helen Hooven Santmyer select a ladies' literary club to tell her story about life in an Ohio town after the Civil War. Most women, tied as they so often were to responsibilities of home and family, had less time than their menfolk for a club life. Without pretext to a scientific sampling, it is probably true that the extent of a woman's activities outside the home depended on her husband's income. The wealthier the family, the more opportunity and responsibility its women had to participate in clubs. Income does not seem to have

---

al. (eds.), *Letters of William Gilmore Simms* (5 vols.; Columbia, S.C., 1952), IV, 524, 535; *New York Times*, October 19, 1865, p. 4, June 28, 1867, p. 8; Allen E. Roberts, *House Undivided: The Story of Freemasonry and the Civil War* (New York, 1961), 287.

43. Sidney Lanier to Mary D. Lanier, October 10, 1873, February 12, October 4, 1874, to Edward Spencer, August 15, 1876, all in Anderson *et al.* (eds.), *Works of Sidney Lanier*, VIII, 399–400, IX, 31, 253–55, 391–92.

been a deciding factor in a man's ability to enjoy the benefits of fraternal organizations.[44]

The upper echelons of polite society served as a sort of club for Confederate social climbers. Admission requirements varied from place to place. Professional status as a physician or lawyer served well enough to join the elite of a town like Cincinnati or Evansville, but places like New York and Philadelphia were different matters. Big city elites required more than money, though money was mandatory; they required more than beauty, though beauty was praised. They required a special blend of lineage, wit, brains, and connections. The chances of securing a reliable identity by this means remained slim, but potential rewards were enormous. People who won the favor of leading society queens entered the magic circle of balls, cotillions, theater parties, and summer resort festivities that marked America's entrance into the Gilded Age. They reigned as national celebrities, the nineteenth century's equivalent of twentieth-century movie stars.[45]

Northern society, particularly in New York, fell into turmoil after the war. Longtime New York social leaders—Astors, Roosevelts, Van Rensselaers—watched horrified as a tidal wave of fortune hunters and social climbers invaded the nation's social and financial capital. A "tide of immigration came pouring from overseas," recalled a surviving dowager, "and mingled with another tide sweeping up from the South, down from the North and, a little later, in from the West." These ambitious people, some having made their fortunes before arriving, others, like most southerners, making or remaking their bankrolls in the North, challenged the prevailing standards of birth, breeding, and "old money" that had been the open sesames to society. Finding their way barred, they established a rival society, hoping in time either to force admission or simply to overwhelm the Old Guard. If Mrs. Astor refused them invitations to her balls, if the boxes at the Academy of Music were family heirlooms, then the *nouveaux riches* would organize their own, even

44. Pryor, *My Day*, 335–40, 364–65, 420–21, 426–46; Helen Hooven Santmyer, ". . . *And Ladies of the Club*" (New York, 1984); Rowland Berthoff, *An Unsettled People: Social Order and Disorder in American History* (New York, 1971), 444–51; William L. O'Neill, *Everyone Was Brave: The Rise and Fall of Feminism in America* (Chicago, 1969), 77–106; Page Smith, *Daughters of the Promised Land: Women in American History* (Boston, 1970), 265–68; Karen J. Blair, *The Clubwoman as Feminist: True Womanhood Redefined, 1868–1914* (New York, 1980), 4, 60–67, 117–19.

45. Mrs. Burton Harrison, "The Myth of the Four Hundred," *Cosmopolitan*, XIX (July, 1895), 329–34; Harrison, *Recollections Grave and Gay*, 278.

more spectacular entertainments; they would build their own opera house, the Metropolitan. Not all Confederate carpetbaggers joined this revolution. The Burton Harrisons, though sympathetic, preferred the "simpler" days and the older standards. But other Confederates, particularly Confederate women, mapped strategy, decided tactics, and led the attack.[46]

Robert E. Lee stayed in Virginia after the war, but Alva Smith proved a worthy substitute on the New York front. Born in Alabama of Virginia and Kentucky parentage, Alva moved to New York with her parents as a child in the late 1850s. Her father, a cotton merchant, prospered in the North during the war but remained a loyal Confederate. Consequently, northern antagonism drove the family to Europe, where Mr. Smith worked for an English exporting firm while Alva and her sisters attended school in Paris. Alva enjoyed the "brilliant" Second Empire of Napoleon III and Empress Eugenie, but her socially ambitious mother knew that the Smith girls must eventually enter New York society. She returned to Gotham with her four daughters in the early 1870s. Two of Alva's sisters eventually married English and French aristocrats, and one later added a Tiffany to her collection of husbands. Alva, by now a pleasantly plump twenty-two-year-old, satisfied herself with a Vanderbilt.[47]

Alva, like her mother, was ambitious, indefatigably so, to the extent that her enemies called her pushy. When she married William Kissam Vanderbilt, her husband's family had not yet been recognized as the social equals of the Astors, thanks largely to the plebian origins of the bumptious, tobacco-chewing commodore. Alva decided to change that. She built a three-million-dollar chateau on Fifth Avenue and a two-million-dollar "cottage" at Newport. She initiated a series of lavish entertainments intended to surpass in glitter and expense anything ever attempted by the Old Guard. Her campaign culminated in March, 1883, with an elaborate costume ball, "the most extravagant entertainment" ever witnessed in New York. She demolished any notion of a "400" by entertaining twelve hundred guests. Even the Astors recognized the ball as a success by permitting several members of the family to attend. Anticipating her victory, Alva dressed as a Venetian princess.

46. Mrs. John King Van Rensselaer, *The Social Ladder* (New York, 1924), 53–57; Harrison, *Recollections Grave and Gay*, 276–78, 310–12, 315–16, 346–48.

47. Alva Belmont, "Memoir" (MS in Matilda Young Papers, DU), 5–6, 19, 47–49; Edward T. James (ed.), *Notable American Women, 1607–1950: A Biographical Dictionary* (3 vols.; Cambridge, Mass., 1971), I, 126–27.

Former President Grant attended (dressed as a former president); so did the most visible up-and-coming *nouveaux riches,* including the Hewitts, Potters, and Whitneys.[48]

Alva's party opened the floodgate. American society never recovered, but Alva was just warming up. She worked hard to maintain her new position as Mrs. Astor's chief social rival. "I know of no art, profession, or work for women more taxing on mental resources than being a leader of society," she declared. Vanderbilt complained that his most taxing work was being Alva's husband. He slipped into an adulterous affair, and Alva demanded a divorce. She got it, thus initiating a feud within the family that grew passionate when Alva assumed custody of the family's darling, Consuelo. Determined to maintain her social clout with or without the Vanderbilt name, Alva used (and that, unfortunately, is the correct word) her daughter to gain international status. Consuelo became the Duchess of Marlborough, a very unwilling and tragically unhappy Duchess of Marlborough. Alva remarried the following year, a Belmont this time (Oliver Hazard Perry), himself recently divorced from a Whitney. The inbreeding was necessary. Neither could afford to marry anyone less wealthy.[49]

Alva never slowed down, although the focus of her activism swerved sharply. She outlived Belmont, five years her junior, and in 1908, in her mid-fifties, became a militant feminist and suffragette. She recalled with satisfaction the sensation caused by her divorce from Vanderbilt, which she regarded as a victory for women's rights. "Women were not supposed to divorce their husbands in those days, whatever their provocation," she explained. "I was the first woman of any prominence to sue for a divorce for adultery, and Society was by turns stunned, horrified, and then savage in its opposition and criticism." Alva defied her attackers. "It was more than a personal matter with me," she insisted. "It was a question of social justice not only to myself but with other women situated as I was." Alva remained devoted to the cause of women's rights until her death in 1933.[50]

Fiery, rebellious Alva may have led the initial charge, but she did not conquer Yankee society alone. Melissa Johnston Wilson, of Virginia and

48. Consuelo Vanderbilt Balsan, *The Glitter and the Gold* (New York, 1952), 5–7; W. A. Swanberg, *Whitney Father, Whitney Heiress* (New York, 1980), 58–61; Alva (Smith) Vanderbilt Belmont Scrapbook (MS in AA), 35–36.
49. Cornelius Vanderbilt, Jr., *Queen of the Golden Age: The Fabulous Story of Grace Wilson Vanderbilt* (New York, 1956), 169; Balsan, *The Glitter and the Gold,* 45–54, 215.
50. James (ed.), *Notable American Women,* I, 127–29; Belmont, "Memoir," 151.

Tennessee, brought up a significant detachment of reserves. Melissa Johnston had been wise enough to marry an ambitious Georgian named Richard T. Wilson before the war. Unlike most Confederates, Major Wilson managed to turn a profit during the war. He served in the commissary department but also spent considerable time and money outfitting blockade runners and representing a group of cotton planters while transacting business for the Confederate government in England. The handsome, dashing major earned close to half a million dollars in these enterprises, plus making valuable social and financial connections in Europe and the South. Legend has it that Margaret Mitchell based her characterization of Rhett Butler on the swashbuckling soldier from Hall County; but Rhett went to California after the war, without Scarlett. Wilson headed for New York with Melissa and three precocious, charming children.[51]

Wilson established his own banking house, R. T. Wilson and Company, in New York while increasing his fortune through shrewd investments in cotton, southern railroads, northern street railways, and chemicals. Like any ambitious businessman, Wilson joined his share of clubs. In partnership with noted turfsman William Whitney, he bought the Saratoga race track, and he helped to establish the upstart Metropolitan Opera. Yet Wilson remained more businessman than clubman. He referred to the *fêtes champêtres* and brilliant balls he was obliged to attend as "the usual hurrah." His closest friend was another self-made man who avoided society, Andrew Carnegie, like Wilson's father a Scots immigrant. For the most part, the major left social maneuvering to Mrs. Wilson, who possessed a decided "social ability." Her talent, combined with her husband's fortune and a determination to secure a place in Yankee society for herself and her children, made Melissa Wilson a legend.[52]

The Wilsons eventually had four children, three girls and a boy. The children married, in turn, a Goelet, an Astor, a Vanderbilt, and an English nobleman. Had not all four children shared the combined charm, vivacity, wit, and savvy of their parents, such matchmaking might have betrayed court intrigues and unsavory financial alliances. Actually, each marriage was a genuine love story, but that did not spare

51. Vanderbilt, *Queen of the Golden Age,* 22–26; New York *Times,* November 27, 1910, p. 13. Margaret Mitchell denied that she had based Rhett Butler on Wilson. See Margaret Mitchell to Herschel Brickwell, July 7, 1936, in Richard Harwell (ed.), *Margaret Mitchell's "Gone with the Wind" Letters, 1936–1946* (New York, 1976), 20–21.

52. Vanderbilt, *Queen of the Golden Age,* 21, 26–27, 46, 148–49.

the family the epithet of "the marrying Wilsons." "Why did the Diamond Match Company fail?" ran the opening line of one popular joke. Answer: "Because Mrs. Richard T. Wilson beat them at making matches." When Melissa's grandchildren began lining up similarly spectacular marriages, old New Yorkers resumed "the usual headshaking" over the Wilsons—"the most successful matrimonial schemers in the world outside the royal House of Denmark."[53]

The Wilsons became responsible for a second schism in the Vanderbilt family when daughter Grace married Cornelius IV. The reason for the feud is not entirely clear. Some say the Vanderbilts scorned the Wilsons as fortune hunters, the Wilsons' treasury being modest in comparison to their own. Moreover, Grace had a reputation for being "fast," an unfair charge probably inspired by those jealous of her beauty and charm; but some Vanderbilts accused her of vamping (if not absolutely bewitching) poor Cornelius. In theory, the two families should have been allies, both trying to hammer down the Old Guard fortress, but the Wilsons by this time were already in the fortress, with marriages to Astors and Goelets. Perhaps the Vanderbilts were simply envious. Grace's son saw the feud as "a kind of rivalry" between his sets of grandparents. "No one is more snobbish about other hopefuls," he correctly observed, "than the parvenu to society."[54]

Meanwhile, the Old Guard did not intend to capitulate without a fight. Certainly the acknowledged leader of New York society, Caroline Schermerhorn Astor, had not folded her tent. Mrs. Astor was wise. Recognizing the determined nature of the southern rebels, she hired her own southerner to thwart them. Samuel Ward McAllister, better known as Ward, a Georgian by birth, served as Mrs. Astor's social secretary from the early 1870s until his death in 1895. It was he who popularized the notion of society as a numerically limited elite by inventing and defining the "400": the number of fashionable people that could comfortably fill Mrs. Astor's ballroom. Outwardly, Mrs. Astor reigned supreme over society. In truth, McAllister played Cardinal Wolsey to Mrs. Astor's young Henry VIII. As the lord chancellor of New York society, he dictated fashions and defined social acceptability.

53. *Ibid.*, 35, 105; Cleveland Amory, *Who Killed Society?* (New York, 1960), 493. Vanderbilt, *Queen of the Golden Age*, 146–48, suggests that Major Wilson was the real matchmaker, but he offers no proof.

54. Swanberg, *Whitney Father, Whitney Heiress*, 141, 211; Vanderbilt, *Queen of the Golden Age*, 91.

McAllister had never really been a Confederate, and perhaps that explains the unhesitating way that he battled Alva, the Wilsons, and the coterie of Confederates who scrambled for social prominence in New York. McAllister had gone to California in 1850 to practice law. He made a small fortune there before moving to New York and doubling his revenues by marrying the daughter of a wealthy Georgian. He then divided his time among New York, Georgia, and Europe before settling at Newport, Rhode Island, in 1859. He caught Mrs. Astor's attention by the way he dominated Newport's postwar summer society. His well-appointed, masterfully managed entertainments marked him as a man who knew how to keep the *nouveaux riches* at bay. He was an un-doubted snob. "I can tell a man from the provinces," he declared, sound-ing like Sherlock Holmes, "simply by his hat." Voicing his opinion of a young swain who asked him to define a cotillion, McAllister exclaimed, "Here was abysmal ignorance with a vengeance!"[55]

But if McAllister was a snob, he was a good snob, no mean achieve-ment. He remained so genial and likable that most people tolerated him with a smile. And he was a smart snob. He knew that the aura of a select group and the discipline needed to keep the parvenus in line came largely from the mystique surrounding his list. McAllister talked about his "400," but he did not announce publicly who it included for over a decade. Speculation ran rampant. One "officially supervised" list, pub-lished in the 1880s, had 617 names, including just five postwar Confed-erate arrivals. People published society directories, too, but these were hundreds of pages long. Wags and pundits had a field day ridiculing socially ambitious people who fancied, without really knowing, that they *must* be on the list. Not until 1892, in conjunction with Mrs. Astor's momentous annual ball, did McAllister release the names of his *crème de la crème* in the New York *Times.* Yet that list included just 307 names, allowing those who had not been included to go on thinking that they must surely be among the remaining 93. The list contained some surprises. McAllister recognized about half a dozen Confederates, in-cluding the Wilsons. Alva and William K. did not make it, but then

55. *Dictionary of American Biography,* XI, 547–48; Ward McAllister, *Society As I Have Found It* (New York, 1890), 3–107, 212–17; Van Rensselaer, *Social Ladder,* 205–207, 228–30, 237; Morris, *Incredible New York,* 144–47; Maud Howe Elliott, *This Was My Newport* (Cambridge, Mass., 1944), 149–50; Frederick Townsend Martin, *Things I Remember* (New York, 1913), 73–74; Moran Tudury, "Ward McAllister," *American Mercury,* VIII (May, 1926), 138–41.

neither did J. P. Morgan, August Belmont, the Huntingtons, or the Pulitzers.[56]

Actually, the number of Confederates in the "400" or any other northern social elite did not matter. Society waxed strong and hearty outside the reaches of the elites. It must have, by necessity, to accommodate the many hundreds of people who could purchase the luxuries, if not the lineage, associated with upper-class life. In truth, society during the Gilded Age splintered into numerous cliques and enclaves in every city, in every town, quite likely in every village. All used the "400" as their model, but each existed self-sufficiently. No other city had so many Confederates displayed so prominently as New York. Chicago, for example, had several antebellum southern arrivals, like the McCormicks and Mrs. Potter Palmer, to lead society, but most postwar arrivals settled into slightly less prestigious groups. The important point is that membership in society, at whatever level, afforded Confederates as useful an identity as membership in a profession or middle-class literary club. Fashionable society had plenty of prejudices, but it largely ignored political and geographic antecedents.[57]

Other clubs and forms of associations provided southerners with very different identities. These alternative associations, almost defying southern attempts to fit into northern life, were intended not to disguise southern origins and Confederate loyalties but to glorify them. Southerners who otherwise adapted well to northern life, people who enjoyed prosperous careers and congenial northern neighbors, joined these groups to preserve their memories of the Old South and to honor their Lost Cause. This intricate network of formal clubs, bolstered by business partnerships and personal friendships, demonstrated undying love for the South and old comrades-in-arms and opened a dramatic new chapter in the South's northern invasion.

56. *The "400"* (New York, 188–); Harrison, "About It and About," 84; Stephen Massett, *Quis, Charge of the "400"! A Society Legend in Rhyme* (New York, 1889); New York *Times*, February 2, 1892, p. 5; Swanberg, *Whitney Father, Whitney Heiress*, 90–94.

57. Frederic Cople Jaher, *The Urban Establishment: Upper Strata in Boston, New York, Charleston, Chicago, and Los Angeles* (Urbana, 1982), 274–79.

5

Comrades Still

Burton Harrison scribbled at his office desk. Suddenly, the sound of the clatter of horses' hooves and the grinding of carriage wheels burst into his sanctum. Before him stood a care-worn, hungry-looking young man. Burton knew the man would speak with a southern accent. Burton had not been in New York very long before his office became a sanctuary for down-and-out Confederate veterans seeking money, jobs, and advice. Constance, despite her tender regard for the South's ragged warriors, balked at these abuses of her husband's generosity. She grew particularly upset with the "so-called Southern survivors of the Lost Cause" who appealed to her husband for passage money home. Far too many "needy" veterans, she fumed, soon reappeared at Burton's door seeking another handout.[1]

Burton knew his countrymen sometimes abused his largess. "I have been a sort of refuge to so many of our oppressed brethren as to more than have my hands full," he complained as late as 1875; yet the kindhearted Louisianian saw little choice but to help whenever he could. Where else should a Confederate in the North seek charity if not among his own people? Harrison felt an obligation to the South. The cause might be dead, but the South must live. Had not southern friends, in addition to his northern acquaintances, helped him during his early days in Yankeedom? Did they not now take pride in his triumphs and achievements? William Preston Johnston, eldest son of slain Confederate hero Albert Sidney Johnston, had been captured with Harrison in Georgia and, like Burton, suffered imprisonment at Fort Delaware. Johnston obtained a professorship at Washington University after his release, but he did not forget his old friend struggling in the North. He sent Harrison

1. Mrs. Burton Harrison, *Recollections Grave and Gay* (New York, 1911), 301–302.

letters of introduction to influential friends in New York. One of them, a fellow named Gwinn, knew "everyone in the Southwest," where he had extensive business connections. Gwinn needed a trustworthy lawyer in New York. "He is an Irish protestant," explained Johnston, "geneal, shrewd, and honest. He is not rich, but a man to be of use to you, and will, for my sake, do a good deal."[2]

Besides, Burton respected the men and women who came north to rebuild their lives. Critics might argue that the South would be better served if one resided in Richmond or Atlanta. Burton himself had been accused of deserting the South, but he could not doubt the conviction and continuing loyalty of the grim-faced veterans who passed through his office. He did not consider them turncoats or scalawags. They were still his countrymen, still his comrades. He certainly respected them more than those southerners who had fled abroad after the war. He could be unusually caustic about "the great mumbo-jumbo" that had established itself as a "Southern set" in Paris. He had warned Constance, while she sojourned in France in early 1867, to stay clear of those "jackals & geese." Vanity alone, Harrison believed, had propelled them to Europe. They fancied their lives endangered by a vengeful northern government when, in reality, most of them were people of little consequence. "They are exiles," he had said, marking an important distinction between Confederates in Europe and Confederates in the North, "& cherish all the petty rancor & egotism which self-elected martyrs have entertained since history began." Southerners who really cared about their homes, Harrison insisted, remained in the United States, in either North or South, to work for the South's restoration from economic depression, political usurpation, and social chaos, "to accomplish for their country the best that is left to be hoped for."[3]

Besides loaning money and helping veterans find work, Burton gave legal assistance to southerners in New York. One instance involved a Virginian named Worsham who had come to the metropolis seeking a job. Worsham could find nothing to suit him, so he returned to Virginia. Shortly thereafter, his New York landlord sued Worsham for failing to pay promissory notes endorsed in lieu of rent. Discrepancies between Virginia and New York laws regarding promissory notes complicated

2. Burton N. Harrison to James Chesnut, April 2, 1875, in Williams-Chesnut-Manning Family Papers, SCL; W. P. Johnston to Burton N. Harrison, August 10, 22, 1867, both in Burton Norvell Harrison Family Papers, LC.

3. Burton N. Harrison to Constance Cary, March 8, 1867, in Harrison Family Papers, LC.

the issue, but Harrison found it a "disagreeable" case in any event because the plaintiff, a Mr. Linthicum, was a first-rate scoundrel and his attorney an ignoramus. Besides that, the notary who heard preliminary testimony was a friend of the rival lawyer, "and, without being corrupt, was so fussy and partial in his rulings as to be insufferable." Once again, Harrison had accepted a case largely because he believed a fellow southerner was being ill-used by Yankee sharpers. He continued decades after the war to provide legal advice and aid to similarly oppressed southerners.[4]

Both of the Harrisons maintained social ties to former comrades. A remarkable number of their wartime acquaintances wandered north after the war. Constance's brother Clarence, a veteran of the Confederate navy, arrived in 1869 and soon joined Burton at the New York bar. John R. Thompson, the Virginia state librarian, who had spared Constance the wind and rain at Jefferson Davis' inauguration, subsequently became her "literary god-father" in New York. Roger and Sarah Pryor, John Mitchel, Colonel Osmun Latrobe, Thomas C. DeLeon, William Washington, William L. Sheppard, and Conrad Wise Chapman were other familiar faces to appear in the city. Henry Kyd Douglas, Robert E. Lee's former aide-de-camp, spent his summers near the Harrisons at Bar Harbor.[5]

Of course, the Harrisons kept in touch with the Jefferson Davis family. Burton tried to see the Chief whenever Davis visited the vicinity of New York. The Davis sons, who spent much time in New York, frequently dropped by Burton's office for a chat. Both of the Harrisons adored Winnie Davis, the "daughter of the Confederacy," and sometimes invited her to spend summers with them at Bar Harbor. When, after President Davis' death, Varina and Winnie moved to New York, the Harrisons formed part of Varina's "court," as she assumed the status of a "dethroned queen in exile." The Harrisons provided sympathy, too. If a queen, Varina was a bankrupt one. She had gone north partly for her health, partly for the same reason as most other southerners: to earn a living. In her case, that meant writing for New York's plethora of tabloids and literary magazines. Burton and Constance understood her position, the wretchedness of her poverty, the "constant effort to

4. Burton N. Harrison to Robert Ould, December 1, 1871, in Isaac Howell Carrington Papers, DU; Burton N. Harrison to Charles S. Fairchild, July 13, 1885, in Charles S. Fairchild Papers, NYHS.

5. Harrison, *Recollections Grave and Gay,* 119–20, 178–81.

keep up appearances." When Winnie died in 1898, Burton accompanied Mrs. Davis to Richmond for the interment. Like the Chief before her, Varina sought comfort and support from Burton. She "leaned upon him like a son."[6]

Nor did the death of Jefferson Davis lessen Burton's loyalty to the Chief or the principles for which Davis had stood. When the Harrisons' second son, Francis, first ran for Congress in 1902, Burton coached him on how to retort when heckled about the Confederacy or his parents' association with the Davis family. Unknown to Francis until years later, Burton frequently stood in the rear of crowds his son was addressing, "ready with a stick to defend the memory of 'Jeff Davis.' " Francis always believed Burton's "sensitiveness" about the Davis family kept his father from seeking a more active political life. Such loyalty formed the heart of Burton's character. "He was preeminently a gentleman," summarized Fairfax Harrison, "satisfying alike the test of Confucius— 'frugal in eating and drinking and lavish to the ghosts of the past.' "[7]

The sociable Harrisons made many new southern friends, too. An unspoken, unbreakable bond linked people who, whatever their true circumstances, often felt like exiles. Even those who, like Burton, wanted to set aside old causes for new opportunities could not exorcise from their hearts or memories the struggle for Confederate nationhood. They could not always suppress a pang of remorse when meeting someone, stranger or friend, who had sacrificed property and loved ones in a common cause. "How do you do Mr. Jones; your servant, sir," might be the public greeting. "Ah, indeed, sir, from Virginia, you say." All the while the mind says: "Yes, I recall you now, with Jackson's brigade at Manassas, in Longstreet's corps at Gettysburg, on Gordon's staff at Appomattox. Yes, I was there, too. My brother died at Malvern Hill. My wife endured the siege of Petersburg; my child . . . my child did not." Words need not be spoken. Affection and shared memories can be communicated with a look, a handshake, the phrasing of the word "Virginia."

6. Burton N. Harrison to Jefferson Davis, October 13, 1869, in Jefferson Davis Papers, AA; Varina Davis to Constance Harrison, December 20, 1886, in Harrison Family Papers, UV; *Confederate Veteran*, X (March, 1902), 100; Ishbel Ross, *First Lady of the South: The Life of Mrs. Jefferson Davis* (New York, 1958), 378–80; Harrison, *Recollections Grave and Gay*, 268–69.

7. Francis B. Harrison, "About It and About" (Typescript in Francis Burton Harrison Papers, UV), 40a; Fairfax Harrison (ed.), *Aris Sonis Focisque: Being a Memoir of an American Family, the Harrisons of Skimino* (New York, 1910), 220–21.

Bonding remained silent during the first few years after the war. The better part of wisdom dictated as much. Southerners in the North wished to draw as little attention as possible to themselves and their activities. Not until October, 1870, did they publicize their numbers and their loyalties. Fittingly, Robert E. Lee, rapidly becoming enshrined as the *beau ideal* of their cause, inspired the occasion. Lee's death, a month after the autumnal equinox, would not pass silently. Confederate carpetbaggers organized memorial services across the North to coincide with the hour Lee would be laid within the sheltering arms of Mother Virginia. Burton Harrison attended the New York ceremony, held at the Cooper Institute, and served as first secretary of the organizing committee. John E. Ward, practicing law in New York with fellow Georgian Charles C. Jones, Jr., served as president. Among Ward's numerous vice-presidents were Enoch L. Lowe, John D. Imboden, John Mitchel, Thomas L. Snead, and R. C. Gardner, all notable Confederates living in the North. Cyrus McCormick traveled from Chicago to attend the service, and prominent northern friends of the South, such as William H. Appleton, Henry Grinnell, and Thomas A. Hoyt, participated. The speakers, including Ward, Imboden, Hoyt, a Mr. Duke, and the Reverend Marshall, of Mississippi, emphasized the occasion as an hour of sectional reconciliation, an opportunity for North and South to join together and honor a great American. For Lee's "soldiers, friends, and supporters," the hour provided their first public opportunity in the North to shed tears over the old cause and exalt their beloved commander.[8]

Such large public gatherings proved rare for many years thereafter, but increasing numbers of Confederates did begin to organize exclusively southern clubs and fraternities in the North. The first organization appeared in Chicago. The Virginia Society announced its formation in the Windy City in 1879 with Cyrus McCormick elected first president. Thomas H. Ellis, who served as the society's first auditor, described its purpose as "social and friendly," but the preamble to its constitution was sufficiently ambiguous to suggest that an unspoken devotion to the Lost Cause and fallen comrades also motivated its founders. These gentlemen sought "a better opportunity of forming acquaintances, cultivating friendships, mutual improvement, and keeping fresh the memory of our common heritage." During the next two decades, similar state societies, "southern associations," and veterans'

8. New York *Times,* October 25, 1870, p. 8.

groups appeared in the North. By then, strident sectional animosities had largely subsided. The war had begun to assume a "rosy glow" of nostalgia, which made it safe to hold veterans' reunions and to form rebel commemorative organizations in Yankeedom.[9]

The New York Southern Society (NYSS), located in the city with the largest and wealthiest concentration of displaced southerners, became the largest, most famous, and best-financed southern organization in the North. "When a vast and cosmopolitan population is brought together in such a city as New York," explained an early chronicler of the society, "a bond of sympathy inevitably develops between those of one nationality and one especial region of the country, and common interests and a love and veneration for the same traditions produce a species of social affinity." In 1886, this desire for southern camaraderie inspired two Virginians and a Louisianian—none of them veterans of the war—to breathe life into the idea. Nearly three hundred southerners whose names appeared on the society's first membership list endorsed the plan. They selected as their first president an Ohioan of southern ancestry and Confederate sympathies who had moved north before the war, Algernon S. Sullivan. Sullivan's selection supposedly deemphasized the society's direct links to the Confederacy, but Burton Harrison served as the first vice-president, and eleven of the society's next twelve presidents had worn the gray. Every one of the two dozen vice-presidents during that period had served the Confederacy. The society renounced all political intentions and avoided all political activity; but it neatly combined dedication to the Confederate cause with its public professions of social purposes.[10]

The society's stated objective was "to promote friendly relations among Southern men resident or sojourning in New York City, and to cherish and perpetuate the memories and traditions of the Southern people." An annual banquet, given on George Washington's birthday, highlighted the social calendar. The remainder of the year witnessed

9. Thomas H. Ellis to Charles Ellis, Jr., February 28, 1880, in Munford-Ellis Family Papers, DU; *Constitution and By-Laws of the Virginia Society of Chicago* (Chicago, 1881), 5; William W. White, *The Confederate Veteran* (Tuscaloosa, 1962), 26–27.

10. Marion J. Verdery, "The Southern Society of New York," *National Magazine*, XV (1892), 530; *Account of Proceedings at the First Annual Banquet of the New York Southern Society* (New York, 1887), 70–72; *Year Book of the New York Southern Society for the Year 1912–1913* (New York, 1912), 10. For a fuller account of southern and Confederate fraternal groups in the North see Daniel E. Sutherland, "Southern Fraternal Organizations in the North," *Journal of Southern History*, LIII (1987), 587–612.

quarterly reunions, a ladies' day reception, and, during winter, fortnightly Saturday evening suppers. The exclusively male membership allowed women to participate in its festivities only at the reception given in their honor. Women could attend the annual banquet but only as onlookers seated in the gallery. The society enjoyed no permanent home until 1889, when it purchased an impressive-looking four-story brownstone on West 25th Street. The new clubhouse contained bedrooms for guests and nonresident members, a café, "card" room, and billiard room. Most club life, however, centered on the building's comfortable parlors. Shining oak and mahogany tables, overstuffed chairs, and plush carpets filled spacious rooms bedecked with portraits of southern and Confederate heroes. A member could relax in these cozy surroundings at any hour with the latest southern newspapers, a book from the society's two-thousand-volume library of southern history and literature, or a cigar and a glass of claret.[11]

The southern spirit that clung to the society and the Confederate spirits that haunted its club rooms provided the camaraderie most members craved. "Love of the South was the dominant sentiment of the occasion," reported one newspaper in describing the society's third annual banquet. "It was on the lip and in the heart; it was in every note of the music; it was in the menu, in the clinking of the glasses, in the fizz of the wine, in the toast, and in the talk. It pervaded everything." Ten years later, the society's president, John A. Wyeth, told the annual gathering, "Sentiment was the chief factor in the organization of this society." Most members were financially secure, as their fifty-dollar initiation fee and thirty-dollar annual dues might suggest. The overwhelming number worked as professional and business men. But this was no group of idle *bon vivants* and sportsmen. Members used their influence to encourage the writing of southern history by men "cognizant of Southern traditions and customs" and to "honor and promote" authors who would "fix and set forth the influence of the Southern element in the development of the national character." They established a relief program to assist needy southerners living in the city. As individuals, they invested large sums of money in southern businesses, charities, and memorials.[12]

11. *First Annual Banquet of the New York Southern Society,* 8–12; *Account of Proceedings at the Third Annual Banquet of the New York Southern Society* (New York, 1889), 63–65.

12. New York *Times,* February 23, 1889, p. 5; *Year Book of the New York Southern Society for the Year 1908–1909* (New York, 1908), 14; *First Annual Banquet of the New*

Northern chapters of the United Confederate Veterans (UCV), founded in 1889, followed hard on the heels of the southern societies. Sixty-five percent of the core group had served in the Confederate military, although they did not represent a proportional cross-section of the Confederate army. Only 38 percent of the group had served in the infantry, the largest combat arm. Nearly as many—32 percent—rode into battle as cavalrymen, the army's elite branch, and most of the others divided fairly evenly between three other branches generally regarded as superior to the infantry: artillery, staff, and medical corps. Two men sailed with the Confederate navy, but both had been officers. In fact, 58 percent of the core group with known military rank served as officers.

Regardless of branch or rank, these veterans joined together in six northern "camps" of the UCV, all but two of them—New York and Boston—located in midwestern states. Camps at Columbus, Ohio; Evansville, Indiana; Chicago and Jerseyville, Illinois, as well as in the two eastern cities, lend credence to one scholar's observation that in the South the distribution of UCV camps followed the distribution of veterans. The establishment of four camps in California and several dozen scattered through the western states and Indian Territory followed the same pattern. Only the absence of camps at Indianapolis, Philadelphia, and Cincinnati, where many veterans settled, mocks the generalization. The northern camps were not the largest ones in the country, but neither were they the smallest. Camps in the South varied in size from four hundred to five members. Only the New York camp approached this upper limit, with a peak membership of between two hundred and three hundred during the 1890s. Chicago, the next largest camp, had seventy-five members in 1894 and probably never exceeded that number by much. The remaining northern camps averaged about fifteen members each, Boston, with ten members, being the smallest.[13]

York Southern Society, 6–7; *Third Annual Banquet of the New York Southern Society,* 50–54; *Account of Proceedings at the Fifth Annual Meeting of the New York Southern Society* (New York, 1891), 8.

13. Gaines M. Foster, *Ghosts of the Confederacy: Defeat, the Lost Cause, and the Emergence of the New South, 1865 to 1913* (New York, 1987), 106–107; Robert C. Wood (comp.), *Confederate Handbook* (New Orleans, 1900), 106, 116; New York *Times,* October 8, 1892, p. 11, January 23, 1898, p. 9; Membership Lists, in United Confederate Veterans Association Records, LSU; *Confederate Veteran,* II (July, 1894), 211, IX (July, 1901), 307. Foster, *Ghosts of the Confederacy,* 93–94, 107–10, 195–96, also stresses the broad social spectrum of UCV membership in the South and the humble origins of UCV founders. Confederates in the North may have been slightly better off socially and financially.

The largest northern camps began primarily as benevolent groups. In welcoming both the New York and Chicago camps into the national organization, UCV commander John B. Gordon instructed them to "take steps to care for and assist the disabled, indigent, helpless, and distressed ex-Confederate soldiers and sailors in their respective departments and to protect their widows and orphans." Additionally, Gordon held each camp responsible for locating and caring for Confederate graves in its department, an assignment that required annual memorial and decoration ceremonies.[14]

Both groups understood the significance of Gordon's directive. The Confederate Veteran Camp (CVC) of New York, which never accepted official induction into the UCV, grew from the death of a former rebel in Gotham who, unknown to former comrades, had been cared for in his final illness by a local post of the Grand Army of the Republic. Confederates in New York, feeling both mortified and outraged, formed their own benevolent society in 1890. The society, under the leadership of Andrew G. Dickinson, a Confederate colonel turned insurance salesman, assembled its own medical staff to render assistance to indigent veterans. It established a mortuary fund to pay the burial costs of "comrades" and their families and eventually purchased a four-hundred-foot plot at Mount Hope Cemetery in which to bury its own. It raised money for these worthy causes by charging modest membership dues, soliciting contributions, and staging benefit theatrical performances organized by the members' wives. The Chicago camp, known officially as the Ex-Confederate Association, operated much the same way, but it faced a particularly difficult chore in locating the graves of more than twenty-three thousand dead Confederates in Illinois, most of them victims of the state's prisoner-of-war camps. The Chicagoans accomplished their task, and they eventually raised nearly twenty-five thousand dollars to erect a handsome monument to six thousand Confederates buried in Chicago's Oakwood Cemetery.[15]

Very soon, however, social fraternization and celebration of the Lost Cause became equally important objects for camp veterans. The New Yorkers, for example, paid ample attention to preserving the "sentiment of fraternity that was born amid the pleasures, hardships, and dangers of the march, bivouac, and battlefield." Briefly in the mid-1890s, it

14. New York *Times,* November 22, 1891, p. 1.
15. *Confederate Veteran,* X (March, 1902), 111–12; New York *Times,* May 15, 1891, p. 8, April 10, 1896, p. 9; White, *Confederate Veteran,* 101.

dropped many of its "semi-military features" as a concession to sectional reconciliation, but the old spirit soon returned and remained unchanged. Members refused to apologize for the war. "We are not met as rebels," explained one member, "or, if rebels, at least we stand unrepentant rebels, in the sense that we are not ashamed of or penitent for the part we bore in the civil war."[16]

To the neutral observer, such outspoken sentiments put the CVC in an awkward position, but the comrades felt no contradiction in glorifying the Confederate States while maintaining their allegiance to the United States, and they expressed bewilderment when people questioned the purity of their loyalties. "This assemblage of scarred veterans," explained Commander Dickinson at the CVC's fifth annual celebration of Lee's birthday, "comprises to their view, as true patriots as have ever written their names in a country's history." "The gallant soldier of the North," he continued, "looks upon our Confederate Veteran Camp with chivalrous admiration, and would laugh to scorn the soldier of the Confederate Army who feared that he might be censured at the North, in his business connections or otherwise, for preserving recollections and incidents of which he should be proud." "The ex-Confederate soldier should be proud of his past," declared Marion J. Verdery at the next year's banquet, "satisfied with his present, and hopeful of his future." The Confederate veteran's "unimpeachable loyalty to our indissoluble Union," Verdery maintained, should exempt him from feeling any "shame" or "regret." "He has made his way to the front in every professional calling, and is today a factor in all the affairs of our common country, and can well afford to muster in dress parade before all the world."[17]

In this sense alone did the veterans' groups differ from the southern societies. NYSS members expressed no shame about their role in the war. Members stood proudly when they sang "Dixie," and rebel yells reverberated through their banquet hall. Nor were the two organizations rivals. Most members of the CVC belonged to the larger NYSS, and a good many of its commanders and lieutenant commanders served as presidents and vice-presidents of the Southern Society. Both types of organizations shared a benevolent as well as fraternal mission. Yet the

16. New York *Times*, December 8, 1893, p. 8; *Confederate Veteran*, III (April, 1895), 114–16, VI (December, 1898), 550, X (March, 1902), 110–11.

17. *Confederate Veteran*, III (February, 1895), 46–47; New York *Times*, January 20, 1897, p. 2.

southern societies never gloried in the war quite so lustily as the veterans' groups. They were bent more on preserving bonds of southern birth than on stoking fires of Confederate passion. Camp comrades, on the other hand, wanted organizations tied more directly to the Lost Cause.

Confederate women maintained a similar dichotomy. On one hand, they busily wove a chain of Dixie clubs in northern cities. Like the male southern societies with which they often affiliated themselves, these clubs, aimed primarily at social intercourse and the preservation of the southern, as opposed to Confederate, heritage. On the other hand, the United Daughters of the Confederacy (UDC) established an impressive network of northern chapters, more numerous even than the UCV camps. Confederate women in San Francisco formed the first UDC chapter outside the South in 1896, only two years after inauguration of the national organization. Constance Harrison helped organize the New York Order of Confederate Women at about the same time, and it became the UDC's first northern chapter in 1897. By 1900, two more chapters had appeared in California, four in Indian Territory, and one in Philadelphia. Chicago, Boston, Cincinnati, and Columbus, Ohio, soon followed.[18]

UDC chapters sponsored well-balanced yearly schedules of social events, philanthropic work, educational programs, and patriotic ceremonies, accomplishing all of these varied undertakings to the tune of "Dixie." One of the first official acts of the Philadelphia chapter was to decorate the graves of 224 unknown Confederate dead at Germantown. The Chicago and Columbus chapters aided their UCV counterparts in caring for Confederate graves and reconsecrating them each Memorial Day. Much UDC fund-raising in the North went toward caring for Confederate veterans and widows and erecting monuments to Confederate glory. Most telling, perhaps, in stressing their Confederate roots, were the mottoes of various UDC chapters and divisions. The Ohio Division swore in typical Confederate spirit: "He wins most who honor saves; success is not the test."[19]

18. Mary B. Poppenheim *et al., History of the United Daughters of the Confederacy* (Raleigh, N.C., 1956), 37; *Confederate Veteran,* VIII (April, 1900), 152, VIII (June, 1900), 272, X (July, 1902), 319, XIII (February, 1905), 82, XXI (January, 1912), 17, XX (June, 1912), 278, XX (August, 1912), 363, XXI (April, 1913), 183, XXII (November, 1914), 492.

19. Poppenheim et al., *History of the United Daughters of the Confederacy,* 37; see all issues of *Confederate Veteran* cited in note 18.

But the veterans' groups and southern societies were only the most visible signs of Confederate camaraderie in the North. Good-hearted men and women had helped each other and the South long before the UCV arrived. The organizations provided vehicles for enjoying southern company, means of identifying southerners who needed help, and sources for distributing aid or money to worthy charities; but all of these had been done before and would continue on an individual basis after the creation of formal organizations. Clannish Confederates, even when they lived without benefit of organized southern associations, sought out other southerners for social and religious affiliation, legal and medical assistance, and business and financial alliances.

Cities with large Confederate populations inevitably spawned southern friendships and informal social gatherings. Some friendships dated back to before the war; others stemmed from business contacts, informal introductions, and chance meetings. Whatever the circumstances, on any given evening or Sunday afternoon small clusters of southerners could be found entertaining each other in new homes across the North. Sarah Pryor would never forget the stormy evening when William Gilmore Simms, John R. Thompson, and Charles C. Jones, Jr., gathered in the Pryor home to tell ghost stories. On a more somber occasion, Jones hurried a note to Josiah C. Nott when a disastrous fire consumed the doctor's house, including much of his irreplaceable library. "We will be very glad to welcome Mrs. Nott and yourself whenever your leisure will permit," assured Jones. Mrs. Jones, he promised, would prepare a dinner designed to make Nott forget his terrible loss, and the doctor must feel free to inspect and borrow from Jones's library. Jones, the thirty-nine-year-old lawyer from Georgia, had little in common with the sixty-six-year-old physician from Alabama other than a Confederate pedigree.[20]

Thomas H. Ellis might never have gone to Chicago had he not been enticed by the opportunity of a real-estate partnership with fellow Confederate George H. Rozet. Once in Chicago, Ellis became a loyal member of the Virginia Society. His ward, Mary Taylor, became a close friend of Cyrus McCormick's daughters, who introduced Miss Taylor to Chicago society. When she married, Ellis did not conceal his pleasure in her

20. Mrs. Roger A. Pryor, *My Day: Reminiscences of a Long Life* (New York, 1909), 391; William G. Simms to John E. Cooke, August 5, 1869, in John Esten Cooke Papers, DU; Charles C. Jones, Jr., to Josiah C. Nott, March 12, 1870, to Roger Pryor, November 3, 1873, both in Charles Colcock Jones, Jr., Papers, DU.

choice of a husband, a handsome, "ingrained rebel" named Isham Randolph from their own state of Virginia. Randolph, a rapidly rising young engineer in Chicago, not only possessed wealth, he gloried in his Confederate service. Ellis confessed, "It tickles me to think of her escape from marrying a 'Yankee'!—a Western pork-packer or a German beer-maker."[21]

A young South Carolinian stopping in New York on his way to California arrived in Gotham with a note of introduction to a Carolina physician, W. Gill Wylie, in practice there. Wylie, a total stranger to the visitor, immediately arranged his busy schedule to serve as enthusiastic host and guide. He directed his charge through New York's streets and Central Park by day and at night escorted him to the theater, including a performance by Edwin Booth in *Hamlet*. Wylie even took his new friend to hear Henry Ward Beecher hold forth from his pulpit at Plymouth Church. They found the unadorned, barnlike structure on Brooklyn's Orange Street packed with Beecher's well-heeled subscribers. "Much disgusted," grumbled the Carolinian, "at finding that in New York salvation is only for the rich." He and Wylie "retired with dignity," doubtless to find salvation at some less crowded sanctuary. "Wylie and I have been inseparable," the young man reported as he neared the end of his visit. "Indeed it could not be other wise for I might get lost if I trusted to myself." He need not fear that with comrades like Wylie on the scene.[22]

Two Virginia brothers, each trying to establish himself in a different northern city, found fellow southerners ready to help. "I had as you know a great many letters of introduction," one brother reminded family members after his arrival in the North, "and I have made through their means & otherwise, a great many acquaintances. I find many Southern men in business here and some are making strong efforts in my behalf." His younger brother, seeking a place in Cincinnati's legal community, met a southern-born lawyer who offered to share his office with the struggling newcomer. In later years, after the Virginian had become

21. Thomas H. Ellis to Powhatan Ellis, August 29, 1881, January 15, 1882, both in Ellis Family Papers, VHS; Thomas H. Ellis to Charles Ellis, Jr., May 7, 1880, to Mrs. T. L. Munford, November 4, 1881, both in Munford-Ellis Family Papers. For Isham Randolph's career see J. Seymour Currey, *Chicago: Its History and Its Builders, A Century of Growth* (5 vols.; Chicago, 1912), V, 304–309; Isham Randolph, *Gleanings from a Harvest of Memories* (Columbia, Mo., 1937).

22. Robert M. Davis to Sallie LeConte, January 30, February 1, 1870, both in Robert Means Davis Papers, SCL.

a prosperous member of the Cincinnati bar, he won a case before a judge who had also served the Confederacy. The opposing attorney complained upon hearing the judge's verdict, "That judge was in the rebel army and he knows you were there too. What chance has a loyal man got under those circumstances, by golly." The former rebel, chuckling as he recalled the episode, thought it "extraordinary, the excuses that lawyers will sometimes give for getting beat in a lawsuit!"[23]

John A. Wyeth arrived in New York with a medical degree from the University of Louisville to pursue postgraduate medical training at Bellevue Medical School. He soon impressed some of the most prominent physicians in the city, including several southerners, who promoted his career. Wyeth, in turn, became famous for assisting struggling but gifted southern students in the North. He married the daughter of J. Marion Sims, the legendary Alabama physician who had moved north before the war. Men and women from across the South traveled to New York to be treated by Wyeth. He befriended Varina Davis when she came north, and he shared her sense of southern unity in his belief that southerners, "our people," should stick together.[24]

An encounter Wyeth had with a southern visitor to Bellevue best illustrates his spirit of camaraderie. The visitor, a North Carolinian seeking admission to one of New York's medical schools, called on a friend in residence at Bellevue. Someone shuffled the young man into Dr. Wyeth's office to await his friend. Possessing the brashness of youth, the fellow seated himself at the doctor's desk, rested his feet on a nearby windowledge, and began reading a medical journal to pass the time. Dr. Wyeth entered. "Good morning," boomed his impressive voice in icy tones; "I hope you find yourself comfortable." It is not easy to totter when seated squarely in a chair, but the young man felt something of the sensation before leaping to his feet and trying to explain his presence to a man whom he knew instinctively he should not trifle with. Wyeth, however, interrupted the trespasser's stammering apologies with a warm smile and a welcoming handshake. The visitor's accent had betrayed his origins and saved his hide. "I was told afterward," reported the Carolinian, "that if I had displayed a nasal New England twang or

23. Raleigh E. Colston to Lou E. Colston, January 6, 1866, in Raleigh Edward Colston Papers, SHC; Edward Colston to John W. Stevenson, July 6, 1869, in Colston Family Papers, CS; *Cincinnati Bar Association: Celebration of Fiftieth Anniversary* (Cincinnati, 1922), 42.

24. John Allan Wyeth, *With Sabre and Scalpel: The Autobiography of a Soldier and Surgeon* (New York, 1914), 347–56, 368–69, 430.

any other intonation belonging north of the Mason and Dixon Line that my reception would have been somewhat cooler than the outside temperature." Instead, Wyeth seated the fellow by the hearth, stoked the fire, handed him a cigar, and sat down to chat until the youth's friend arrived. Little did the visitor realize that he had stumbled into "one of the most useful and pleasant friendships" he would ever know. Wyeth invited him to attend surgical demonstrations at his private clinic, to visit the Southern Society, and "to call upon him for any service that he might be able to render." Thereafter, Wyeth's personal calling card became a powerful " 'open Sesame' on a great many occasions."[25]

Being religious people in a religious century, southerners far from home and friends clung to their God and their church as a refuge. Southerners in the North erred at first in thinking that the northern God was the same as their God. He was not, or so it sometimes seemed. A Tennessean became so riled when she heard a northern preacher call former Confederates "traitors" that she walked out of the church. She made up her mind to find a southern preacher with a southern congregation. "Never mind what distance it is," she swore to a relative back in Tennessee, "I will go to it. I can never feel any other way towards a northerner but a bitter hatred. I never expect to associate with any of them."[26]

A Kentuckian newly arrived in New York could not resist the temptation, like Dr. Wylie's friend, of attending a Sunday service at Beecher's Plymouth Church. "The people flock there," she marveled, "like they were going to a show." The woman waited an hour before winning admission to the performance, but she went away unimpressed. The unfamiliar service and the alien hymnal added to her keen disappointment with Beecher's sermon. The Kentuckian judged his performance "very poor," and he not at all handsome, as she assumed he would be. All in all, she felt called upon to ask God's forbearance in her caprice, "& if I get forgiveness for that," she confessed to her father, "shall not try the same thing again soon." Thereafter, she, like the Tennessean, would sit in southern congregations presided over by southern pastors.[27]

25. Charles T. Nesbitt, "Autobiography" (MS in Charles Torrence Nesbitt Papers, DU), 73–76.

26. Mrs. B. F. DeBow to Martha DeBow, December 4 [1865], in James D. B. DeBow Papers, DU.

27. Sophonisba Steele to Robert J. Breckinridge, November 20, 1865, in Breckinridge Family Papers, LC.

One man to whom they flocked was Reverend Francis L. Hawks, an Episcopal clergyman from North Carolina. Hawks first went north in 1829 to serve as assistant rector at Trinity Church, New Haven, Connecticut. During the next thirty-three years, he served his faith in various capacities in six states, four of them northern. When the war came, he had been pastor of New York's Church of the Mediator for twelve years, but in 1862 Hawks's congregation took exception to his Confederate sympathies and forced him to resign. He spent the rest of the war in Baltimore, but in the spring of 1865 Hawks returned to New York, where he formed a congregation composed of southerners and southern sympathizers in the small chapel of New York University. Hawks believed that the hundreds of Confederates already in New York required spiritual guidance and a haven from the "contempt and hatred felt by the masses at the North," which he judged was "more intense than before the war." Hawks provided the precise atmosphere exiled southerners sought. One girl wrote in her diary after attending one of the clergyman's sermons: "I could never have believed that I would feel so much at ease in any church in a Northern city." By early September, 1866, Hawks had raised enough money to construct a larger chapel for his newly formed Parish of the Saviour. He died three weeks after the cornerstone had been laid.[28]

Stepping almost immediately into the gap left by Hawks strode Methodist clergyman Charles Force Deems. Hawks had befriended Deems when the latter arrived in New York to establish a "family newspaper," the *Watchman*. The two pastors, though representing different denominations, were both North Carolinians and Confederates. During the last weeks of Hawks's life, he had discussed with Deems the spiritual needs of southerners in the metropolis and encouraged Deems to assemble a congregation, like his own, of southerners and southern sympathizers. Encouraged also by his wife, Deems accepted the challenge. At first Deems continued to devote most of his time to the *Watchman*, but when it failed in 1867, he turned all of his attention and affection on the thirty-odd souls who attended his small chapel in Washington Square. Recognizing that his flock came from various denominations,

28. Francis L. Hawks to David L. Swain, August 14, 1865, in David Lowry Swain Papers, SHC; Maggie N. Tucker to Maggie N. Munford, December 8, 1865, in Munford-Ellis Family Papers; *Dictionary of American Biography* (26 vols. and index; New York, 1928–80), VIII, 416–17; James Grant Wilson and John Fiske (eds.), *Appleton's Cyclopedia of American Biography* (6 vols.; New York, 1891–93), III, 121–22.

Deems decided to establish a nondenominational church, to be called the Church of the Strangers. "The wants of many strangers visiting New York," he reasoned, "and of many residents whose ecclesiastical connections have not been permanently formed, seem to demand the existence of such an institution." The bishops of the Southern Methodist synod approved the project.[29]

Deems and his church were well-known institutions for a quarter century. "Dr. Deems draws a crowded church and commands the attention of his audience," reported a newcomer to the city in the early 1870s. Deems, described as "rather a sensational preacher," and the Church of the Strangers even became subjects of poems and fiction. The church was "open," with no rental fees or buying of pews. Southerners, both humble and affluent, rubbed shoulders as they passed the collection plate. The first executive committee included such notable financiers as James Gardner, Kenneth M. Murchison, R. C. Daniels, and James L. Gaines, all Confederates. When Deems celebrated his twenty-first year as pastor in 1887, the congregation included such prominent and prosperous transplanted southerners as Roger Pryor and John H. Inman, as well as prominent northerners with southern sympathies such as Algernon S. Sullivan, Abram S. Hewitt, William E. Dodge, Thomas F. Bayard, and Cornelius Vanderbilt, Jr. Indeed, Vanderbilt's father, the old commodore, who headed that gilded clan, had ensured the survival of Deems's church shortly after its establishment.[30]

In 1868, Deems met a sprightly Mobile belle named Frank Crawford, who attended his church while visiting New York with her parents. Shortly thereafter, Miss Crawford settled permanently in New York and joined the congregation. A year later, in August, 1869, Miss Crawford became Mrs. Cornelius Vanderbilt, and she promptly asked her husband to help the financially strapped church. Mrs. Vanderbilt even introduced her husband to Deems, and, although each man was initially wary of the other, they soon became close friends. Deems and Mrs. Vanderbilt worked subtly on the crotchety old commodore to break down his dislike of charitable and clerical beggars. Vanderbilt finally

29. Charles Force Deems, *Autobiography of Charles Force Deems and Memoir by His Sons, Rev. Edward M. Deems and Francis M. Deems* (New York, 1897), 192–203.

30. John Grimball to John B. Grimball, October 29, 1871, in John Berkley Grimball Papers, DU; Mary Eliza Tucker, *Loew's Bridge, a Broadway Idyl* (New York, 1867), 34–35, 74 n. 9; Sallie F. Chapin, *Fitz-Hugh St. Clair, the South Carolina Rebel Boy; or, It's No Crime to Be Born a Gentleman* (Philadelphia, 1872), 173, 179; Deems, *Autobiography,* 197–99, 331.

responded with fifty thousand dollars to purchase a vacant church near Mercer Street, which became the Church of the Strangers' permanent home. A few years later, in 1873, Deems and Mrs. Vanderbilt again joined forces to persuade the commodore to bestow a half-million dollars on the Central University of the Methodist Episcopal church, located at Nashville. In gratitude, the school changed its name to Vanderbilt University, and the commodore promptly donated another half-million dollars. On January 7, 1877, Deems conducted Vanderbilt's funeral service, highlighted by an eloquent oration, at the Church of the Strangers.[31]

One explanation for the close southern associations is that southerners distrusted northerners. Even smiling northerners who did not refer to southerners as "rebels" or treat them like second-class citizens might not be desirable as friends or business associates. Businessmen and investors had to be especially wary. "One will find hundreds of men who will profess to be able to handle your property for a consideration," complained a Tennessee businessman, "but I have always found such 'curbstone brokers' totally inefficient, worthless and untrustworthy in every way."[32]

One Georgian learned his lesson the hard way. Richard M. Cuyler had been suspicious of northerners when he moved to New York in 1866. "I am a little distrustful of the breed," he admitted. Still, he formed a cotton commission firm with a northerner, John Potts Brown. Cuyler had every reason to trust Brown. The northerner, a veteran in the commission business, had been a partner of Armand DeRosset, of North Carolina, before the war, and he had helped to smuggle men and merchandise south through Union lines during the war. Brown promised to provide the firm with invaluable experience and financial backing if Cuyler would find southern customers. The arrangement worked at first, although Cuyler quickly learned he was to be treated as a junior partner. "My opinion is not worth shucks *yet*," he wrote scowlingly to an old Georgia friend and customer, "so if ever you are dissatisfied with rules, complain of Mr B.—— & not me, but give me half the credit when you are pleased." From the firm's office, first on Beaver Street, then on

31. Wheaton J. Lane, *Commodore Vanderbilt: An Epic of the Steam Age* (New York, 1942), 308–309, 312–17, 320, 322; Deems, *Autobiography*, 205–209.

32. Joseph B. Killebrew, "Recollections of My Life: An Autobiography" (2 vols.; Typescript in Joseph Buckner Killebrew Papers, TL), II, 8.

Pearl, Cuyler helped southern friends market their cotton and kept them informed on prices in New York and Liverpool for cotton, naval stores, rice, and grain.[33]

The honeymoon continued for one year, until the company started losing more money than it made. Cuyler, suspicious about where the money had gone, investigated. He discovered that Brown had been stealing him blind. Cuyler spent much time in the South lining up customers and inspecting cotton. In his absences, Brown had written large drafts against the company. These drafts probably would have gone unnoticed had not the cotton market dipped sharply in the autumn of 1867, following a period during which the firm had made large loans to its customers. The resulting losses revealed Brown's withdrawals. Cuyler wanted to dissolve the partnership immediately, but Brown convinced him to continue a little longer, and he promised to repay the drafts. Brown behaved for awhile, but then small amounts of money began disappearing from the firm's petty cash fund. Soon the large drafts resumed. Subsequent investigation convinced Cuyler that Brown had "grossly deceived" him and that Brown's "specious, oily arrangements" had cost the firm tens of thousands of dollars. During Cuyler's final trip south, Brown had given extravagant champagne suppers at his home and at Delmonico's swanky restaurant. Company funds purchased expensive dresses and accessories for Brown's wife, daughters, and "lady friends." "I am not quite certain," fumed Cuyler, "that he has not speculated & lost my money in stocks."[34]

Cuyler learned the dangers of northern association in time. He admitted being "a fool" for not having investigated Brown's background more thoroughly and for not drawing up a detailed contract at the start of their partnership, but he had never worried about such things, he claimed, when dealing with southerners. In any case, he had been "deceived, swindled, but not ruined." His lesson learned, Cuyler expressed gratitude at finding his southern customers still loyal to him despite Brown's efforts to draw them off to his new company. When Cuyler

33. Richard M. Cuyler to William W. Gordon, July 7, June 21, 1866, both in Gordon Family Papers, GHS; *Confederate Veteran,* XVIII (September, 1910), 424–26; New York *Daily News,* April 22, 1866, p. 3, May 19, 1866, p. 6; Brown & Cuyler to John L. Manning, October 5, September 14, 1867, both in Williams-Chesnut-Manning Family Papers.

34. Richard M. Cuyler to William W. Gordon, January 4, February 10, 1869, both in Gordon Family Papers, GHS.

formed a new partnership later that year, he selected another southerner in New York with whom to associate.[35]

One had only to stroll through the business district of a city with a good-sized southern population to realize how many friendly faces Confederate shoppers and businessmen could expect to meet. Word spread quickly about who were the most reliable, that is, southern, merchants and financiers. In New York, the northern city with the largest concentration of Confederate businessmen, it became possible as early as 1867 to tour lower Manhattan via southern stores, shops, offices, and banks. Pretend you are walking up Broadway in 1867. At Nos. 40–42 you encounter the commission merchants Fitzhugh, Wilmer and Company. With partners from Missouri, Kentucky, and Virginia, they stand ready to help old comrades. James D. B. DeBow has set up the business offices of his *Review* in the same building. DeBow spends much of his time in New York, and when he is away, his brother and a platoon of Confederate friends handle affairs. Also at No. 42, Salomon, Root and Company operate a general commission and banking business in cooperation with firms in Liverpool and Charleston. Salomon hails from New Orleans. Sidney Root, father of rising young architectural star John Wellborn Root, came north with his family from Atlanta.[36]

Continuing north along Broadway you pass E. S. Jaffrey's giant dry goods store, the third largest in the city, at No. 350. Jaffrey is an Englishman, but two Virginians ably direct the store's daily management. At No. 380, on the corner of White Street, stands the wholesale dry goods house of Evans, Gardner & Company, operated by two affable, good-humored southerners from North Carolina and Tennessee who seemingly hire none but former rebels. Five Tennesseans, a Kentuckian who rode with John Hunt Morgan, four Alabamians, a Virginian, a Calhoun from South Carolina, a Tar Heel, and three Georgians handle sales, and a Major Pryor, late of the Confederate army, works as cashier. A block along, at No. 418 Broadway, Murfrey Bros. & Ludlow, dealer in fancy goods and varieties, is a staunchly Democratic, prosouthern concern at which customers are served by a South Carolinian, a Georgian, and an Alabamian. E. J. Hale and Sons operate their newly opened

35. *Ibid.*, February 10, October 1, 1869.

36. *Metropolitan Record and New York Vindicator*, March 31, 1867, p. 15; *DeBow's Review* circular, dated September 1, 1865, in Hampton Family Papers, SCL; Sidney Root to Mary Ann Cobb, May 29, 1867, in Howell Cobb Papers, UG.

bookstore at No. 496. They are North Carolinia Confederates. The home of the world-famous carriage makers Tomlinson, Demorest & Company stands at No. 620 Broadway. An Alabamian, William L. McDonald, and a Georgian, W. W. Woodruff, serve the customers.[37]

Crossing Broadway from No. 620, you cannot help but be impressed by the five-story white marble Southern Hotel, just up the street. The Southern has been purchased and refurbished by Eli Metcalfe Bruce, a Kentucky businessman and former Confederate congressman. Bruce died in 1866, but his hotel retains its reputation, which he established, as a place where no former Confederate, regardless of financial condition, is ever turned away. Retreating back down the western side of Broadway, you run another gauntlet of southern concerns. At No. 501, Cady, Morrison & Cady, a gentlemen's haberdashery, is managed by Charles H. Betts, late of Richmond, where he managed the famous Spotswood Hotel. Further along, passing opposite Murfrey Bros., you see, around the corner on Canal Street, the sign of Baskerville and Sherman, wholesale grocers. Baskerville is a Virginian who convinced his New York partner—more honest, we trust, than John Potts Brown— to employ a pair of Confederates from Mississippi. Alston B. Estis, a Tennessean with twenty years' experience in commercial pursuits, operates a general commission office at No. 377 Broadway. At No. 319, Lathrop, Cady & Burtis deal in trimmings and varieties. The owners are northerners but loyal Democrats and southern sympathizers. The concern has a distinct southern air as customers hear employees speaking in the warm, friendly accents of South Carolina, Texas, Kentucky, Tennessee, and Virginia. At the same address, one floor up, Gould & Betts, northern-born dealers in hats and caps, wisely and sympathetically employ two southerners, and on the building's street floor, F. B. Betts and Company employs a Georgian and a Texan.[38]

Continuing on toward the heart of the city's financial district you come to Murray Street. Across Broadway stands City Hall Park. People, carriages, and horsecars fill the thoroughfare. Here and there men—and nearly all the people one sees in this part of town are men—pause to

37. *Metropolitan Record and New York Vindicator*, October 5, 1867, p. 2, October 12, 1867, p. 6, October 19, 1867, p. 4, November 23, 1867, p. 11.

38. Jon L. Wakelyn, *Biographical Dictionary of the Confederacy* (Westport, Conn., 1977), 114–15; New York *Daily News*, June 27, 1866, pp. 4–5; telephone conversation between author and George S. Bruce, February 20, 1978; *Watchman* February 17, 1866, p. 48; *Metropolitan Record and New York Vindicator*, October 12, 1867, p. 6, November 23, 1867, p. 11.

speak in confidential tones, heads close together, of weighty affairs, financial and political. The proud cupola of City Hall, clearly visible above the trees, crowns one of the nation's most beautiful public build- ings, its French-influenced Federal style seeking vainly to maintain the nationalistic spirit of a half century earlier. Looking to the right, down Murray Street, you see the store of Wesson & Huntling, where Major Alfred M. Watkins of Tennessee, W. D. Benton of Texas, Robert Bonner of Georgia, and A. M. Carter of North Carolina provide a distinct southern tone to the firm's wholesale boots and shoes enterprise. Across the street, H. E. Diblee & Company sells dry goods. Mr. Diblee, a New Yorker, works in partnership with Mr. Bingly of South Carolina and Mr. Kraus from the Old North State. Among their salesmen labor former Confederates from Texas, Alabama, Georgia, and North Carolina. A few doors down, at No. 18 Murray, the hardware store of Yale, Mac- farlane & Ingoldaby places its southern customers in the capable hands of Captain Herme of Florida and Messrs. Burnley and Carter of Virginia.[39]

Still further down Broadway, if you have the stamina to continue, you might turn left onto Ann Street, where it converges with Broadway and Park Row to form the busiest intersection in the city. Several horsecar lines terminate here, on the edge of the city's financial and commercial district. P. T. Barnum's museum stood here until consumed by fire two years ago. You can avoid the traffic hazards of hundreds of people and dozens of horsecars at this point by walking down one more block and crossing Broadway on Loew's Bridge, the first of several "aerial bridges" to be constructed across this heavily traveled portion of the metropolis. Crossing the bridge, however, has its own hazards. It seems to attract what local merchants call "disreputable loiterers," a group that gener- ally includes a tattered and occasionally disabled Confederate veteran, and all are looking for handouts. The bridge is destined to be torn down. Better to make a mad dash across Broadway to Ann Street.[40]

You can catch your breath as you walk east on Ann to Nassau Street, one block over from Broadway. Glancing to the right down Nassau you see a wonderful contrast to Broadway. Nassau is one of New York's narrowest and most inconvenient commercial avenues. Its tall buildings keep the street in almost constant shade, yet several ambitious Confed-

39. Frederick S. Lightfoot (ed.), *Nineteenth-Century New York in Rare Photographic Views* (New York, 1981), 32–33; *Metropolitan Record and New York Vindicator*, Oc- tober 26, 1867, p. 6.
40. Lightfoot (ed.), *Nineteenth-Century New York,* 17–18.

erates flourish here. Burton Harrison has just moved into No. 20 from his Pine Street cubbyhole. Roger Pryor will soon move into Nos. 37–39. Charles Force Deems published the *Watchman* from No. 119 (Room 20) until forced to close. Glancing to the left you can look down the short end of Nassau to Beekman Street, where, at No. 39, H. St. George Offutt of Virginia and John McAnerney of Alabama, both late of the Confederate Post-Office Department, operate a commercial hardware store. They are known for supplying railroad and steamboat equipment to southern customers "at the lowest prices."[41]

Approaching the end of Fulton you see Walt Whitman's Brooklyn ferry docked at the wharf on South Street. A few southern concerns, including Shackleford, Haas & Company and Murray, Ferris & Company, dot the busy wharf area, piled high with crates, barrels, boxes, and bales and canopied by the bowsprits of proud sailing schooners; but Front Street, one block before South, holds more interest for a southerner seeking business contacts. By turning right off Fulton, you pass J. T. Murray & Company, commission merchants, who maintain close ties with E. Murray, wholesale grocers and commission merchants, in Wilmington, North Carolina. The New York Murray proudly announces in advertisements: "All consignments to me in New-York will be forwarded through Wilmington free of Commission, and covered by Insurance from point of shipment." Moving further north, you find Tannahill, McIlwaine & Company, commission merchants, at No. 79 Front Street. Both men hail from Petersburg, Virginia.[42]

Turning right up the Old Slip, you come to Water Street and the heart of New York's mercantile/financial scene. At No. 196 Water, Harris & Howell, shipping commission merchants, operate a packet service between the South Street docks and North Carolina. The next street up, Pearl, is crowded with commission merchants. James L. Hathaway & Utley (formerly Hathaway & Company, Wilmington, North Carolina), Stenhouse & Macauly, and Brown & Cuyler (not yet disbanded) grace this busy street. Two more blocks take you to Beaver Street, where Harris, Gaines & Company, wholesale grocers, proudly declares itself a "Southern House." W. Hooper Harris is from Nashville; James L.

41. James D. McCabe, Jr., *Lights and Shadows of New York Life; or, the Sights and Sensations of the Great City* (Philadelphia, 1872), 426–27; *Metropolitan Record and New York Vindicator,* December 2, 1865, pp. 3, 14; Thomas F. Greene to Charles Ellis, September 25, 1865, in Munford-Ellis Family Papers.

42. *Watchman,* January 13, 1866, p. 8, February 10, 1866, p. 40, February 17, 1866, p. 48, July 14, 1866, p. 216.

Gaines, late colonel of the 2nd North Carolina Cavalry, is from Asheville. Bear right up the Old Slip and you come to Wall Street. One block to the left is Broad, where the newly constructed stock exchange stands four buildings from the corner. More southern commission merchants are strung along Wall, including E. E. Blake of North Carolina and Mr. Palmore of Virginia. A rapidly growing cadre of southern bankers and brokers is beginning to accumulate, too. The most prominent brokers at this early date include Hatch & Phelps of Georgia and Cherry, Daniel & Company, whose partners hail from Tennessee and Kentucky.[43]

Such was the complex nature of southern society in the North. Friends were everywhere and could serve any need, if only one knew where to find them and whom to contact. One southern magazine reported that "Southronism" in New York, far from declining since the war, had reached new heights. "There is hardly a trade or profession in which a large number of Southern men are not engaged," the correspondent insisted, "and most of these have come North since the war. . . . Then there are large and constantly increasing social circles, composed almost exclusively of Southern men and women, large fashionable boarding houses, where one meets hardly any but Southern people, a church attended by Southern people only, and two hotels known by every one to be patronized almost solely by Southerners." Southern influence, he continued, permeated "the whole business circle," no doubt very annoying to the " 'loyal' element," but, he concluded, "I don't see how that element is going to get rid of it." He wrote of New York, always the most highly visible southern center in the North, but the same observation might be made of dozens of northern urban and rural communities. Southerners probably composed no more than 6 percent of any single northern community's white population and, by 1880, only 3 percent of the entire region's white population, but that made their vitality all the more remarkable.[44]

Still, it would be wrong to imagine a single, exclusive "southern colony" in any northern town or city, let alone in the countryside.

43. *Ibid.*, January 27, 1866, p. 21, February 3, 1866, p. 32, February 10, 1866, p. 40, July 21, 1866, p. 244; William S. Speer (comp. and ed.), *Sketches of Prominent Tennesseans* (Nashville, 1888), 100–101; E. P. Clayton to Howell Cobb, September 25, 1868, in Cobb Papers.

44. "Editorial Miscellany," *Scott's Monthly*, VI (December, 1868), 392; U.S. Bureau of the Census, *Ninth Census of the United States: Population* (Washington, D.C., 1872), I, 380–85, *Tenth Census of the United States: Population* (Washington, D.C., 1883), I, 472–95.

Despite the large numbers of southerners living near to one another, they often knew little about other southerners in their community. Rather, southerners were fragmented by occupation, social position, income, religion, and any number of other categories into numerous "colonies," even in the same neighborhood. Despite their common identities as southerners and Confederates, they frequently had little contact with more than a handful, if that many, of the emigrants living near them. Even fellow members of the southern societies and veterans' groups might meet only at club functions.

This isolation is understandable. A veteran would not rush up to a man and embrace him as a brother just because he spoke with a Mississippi drawl or wore a Confederate campaign hat. An introduction, some common ground, was required. The clubs and societies served that purpose. Many southerners, especially those who had moved north before the war, had not been Confederates. One had to be careful; not every southerner could be trusted or was worthy of association. One woman could lament from New York, surrounded by thousands of southerners, "I have found no friends here, except some Kentuckians that have moved here about the time we did." A former rebel living in Chicago reported that he was "not acquainted with more than two or three" of the many men attending a meeting to organize a southern memorial society in the city. Many people, especially those living in rural areas or in small towns, grew desperate for southern associates. "Pray send me any pretty pieces that are published on the times," begged a woman of friends at home. "I dare say that it seems to you we are too far removed from home troubles to feel them," she continued. "Yet in reality we do nothing but think of and with the people at home . . . and we feel the want of a circle of friends."[45]

This woman's remarks suggest a second dimension to the ties transplanted Confederates worked so feverishly to maintain. The real object of southerners in the North, the real purpose behind the clubs and business partnerships they formed, was to preserve their links to the past and to the South. Many carpetbaggers recognized the true object of their affection. Besides maintaining old loyalties and helping fellow southerners in the North, these Confederates aided the South and comrades who

45. Sophonisba Steele to Robert J. Breckinridge, November 20, 1865, in Breckinridge Family Papers; Theophilus Noel, *Autobiography and Reminiscences of Theophilus Noel* (Chicago, 1904), 169; Harriet Middleton to Susan Middleton, January 4 [1866], in Cheves-Middleton Papers, SCHS.

remained behind. It was noble and good to assist needy veterans, help people find employment, and provide financial aid or advice to fellow emigrants. In the end, this may have been the most important help Confederates in the North could provide. But the South, too, required aid, and Confederate carpetbaggers who were able assisted their homeland through business investments, philanthropic activities, and political action. Conscience demanded as much.

6

For Conscience' Sake

Everyone has a lurking desire to appear important in the eyes of old friends, particularly old friends in one's native place. Burton Harrison took a certain pride in his accomplishments; he enjoyed using his position to help fellow southerners in New York. His legal advice to them had been invaluable. His financial aid, though modest, sometimes proved crucial. His social influence was considerable. Burton had not been showing off. He simply felt obligated to assist Confederates in need. Like many other Confederate carpetbaggers, Burton also knew that his identity and happiness depended ultimately not just on his personal success but on the survival and vitality of the South. Folks at home needed help, too. So, despite the distance from his native Louisiana and adopted Virginia, Burton did what he could to further the South's interests.

Burton's political activities betrayed his concern. "My father often had a melancholy look in his eyes," recalled Francis Harrison, "particularly did I notice this when at all civic parades the interminable ranks of the veterans of the Grand Army of the Republic in their blue uniforms marched by." Burton had joined the Tammany Society at least partly to resist the growing political power of the GAR. As part of Samuel J. Tilden's "inner circle" in 1876, he campaigned not only for a neighbor and fellow Democrat but for a man whose concern for the South appeared more genuine than that of his opponent.[1]

When Rutherford B. Hayes carried the disputed election of that centennial year, Burton Harrison looked on the bright side. "Hayes *must* be moderate and reasonable" toward the South, he assured friends. The

---

1. Francis B. Harrison, "About It and About" (Typescript in Francis Burton Harrison Papers, UV), 22, 33, 138.

nature of the Republican victory required nothing less. Hayes had made deals. He had made promises to gain southern cooperation. Southerners must make him respect those promises. In any case, observed lawyer Harrison, the South must respect the constitutional process that put Hayes in office. The outcome of that process, no matter how distressing, "was better than having Hayes declared President by violence and having him put in the White House by Grant and the army. . . . Had they done so," Harrison continued, "the whole country would have been in a tumult and the Carpet-baggers would still be in possession of South Carolina and Louisiana & striving to get possession of other Southern States." Nor did Burton express any rancor toward misguided southerners who had supported Hayes. "They were wise and patriotic in all they have done," he judged, "& South Carolina and Louisiana are the first results."[2]

As a lawyer, too, Harrison found abundant opportunity to serve southern interests. His first big court case had involved the defense of a Confederate comrade against charges of financial shenanigans. Other cases involving southerners in both New York and the South came Harrison's way in the following years. Friends across the South sought his counsel. He specialized in business litigation and cases involving tangled North/South investments and partnerships. He also represented Virginia's financial interests in New York and abroad. The "good name & credit of the State" concerned him enough to travel to Richmond on one occasion and address the legislature on the issue of Virginia's debts. He conveyed his sense of shame, shared by other Confederates in the North, that southern solons should consider default and bankruptcy an honorable way out of their postwar financial problems.[3]

As he did in so many other ways, Burton Harrison typified the spirit of continuing loyalty felt by other Confederate carpetbaggers who provided political, professional, and even financial aid to the South. Some of this support assumed spectacular forms, particularly as financial investments and charitable contributions. Confederate carpetbaggers, good farm boys that many of them had been, knew that money, like manure, is not much use unless spread around. Even Confederates of

---

2. Burton N. Harrison to sister, April 26, 1877, in Fairfax Harrison (ed.), *Aris Sonis Focisque: Being a Memoir of an American Family, the Harrisons of Skimino* (New York, 1910), 214–15.

3. Burton N. Harrison to William W. Glenn, May 27, 1867, in Glenn Family Papers, MHS; Burton N. Harrison to Alexander H. H. Stuart, March 2, 1874, in Stuart Family Papers, VHS.

modest economic means and lowly social standing did what they could to prove their move to the North had been not a desertion but a tactical withdrawal. Conscientious emigrants believed they could do more for the South in the North than had they stayed timidly at home.

Charles Broadway Rouss may have been the biggest financial contributor to memorialize the Lost Cause, becoming a legend in his own time. He had been a prosperous merchant in Winchester, Virginia, worth sixty thousand dollars, when the war started. In 1861 he moved his dry goods business to Richmond, where he established two stores, one on Main Street, between 12th and 13th, the other on East Broad. Rouss engaged in blockade running for awhile before selling his business and joining Company B, 12th Virginia Cavalry, as a private. He remained a private. Speaking of himself and his best friend in Company B, William L. Wilson, later postmaster-general of the United States, Rouss liked to recall, "Billy and I were the only two surviving privates of the Confederacy, the balance having been killed and the others all claiming to be officers."[4]

Charley, as everyone called him, did not have much use for officers— or for quite a few people. He was a professed agnostic who tended to such remarks as, "I'd rather be sumbody in Hel than nobody in Heven." That attitude had cost him a few customers in Winchester. He could be abrasive and vulgar, too. He was brash, boisterous, blunt, egotistical, and ambitious. Rumors circulated that he had illegitimate children. Enemies called him an "uncouth racketeer," but his friends knew Charley had a heart of gold. Charley was just unsophisticated, and he very likely cultivated his rough exterior. He was obscurely wise and coarsely kind, the sort of fellow who referred even to his best friends as "horse thieves." His increasingly poor eyesight (caused by syphilis, sneered his enemies) made him even more crotchety in later years, but his friends accepted that. Charley was one of a kind.[5]

Charley Rouss returned to his father's farm near Charles Town, in the area that had become West Virginia, after the war. All he had left from his dry goods business was a quarter of a million dollars in Confederate bonds and eleven thousand dollars in debts to northern suppliers. Rouss worked his father's farm for nearly a year before moving north. He had

4. James V. Hutton, "The Barefoot Boy of Apple Pie Ridge: Life of Charles Broadway Rouss" (Typescript in VHS), 1–9.

5. Larry A. Mullin, *The Napoleon of Gotham: A Study of the Life of Charles Broadway Rouss* (Winchester, Va., 1974), 21; *Confederate Veteran*, X (March, 1902), 131–32.

contemplated moving his store north shortly before the war. Now he saw little alternative. He left Virginia with only twenty-eight dollars and one suit of clothes—his old Confederate uniform. After stops in Baltimore and Philadelphia, seeking loans and credit, Rouss reached New York having acquired neither and with less than two dollars in his pocket. He contacted several merchants with whom he had done business before the war, including A. T. Stewart, the nation's wealthiest merchant and owner of the nation's first "department store." All refused Rouss further credit until he paid his old debts.[6]

"I slept in wagons, under carts, in parks, at the Oak Street Police Station close to the big stove and the tramps full of fleas and lunched at the free lunch tables of the Astor and the St. Nicholas Hotels," Rouss recalled of those days on the ragged edge. No one cared to help a "carpetbagger who had come north." Finally, after Rouss had roamed the streets soliciting help for three months, an old business acquaintance gave him his outdated stock to sell on a percentage basis. He also took Rouss home to sleep in a real bed and eat a decent meal. Four months later, Rouss left the concern with a six thousand dollar profit. He purchased his own stock and opened a wholesale auction business. The next year, his wife and children joined him in New York. By 1873, he had paid off his antebellum debts and established branch stores in forty different cities around the country.[7]

Alas, life enjoyed playing tricks on Charley Rouss. He lost a fortune in the depression of the 1870s. Unable to pay creditors, he spent several weeks in the Ludlow Street jail, until friends arranged a settlement. Like the Battle of Warrenton Bridge, in which Rouss had ridden in a gallant cavalry charge, the depression had been a devilish close-run thing. Even with loans from friends, Charley still owed creditors fifty-one thousand dollars. Yet his morale remained high. If Rouss was not actually singing as he stepped from jail, his sunny smile and sparkling eyes did express great confidence. He set to work once more and sold one and a half million dollars worth of dry goods in eighteen months. In late 1877, he opened a new store on Broadway and adopted the street's name as his own middle name. By 1888, he had paid off his debt with interest. Determined to be the biggest merchant in New York, Rouss constructed, in 1889–1890, the largest—ten stories—mercantile em-

6. Mullin, *Napoleon of Gotham,* 17.
7. Hutton, "Barefoot Boy of Apple Pie Ridge," 1–9; Mullin, *Napoleon of Gotham,* 17.

porium in the city. It cost half a million dollars, but only the Pulitzer Building stood taller.[8]

Charley Rouss's money did not go to his head. He remained a southern boy, and nobody was more dedicated to the Lost Cause than old "Broadway." He spent his summers in Virginia and visited the South frequently. Other Confederate carpetbaggers built cottages in Rhode Island and Maine or checked into the U.S. Hotel at Saratoga; Rouss retreated to his twenty-three-room Shannon Park, just a few hundred yards from his father's house, Shannon Hill. Both houses sat perched above the winding Shenandoah River. But what endeared Rouss most to his Confederate friends was his unstinted generosity. Every Sunday afternoon Rouss held open house at his Fifth Avenue mansion. He provided "splendid dinners" for fifty people, though he rarely ate anything but corn bread and browned ham gravy. After dinner he inevitably slipped away to work at his store while guests continued to sing "old-time music" and enjoy his hospitality. Rouss literally threw money away to beggars and street urchins. He gave his employees extravagant parties. He donated twenty-five thousand dollars to victims of the Johnstown flood, and no one knew the number of charities and philanthropic organizations he supported anonymously. Not so anonymous was the five thousand dollars he proudly donated for construction of a monument to Confederate dead in Mount Hope Cemetery, New York. Hundreds of thousands of dollars went to construct universities, churches, cemeteries, and public buildings in his native Virginia, particularly in his old home, Winchester.[9]

Rouss's greatest monument to the Confederacy, the Battle Abbey in Richmond, remains the most impressive of all Confederate memorials. The monument grew out of Rouss's desire to preserve Confederate history. In 1894, he began contacting friends and urging the formation of a national association of Confederate veterans. The association's object would be "the collection and preservation of those records and relics" that told of the South's struggle for independence. Local United Confederate Veterans' camps, memorial associations, and historical societies should join forces, he said, to erect a Confederate museum and library to house the precious collections. Rouss pledged one hundred thousand

8. Mullin, *Napoleon of Gotham,* 18–27.

9. *Confederate Veteran,* X (March, 1902), 131–32; Mullin, *Napoleon of Gotham,* 57ff.; New York *Times,* March 25, 1896, p. 14.

dollars to the project, under condition that the southern people match his donation. The Temple of the Lost Cause, as he called it, consumed Rouss's time and energy for three uncomfortable years. He did not want to be in charge of the project. "It is a singular change in the situation with me," he confided to a friend. "From being a rather liberal giver, I hav turned begar—it dus not take wel—I do not like it. I have gone into this, however, and wil make it go, if it can be dun." It was done, although not completed until 1913, eleven years after Rouss crossed over the river. Sadly, even had he lived to its completion, Rouss never would have seen the beautiful Greek Revival edifice. By 1898, Rouss lived in darkness, his eyesight completely gone. Few sparks remained in the eyes that once would have twinkled merrily at the sight of his temple. His old comrades did not forget Charley. He became the only Confederate carpetbagger to have a UCV camp named in his honor.[10]

Richard T. Wilson, head of the "marrying Wilsons," did not forget the South either. Although not so sentimental about the Lost Cause as Rouss, Wilson wanted to see the South prosper, even though his invest-ments in southern railroads and industries promoted a New South at odds with the pastoral peace of Charley Rouss's Shenandoah Valley. Wilson established his own banking house in New York and surrounded himself with bright young southerners who had followed him north. R. T. Wilson and Company helped in rebuilding and expanding rail-roads, renovating mining industries, and resurrecting mercantile ac-tivity in the postwar South. Wilson financed the Mathieson Alkali Works at Saltville, Virginia. He helped reorganize the near bankrupt East Tennessee, Virginia, and Georgia Railroad in 1868. His shrewd political and financial maneuverings expanded the railroad into Ala-bama and Georgia, and he saved other southern railroads from eco-nomic collapse through timely investments and wise management. Crit-ics of his daring stock market deals claimed that Wilson looked after his own interests, rather than the South's, as on the occasion when he sold short on some Tennessee railroad bonds so as to drive down the price and rebuy them at a profit. But Wilson had pulled this neat trick when Republicans still ruled in Tennessee; his victims had been not Confeder-ates but scalawags and Yankee carpetbaggers. In Virginia's heated 1868

10. Charles B. Rouss to Frederick W. M. Holliday, November 2, December 24, 1894, March 5, 1897, all in Frederick William Mackey Holliday Papers, DU; United Confeder-ate Veterans, *Minutes of Sixth Annual Meeting and Reunion* (New Orleans, 1897), 104–106; *Confederate Veteran*, VIII (January, 1900), 17.

elections, in which railroad consolidation emerged as a prime issue, Wilson corresponded with leading politicians and businessmen to fashion a satisfactory result for southern interests.[11]

The *Confederate Veteran* delivered what should stand as the final evaluation of Wilson's loyalties. At the time of his death, some people criticized Wilson for having gone north to start his career with Confederate government funds. Wilson had returned to Richmond from England, where he had operated as a financial agent, during the evacuation of the rebel capital. He supposedly carried with him proceeds from the sale of government cotton in Europe. When he went north, charged enemies, Wilson used this money to establish his banking company. The *Confederate Veteran* defended Wilson's actions—if, indeed, the stories were true—by pointing out that he had little alternative but to keep the money. No Confederate government existed to receive it. Rather than hand the money over to the United States government, he kept it and invested it. His investments permitted Wilson to become "one of the most liberal supporters of charities, education, and religion" in the South. "What he gave away," concluded the *Confederate Veteran*, "a hundred times exceeds what events laid in his lap."[12]

John H. Inman was another man proud of his heritage. Inman's rise to financial power, if not so colorful as Wilson's or Rouss's, was nonetheless impressive. Inman had been among the East Tennessee Confederates unable to return home after the war. "The bitterness against us by union people and bushwackers in East Tennessee was so great that we could not live there," he recalled. He moved with his family and another veteran and lifelong friend, James Swann, to Atlanta, where a branch of the Inman family resided. Inman had been working as a clerk in an uncle's bank at Ringgold, Georgia, when the war began. Service in Brazelton's Tennessee cavalry as a quartermaster sergeant known for "his thorough business methods" sharpened Inman's business acumen. When in late 1865, his Georgia uncle, William H. Inman, joined forces

11. Daniel Van Pelt (comp.), *Leslie's History of the Greater New York* (3 vols.; New York, 1898), III, 159–60; Henry Hall (ed.), *America's Successful Men of Affairs: An Encyclopedia of Contemporaneous Biography* (2 vols.; New York, 1895), I, 103; William Joseph MacArthur, Jr., "Charles McClung McGhee, Southern Financier" (Ph.D. dissertation, University of Tennessee, 1975), 14, 41, 57–58, 99–100; William G. Raoul to Richard T. Wilson, August 28, 1893, February 19, 1894, both in William Greene Raoul Papers, EU; Richard T. Wilson to Thomas H. Callaway, October 29, 1868, in William Mahone Papers, DU.

12. *Confederate Veteran*, XIX (April, 1911), 158.

with former Confederate general Alfred Austell to establish a cotton house in New York, John went to Gotham as a clerk in the firm. Just twenty-one years old at the time, he soon became a driving force in the company.[13]

Inman worked sixteen-hour days in his uncle's warehouse. He delivered cotton shipments by day and maintained the books and correspondence at night. By 1867, Austell and Inman became Austell, Inman and Company, with John as a junior partner. In 1870, John bought out Austell and joined forces with Swann, who had been soliciting southern business for Austell and Inman since 1865, to direct Inman, Swann and Company. The new firm coordinated an intricate kith-and-kin network of businesses. John's brother Samuel Inman operated a cotton shipping firm in Savannah with his brother-in-law Sam Dick. Hugh T. Inman worked for the firm at various times in New York, Savannah, and Atlanta. General Austell, whose daughter married Swann, continued to finance the company through his Atlanta National Bank.[14]

John Inman made a quick fortune in the cotton trade and used his influence to become the first Confederate living in the North to influence backstage political maneuverings on a national level. Northern critics called Inman a "carpet bagger in Wall Street," an aspersion on his well-known talent for wheeling and dealing in the cotton trade, but Inman also possessed the political clout associated with northern politicos in the South. Not much is known of Inman's political activities. Even his public financial career is extremely murky, not to say controversial. Yet as early as 1876, Inman was influential enough in Democratic party affairs to work closely in coordinating the negotiations of presidential hopeful Samuel J. Tilden, Democratic National Executive Committee chairman Abram S. Hewitt, and Georgia governor Joseph E. Brown during the postelection crisis of that disputed-election year. Inman's service on the executive committee of the Association of Southern Democrats in New York was the most public role he ever took in politics.[15]

Inman eventually invested millions of dollars—one estimate is one hundred million—in southern railroads, insurance firms, coal, iron,

13. Interviews with James P. Coffin and James Harle, in Arthur C. Inman Notebooks (MS in AHS); Inman Biographical and Genealogical Folders (MS in AHS); Hall (ed.), *America's Successful Men of Affairs*, I, 345–46.

14. Interviews with Coffin and Harle, in Inman Notebooks; Inman Biographical and Genealogical Folders; Hall (ed.), *America's Successful Men of Affairs*, I, 345–46.

15. *Dictionary of American Biography* (26 vols. and index; New York, 1928–80), IX, 484; Joseph H. Parks, *Joseph E. Brown of Georgia* (Baton Rouge, 1977), 486–87.

and cotton. He caused millions more to be invested. He guided more than one bewildered cotton planter through the rapidly changing postwar cotton business with its need for diversification, futures buying, and replacement of the old factorage system. He helped establish the New York Cotton Exchange in 1870, bringing order to the chaotic postwar trade and providing wider investment opportunities for planters. He delighted in taking northern investors on tours of the South in his private railroad car. As the car rumbled through the countryside, Inman pointed out choice agricultural lands, the improved railroad system, and the giant iron furnaces that he had helped to build. As in the case of R. T. Wilson, some people misjudged Inman's character and spirit. They claimed that his southern investments benefited only John Inman, that he was ruthless and calculating, concerned only with profit. Such charges are generally hurled at successful financiers, and must, to some extent, be true. The business world requires a certain degree of ruthlessness, cunning, and opportunism. If Inman ever expressed any concern over the allegations, however, he betrayed it only with an occasional furrow of his high-arched eyebrows. He had a clear conscience.[16]

Thomas Fortune Ryan, like Wilson and Inman, was a subject of controversy. Ryan's family had been devastated, both financially and personally, by the war. It left him an orphan and wrecked the family's Virginia farm. Tom came from Nelson County, wedged between the southern flanks of Albemarle and Augusta counties, at the eastern foot of the Blue Ridge Mountains. Two other Thomases hailed from those neighboring counties. Thomas Jefferson, a president Ryan admired immensely, came from Albemarle; Thomas Woodrow Wilson, whom Ryan helped to make president, came from Augusta. Tom Ryan did not want to be president; he wanted to be rich. He worked his grandmother's farm for nearly three years after the war before moving to Baltimore, where a kindly dry goods merchant, John D. Barry, gave the Virginian a job as clerk. Ryan stayed in Baltimore four years, learning

16. Interview with S. T. Hubbard in Inman Notebooks; *Confederate Veteran,* IV (December, 1896), 418; Parks, *Joseph E. Brown,* 486–87; Harold D. Woodman, *King Cotton and His Retainers: Financing and Marketing the Cotton Crop of the South, 1800–1925* (Lexington, 1968), 278, 331; E. G. Campbell, *The Reorganization of the American Railroad System, 1893–1900: A Study of the Effects of the Panic of 1893, the Ensuing Depression, and the First Years of Recovery on Railroad Organization and Financing* (New York, 1938), 97–106; Justin Fuller, "History of Tennessee Coal, Iron, and Railroad Company, 1852–1907" (Ph.D. dissertation, University of North Carolina at Chapel Hill, 1966), 43–45, 75–89.

something about business and courting Barry's pretty daughter Ida. Ryan moved to New York in 1872 to try his luck on Wall Street. He began his financial life as a "pad-shover," or messenger, for a brokerage firm. A year later, newly wed to Ida, he became a partner in Lee, Ryan, and Warren. In 1874, he purchased a seat on the stock exchange.[17]

Ryan attributed his early success on Wall Street to John Barry and his southern friends in Baltimore, who allowed him to invest their money. His investments produced spectacular results and established his reputation as a shrewd operator. Always fashionably but discreetly dressed, Ryan prowled the floor of the stock exchange noiselessly, stealthily, like a fox in a chicken coop, his six feet plus and broad-shouldered frame clearly visible above the fray. He had an uncanny knack for making the right investment at the right moment. Good-natured Ryan was the soul of courtesy. He never gave or took offense publicly. He worked long hours but never appeared rushed or haggard. He said little, but his eyes never rested. He saw everything; he constantly observed and interpreted the world around him. He expanded his already considerable fortune in the 1880s by investing in New York's fast-developing street railways. Some questioned his tactics and investment practices; they called him a robber baron. Even his friends referred to him as the "old pirate," and William C. Whitney, a friend of three decades, called Ryan an "adroit, suave, and noiseless man," an open-ended compliment if ever there was one. But Ryan succeeded. He became rich and richer still by extending his investments to gas, coal, lead, utilities, tobacco, banking, insurance, and southern railroads.[18]

Equally important, from the time he invested the money of those Baltimore capitalists, Ryan proved his southern loyalties. Younger than Inman by seven years and slower to grab his fortune, Ryan did not achieve political power until the 1880s. Like Inman, he served on the Association of Southern Democrats executive committee, but that was small potatoes for Ryan by 1892. With close friends, including Whitney, Oliver H. Payne, Peter A. B. Widener, and Elihu Root, Ryan formed "one of the most powerful groups in the country," financial or political. As his wealth and political power reached immense levels, Ryan contrib-

17. Alfred Henry Lewis, "Owners of America: II. Thomas F. Ryan," *Cosmopolitan*, XLV (July, 1908), 141–42.

18. Burton J. Hendrick, "Great American Fortunes and Their Making: Street-Railway Financiers," *McClure's Magazine*, XXX (November, 1907), 38–39; B. L. Reid, *The Man from New York: John Quinn and His Friends* (New York, 1968), 91; *Dictionary of American Biography*, XVI, 265–68.

uted generously to southern education, advised southern politicians, helped build southern railroads, constructed, like Rouss, an impressive summer home in Virginia, built an awe-inspiring cathedral in Richmond, and, in 1912, helped elect the first southern president of the United States in over half a century. He also kept tabs on politics in his native Virginia. Influential Virginia politicians sought his advice on appointments, candidates, and policies. He even represented Virginia at Democratic national conventions. When the pressures of business and politics bore too heavily on Ryan, he journeyed to his Virginia farm. There, refreshed by the clear mountain air and magically rejuvenated by the soil, Ryan claimed he could see life more clearly, place his business and personal life in sharper perspective, and find the strength and wisdom to continue his northern life.[19]

John C. Latham, despite membership in both the New York Southern Society and Confederate Veteran Camp of New York, had a reputation as a pretty unclubable fellow. He remained one of the few extremely successful Confederates in New York who never accepted office in either organization. Latham's staid, overly dignified bearing put off some people. He disliked large social gatherings and only rarely attended the Southern Society's annual banquets. He had few close friends; many people claimed he had no sense of humor. The latter charge was not entirely fair. There was, for instance, one memorable occasion when Latham gave a grand reception. After tasting the bland punch prepared by his servants, Latham slipped a generous measure of champagne into the punch bowl. Later that evening, Latham's old schoolmarm, who had taken several turns through the refreshment line, rushed up to her former pupil, embraced him, and gushed, "John, that is the finest lemonade I ever drank!" Even Latham had to smile.[20]

Latham's inability to express personal warmth and pleasure led him to demonstrate his sentiments in other ways. If distant and aloof, he

19. Mark D. Hirsch, *William C. Whitney: Modern Warwick* (New York, 1948), 423; Thomas F. Ryan to James T. Ellyson, February 26, 1907, January 26, 1908, both in James Taylor Ellyson Papers, UV; Thomas F. Ryan to Edwin A. Alderman, June 19, 1905, November 29, 1913, April 13, 1916, all in Edwin A. Alderman Papers, UV; Thomas F. Ryan and Samuel Thomas to Richard T. Wilson, May 28, 1894, Richard T. Wilson to Thomas F. Ryan and Samuel Thomas, June 8, 1894, Patrick Calhoun to William G. Raoul, June 13, 1894, all in Raoul Papers; Thomas Fortune Ryan, "Why I Bought the Equitable," *North American Review*, CXCVIII (August, 1913), 165.

20. *National Cyclopaedia of American Biography* (59 vols. and index; New York, 1898–1980), IX, 505; Christian County, Kentucky, Folder (MS in FC).

remained uncompromisingly loyal to his convictions. Certainly no one could doubt his love for the South and the Lost Cause. From the moment he moved north to establish Latham, Alexander and Company in 1871, he nurtured the South. A native Kentuckian, Latham operated a dry goods store at Hopkinsville immediately following service in the Confederate army. He gained further mercantile experience during a residence in Memphis, where he learned the cotton brokerage business. In New York, Latham joined Inman and Swann in helping more than a few planters recoup their wartime losses. He gave generously to the development of his native Christian County. Hundreds of thousands of dollars helped construct new turnpikes, erect a huge tobacco warehouse, build a hotel, construct and refurbish churches, outfit a local militia unit, and maintain cemeteries. Latham always spent part of each summer at Hopkinsville. During one summer visit he noticed the deplorably unkempt and neglected graves of the unknown Confederate dead buried in the local potter's field. He initiated a campaign to erect a memorial to these unknown comrades. The resulting thirty-seven-foot-high granite shaft commemorated not only the decayed remnants of once proud rebel armies but, more important, the heroism embodied in their ranks. The momument allowed Latham "to honor the memory of my comrades in arms who left their homes and lost their lives 'for conscience sake.'" John Latham, shrewd, tight-lipped New York millionaire, knew something about conscience.[21]

Many other merchants and investors, if less wealthy than Rouss, Wilson, Inman, Ryan, or Latham, aided southern economic development. The list seems never-ending. Joseph L. Robertson, Charles H. Bosher, and Kenneth M. Murchison were known and appreciated in the South. William P. Thompson, James H. Parker, and John C. Calhoun, Jr., came north after 1880, but they, too, quickly took up the financial cause of their native section. Even W. Gill Wylie, the South Carolina physician who had been so attentive to a visiting Carolinian in New York, played an important role in building the New South. In 1896, toward the end of his active days as a surgeon. Wylie became interested in developing hydroelectric power in his native state. With a brother, Wylie invested money in a power plant at Anderson, South Carolina,

21. *National Cyclopaedia of American Biography,* IX, 505; Christian County, Kentucky, Folder (MS in FC); Woodman, *King Cotton and His Retainers,* 329; New York *Times,* May 20, 1887, p. 3; *Confederate Veteran,* II (December, 1894), 376–77, XVII (September, 1909), 470.

supplying light, water, and electric power to industries, mostly cotton mills, in the vicinity. Success there led Wylie to undertake more ambitious projects on the Catawba River and at Great Falls and finally to combine all three projects into the Southern Power Company. Wylie, who served the company as president for several years, reaped criticism for his administration of the enterprise, and, in truth, he was a better doctor than businessman. His chief engineer at the Catawba station resigned and sold his stock in protest over managerial organization. Yet Wylie remained a pioneer developer of hydroelectric power in his state.[22]

Expensive monuments, turnpikes, railroads, and power stations were nice if you could afford them, but Confederate carpetbaggers in more humble financial circumstances found other ways to help former comrades and pay homage to the South. For instance, transplanted southerners in the North provided life-saving aid to victims of starvation and famine in the South. In 1867, many parts of the old Confederacy suffered serious crop failures. When Yankee philanthropists organized to relieve the South's suffering, southerners in the North—both antebellum and postbellum arrivals—helped direct their campaign. William T. Coleman, a Kentucky merchant who arrived in New York during the 1850s, conceived and managed the largest relief organization, the Southern Famine Relief Commission. His labors produced a quarter of a million dollars between February and August, 1867, the bulk of which paid for the shipment of corn to the South. Coleman was the only southerner in a prominent position on the commission, but southerners packed the other principal relief organization, the Ladies' Southern Relief Association. Mrs. Algernon S. Sullivan, a Virginian and wife of the New York Southern Society's first president, organized Gotham's southern ladies and friends. The former, most of them antebellum arrivals like Mrs. Sullivan, canvassed door to door, sponsored theatrical benefits and public lectures, and helped at fairs and teas to raise seventy-one thousand dollars. The amount was not as impressive as the Southern Relief Commission's contribution, but it may have been more heartfelt.[23]

22. Hall (ed.), *America's Successful Men of Affairs*, I, 103, 471, 546–48, 650–54; James Sprunt, *Chronicles of the Cape Fear River, 1660–1916* (2nd ed.; Raleigh, N.C., 1916), 347–49; *National Cyclopaedia of American Biography*, XIII, 506–507, XVI, 139–40, XXXVII, 88; William C. Whitner to W. Gill Wylie, July 28, 1902, in Whitner Family Papers, SCL.
23. Robert H. Bremner, *The Public Good: Philanthropy and Welfare in the Civil War Era* (New York, 1980), 121–24; Treasurer Report, August 28, 1867 (MS in Southern

Some former Confederates promoted the South. Edward A. Pollard and Sidney Lanier wrote guidebooks to encourage tourism and stimulate northern investment. Pollard, a Virginian, published *The Virginia Tourist* in 1870. In a letter to a northern acquaintance Pollard explained his purpose: "I hope it will give you a taste for a visit, some time, to Virginia. . . . I want Virginia known to Northern *tourists,* to men of culture who can appreciate the grandest scenery and most charming spots *in the world* (!)" Lanier promoted not his home state of Georgia but neighboring Florida. His purpose differed from Pollard's. Lanier wrote his "potboiler" on commission; he needed the money. Completion of the work produced an ecstatic sigh of relief. Yet the result, *Florida,* published in 1876 with some chapters selected for publication in *Lippincott's Magazine* a year earlier, promoted Lanier's South to an extent his poetry and music never achieved in his lifetime.[24]

Visits to the South were the most obvious way of maintaining old ties. Affluent people such as Rouss and Ryan could afford to keep second homes in the South. Humbler folks had to content themselves with brief vacations, usually in conjunction with holidays, battlefield reunions, burial of old comrades, veterans meetings, or some other special occasion. These visits, they claimed, reminded them of their heritage and stirred anew their dedication to the South and the Confederacy. Some visits could be dramatic. A South Carolinian residing in Pennsylvania kept close watch on political events in his home state. The "negro problem," especially its interpretation by northern newspapers, troubled him deeply. He bitterly denounced a repetition of the moral arrogance that had infuriated antebellum southerners when Yankees, with their small black populations, had spoken so authoritatively of how southerners should handle their "peculiar institution." He grew so concerned that he traveled home, some fifteen hundred miles round trip, just to vote in that year's election. While in Carolina, he sent a letter

---

Famine Relief Commission Papers, NYHS); Mary Elizabeth Massey, *Bonnet Brigades: American Women and the Civil War* (New York, 1966), 324–25; Anne Middleton Holmes, *The New York Ladies' Southern Relief Association, 1866–67* (New York, 1926), 7–9, 19–23, 84–95, 111–13.

24. Edward A. Pollard to William C. Church [1870], in William Conant Church Papers, NYPL; Sidney Lanier to Mary D. Lanier, September 5, 1875, in Charles R. Anderson *et al.* (eds.), *The Centennial Edition of the Works of Sidney Lanier* (10 vols.; Baltimore, 1945), IX, 240.

describing conditions to the Chicago *Times* so that northerners should read a "true" account of southern political and racial problems.[25]

Old southern friends could help returning sons, too. By 1890 Roger A. Pryor was near the peak of his legal career. He had earned a reputation as one of the nation's foremost attorneys, and he would shortly sit on the New York Supreme Court. Yet perhaps Pryor's most memorable moment of the year came on a summer trip to White Sulphur Springs in Virginia. He spent time there with George W. Bagby, an old Virginia friend, who helped Pryor through a crisis in his professional life. "I feel much invigorated," he reported to Bagby upon his return to New York. "I am much happier here than anywhere else. I believe I have fully recovered my peace of mind and I have returned to my work quite enthusiastically." His talks with Bagby, away from the artificial whirl of northern life, had turned the trick, "and it is surely most gratifying to me," explained a grateful Pryor, "to feel that I can rely upon your friendship at all times."[26]

The *Confederate Veteran,* published at Nashville from 1897 through 1932 as the unofficial magazine of the United Confederate Veterans, provided northern Confederates with moral support. Its articles on southern history, wartime reminiscences, and news about veterans' activities around the country kept transplanted southerners in touch with their heritage. The *Veteran* maintained the spirits of Confederates who could not participate actively in local Confederate or southern societies or who lived where no such organizations existed. Veterans in the North supported only six camps in five states, but by 1900, the *Veteran* reached 139 northern cities, towns, and villages in fourteen states. One lonesome old carpetbagger told the magazine's editor, "There is nothing I enjoy in my isolation so much as the coming of your delightful, refreshing news from the dear Southland."[27]

More frequently, Confederates in the North helped the folks back home by serving the employment, financial, and legal needs of southern friends and relations. Letters seeking counsel, introductions, and information about jobs flowed northward. Advice on investment oppor-

25. Daniel A. Tompkins to Harriet Brigham, July, November 27, December [7], 1876, all in Daniel Augustus Tompkins Papers, DU.

26. Roger A. Pryor to George W. Bagby, August 24, 1890, in Bagby Family Papers, VHS.

27. *Confederate Veteran,* VIII (March, 1900), 126, XXXV (July, 1927), 249.

tunities, legal questions, and political conditions went southward. John A. Wyeth earned a reputation as a wise, kindly spirit in whose hands southerners might place their affairs without tremor. Did southerners need Wyeth's influence to press a claim against the government? The doctor would help. Were donations needed for a Confederate memorial? Wyeth would contribute. Did a seriously ill Confederate need expert medical attention? Wyeth invited him to his private clinic. Similarly, lawyers, including Roger A. Pryor, John E. Ward, Charles C. Jones, Jr., and Thomas L. Snead, catered to the needs of southerners involved in northern litigations but unfamiliar with northern courts and legal procedures.[28]

Southern editors, journalists, and publishers working in the North found opportunities to help struggling southern writers and to ensure that southern views on the war, politics, the economy, and other crucial subjects received fair hearings. Southerners in influential positions sometimes complained about the unceasing requests for literary favors, many from total strangers, but they generally tried to accommodate. Because of his own early postwar experience, John R. Thompson understood the desperation of struggling southern writers to establish themselves. He delighted in helping them or, if he could not help, recommending someone who could, usually another southerner. James Maurice Thompson (no relation to John) swore to Paul H. Hayne, "I never forget you, nor any of my friends, indeed when I'm where I can make a stroke for them and as my field of influence slowly widens the sweetest liberty it gives me is that of reaching my hand to a brother." Other southern writers and editors, including Charles Force Deems, George C. Eggleston, Moses P. Handy, Thomas L. Snead, and Sophie Bledsoe Herrick, helped, too.[29]

28. John A. Wyeth to Joseph Wheeler, June 6, 1891, November 11, 1895, April 16, 1896, all in Joseph G. Wheeler Papers, AA; Roger A. Pryor to Alexander R. Boteler, October 2, 1876, in Alexander Robinson Boteler Papers, DU; Thomas C. DeLeon, *Belles, Beaux and Brains of the Sixties* (New York, 1907), 241; John E. Ward and Charles C. Jones, Jr., to Gazaway B. Lamar, April 27, 1866, in Gazaway Bugg Lamar Papers, UG; Robert T. Paine, Jr., to John E. Ward, November 9, 1866, in Arnold and Appleton Family Papers, SHC; Thomas L. Snead to John O. F. Delany, 1871–72, in Mullanphy Family Collection, MOHS.

29. Gerald M. Garmon, *John Reuben Thompson* (Boston, 1979), 134–35; John R. Thompson to John H. Chamberlayne, [c. 1870], in Chamberlayne Family Papers, VHS; John R. Thompson to George W. Bagby, April 4, 1868, in Bagby Family Papers; William G. Simms to John R. Thompson, May 8, 1869, in Mary C. Simms Oliphant *et al.* (eds.), *The Letters of William Gilmore Simms* (5 vols.; Columbia, S.C., 1952), V, 220; James M.

Edward J. Hale ranks as the most helpful early southern literary promoter in the North. Hale, a North Carolinian thrice wounded in defense of the Confederacy, did not want to go north, and his friends advised him against it. He enjoyed the benefits of property, influence, and position as publisher of the Fayetteville *Observer,* but in early 1866, Hale decided that the South's poverty and the disruption of mail service made publication of his paper and operation of his small book business an impossible task. A son and brother-in-law in New York urged him to come and establish a wholesale southern bookstore. "They say that there is not only no Southern bookseller in New York, but not even a Southern salesman in a book store," reported Hale, and they convinced him that his "extensive Southern acquaintance" would ensure a profitable venture. That, indeed, proved the case. In addition to a book shop, Hale, in partnership with his sons, established a thriving publishing firm devoted to southern interests. E. J. Hale and Sons specialized in novels, poetry, biography, and history untainted by "matter offensive to Southern people." Between 1867 and 1875, when the elder Hale's health forced his return to North Carolina, they published volumes of poetry by Henry Timrod and Emily V. Mason, a biography of Stonewall Jackson, a history of North Carolina by Francis L. Hawks, the wartime experiences of southern refugees and civilian prisoners of war, and histories of the United States that referred to the war by its proper title: the "War Between the States."[30]

Southerners in North and South also formed extensive business connections. Such contacts, of course, were not new, but they seemed to proliferate after the war. The cotton trade provided the most examples,

---

Thompson to Paul H. Hayne, February 16, 1875, in Paul Hamilton Hayne Papers, DU; Charles F. Deems to David L. Swain, November 15, 1865, in David Lowry Swain Papers, SHC; Charles F. Deems to Cornelia P. Spencer, January 19, 1866, in Cornelia Phillips Spencer Papers, SHC; Sidney Lanier to Gibson Peacock, December 27, 1876. in Anderson *et al.* (eds.), *Works of Sidney Lanier,* IX, 421; Moses P. Handy to John H. Chamberlayne, March 8, 1875, in Chamberlayne Family Papers; W. N. Pendleton to Thomas L. Snead, January 16, 1866, in W. N. Pendleton Correspondence, NYHS; James Grant Wilson and John Fiske (eds.), *Appleton's Cyclopedia of American Biography* (6 vols.; New York, 1891–93), III, 187; Jay B. Hubbell, *The South in American Literature, 1607–1900* (Durham, 1954), 718, 727, 780, 800; Clifton Wharton to Edward C. Wharton, February 7, 1881, in Edward Clifton Wharton and Family Papers, LSU.

30. James McCarter to Edward J. Hale, November 24 [1865], in Edward Joseph Hale Papers, SHC; Edward J. Hale to Cornelia P. Spencer, April 9, 1866, January 23, 1871, both in Cornelia Phillips Spencer Papers, NCA; Edward J. Hale to Eli J. Capell, May 30, 1868, in Eli J. Capell Papers, LSU.

but bankers and merchants dealing in groceries, naval stores, dry goods, and hardware also promoted and enjoyed North/South cooperation. Admittedly, many of these merchants enjoyed a certain measure of Yankee financial backing, and some men, like Richard M. Cuyler, had northern partners; but in many other cases, the profits and benefits of the trade went to southerners. "This may seem a bold enterprise," explained a former Confederate colonel attempting to establish a shipping firm between New York, Liverpool, and Charleston, "but we know what we are about." He admitted to heavy financial backing by a northern bank, "but," he emphasized, "it is *our line, not theirs.*"[31]

Business correspondence often contained numerous references to personal affairs and family matters. Cheery hellos to friends not seen in years and invitations to visit betrayed close personal bonds between many business associates. Two correspondents, one in New York, the other in South Carolina, found space in their exchanges about railroads and litigations to discuss mutual problems encountered writing Confederate history without access to necessary records. Another gentleman promised a business friend that, should he visit the North, he would be treated to "good *old Country* hospitality, none of your city frigidty & formality but the expression of pure friendship." One transplanted Confederate, using an old southern expression of welcome, promised that visitors would find the "latch string outside." Responding to a fellow Confederate's request for legal advice, a Virginian concluded by saying, "I am glad to hear from you, for I cherish toward you a very sincere friendship." Come north, he told his correspondent, and he would be treated to "old Virginia hospitality."[32]

Unfortunately, given the state of southern financial resources after the war, many cooperative business ventures went awry. The short-lived American Cotton Planters' Association exemplifies the fate of many such projects. In September, 1865, three Tennesseans, Gideon J. Pillow,

31. Alexander R. Chisolm to John L. Manning, August 12, 1865, in Williams-Chesnut-Manning Family Papers, SCL; Beach, Marshall, Root, and Salomon circular, dated September 1, 1865, in Hampton Family Papers, SCL; Thomas L. Greene to Charles Ellis, September 25, 1865, in Munford-Ellis Family Papers, DU; E. P. Clayton to Howell Cobb, September 25, 1868, James T. Cleveland to Howell Cobb, September 13, 1867, both in Howell Cobb Papers, UG.

32. Charles C. Jones, Jr., to E. P. Alexander, February 28, 1870, May 12, 23, 1874, all in Charles Colcock Jones, Jr., Papers, DU; Thomas Cottman to John L. Manning, January 3, 1870, in Williams-Chesnut-Manning Family Papers; Eugenia J. Bacon to Michael L. Woods, March 22, 1890, in Michael Leonard Woods Papers, AA; Roger A. Pryor to Alexander R. Boteler, October 2, 1876, in Boteler Papers.

Robert V. Richardson, and Thomas J. Brown, and a Georgian, Charles G. Baylor, assembled in New York to launch an ambitious project in aid of southern planters. They intended, by negotiating loans for planters at the best available terms with northern and European investors, to revitalize the cotton economy and, by extension, redirect the South's "industrial interests." They assumed that most of the money obtained would be used to employ Negro labor. Richardson, the association's treasurer, also served as vice-president of the United States Cotton Company. He hoped that his connections in that capacity would make it easier to obtain the needed capital.[33]

The association had an uphill fight. Northern and European banks demanded stiff terms before they would grant the amounts of money required. They wanted participating planters to pay 10 percent annual interest on their loans, sign over the mortgages on their lands, divide the profits from their crops, consign all crops to the mortgaging agency, and pay the "customary commercial commissions." Despite these outrageous terms, the association had high hopes. The partners spoke of acquiring loans amounting to sixty million dollars. They sought, and sometimes acquired, the cooperation and endorsement of well-known Confederate leaders. Yet the project was doomed to failure. Too few capitalists considered southern investments a safe bet so soon after the war. Too few planters would agree to the exorbitant terms. The scheme died in less than a year, yet its vast web of American and foreign financial connections showed the inroads barely reconstructed rebels could make and illustrated the efforts of Confederates to maintain close ties between their southern and northern communities.[34]

Southern land and emigration companies seemed like another promising way to stimulate the South's economy. Most such companies had agents working and living in both North and South. One of the earliest ventures to be established after the war, the General Southern Land Agency, offered lands in North Carolina, South Carolina, Georgia, and Florida and encouraged white emigration to North Carolina. The principal needs of the South, the companies' directors believed, were dependable labor—which freedmen could not be expected to provide—and payment of planters' debts through the sale of part of their lands.

33. Mary Wilkins (ed.), "Some Papers of the American Cotton Planters' Association, 1865–1866," *Tennessee Historical Quarterly,* VII (1948), 335–61, VIII (1949), 49–62.
34. *Ibid.;* Robert E. Lee to Robert V. Richardson, May 9, 1866, in Robert E. Lee Papers, VHS.

Emigrants, both northern and European, could serve the South as plantation hands and independent yeomen who would purchase their own land. Railroads, too, might be attracted through reasonably priced private and public lands.[35]

Other firms, such as the Southern Land and Immigration Company, grew from the efforts of southerners in the North. It was incorporated under New York law in 1872 "to deal in lands in all parts of the South, to form colonies, and to do a general real estate business." In addition to its obvious economic object, the company had a political goal. By 1872, northern carpetbaggers, aligned with freedmen and scalawags, still politically controlled much of the South through the Republican party. The only way to unseat this triumvirate was to change the racial balance of the South's voting population. "To be pre-eminently prosperous," explained the company's New York agent, "you must have State governments which reflect the will of the better classes, and this can only be brought about in one way, viz., immigration." White emigrants from the North and Europe, if welcomed to the South "in a hospitable manner," would soon join forces with native whites in the Democratic party and oust the Republicans from power.[36]

Few of these agencies prospered, and the men who organized them soon turned to other projects. The case of Edwin DeLeon is typical. Born in South Carolina, DeLeon had served the political and financial interests of the South and the Confederacy as a journalist and diplomat. Settling in New York shortly after the war, DeLeon supported himself and his wife by writing for northern magazines and newspapers. In 1868, he campaigned through the South for presidential candidate Horatio Seymour. In the autumn of that year, upon his return north, he joined John D. Imboden as a partner in the Virginia Lands and Southern Real Estate Company. DeLeon operated the New York office while Imboden handled affairs in Richmond. Other branches soon opened in Philadelphia, Boston, Baltimore, and Liverpool. DeLeon drummed up investors and encouraged emigration from the North; Imboden in-

35. Rowland T. Berthoff, "Southern Attitudes Towards Immigration, 1865–1914," *Journal of Southern History,* XVIII (1951), 337–38; Dan T. Carter, *When the War Was Over: The Failure of Self-Reconstruction in the South, 1865–1867* (Baton Rouge, 1985), 168–75; Battle, Heck & Company to Dear Sir, September 11, November 20, 1865, Edmund Morris to Kemp P. Battle, June 28, 1865, Kemp P. Battle to wife, July 22, 1865, J. M. Heck to Kemp P. Battle, September 2, 1865, all in Battle Family Papers, SHC.

36. Augusta (Ga.) *Daily Chronicle and Sentinel,* July 2, 1872, p. 4. See Michael Perman, *The Road to Redemption: Southern Politics, 1869–1879* (Chapel Hill, 1984), 149–51, for the southern Democratic party's shift toward racial politics after 1872.

spected and purchased lands in the South and encouraged foreign emigration directly to Virginia. "Business here & in Richmond getting brisker & things look well for us," DeLeon reported in the summer of 1869. In 1870, the company changed its name to DeLeon & Imboden in New York, and Imboden's Office of Virginia Lands in Richmond. A more substantial change occurred when DeLeon became responsible for most of the company's daily management. Imboden, recently drawn into the service of the Virginia International Land Loan & Trust Company, felt more comfortable as a silent partner. A brother, F. M. Imboden, conducted the Richmond business.[37]

DeLeon's active partnership ended in 1872, when he entered presidential politics once more, but his interest in promoting emigration died slowly. DeLeon accepted a job as editor of the Savannah *Daily Republican* in the spring of 1872, a post he intended to use to promote the presidential ambitions of Horace Greeley. Greeley, DeLeon believed, represented the best hope of defeating incumbent president Ulysses S. Grant and ending Republican rule in the South. His post as editor also gave DeLeon an opportunity to promote emigration in Georgia. Though no longer actively participating in the firm of DeLeon & Imboden, he maintained an interest in emigration, partly because he still owned stock in the company. DeLeon joined the chorus of Georgians calling for the promotion of emigration and strengthened their case by stressing the benefits of direct trade links with European ports. His editorials described the prosperity enjoyed by Norfolk since that city, at the instigation of General Imboden, had begun direct trade to Europe. Charleston, too, was moving in the same direction. Soon Savannah and Georgia would be "left behind" in the race for "progress and population." DeLeon's editorials caught the attention of Georgia legislators, who summoned him to Atlanta to confer with a committee addressing the issues of emigration and trade promotion. Meanwhile, Greeley lost his presidential bid by a landslide, though he won Georgia, thanks in large part to DeLeon's efforts.[38]

The end of Greeley's crusade focused DeLeon's attention once more

37. Helen Kohn Henning, "Edwin DeLeon" (M.A. thesis, University of South Carolina, 1928); Charles W. McCaskill, "An Estimate of Edwin DeLeon's Report of His Services to the Confederacy" (M.A. thesis, University of South Carolina, 1950); Charles P. Cullop, "Edwin DeLeon, Jefferson Davis' Propagandist," *Civil War History*, VIII (1962), 386–400; Edwin DeLeon to wife, September 6, 1868, August 31, 1869, contract dated August 4, 1870, all in Edwin DeLeon Papers, SCL.

38. Augusta (Ga.) *Daily Chronicle and Sentinel*, May 22, 1872, p. 4; F. Schaller, "Immigration of Capital and of Population to the South," *Southern Magazine*, III (1872),

on emigration, but with slight complications. During the presidential contest, Georgians became involved in a fierce debate over their state's debt. Many Georgians—Democrats anyway—blamed the debt on the recently ousted carpetbagger governor, Rufus Bullock, who had issued the larger part of thirty-two million dollars in state bonds. Following the pattern of all "redeemed" southern states, Georgia's legislature stopped further issue of bonds and appointed a committee to investigate charges of fraud against the late Republican administration and to determine the size of the carpetbagger debt. The investigation uncovered nearly nine million dollars worth of carpetbagger fraud, and the committee recommended repudiation of that portion of the debt. The legislature complied in August, 1872.[39]

Repudiation engulfed the state in controversy. Georgia businessmen and investors, concerned for the state's financial reputation, requested that a committee be sent to New York to renegotiate the bonds with northern and foreign bondholders. The legislature complied and asked Thomas L. Snead, who had advised the original investigating committee, to act as principal negotiating agent. Colonel Snead, former Confederate soldier and congressman, had opened a law practice in New York after working as managing editor of the New York *Daily News* in 1865–1866. Snead spent considerable time helping southern friends with legal and financial problems; his assistance to the Georgia legislature was only one instance of his continuing spirit of camaraderie. DeLeon, whose earlier business associations in New York were widely known and whose editorials had previously backed legislative repudiation, joined Snead as part of the Georgia delegation. DeLeon also had instructions to use the negotiations to test foreign support for a Georgia emigration program.[40]

385–410; Clara Mildred Thompson, *Reconstruction in Georgia: Economic, Social, Political, 1865–1872* (New York, 1915), 91–94; Savannah *Daily Republican,* August 3, 1872, p. 2; Edwin DeLeon to wife, August 10, 1872, in DeLeon Papers; Atlanta *Constitution,* August 20, 1872, p. 2; Daniel E. Sutherland, "Edwin DeLeon and Liberal Republicanism in Georgia: Horace Greeley's Campaign for President in a Southern State," *Historian,* XLVII (1984), 38–57.

39. B. U. Ratchford, *American State Debts* (Durham, 1941), 171–74, 180, 183–84; Reginald C. McGrane, *Foreign Bondholders and American State Debts* (New York, 1935), 304–11; Thompson, *Reconstruction in Georgia,* 226–35; Savannah *Daily Republican,* August 7, 1872, p. 2, October 15, 1872, p. 2, November 9, 1872, p. 2, December 8, 1872, p. 2.

40. Robert E. Miller, "Proud Confederate: Thomas Lowndes Snead of Missouri," *Missouri Historical Review,* LXXIX (1985), 167–69; Savannah *Daily Republican,* Sep-

DeLeon felt at home when he checked into New York's Irving House, where he paid $1.50 per day for lodging. The trip gave him ample opportunity to visit and dine with friends because negotiations over the bonds began slowly. First, Snead took ill. Then a deadlock ensued between American and foreign bondholders. Each group proposed its own plan for refinancing the bonds, and DeLeon found himself in the middle of high-powered political and financial machinations. He first sided with the foreign bondholders because of his desire to placate men who might advance his emigration scheme. Snead, who leaned toward the American plan, impressed DeLeon as a genial fellow, but DeLeon did not completely trust him. Snead courted DeLeon's support as vigorously as the foreign interests and promised, like the Europeans, to press DeLeon's emigration plan in return for his support of the American delegation's bond proposal. Both sides spoke of DeLeon as the logical person to direct any resulting Georgia emigration board. "I am compelled to watch my own interests," DeLeon explained to his wife, "and am being as polite as I can." He smoked and drank very little as the conference progressed. He wanted to keep a clear head.[41]

DeLeon shifted sides as the negotiations dragged on. " 'Tom' is honest & straightforward," he decided of Snead. "The other side . . . are the reverse." On Christmas Day, nearly a fortnight after he arrived in New York, DeLeon met with Snead and Benjamin Wood at the Manhattan Club. Both DeLeon and Snead knew Wood. Snead had worked for him when Wood owned the *Daily News;* DeLeon had cooperated with him in Greeley's campaign. Now DeLeon and Snead wanted Wood to use his influence to force the foreign and American bondholders to approve Snead's compromise plan for renegotiating Georgia's bonds. Wood moved in mysterious ways his wonders to perform, even when impeded by capricious acts of God. A raging snowstorm, "worthy of Russia or Siberia," slowed Wood's efforts. Traffic ground to a halt, and many of the negotiators could not reach the sessions in lower Manhattan from their uptown hotels. Finally, however, all parties agreed to Snead's plan. If the Georgia legislature would repay *bona fide* bondholders their original investments in new bonds issued at ninety cents on the dollar, repay cash advances from New York banks originally funding the loans in new bonds, recognize the validity of all gold quarterly bonds (not currency bonds or railroad bonds) issued by Bullock, and guarantee two railroad

tember 28, 1872, p. 1; Thomas L. Snead to John O. F. Delany, January 21, April 22, 1871, November 8, 1872, all in Mullanphy Family Collection.

41. Edwin DeLeon to wife, December 15, 18, 1872, both in DeLeon Papers.

mortgage bond issues (totaling $3.6 million) if those railroads were actually completed, all bondholders would pledge the cash necessary to repay past interest and guarantee Georgia's credit. Snead and DeLeon rushed to Atlanta to win agreement from the legislature and, incidentally, to convince the solons of European eagerness for direct trade and emigration routes to Georgia.[42]

Unfortunately for all concerned, the legislature rejected the entire package. Snead worked hard to convince the politicians of the consequences in lost investments. DeLeon, reversing his earlier position on repudiation, railed in editorials against the dangers of antagonizing foreign investors. "We cannot afford to disregard the assaults of 'the enemies of Georgia,' either at home or abroad," he warned, "for candor and truth compel us to make the admission that they have told terribly on the character and credit of our State, and discredited us in the money markets of the North and of Europe, in some of which our State bonds are not allowed to be put on the [stock] lists." Georgia legislators were not interested. They stood by their rejection of Snead's plan and shelved DeLeon's emigration bureau. DeLeon subsequently abandoned all interest in emigration. In September, the Panic of 1873 struck, and by the next summer the country was settled into a severe financial depression. "I am afraid our Land Co. stock will never be worth a farthing," F. M. Imboden reported to DeLeon in July. DeLeon's last hope to sell his stock had rested on a proposed railroad passing through the firm's Virginia lands, but the project failed. "In its death," admitted DeLeon, "the Land Co. receives a fatal blow as well."[43]

Ungenerous persons might question DeLeon's "conscience" in these proceedings. His partnership with the Imbodens, his support for Greeley, his Georgia emigration scheme, and his New York negotiations all promised potential gain for DeLeon. The same could be said of any of the businessmen mentioned in the foregoing pages. Livings had to be made, lives must continue. None of these southerners so fell to grief as to be incapacitated. Other than Varina Davis, no Queen Victorias, draped in mourning for decades, haunt this story. Yet probably most Confederate carpetbaggers, even those who, like DeLeon, made their livings through southern business interests, felt deeply the wounds of the war

---

42. *Ibid.*, December 21, 25, 28, 31, 1872, January 2, 1873; Savannah *Daily Republican,* January 1, 1873, p. 2, January 29, 1873, p. 2, January 30, 1873, p. 1.

43. Savannah *Daily Republican,* January 21, 1873, p. 2, April 13, 1873, p. 1; F. M. Imboden to Edwin DeLeon, April 14, 1873, July 25, 1874, both in DeLeon Papers.

and grieved for the South's postwar suffering. However well one adapted to northern life, it was reassuring to know that some semblance of the old ways would be preserved and shared. Some emigrants, it is true, wanted to forget the past, but the vast majority cherished the South. Even with new homes, new lives, and new identities, they remained southerners, even Confederates. "I am an American," insisted a South Carolina veteran living in Massachusetts, "and I have gained all that I own in the North; but once a Southerner, always a Southerner, and I was born in Charleston." In dreams and memories, Confederate hearts heard the South beckoning, even as the Irish poet heard the winds of Erin:

> Go where glory waits thee,
> But, while fame elates thee,
> O! still remember me.[44]

44. *Confederate Veteran,* XXXVII (April, 1929), 124.

7

The Scythe of Time

"Whatever shall we do in this remote spot? Well, we will write our Memoirs. Work is the scythe of time." So wrote Napoleon Bonaparte, bound for exile on St. Helena, but his words might have been muttered by any number of former Confederates as they set down their carpetbags on Yankee soil. They had come to find work and to make new homes. An unusually large number of them would also write their memoirs. Their purposes in writing varied. Some people wanted to defend and perpetuate the Lost Cause. Others sought to memorialize the Old South. Military men frequently concerned themselves with the war years. Appalled by northern versions of the origins and progress of the war, they wanted to set the record straight. Not all people wrote conventional histories and reminiscences. Some disguised their personal experiences in fictional forms; others wrote histories of antebellum and wartime civilian life; still others produced or collected poems, ballads, and songs. Yet all of these men and women based their writings on personal experience. Writing became another way of holding on to the past, of maintaining tenuous ties to a time, a place, and a people that became less real and more mythical with each passing year. Most writers approached their task with nostalgia. They wrote not just of the South or the war but of their lost youth and the passing of scenes and people that had impressed them at an age when impressions are apt to be deep and lasting. In conjunction with comrades in the South, they produced an impressive body of Confederate literature that created and defined the Lost Cause.

The Burton Harrisons did their part, Constance more so than Burton. Burton had strong opinions about the war, but he rarely expressed them publicly. For instance, he privately criticized Joseph E. Johnston for surrendering his army in North Carolina, believing Johnston had blatantly disobeyed orders and that his action resulted in President Davis' capture. Yet Harrison never denigrated Johnston in print or even privately to a northerner. Likewise, he remained close-lipped about the private life of the Confederacy's First Family. Having lived as an intimate in the Davis household, and being privy to family secrets long after Appomattox, Burton could have earned sizable sums of money writing tattletale magazine articles about their affairs. But woe be to the ambitious editor who suggested such a betrayal of the Chief. Harrison, known for his cool manner and self-control, would have been hard-pressed to resist throttling the miscreant. Harrison did not even reveal his considerable knowledge about the impersonal machinations of the Confederate executive branch, which alone would have proved a valuable and fascinating study. His only contribution to the volumes of wartime reminiscences being published all around him was a pedestrian account of the capture of President Davis, published in 1883, and even this he submitted to the Chief for approval before handing it over to the editors.[1]

If not much of a quill dipper himself, Burton nonetheless realized the necessity of preserving Confederate history, and he became involved in one of the most controversial and embarrassing episodes in Confederate literary history. Burton had been charged during the evacuation of Richmond with salvaging part of Jefferson Davis' confidential correspondence and official papers. Someone, Harrison or perhaps a clerk, placed a bundle of these valuable papers in Burton's personal trunk. The trunk was on the baggage train that followed the president on his exodus and eventually ended up in Washington, Georgia, where it remained in a "safe place" until claimed by Harrison after his release from Fort Delaware. When Harrison visited New Orleans to investigate the possibilities of settling there, a woman entrusted him with a trunk of executive documents that had come into her possession. He forwarded both sets of papers to New York, where they sat in a warehouse until 1870. In the summer of that year, Charles C. Jones, Jr., a Georgian living in Brooklyn, volunteered to store the papers in his commodious, and presumably secure, attic. Jones, a budding amateur historian, promised he

---

1. Bayly Ellen Marks and Mark Norton Schatz (eds.), *Between North and South: A Maryland Journalist Views the Civil War, The Narrative of William Wilkins Glenn, 1861–1869* (Rutherford, N.J., 1976), 268–69, entry of May 9, 1866; Burton N. Harrison, "The Capture of Jefferson Davis," *Century Magazine*, XXVII (November, 1883), 130–45; Fairfax Harrison (ed.), *Aris Sonis Focisque: Being a Memoir of an American Family, the Harrisons of Skimino* (New York, 1910), 160–61, 238.

would organize the papers, a task Harrison had never found time to accomplish.[2]

Harrison gave no further thought to the papers until 1876, when Jones published a confidential wartime letter from Robert E. Lee to Davis in *Scribner's Magazine*. Burton expressed surprise that Jones should publish such a letter, which he recalled being in the trunk, without permission. Jones claimed he had acquired the dispatch from a friend in Richmond. Shortly thereafter, Davis contacted Harrison, asking how Jones had obtained the dispatch from Lee and requesting that all remaining correspondence be returned to him.[3]

Burton now became enmeshed in a three-way debate with Jones and the Chief. "Col. Jones seemed to be a very proper person to take charge of them," Burton told Davis, justifying his original decision to move the papers, "and his house, a very safe one, was already the place of deposit of other things of such value as probably to be sure of supervision against either fire or thieves." Harrison assured Davis that Jones was an honorable, cultivated man who would return the president's papers. But Davis did not get them all. When Burton reclaimed the trunk for inspection, he discovered that many documents were missing. Jones picked this particular time to return to Georgia. Most scholars seem convinced that Jones profited financially from the purloined letters. Douglas Southall Freeman finally tracked down the missing Lee dispatches in 1915 in a private collection in Georgia. The owner would say only that he had purchased them "from a well-known Southern writer."[4]

Normally, Burton remained in the literary shadows, content to let Constance do the writing while he served as her proofreader and chief enthusiast. Constance, with an outpouring of reminiscences, history, social commentary, short stories, novels, and plays, proved to be one of the most prolific of all Confederate authors in the North. Except for the novel destroyed in the evacuation of Richmond, she had confined her wartime writings to sketches for local newspapers and periodicals. The challenge of establishing a family in the North disrupted her literary

2. Dallas D. Irvine, "The Fate of Confederate Archives," *American Historical Review,* XLIV (1939), 823–27; Douglas Southall Freeman, *The South to Posterity: An Introduction to the Writing of Confederate History* (New York, 1939), 96–101; Burton N. Harrison to Jefferson Davis, May 24, 1877, in Burton Norvell Harrison Family Papers, LC.

3. Irvine, "Fate of Confederate Archives," 823–27; Freeman, *The South to Posterity,* 96–101; Harrison to Davis, May 24, 1877, in Harison Family Papers, LC.

4. Irvine, "Fate of Confederate Archives," 823–27; Freeman, *The South to Posterity,* 96–101; Harrison to Davis, May 24, 1877, in Harrison Family Papers, LC.

efforts. A spatter of European travel tales published anonymously in a New York magazine at the urging of her pastor are her sole output during the early northern years. Not until 1876, nine years after arriving in New York, did she resume writing in earnest. During the next three decades she produced more than thirty books, mostly novels, and scores of magazine contributions. She became one of only two women to contribute to *Century Magazine*'s monumental "Battles and Leaders of the Civil War" series. Her fiction contained a mixture of fact and fancy, and she drew much of the fact from her own and her family's history before, during, and after the war. The best of her work falls into two categories: romantic fiction and historical essays about the Old South, and satirical fictional glimpses of northern society. Both reflect her experience as a southerner living in Yankeedom and serve as her testament to the war and its aftermath.[5]

Few authors, save perhaps Thomas Nelson Page, have painted such a deliciously languid picture of antebellum plantation life as Constance Harrison. And to Constance the South meant Virginia. Antebellum Virginia in her writings achieves the combined glories of Olympus, Valhalla, and the Garden of Eden, a world apart, unsullied by the feet of mere mortals and the vices of the "modern" age. In Constance's Virginia all the men are brave, all the women beautiful, and everyone is loyal to the South and the Confederate cause. Harrison's southerners are generally wiser and more virtuous than her northern characters. Even when recalling the tragedy of postwar Virginia, a theme found in several of her writings, Harrison's southerners are always able to outwit the scalawags and Yankee carpetbaggers with whom they do battle. As one commentator put it, if the South does not exactly win the war in Harrison's stories, it certainly does not lose it.[6]

Constance's best southern novel is *Flower De Hundred: The Story of a Virginia Plantation*. The story revolves around the ladies and gentlemen of the Throckmorton family, through whom Harrison recreates the joys of plantation life too suddenly and brutally wrecked by the pain of secession and the chaos of war. Constance bestows upon her heroine,

5. Mrs. Burton Harrison, *Recollections Grave and Gay* (New York, 1911), 302–303; Dorothy M. Scura, "Homage to Constance Cary Harrison," *Southern Humanities Review*, X (1976), 36; Henry N. Snyder, "Mrs. Burton Harrison," in William Malone Baskervill (ed.), *Southern Writers: Biographical and Critical Studies* (2 vols.; New York, 1903), II, 250, 262–63.

6. Snyder, "Mrs. Burton Harrison," 264–67; Scura, "Homage to Constance Cary Harrison," 39–42.

Ursula, some of her own physical traits, including "reddish hair," and Ursula relives many of her own experiences. Ursula goes to Virginia from Maryland following the death of her parents (Constance had lost only her father); she has relatives in the North; she nurses Confederate wounded during the war. Perhaps most riveting are the scenes of Richmond during the final months of the war. Constance describes the "starvation parties," the plight of refugees, the overcrowding, the outrageous prices, the undying spirit of the inhabitants. Men, women, and children all exude that "same element of fearless vivacity, born of Southern soil, which in all times has been difficult for the Northern mind to accept as anything more than frivolity." A scene during the secession crisis sets the novel's tone. As echoes of war drums disrupt the tranquil flow of plantation life, old Colonel Throckmorton, family patriarch and hitherto a loyal Unionist, is asked what he will do if Virginia secedes. " 'Virginia!' " he exclaims in reverent voice. " 'I shall feel as if my mother called me to come to her in need.' "[7]

The same tone haunts Constance's other southern fiction. "Crow's Nest," a short story published in 1885, contains all of the stock features needed to recreate the aura of Virginia's golden age: faithful slaves; benevolent, romantically inclined planters; virile, courageous men; beautiful, emotionally strong women; and scenery unimaginable in any other time or place. As in *Flower De Hundred,* an old Virginia colonel opposes secession but stands by his state when it joins the Confederacy. *A Daughter of the South* and *A Son of the Old Dominion,* both published in the 1890s, continue this theme. The first of these two novels opens in New Orleans but shifts quickly, after the outbreak of the war, to a description of life among Confederate exiles in France. Constance fills the story with details of her own postwar year in Paris. The second work is set in prerevolutionary Virginia and emphasizes the patriotism of such young Virginians as George Washington, Thomas Jefferson, George Mason, and the Lees, brave men all, who are reluctantly drawn into a struggle to preserve their native soil against England's tyranny, just as their descendants, in 1861, would battle against Yankee aggression.[8]

Constance touches on wartime military events only from afar. Ex-

7. Mrs. Burton Harrison, *Flower De Hundred: The Story of a Virginia Plantation* (New York, 1890), 187, 262–63.

8. Mrs. Burton Harrison, *Crow's Nest and Bellhaven Tales* (New York, 1892), *A Daughter of the South and Shorter Stories* (New York, 1892), and *A Son of the Old Dominion* (Boston, 1897).

cluding third-person narrations, she usually relays information about the war's bloodier aspects by such devices as messengers from the front, wounded soldiers on convalescence, and rumors circulating through the civilian population. For the most part, her war is the struggle of civilians and the actions of government. That, after all, is how Constance experienced the war. More often than not, her "war" stories are set in the days preceding or following the fighting. For instance, the novel in which she spends the most time discussing the Confederacy and the war is *The Carlyles,* subtitled, significantly, *A Story of the Fall of the Confederacy,* indicating a setting in the late war and early postwar years.[9]

The Carlyles is also a good example of how Constance's fiction is based on genuine reminiscences, almost to the point of autobiography. Early in the story, Harrison places her heroine, Monimia Carlyle (Monimia was Constance's mother's name), in a pew at St. Paul's Church on the morning of April 2, 1865, the morning President Davis was informed midway through holy devotions that Petersburg had fallen to General Grant. Monimia witnesses the fictional reenactment of that scene, just as Constance witnessed the real event. Moreover, Constance describes the fictional scene in language strikingly similar to her nonfictional reminiscences of the event. In the novel, President Davis looks "pale, grave"; in Constance's memoirs, his countenance bears a "gray pallor." In the novel, "a messenger strode up the aisle, presenting a note to the President." In the memoirs, Davis "read a scrap of paper thrust into his hand by a messenger hurrying up the middle aisle." In both novel and memoirs, a "tremor" passes through the congregation as the president immediately departs the church. In both novel and memoirs, the rector restores the proper atmosphere and concludes the service. In the novel, he does so by "advancing to the altar-rail" and urging his people "to remain for the Holy Communion." In her memoirs, Constance recalls how the rector "came down to the altar rail and tenderly begged his people to remain and finish the service."[10]

Later in the novel, its hero, Colonel Lancelot Carlyle, like Burton Harrison, is imprisoned, first in the Old Capitol Prison, later in Fort Delaware. Constance's vivid descriptions of prison life must have come from her husband. Certainly Colonel Carlyle's prison experience sounds strikingly similar to Burton's, as described in Constance's

9. Mrs. Burton Harrison, *The Carlyles: A Story of the Fall of the Confederacy* (New York, 1905).

10. *Ibid.,* 9–10; Harrison, *Recollections Grave and Gay,* 207.

memoirs. Finally, Constance's description of the life led by Confederate exiles in Paris uses details of her own experiences there after the war.[11]

Although fictional and not to be relied on as true representations of the Old South, Constance's southern stories filled an emotional void for her. She, like Confederate soldiers who wrote wartime reminiscences, sought to recapture a cherished past. Both Constance and the soldiers embellished and romanticized that past, Constance by using fictional characters and episodes, the soldiers by sometimes describing events they never witnessed or omitting events they wished to forget. Both, whether describing plantation life or the brotherhood of arms, conveyed the spirit of the Old South. Additionally, each sought to justify the old order. Each—and this was true of nearly all Confederate writers in the North—wanted to "tell about the South." They wrote always with an eye to their northern audience. They believed northerners still did not understand southerners or the South and did not appreciate the heartfelt reasons southerners had gone to war. Quite likely they never would understand, but Constance and other southerners believed they must try to explain.[12]

Only on the issue of slavery did Constance speak against the old order, and even then her remarks reflected personal preference rather than criticism. Information about slaveholding in the core group is sketchy. Burton's family, like 24 percent of the core group, owned slaves; Constance's family hired slaves. Only 8 percent of the core group owned no slaves, but that leaves nearly 70 percent to be labeled "unknown." Colonel Throckmorton opposed slavery. " 'I don't sympathize with the sentimentalists who cry out on us as fiends, because we accept the conditions of life and society transmitted to us by our fathers,' " he explained. " 'But I'd have been glad to have been born free of the responsibility of slaves. I wish my great-grandchildren could live free of it.' " Thomas Jefferson could not have said it any better. Constance never condemned the South for its peculiar institution. The slaves that wander into her stories are as happy and well-treated as any to be found in Margaret Mitchell. Yet in numerous ways, in different forms, Constance expressed her "detestation of the curse of slavery upon our beautiful Southern land."[13]

11. Harrison, *The Carlyles,* 129–37, 148–51, 162–66, 232–40, and *Recollections Grave and Gay,* 228–36, 245–59.

12. Fred Hobson, *Tell About the South: The Southern Rage to Explain* (Baton Rouge, 1983), is the best description of this tradition.

13. Harrison, *Flower De Hundred,* 186, and *Recollections Grave and Gay,* 42.

Constance's northern satires, in the form of short stories and novels of manners, often served to magnify southern superiority. Her best effort is *The Anglomaniacs*, a satire of the *nouveaux riches* in New York society and their passion for imitating English aristocrats. Northern swells, as described by Constance, live in a world of "watering places and ocean liners," bathed in a "glaring display of wealth, plenty of leisure, inordinate social ambition, an openness to every whim and fad and freak." Their world is exciting and glittering, yet it is also decadent, ignorant, cold, and calloused. It stands in dramatic contrast to Harrison's southern world, a point she emphasizes in the satires by slyly inserting southern characters in northern settings to expose the moral and ethical bankruptcy of the Yankee world. Constance believed that New York's upper crust had at one time, back in the colonial period, shared many of the best qualities of Virginia society. New Yorkers, however, with the rise of the *nouveaux riches*, had fallen into the clutches of Mammon. They had chosen crass materialism over studied leisure, power and self-aggrandizement over *noblesse oblige*.[14]

Constance follows the same tack in *Good Americans*, a novel dedicated to Burton ("My Trooper") and featuring a hero, Peter Davenant, strikingly reminiscent of her husband. Davenant is a southern lawyer who moves to New York after the war from "a dead Southern town." He is as "poor as a church-mouse" and knows not a soul in the huge metropolis. Yet this brave Confederate veteran stands head and shoulders above his northern competitors. He is a "type of the best latter-day American . . . and looks like an 1840 'portrait of a gentleman,' with manners to match—old-fashioned and courtly." The heroine, Gwynne Sybil, is a beautiful but willful and conceited New York debutante, educated abroad and "presented at half the courts of Europe." The story's essential moral, repeated over and over again, is that Davenant is the first true "American"—measured by his strict moral and ethical values—that Gwynne has ever encountered. "It is so hard," explains one character, "to be a good American when one knows only New York, Boston, Washington, a little of Baltimore, and all of Newport." Naturally, Gwynne falls in love with the southern gallant. Following a stormy courtship (much of the story is here again autobiographical, save that the heroine is northern-born), Gwynne marries Davenant and learns from him a new code of "American" values and behavior. She becomes, in the end, "a more contented daughter of the Great Republic."[15]

14. Snyder, "Mrs. Burton Harrison," 254–55.
15. Mrs. Burton Harrison, *Good Americans* (New York, 1898), 6–8, 13, 220.

One might suppose that dowdy northern dowagers and self-centered sycophants, securely hoisted upon Constance's literary lampoons, would be enraged by such portrayals (or betrayals) of her adopted home, but it was not so. "On the contrary," wrote one contemporary observer; "society is enchanted. It sees everyone satirized but itself." Her satires, rather than making Constance *persona non grata,* made her one of the best-paid authors of the day. *Scribner's Monthly, Century Magazine, Cosmopolitan, Harper's Magazine,* and *Lippincott's Magazine* scrambled for her offerings, *Cosmopolitan* going so far as to publish her blasphemous article "The Myth of the 'Four Hundred.'" Some commentators, in admittedly excessive comparisons, ranked her work with that of William Dean Howells and William Makepeace Thackeray, Jane Austen and George Eliot. No one was more amazed than Constance, who never claimed any great gift as a writer and who insisted that she wrote for her own pleasure, not as a profession but as an avocation.[16]

Constance also wrote several successful nonfictional reminiscences. Two descriptive narratives of wartime Virginia published in *Century Magazine* capture a young woman's perspective on the whirlwind of great events during the early, heady days of Confederate victory. More important is her last published work, *Recollections Grave and Gay,* an autobiography that dwells most lovingly on the antebellum and war years. Nearly two-thirds of the book is devoted to her twenty-three years of life before 1866, up to Burton's release from Fort Delaware. The next forty-five years are packed into the last third of the book. Constance wrote her recollections late in life. Consequently, they occasionally suffer from confusion of dates (or total lack of dates), misidentification of persons, and so on. They also lack the energy of a work like Mary Chesnut's diary/reminiscences, but she never snaps at individuals in the manner of her South Carolina contemporary. She includes snatches from her letters and diaries that evoke a sense of immediacy, and, of course, she writes with the grace and ease of a novelist. Constance had a talent for telling stories, and she tells the story of her life in as vivid a fashion as she creates the lives of her fictional characters. All in all, Constance's recollections rate among the best female Confederate memoirs.[17]

16. Mrs. Burton Harrison, "The Myth of the Four Hundred," *Cosmopolitan,* XIX (July, 1895), 329–34; Caroline Wardlaw Martin, "A Favored Daughter of the South," *Southern Magazine,* V (July, 1894), 74–75; Snyder, "Mrs. Burton Harrison," 252, 260–61.

17. Mrs. Burton Harrison, "Virginia Scenes in '61," and "Richmond Scenes in '62,"

Her romanticization of Old South civilization, her defense of the Confederacy, and her almost mystical sense of what it meant to be southern made Constance Harrison a principal architect of the Lost Cause, but she was by no means a pioneer. Former Confederates, including Confederate carpetbaggers, loaded their pens before the last stand of rebel arms had been stacked; they marshaled their literary arguments as the Confederacy's last valiant brigades lined up to be discharged; they plotted their strategy and adopted their tactics even while northern politicians prepared their postwar assaults on southern sovereignty. Recent scholars have noted fine distinctions between different phases and strategies of Lost Cause mythology. Some of their contentions merit attention. Yet in viewing the larger picture, particularly when considering Confederate writings from the North, nuances can obscure larger truths. Confederates in the North cut across all possible phases and motivations in the Lost Cause catechism; oftentimes individuals displayed characteristics of supposedly conflicting categories in the canon. All shared a desire to justify the Confederacy, whether they expressed that desire by writing plantation novels and memoirs, delivering sermons, addressing public meetings, or inveighing against Republican radicalism in editorials, essays, and treatises. Actually, the phrase "Lost Cause" is misleading. The South may have lost its fight for independence, but former Confederates soberly agreed that they would never forsake their cause.[18]

Sixty-seven Confederates in the core group published their reminiscences in some form—as memoirs, history, biography, fiction, or poetry. The number needs to be qualified somewhat, for seven people published their most important work before or after their northern residence, and it does not include seven important Confederate writers who moved north after 1880. Nor does it include people who wrote historical or personal sketches for local newspapers or obscure periodicals or three people who wrote their reminiscences but never published them. Like a child trying to pick just a few pieces of candy from a counter laden with scrumptious treats, one finds it difficult to select only a few writers to represent the

---

both in Robert Underwood Johnson and Clarence Clough Buel (eds.), *Battles and Leaders of the Civil War* (4 vols.; New York, 1887), I, 160–66, II, 439–48.

18. Thomas L. Connelly and Barbara L. Bellows, *God and General Longstreet: The Lost Cause and the Southern Mind* (Baton Rouge, 1982), 1–7; Gaines M. Foster, *Ghosts of the Confederacy: Defeat, the Lost Cause, and the Emergence of the New South* (New York, 1987), 4–8.

whole. An entire volume could be devoted to Confederate writers in the North. Some of them have merited their own biographers. The most important writers, certainly the most numerous, are those who wrote reminiscences in traditional, autobiographical style. Their stories appeared either in book form or in the nation's magazines. Eleven writers produced twenty-six contributions for *Century Magazine*'s Civil War series. The majority of all reminiscences concentrated on the war years, although several included sketches of antebellum life, and nine people wrote about their postwar experiences in the North.

Most scholars agree that Edward Pollard fired the first shot in the new "war of ideas," as Pollard himself described it. *The Lost Cause,* published in 1866, not only launched a Confederate compulsion for self-justification, it christened the theme. Pollard, a fiery polemicist and womanizer, edited the Richmond *Examiner* during the war. He used the paper to attack Jefferson Davis, whose timidity and lethargy Pollard blamed for Confederate defeat. *The Lost Cause* continued the attack with a bruising assault on the president and certain Confederate military leaders, a theme also stressed in Pollard's *Southern History of the War,* written during the conflict and published in 1865. Pollard intended *The Lost Cause* as a forceful elaboration of his southern history, an explanation of why southerners, the "better men," had been whipped by the neanderthals of Yankeedom. To this he joined a defense of southern civilization. "Defeat has not made 'all our sacred things profane,'" Pollard insisted. "The war has left the South its own memories, its own heroes, its own tears, its own dead. Under these traditions, sons will grow to manhood, and lessons sink deep that are learned from the lips of widowed mothers."[19]

Pollard flitted between North and South after the war, finally settling in New York in 1868. By that time, he was a fairly well reconstructed rebel who better appreciated southern faults. He had not changed his mind about why the South lost the war; he still blamed Jefferson Davis. But he no longer thought of Confederate defeat as bad. He did not forsake the South; he merely shifted his loyalty from southern nationalism to American nationalism, to a nation in which southerners enjoyed an honored place within the larger Union.[20]

19. Edward A. Pollard, *The Lost Cause: A New Southern History of the War of the Confederates* (New York, 1867), 751. The best evaluation of Pollard's writings is Jack P. Maddex, Jr., *The Reconstruction of Edward A. Pollard: A Rebel's Conversion to Postbellum Unionism* (Chapel Hill, 1974).

20. Maddex, *Reconstruction of Edward A. Pollard,* 69–70.

George Cary Eggleston deserves attention as probably the most versatile Confederate writer in the North. Eggleston had not been born in the South, but, as in the case of many converts, he became fiercely devoted to his adopted cause. Eggleston's father was a Virginian, as were his father's father and his grandfather's father—all the way back to 1635. His mother was a Virginian, too, and it was only by chance—a poor chance Eggleston would say—that he had been born on the wrong side of the Ohio River. He spent his first seventeen years in Indiana, but in 1856 he moved to his uncle's home in Amelia County, Virginia, where he studied law and became a Virginian. When his state seceded, Eggleston and a younger brother, Joseph, enlisted in Company G, 1st Virginia Cavalry, Army of Northern Virginia. George served at the heart of action, first as a clerk to James E. B. Stuart, later as a sergeant-major in the Wilderness, at Petersburg, and at Appomattox.[21]

The war over, Joseph returned to Virginia, where he became a prominent Richmond physician, but George, seized by uncertainty about Virginia's future, started to drift. After the usual talk about going to Brazil, he returned briefly to Indiana before settling at Cairo, Illinois, to work as legal counsel for a banking and steamship company. A good many former Confederates settled in that hospitable river town. George fell in love with a local girl, Marion Craggs, and married her in 1868. But he yearned for the South. He traveled to Memphis, then to Mississippi, where he established a law practice. Nothing suited him, so, in 1870, at the invitation of an older brother, Edward, he journeyed with his wife and newborn child to New York City.[22]

Eggleston enjoyed a successful forty-year journalistic career in the North, but his literary career, the one he preferred, provided more opportunity to express his loyalties and loves. Eggleston's creative work included both fiction and nonfiction. Novels, a series of boys' adventure stories, a series of wartime sketches, an autobiography, a collection of war songs and ballads, and a two-volume history of the war indicate the range and bulk of his work. His magazine contributions appeared in such premier northern journals as *Harper's, Appleton's, Galaxy,* and the *Atlantic.* His favorite topics, both in fiction and nonfiction, were the South and the war. His novels included stories set in the colonial, ante-

21. John Calvin Metcalf, "George Cary Eggleston," in Edwin Anderson Alderman and Joel Chandler Harris (eds.), *Library of Southern Literature* (17 vols.; Atlanta, 1909), IV, 1525–26; George C. Eggleston to Paul H. Hayne, May 10, 1889, in Paul Hamilton Hayne Papers, DU.

22. Metcalf, "George Cary Eggleston," 1525–26; Eggleston to Hayne, May 10, 1889.

bellum, wartime, and postwar South, and all paid homage to the southern past, particularly the Tidewater Virginian past.

"It was a very beautiful and enjoyable life that the Virginians led in that ancient time," begins Eggleston's first historical sketch, "for it certainly seems ages ago, before the war came to turn ideas upside down and convert the picturesque commonwealth into a commonplace, modern state." Eggleston disapproved of modern notions. "It was a soft, dreamy, deliciously quiet life," he continued, "a life of repose, an old life, with all its sharp corners and rough surfaces long ago worn round and smooth." Eggleston approved of a quiet life. Throughout his northern residence, he sought to maintain something of that pastoral Virginia tradition. He disliked city life and avoided Manhattan whenever possible. During the mid-1870s, he retired to rural New Jersey, where he planted flowers and fruit trees on his modest farm. Even in later years, after he was forced once more to live in town, he spent his summers at a cottage on Lake George. He never returned to the South. He was afraid of what he might find. The Old South had its faults, Eggleston admitted. Southerners could be idle, prodigal, and altogether worthless, in a New England sense. Yet, even as Eggleston lists these flaws, his tone is wistful, like a man recalling the imperfections of a former lover.[23]

Eggleston wrote nearly a dozen novels about the South. They are not great literature. Neither their plots nor their characters are particularly memorable. Their immense popularity at the time of publication grew from the "atmosphere" they conjured up, "the purple haze of romance, which invests the life of a vanished time." Eggleston knew those vanished times well. Much of his work, if not blatantly autobiographical, is based on his memories of antebellum Virginia. "The greatest joy I have known in life," he insisted, "has come from my efforts to depict it [old Virginia] in romances that are only a veiled record of the facts."[24]

Eggleston centered his first—and worst—novel, *A Man of Honor,* on a character who, like himself, was born in "a western state" of Virginia parents. Robert Pagebrook, like Eggleston, had "been knocked about in the world until he had acquired considerable confidence in his ability to earn a living at almost anything he might undertake." Pagebrook goes to New York seeking literary fame, but much of the story unfolds during a visit he makes to Virginia. Eggleston's main premise is that Virginians,

23. George Cary Eggleston, "The Old Régime in the Old Dominion," *Atlantic Monthly,* XXXVI (November, 1875), 603–604.

24. George Cary Eggleston, *Recollections of a Varied Life* (New York, 1910), 72.

and southerners generally, are men of honor, in striking contrast to deceitful, conniving Yankees. The story is filled with diversionary essays that run off from the plot and are intended to acquaint northern readers with the customs and manners of Virginia civilization. Eggleston's readers learn that a Virginia village is called a "court house." They learn that honor is the most important characteristic a gentleman can possess. They learn that southerners take up their carpets in the spring and replace them in the fall, when more warmth is required. They learn the nuances of domestic relations between house servants and mistresses. They learn a host of "Virginianisms," such as "you all." Pagebrook falls in love with these good-hearted people and their intoxicating landscape, and Eggleston tries to seduce his readers with the same wiles.[25]

Eggleston's later works, both fiction and nonfiction, voice even more emphatic approval of the Old South, and nearly all touch on the theme of southern honor. He published *A Man of Honor* unsure of its reception. Not wanting to seem overly partisan, he suggested rather than asserted his belief that southerners were, by nature, more noble and courageous than northerners. In later novels, like *Dorothy South* and *Evelyn Byrd,* he leaves no doubt. His growing boldness partly reflects a more polished style, but Eggleston had also determined to portray the South and the Confederacy in the most favorable light possible. At the same time, he tried to be fair to the North. He was not so much anti-northern as prosouthern. When he writes of the war, for example, he depicts the courage and bravery of soldiers on both sides; both northern and southern climates spawned honest, likable people. Yet his southerners are always a little more brave, a shade more honest than Ohio farmers and New England merchants.[26]

Eggleston's honesty enabled him to see shortcomings in the Confederate cause, but even these served to enhance southern honor. Eggleston could recall some aspects of the South's vaunted struggle for independence, "a very ridiculous affair." Southerners, Virginians especially, had "made war upon a catch-word, and fought until they were hopelessly ruined for the sake of an abstraction." They had been brave; they had shown pluck; but they had fought a war "they knew must work hopeless ruin to themselves, whatever its other results might be." Most tragic of all, many southerners had not wished to dissolve the Union. Divided

25. George Cary Eggleston, *A Man of Honor* (New York, 1873), 15–16.
26. Francis Pendleton Gaines, *The Southern Plantation: A Study in the Development and the Accuracy of a Tradition* (New York, 1924), 64–65.

patriotism—love of country versus love of section—had split southern hearts and tortured southern souls. "Noisy speech-makers" and "clamorous demagogues," totally unrepresentative of the southern people, had seized on the passions of the moment to disrupt the tranquillity of the Union. By disassociating the majority of Confederates from the fire-eaters, Eggleston maintained the purity of southern motives and preserved southern honor. And who, he asked, dared gainsay the potential glory of such a desperate war? To battle for honor regardless of consequences, to sacrifice life in almost certain defeat, was the stuff of legends, and Eggleston, despite the truth of much of his analysis, helped to create a Confederate legend.[27]

Placing responsibility for Confederate defeat followed with unfaltering logic. Eggleston had little patience with braggarts who claimed one rebel could lick a dozen Yankees. He knew better; Yankees were brave soldiers. More important, however, they had enjoyed unlimited manpower, food, guns, and equipment during the war. The South could have defeated such a juggernaut only by sending its bravest men to the front. The South had met the challenge, yet precisely there lay the answer to Confederate defeat. While the bravest and the brightest southern men rushed to be slaughtered, smaller men lagged behind to operate the government. An "incompetent" government and a "meddling" president had wasted the flower of Confederate manhood. Mismanagement and politics, not want of courage, had undone the South's dream.[28]

Sarah Pryor, wife of General Roger A. Pryor, would never say anything so harsh. Sarah's father, like Roger's, was a Presbyterian clergyman. As a consequence of the Reverend Samuel Blair Rice's large family and his wife's poor health, Sarah went at an early age to live with a childless aunt in Charlottesville, Virginia. Her aunt, Mrs. Samuel Pleasants Hargrave, gave Sarah a superb education, personally reading with her in history, poetry, and fiction and providing tutors in philosophy, music, and French literature. Sarah first met Roger at Charlottesville in 1846. She was fourteen; he was sixteen. Roger could not be called handsome. Tall, lean, and big-boned with a large nose and long, straight black hair, he resembled an Indian. Sarah, small, delicate, with dark brown eyes, high forehead, and long dark hair, was a beauty, her

27. George Cary Eggleston, *A Rebel's Recollections,* ed. David H. Donald (1875; rpr. Bloomington, 1959), 57, 61–62, 77–78; Richard M. Weaver, *The Southern Tradition at Bay: A History of Postbellum Thought,* ed. George Core and M. E. Bradford (New Rochelle, N.Y., 1968), 238–39.

28. Eggleston, *Rebel's Recollections,* 77–78, 155–57.

only imperfection being a bend in a nose only slightly too large for her face. Pulses quickened at their first meeting, and they wed just two years later, following Roger's graduation from the University of Virginia. The couple remained in love for sixty-three years, until Sarah's death in 1912. They produced seven children, fought a war, and, in middle age, uprooted themselves from the land and people they cherished to live in Yankeedom.[29]

Sarah unintentionally caused her family's removal to the North. "A deadly silence and apathy had succeeded the storm," she recalled of the weeks and months following Lee's surrender. "It was for a long time before the community waked up from this apathy—not, indeed, until the cool, invigorating weather of autumn." Even then, it remained for winter frosts to disguise the final odors of war—the blood-soaked fields and still dying or unburied animals. In September, Sarah persuaded her husband to visit New York, ostensibly to shake off his lingering malaria, a plague of which had recently swept through the Virginia countryside. She pawned her jewelry to buy him quinine, a new suit of clothes, and passage northward, her real hope being that something might turn up among his friends—northern and southern—in Gotham. "Nothing was further from my thought or wishes," she insisted, "than a permanent residence in New York."[30]

General's Pryor's sudden enthusiasm for New York jolted Sarah. It paralyzed her; Lot's wife could not have been stiffer. Was her darling feeling well? Had he suffered another touch of fever? No, he was perfectly well, never felt better. Would not Sarah and the children hurry along? The rest of the Pryor clan joined him in the spring of 1867. "My heart was heavier than my boxes, as I waited for the boat," recalled Sarah of her departure day. What little cheerfulness she mustered for the children's sake was nearly destroyed when a fellow passenger, a southerner who had lived in New York before and during the war, asked what had possessed her husband to engage in such a "desperate venture." "New York you will find," he emphasized slowly, "has *no use for the unsuccessful man.*" Sarah felt her courage ebb, and it would be several years before the anxiety caused by those words left her. As her husband

29. Robert S. Holzman, *Adapt or Perish: The Life of General Roger A. Pryor, C.S.A.* (Hamden, Conn., 1976), 11–13, 153–54; Mrs. Roger A. Pryor, *My Day: Reminiscences of a Long Life* (New York, 1909), 65–68; Marie Gordon Pryor Rice, "Sarah Agnes Pryor," in Alderman and Harris (eds.), *Library of Southern Literature,* X, 4273.

30. Mrs. Roger A. Pryor, *Reminiscences of Peace and War* (New York, 1924), 383, 394, and *My Day,* 277–79.

whisked her off to their new domicile, an "unsubstantial," narrow Brooklyn row house in a "sparsely settled" neighborhood, she anticipated an existence far more trying than the war years.[31]

Sarah had little time for literature during the next decade. She found time to do occasional charity work, as when raising funds for a "home" in Brooklyn to house homeless women and children, many of them southerners. Most of her time and energy, however, went to her own household and only slightly better-off family. The Pryors had seven children, aged seven to twenty, and for their first ten years in Brooklyn, the family motto remained "work, work, work." Washing, ironing, cleaning, and cooking, with only minimal help from domestic servants, occupied Sarah's days. With these chores done, Sarah and the older children pitched in to help the general establish his law practice. The children read to him when his eyes, weary from excessive reading, refused to focus. Sarah transcribed borrowed law books that he lacked money to purchase. Then, with the children abed and the general dozing in his chair, Sarah mended Roger's suits and altered and patched the children's clothing until two or three o'clock in the morning.[32]

Not until the 1880s, when most of her children were making their own ways in the world and her husband was firmly entrenched as a prominent attorney, did Sarah find time to write. Her early work did not feature southern life and history. Indeed, she began by writing mere fluff—society sketches and gossip—over the signature "Alpha" for New York's *Home Journal.* A variety of poems, essays, and short stories flowed from her pen shortly thereafter for such popular magazines as *Century* and *Cosmopolitan,* but not until a heart attack, suffered in 1893, forced Sarah to spend large portions of each day in relative inactivity did she begin to read, reminisce, and write about the South's past. She produced two books on Virginia's colonial history, one recreating the hardships of seventeenth-century Jamestown, the other transmitting the delicate fragrance and spirited gaiety of the eighteenth century. Neither volume would pass muster in a modern college seminar. It remained for Sarah's personal reminiscences about the Old South, the Confederacy, and the postbellum years to secure her reputation as a literary craftsman and curator of the Lost Cause.[33]

31. Pryor, *My Day,* 306–11.
32. Holzman, *Adapt or Perish,* 97; Pryor, *My Day,* 335–40.
33. Pryor, *My Day,* 410–11, 420–21, 426–46; Rice, "Sarah Agnes Pryor," 4276; Mrs. Roger A. Pryor, *The Birth of a Nation: Jamestown, 1607* (New York, 1907), and *The Mother of Washington and Her Times* (New York, 1903).

Sarah's graceful, melodious *Reminiscences of War and Peace* and *My Day: Reminiscences of a Long Life,* published in 1904 and 1909, respectively, expressed no bitterness or anger over the war. Like her husband, Sarah believed that, although the South had been entirely justified in its rebellion, the results of the war must be accepted. Indeed, from the perspective of the twentieth century, those results seemed almost desirable. Yet Sarah's story, if told with a lightness of tone and spirit, betrayed the strain of her life. Like many old Confederates, she felt a void that God, family, and work could not adequately fill. Life would never again be so bright, hearts never again so buoyant as before the war. She no longer grieved for all that the South and she personally had lost in the war, but the Lost Cause remained serious business for Sarah Pryor. Commenting on a recently unveiled statue of William T. Sherman, Sarah observed, "No Southerner . . . can wholly forget, as he stands before the splendid statue . . . at what price the honors to this man were bought. The angel may bear, to some eyes, a palm of victory, and proclaim, 'Fame, Honor, Immortality, to him whom I lead.' To the eye of the Southerner the winged figure bears a rod, and the bronze lips a warning—'Beware.' "[34]

Sarah expressed her conflicting emotions most concisely in fifty-two lines of poetry, written sometime during the 1890s. "My Day," the same title as her second volume of reminiscences, reviews the guiding forces in Sarah's life: her religion, her love for Roger, her southern loyalties. Most interesting, however, is Sarah's reaction to the war, the "Famine and Fever and Shuddering Fear" that had swept over the land. When the war screams had died and the guns had grown silent, as the drifters and floaters lightly touched earth, God's voice spoke to her:

> And the Voice said: "Take up your lives again!
> Quit yourselves manfully! Stand in your lot!
> Let the Famine, the Fever, and Peril, the Pain
> Be all forgot!
> Weep no more for the lovely, the brave,
> The young head pillowed on a blood-stained sod;
> The daisy that grows in the soldier's grave
> Looks up to God!"

Then, repeating a phrase ("my rose . . . my song") used earlier to symbolize her awakening love for Roger, an awakening that coincided with

34. Rice, "Sarah Agnes Pryor," 4276; Pryor, *My Day,* 403.

the end of adolescence and her entrance into the land of adult remembrance, she concludes:

> I have lost my rose, forgotten my song,
> But the true heart that loved me is mine alway.
> The stars are alight—the way not long—
> I had my day![35]

Virginuis Dabney had his day, too. A plantation boyhood, tutors, a
university education, the Grand Tour of Europe, and a successful law
practice outline the contours of Dabney's life before the war. It was a
happy life until the death of his first wife in 1860. That event devastated
Dabney, disrupted his law practice, and cast a pall over the months
preceding the war. Dabney embraced war with relief; the excitement of
Confederate service lessened his personal tragedy. Captain Dabney established a school at Middleburg, Virginia, after the war. Achieving
only moderate financial success, he left to teach at a preparatory school
in Princeton, New Jersey, for one year before moving to New York City
in 1875.[36]

Dabney had a rough time during his first few years in Gotham. He
opened a new school but attracted only eleven pupils the first year and
thirteen the second. Yet Dabney was an unflappable, cheery sort who
never seemed to get depressed. With his thirteen students in hand, he
could say confidently, "I look upon myself as having fairly taken root
here." When he finally gave up the school in 1883 to devote himself to
journalism and literature, Dabney had more than fifty students and
reported contentedly to his eldest son, "The way I have not had any
money in my pockets has been perfectly ludikerous, for some time; but
my emotions readjusted themselves to meet the environment; and I have
been chirpy as a millionaire and minus some of the worries of wealth."[37]

What unhappiness Dabney experienced in the North may well have
been caused, untypically, by fellow southerners rather than Yankees.
Nothing in Dabney's surviving correspondence verifies this impression,
but circumstances and one of his two novels suggest it. *Gold That Did*

35. Mrs. Roger A. Pryor, "My Day," in Alderman and Harris (eds.), *Library of Southern Literature*, X, 4294.

36. *Dictionary of American Biography* (26 vols. and index; New York, 1928–80), V, 22.

37. Thomas C. DeLeon, *Belles, Beaux and Brains of the Sixties* (New York, 1907), 313;
Virginius Dabney to John Chamberlayne. November 14, 1875, in Chamberlayne Family
Papers, VHS; Virginius Dabney to Richard H. Dabney, June 28, 1883, in Richard Heath
Dabney Papers, UV.

Not Glitter revolves around a young Virginian who, seeking aid for his
financially distraught parents, looks for work in New York. " 'I came
with a light heart, and with scarcely a misgiving,' " claims Dabney's
hero, " 'for a number of our acquaintances had removed to New York,
after the war, and several of them had greatly prospered; and as more
than one of them had always professed to be warm friends of our family,
I had no doubt that some one among them would put me in the way of
finding something to do.' " Understandably, the Virginian's un-
enthusiastic reception by these supposedly "warm friends" stunned
him. They were all exceedingly polite over cigars and sherry, but none
had a job for him or knew where he might find one. " 'A well-established
emigré,' " the fellow learned, " 'looks upon every new-comer as an im-
pertinent interloper . . . who cheapens his success by assuming that it is
possible for another.' "[38]

Whatever his experience with a few renegade southerners, Dabney
never renounced his beloved Virginia or the Confederacy. *The Story of
Don Miff,* Dabney's other novel, is a good example of his passion. The
book is a marvel. Ostensibly, it is a record of Virginia during the war
years, written for the narrator's fictional descendants in the year 2200. It
was considered a profound work when first published in 1886, and even
today's reader is struck by its originality, not to say eccentricity. It is
heavily philosophical as well as "whimiscal, shrewd, and wise" in its
criticism of America's social order. Dabney excelled at philosophical
analysis and at ridiculing, through wit and sarcasm, social fallacies and
human foibles. "A fallacy could not live under the light of his eyes. A
falsehood or a false pretence flashed into sudden deformity under the
illumination of his humorous exposure." In his preface, Dabney lamely
disavows having written the book. He is merely presenting it to the
public, he says, as a favor to its author, John Bouche Whacker. The name
sets the book's tone.[39]

"And this is the thing that I feel that I have to say," Mr. Whacker tells
his descendants. "I would tell you something of the land of your fore-
fathers. Something of Virginia. Not new Virginia,—not West Vir-

38. Virginius Dabney, *Gold That Did Not Glitter: A Novel* (Philadelphia, 1889),
59–61.

39. *Dictionary of American Biography,* V, 22; Lyon Gardiner Tyler, *Encyclopedia of
Virginia Biography* (5 vols.; New York, 1915), III, 190; Virginius Dabney, *The Story of
Don Miff, as Told by His Friend John Bouche Whacker: A Symphony of Life* (2nd ed.;
Philadelphia, 1886), 3–4.

Burton N. Harrison, painted by Marrietta Minnigerode Andrews in 1915 from a photograph
Courtesy Virginia Historical Society, Richmond

Constance Cary Harrison, painted by Alice Pike Barney, ca. *1900*
Courtesy Virginia Historical Society, Richmond

George Cary Eggleston, who believed the South and southerners were "sadly misunderstood"
Courtesy Virginia Historical Society, Richmond

Roger A. Pryor, Confederate
general, Confederate
congressman, and justice on
the New York Supreme Court
Courtesy Museum of the City of
New York

Sarah Rice Pryor, who counted
her Brooklyn neighbors among
the "noblest men and women"
she had ever known
Courtesy Virginia Historical
Society, Richmond

William R. O'Donovan in 1891 as he fashioned a bust of Walt Whitman

Courtesy Photos of Artists, Collection II, Archives of American Art, Smithsonian Institution. Photographer: Thomas Eakins

Richard T. Wilson and his dog Romeo, the only canine ever to enjoy the services of the Union Club dining room
Courtesy Orme Wilson, Jr.

Sidney Lanier in 1874, the year
he wrote "Civil Rights" and
"Corn"
Courtesy Sidney Lanier Collection
Ms. 7, Special Collections, Milton
S. Eisenhower Library, The Johns
Hopkins University

Charles Broadway Rouss, also
known as the Napoleon of
Gotham
Courtesy the Handley Library
Collection, Winchester, Virginia

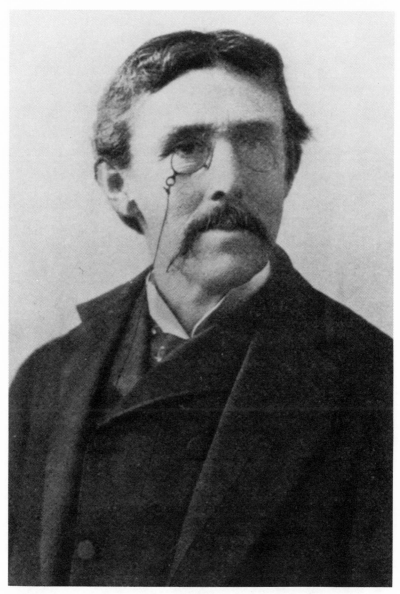

James Maurice Thompson wanted "no sectionalism East, West, North or South."
Courtesy Indiana Division, Indiana State Library

John H. Inman.
Northerners called him
a "carpetbagger in Wall
Street."
From *Munsey's Magazine*,
XLII (November, 1909),
237

Thomas Fortune Ryan in 1908
Courtesy Museum of the City of New York

ginia,—but the Old Dominion and her people." "Yes, my lad," he re-counts elsewhere, "I think the glimpses I am about to give you of the old Virginia life will refresh your tired soul. Just as it refreshes mine to draw the pictures for you." With fire in his heart and a good head of steam piping in his soul, Dabney plunges into the details of that faraway, long ago place called Old Virginia. Its preservation, he says, inspired young men to take up arms in 1861. The collapse of the Confederacy did not pain Virginians so much as the ruination of their state. The Confederacy, after all, was ephemeral; it, perhaps, was destined to die; but Virginia! That was real; that should have endured. Yet even as Dabney wrote, twenty years after the war, Old Virginia, too, seemed like a dream world. "For from me, as well," sighs Dabney, "the reality has vanished. Our civil war (war of the rebellion, as the underbred among the victors still call it) swept that into the abyss of the past; but let me with such poor wand as I yield summon it before you."[40]

Other Confederates, blessed with only slightly less wonder wands than Dabney, Harrison, Eggleston, and Pryor, also turned their hands to recreating those ancient scenes and honoring the Confederacy. Gustavus W. Smith dearly loved his native Kentucky, but he lacked the flair for imaginative detail that sparked many fictional reminiscences of the South. Smith was a soldier, a West Pointer, and his reminiscences, writ-ten in the 1870s and 1880s, are military memoirs. Smith had a good many memories, too. A veteran of the Mexican War, Smith, like so many West Pointers in the old army, resigned his commission to take a more lucrative job with a civilian engineering firm. He had married a Con-necticut girl and settled in New York by the mid-1850s, and his posi-tions as chief engineer of the Trenton Iron Works and as New York City's street commissioner promised a secure future. Wars, however, have a habit of disrupting secure futures. Smith left New York with his good friend Mansfield Lovell in the spring of 1861 to join the Confederacy. Both men received commissions as major generals, Lovell to command defenses at New Orleans, Smith to command a corps in Virginia. For a brief time in May 1862, Smith even commanded the Army of Northern Virginia.[41]

Smith's service in the Confederate army ended abruptly in early 1863. Believing that Jefferson Davis lacked confidence in him, Smith resigned

40. Dabney, *Story of Don Miff*, 8–9.
41. C. Seaforth Stewart, "Gustavus Woodson Smith," in *Annual Reunion of the Asso-ciation of the Graduates of the United States Military Academy at West Point, New York, 1897* (Saginaw, Mich., 1897), 13–22.

his commission to accept the presidency of the Etowah Manufacturing and Mining Company in Georgia. Partly for reasons of poor health, Smith fully intended to forsake further military service, but once again circumstances shattered his plans. William T. Sherman's invasion of Georgia and the subsequent destruction of the Etowah iron works, second only to Richmond's Tredegar works in importance to the Confederacy, put Smith back in military harness. The Georgia militia drafted him to organize that state's defenses. Not even Smith, muscular, broad-chested, thick-necked, with a bulldog countenance, could thwart Sherman, but he served the dying Confederacy faithfully as a major general until captured and paroled at Macon in April, 1865.[42]

Energetic and impatient, Smith tried a number of postwar careers. He operated the South Western Iron Company at Chattanooga for five years. In 1870, he returned to his native Kentucky and served as the state's insurance commissioner until 1876. He became a nationally recognized authority on life insurance, contributing articles on the subject to various journals and penning two volumes that remained standard literature in the insurance business for many years. Smith then moved to New York, where, after several profitable ventures, he retired from business in the early 1880s.[43]

In retirement, Smith began to write about Confederate service. He produced memorable accounts of several important battles for *Century*'s "Battles and Leaders" series: the Battle of Seven Pines and the Georgia militia's activities in the Atlanta campaign and during Sherman's March to the Sea. In 1892, he published an account of Confederate strategy and tactics at Manassas, a battle in which he had not participated, and during the 1880s and 1890s, he wrote several unpublished papers on Gettysburg, Chickamauga, and the causes of the war. Candor characterized Smith's writing. He pulled few punches in criticizing leaders he held responsible for Confederate defeat. Jefferson Davis received a good dose of blame for faulty judgments in strategy and promotions. Leading generals also received more or less gentlemanly rebukes. For instance, Smith blamed James Longstreet's refusal to counterattack at Seven Pines, as Longstreet had been ordered to do, for the Confederate army's failure to destroy a federal corps.[44]

42. *Ibid.;* Marks and Schatz (eds.), *Between North and South,* 246–47, entry of November 29, 1865.

43. Stewart, "Gustavus Woodson Smith," 20–21.

44. *Ibid.,* 21; Gustavus W. Smith, "Two Days of Battle at Seven Pines," in Johnson and Buel (eds.), *Battles and Leaders of the Civil War,* II, 263.

Smith's best published volume is a collection of essays entitled *Confederate War Papers*. One of the most interesting essays examines the fall of New Orleans. Smith had not been at New Orleans when federal forces captured the city in April, 1862, but his friend Mansfield Lovell had commanded the military forces there, and Lovell had been blamed for the collapse of the strategically vital city. Lovell blamed Jefferson Davis. Smith prepared twin briefs, one for Lovell's defense, the other for Davis' prosecution. Smith based his story on official Confederate documents, Lovell's correspondence, and Lovell's own unpublished account of events. If ever Smith refused to mince words, it was in this spirited interpretation of the New Orleans debacle. Smith charged that Davis had "actively promoted the unjust hue and cry" against Lovell when the city surrendered. When the general asked for a public hearing to exonerate himself, Davis stalled. When he could stall no longer, Davis rigged the court of inquiry so that he and his government escaped blame. In his self-serving memoirs, published in 1881, Davis continued to lay blame on Lovell, charged Smith, and the president's conduct throughout the twenty years since 1862 had been "characterized by a spirit born of wounded vanity and nursed by fear of the truth."[45]

Theophilus Noel had little good to say about Davis either. Actually, Noel had little good to say about anybody, but Davis, in particular, seemed to raise his ire. Noel, a bookish man with a flair for language, left his birthplace in rural southwestern Michigan as a teenager, bound for Texas. There he operated a bookstore and newsstand until the war began. His service to the Confederacy as a scout, mostly with Sibley's Texas Brigade, seemed perfectly natural, given his father's Virginia heritage. In later years, Noel decided that gradual emancipation and the restriction of slavery to "certain territory" might have been the best course for the nation to pursue in 1860, but that all occurred to him after the gods of war had settled the issue of southern independence. Not being a slaveowner himself, Noel had given the matter little consideration at the time.[46]

Noel became a journalist and newspaper editor in Texas after the war. In 1865, he published a good history of the Sibley brigade, based on the

45. Daniel E. Sutherland, "Mansfield Lovell's Quest for Justice: Another Look at the Fall of New Orleans," *Louisiana History,* XXIV (1983), 233–59; Gustavus W. Smith, *Confederate War Papers* (2nd ed.; New York, 1884), 135–38.

46. Theophilus Noel, *Autobiography and Reminiscences of Theophilus Noel* (Chicago, 1904), 7, 55–57, 154.

diary of a wartime comrade-in-arms. Noel joined the Condeferate migration northward sometime during the 1870s, finally stopping at Chicago, where he prospered as a journalist and publisher. Noel had been quite generous to the Confederate cause in his account of the war in the Southwest, but the political direction of Reconstruction and the South's seemingly unsolvable economic and racial problems combined to make him exceedingly bitter toward the Democratic party and all but a few Confederate leaders.[47]

Noel presented his reevaluation of Confederate leadership in an autobiography published in 1904. "It was the old Democratic party and its leaders," he declared, "who . . . robbed me of four years of the hardest service that a man ever put in." *"Had the Confederate army been properly officered and supported by a proper, generous and brave government,"* Noel added with emphasis, *"no army on earth could have conquered it."* The South's leaders had deceived and betrayed their people. Noel's heroes were men who had opposed Davis' policies or who had been slighted by pro-Davis historians. James Longstreet, for example, the whipping boy of many early Confederate histories, received extraordinary praise from Noel. "None enjoyed the esteem, confidence, and love of the people of the South more than he," gushed Noel of "Old Pete." Joseph E. Johnston, a leading critic of Davis, he decreed "one of the great men of the Confederacy." Among Davis' friends, only Braxton Bragg wins Noel's approval, although here Noel may have recognized a kindred spirit, for Bragg's dour, prickly personality seems a mirror image of his own caustic style. In retrospect, Noel believed southern women, if given the opportunity, would have displayed more "real backbone" in leading the Confederacy. "The 'lost cause,'" he decided, "would not have been so reported to the world around had it been for the women of the South instead of the men."[48]

Despite the disaster, Noel held high hopes for some phoenixlike resurgence of southern vitality after the war. Symbolically, he invested money in "New South" magazines, hoping they would sound the clarion call for a new, wiser southern army of politicians and investors. Instead, he witnessed the continuing and seemingly fixed poverty of the southern people. He blamed the unhappy circumstances on the tendency of new southern leaders to follow the same disastrous policies of

47. Theophilus Noel, *A Campaign from Santa Fe to the Mississippi; Being a History of the Old Sibley Brigade* (Shreveport, La., 1865), Introduction.
48. Noel, *Autobiography,* 40, 58, 78, 80, 306, 309–10, 279–80.

their antebellum and Confederate predecessors. Noel even felt sorry for southern blacks, whom he believed naturally indolent and innately inferior to whites. Black sharecroppers had fared better under slavery, he insisted, and the "negro question" had become the South's most difficult problem of postwar adjustment. Noel's most heartfelt sympathy, however, went to aging Confederate veterans. Feeble, tottering, hungry, sometimes maimed, their suffering diluted even his cynicism. Visits to soldiers' homes during his frequent trips to the South tested all of Noel's courage. These men, some of whom pathetically begged him to save them from "those worse than accursed prison pens," typified for Noel the "ruin, misery, desolation, destruction and all else but peace, comfort and happiness" wrought upon the South by the legacy of Jefferson Davis and his band of piranhas.[49]

Constance Harrison would have considered Noel an old curmudgeon, and, in truth, he cannot be considered a typical Confederate writer. Even most critics of Confederate policy and leadership retained a rosy picture of the Confederate era, particularly if they wrote a decade or more after events. A general rule of thumb is that the longer after the war people wrote their recollections, the less they recalled of the horrors of war and the inconveniences of antebellum life. The older they became, the more they dwelled on life's joys, the more they cloaked the Lost Cause in garlands and roses.[50]

Some, whether writing early or late, refused to say an unkind word about the Confederate cause. Allen C. Redwood may have been the most cheerful disciple ever to serve in gray. He joined the 55th Virginia Infantry at age seventeen and served in some of the heaviest fighting of the war. Thrice wounded and twice captured, Redwood was sitting in a northern prison camp when the war ended. Legend has it that he was the last prisoner of war to take the amnesty oath. Even then, Redwood never stopped being a Confederate. He became a popular illustrator for *Scribner's* and *Century* after the war and lived off and on in New York. Some of his illustrations, particularly the dozens he contributed to the "Battles and Leaders" series, are classics. His portrayal of Confederate defenders at the stone wall below Marye's Heights and his portrait of Stonewall Jackson on "Old Sorrel" as he galloped along the plank road hours before his death at Chancellorsville still stir Confederate pride. And no one surpassed Redwood at catching private moments in the

49. *Ibid.,* 78–81, 110–11, 322.
50. Freeman, *The South to Posterity,* 170–72.

Confederate ranks. Weary artillerymen lounging beside a campfire as they smoke their pipes and drink cups of "Confederate coffee" after a hard day of war; the occupant of a field ambulance, a bandage wound round his head, as he grips hands with his messmate in a touching farewell—these were Redwood's specialty and his claim to immortality.[51]

Equally enduring are Redwood's written tributes to the common soldier. Redwood's reminiscences of life in camp, on the march, and in the field represent some of the earliest "social histories" of the war. He recalled how soldiers relieved the "tedium" of campaigning by playing "seven up" with a "greasy, well-thumbed deck" of cards. When a sergeant called for a volunteer to fill the company's canteens under fire, a hand was dealt to determine who would receive the honor. The loser accepted his ill luck "without demur." Describing Jackson's troops as they liberated federal supplies at Manassas Junction, Redwood conveyed the foot soldier's joy when chance dealt such a lucky hand. "What a prize it was! Here were long warehouses full of stores; cars loaded with boxes of new clothing." Jackson's men could not possibly eat, drink, wear, or carry all they had seized, but as the day wore on, Redwood recalled, "an equitable distribution of our wealth was effected by barter, upon a crude and irregular tariff in which the rule of supply and demand was somewhat complicated by fluctuating estimates of the imminence of marching orders." Redwood also conveyed, again from experience, the chill of being captured by the enemy. He recalled how, once finding himself surrounded by Yankees, hasty efforts to reload his weapon had been "arrested by the dry click of several gunlocks" and the sight of half a dozen rifle barrels pointed more or less in the direction of his heart.[52]

Thomas L. Snead, Edwin DeLeon's fellow negotiator for Georgia bonds, wrote his military recollections on a loftier, more clinical plane. Snead had enjoyed a privileged position in the Confederacy's western

51. Melany Neilson, "Old Times Here: A Richmond Exhibition," *Civil War Times Illustrated,* XXII (December, 1983), 18–33; Stephen Davis, "A. C. Redwood and the Confederate Image," *Civil War Times Illustrated,* XXIII (June, 1984), 30–36; Allen C. Redwood, "The Horsemen in Gray," *Civil War Times Illustrated,* IX (June, 1970), 5; Johnson and Buel (eds.), *Battles and Leaders of the Civil War,* II, 530, 532, III, 80, 210, 250, 359, 423.

52. Stephen Davis, "'A Matter of Sensational Interest': The *Century* 'Battles and Leaders' Series," *Civil War History,* XXVII (1981), 338–39, 346–47; Redwood, "Horsemen in Gray," 5–8, 45–48, and "Jackson's 'Foot-Cavalry' at the Second Bull Run," in Johnson and Buel (eds.), *Battles and Leaders of the Civil War,* II, 533, 535–36.

theater, first as aide-de-camp to Governor Claiborne F. Jackson of Missouri, later as chief of staff to General Sterling Price. In 1864–1865, he served Missouri Confederates in the Second Confederate Congress. After the war, Snead wrote four recollections of his experiences. The most important one, *The Fight for Missouri,* describes the secession movement and early fighting (up to August, 1861) in Missouri. The other three pieces appeared in the "Battles and Leaders" series. Although Snead remained unswervingly loyal to the Confederate cause, his memoirs are notable for their impartial tone. Indeed, some old southern friends complained of his balanced views and accused him of having been "Yankee-ized" by his northern residence.[53]

Snead also prided himself on his meticulous research. He consulted official documents and old comrades whenever possible to garner facts and check his recollections. He took particular pride in his book on Missouri, believing it "the most *truthful* book" ever written on the subject. He felt obliged to write an honest account of the war in the West, he told a former comrade; he saw it as his "duty to Gen. Price, to Gov. Jackson, & to all of us who fought with them for our rights & our honor." He then gave his friend one of the most direct and eloquent justifications ever expressed by a Confederate for writing his memories of the war: "I am not willing that they & we shall go down in history as we are painted either by our foes—or by those who have heretofore written on our side. I don't want my children to feel that their father was either a fool or a traitor, or a marauder. I shall write the *truth.*"[54]

Poetry formed an important part of Confederate literature, both during and after the war. Douglas Southall Freeman estimated that southerners wrote thousands of poems glorifying the Lost Cause, and those were only the ones that had been unearthed. How many countless others remain buried in diaries and small-town newspapers is anyone's guess. Sidney Lanier, John W. Palmer, John R. Thompson, Irwin Russell, James M. Thompson, and Augustus J. Requier rate as the best-known Confederate poets to move north. Generally, however, poets did not dwell on the past so much as did novelists and memoir writers. Poets, perhaps,

53. Robert E. Miller, "Proud Confederate: Thomas Lowndes Snead of Missouri," *Missouri Historical Review,* LXXIX (1985), 167–91; Samuel B. Paul, *Memorial of Thomas Lowndes Snead* (New York, 1890), 1–14; Basil W. Duke to Thomas L. Snead, January 6, 1882, in Thomas L. Snead Papers, MOHS.

54. Thomas L. Snead to John F. Snyder, April 21, 1882, December 8, 1885, June 10, 1886, all in John F. Snyder Papers, MOHS.

are more concerned with expressing their feelings or describing events at the moment of composition. Lanier's most powerful poems deal with the political horrors of Reconstruction and the spiritual destructiveness of the war. He invariably wrote these poems before moving north or on return visits to the South. Palmer wrote prose and poetry for nearly forty years in the postwar North. His short stories and essays frequently use southern themes, but never again would he capture the Confederate spirit as he had in "Stonewall Jackson's Way," written during the Antietam campaign in 1862. John Thompson, like Lanier, dwelled more on the South's postwar problems than on its glorious past. Pathetic little Irwin Russell, alcoholic and nearly blind, wrote brilliant poems that captured the character of southern blacks, but he wrote his best lines before his brief northern residence and untimely death.[55]

Maurice Thompson is another story. Thompson resided for thirty-five years in Indiana and wrote nearly all of his finest work in a northern clime. Maurice, like John Thompson and Palmer, was more than a poet. Many of his half dozen novels and scores of his shorter prose pieces pay homage to the Old South and recreate events of the war in semi-autobiographical fashion. Yet Thompson's poetry, easily the most romantic southern poetry written in the North, won him his greatest fame. This transplanted Confederate veteran worshiped the South as

> Land where our Washington was born,
> When truth in hearts of gold was worn;
> Mother of Marion, Moultrie, Lee
> Widow of fallen chivalry!

Thompson was not uncritical of the South. He became disillusioned with the war in its closing phases, primarily because growing maturity (he was just seventeen when the war started) prompted second thoughts about slavery. Thus could he write without contradiction:

> I am a Southerner;
> I love the South: I dared for her
> To fight from Lookout to the sea,
> With her proud banners over me:
> But from my lips Thanksgiving broke,
> As God in battle thunder spoke,

55. Freeman, *The South to Posterity*, 13.

> And that Black Idol, breeding drouth
> And dearth of human sympathy
> Throughout the sweet and sensuous South,
> Was, with its chains and human yoke,
> Blown hellward from the cannon's mouth,
> While Freedom cheered behind the smoke.[56]

Augustus Requier could turn a good phrase, too. Born in South Carolina and resident in Alabama for a decade preceding the war, Requirer gave his principal postwar attention to law and politics, but he had been writing poetry since the 1840s, and he found it a difficult habit to break. Easily one of his best poems, even included in William Gilmore Simms's *War Poetry of the South,* is his reply to Abram J. Ryan's "The Conquered Banner." Father Ryan's immensely popular poem, thought Requirer, betrayed a defeatist attitude ("Let it droop there, furled forever,—/For its people's hopes have fled"). His reply, "Ashes of Glory," denied that the Confederate war flag or the Confederate cause would ever be conquered. Even with its armies surrendered, the cause maintained a glory and purity comparable to that achieved by Nelson at Trafalgar and Arthur at Camlann. The Confederate banner conquered? Never!

> It was outnumbered—not outdone;
> And they shall shuddering tell,
> Who struck the blow, its latest gun
> Flashed ruin as it fell.
> . . . .
> Sleep! in thine own historic night—
> And be thy blazoned scroll,
> A warrior's Banner takes it flight,
> To greet the warrior's soul![57]

Mary Tucker was one of the earliest Confederate poets to find sanctuary in the North. As Miss Mary Perine, born at Catawla, Alabama, she had been educated at a New York boarding school during the 1850s. She married John M. Tucker of Milledgeville, Georgia, shortly before the war. Both her husband and her father lost their property after the

56. Otis B. Wheeler, *The Literary Career of Maurice Thompson* (Baton Rouge, 1965), 14–15, 121–26; William Malone Baskervill, "Maurice Thompson," in Baskervill (ed.), *Southern Writers,* I, 102–103.

57. James Grant Wilson and John Fiske (eds.), *Appleton's Cyclopedia of American Biography* (6 vols.; New York, 1891–93), V, 223; New York *Daily News,* December 11, 1865, pp. 2, 4.

war. Perhaps because of the strain of war and financial crisis, her marriage ended in divorce. Mary moved north, seeking a publisher for her poetry and work as a journalist, in 1866. Drifting to New York, she experienced poverty and loneliness, but she managed, by 1867, to publish her first volume of poetry. A second volume of poems and a novel followed the next year, and soon Mary became a regular contributor to several New York newspapers. In 1871, she married James H. Lambert, editor of the Philadelphia *Press,* and moved to the Quaker City.[58]

Mary dedicated her first published volume, *Poems,* to Georgia's wartime governor, Charles J. Jenkins. Its verses, written during and after the war, explore many subjects—love, death, divorce, nature—but they express "southern" sentiments, too. Typical is "Christmas, South, 1865," describing Mary's last Christmas in the South. She weaves together several themes: the South's desolation, love between mother and child, the South's will to survive, and the loyalty of old family slaves. Christmas begins as a joyless holiday. The children leap from their beds laughing and singing, trembling in anticipation of what Santa Claus has left in their stockings. They find, instead, their mother in tears, for she has little but love to give them on this somber Christmas:

"Sissie," said the bravest rebel, "did Santa have his cotton burned?"
"Hush, hush, Buddie; don't say nothing; just see how poor mamma cries."

The repentant boy rushes to hug his mother:

"I'm so sorry, mother darling: when I'm grown you shan't be poor;
I'll write for the Yankee papers, that will make us rich once more."

Enter two freedmen, asking, " 'Why, what fur you white folks weep?' "

"All dis time you give us Christmas; now we going to give to you:
Here, old Missus, here, Miss Annie—children, here's your Christmas, too!"
In black bosoms true love lingers, deeply by our kindness riven,
And the tender tie that binds us, can be severed save by heaven.[59]

Clearly, Confederate carpetbaggers produced a large volume of literature. Yet one is hard-pressed to find any single theme in this outpouring of memoirs. The fictional writers closely resemble a group of 371 Civil War novelists analyzed in a literary study of the mid-1950s, which found that the novelists with personal recollections of the war invariably based

58. Wilson and Fiske (eds.), *Appleton's Cyclopedia of American Biography,* VI, 173–74.
59. Mary E. Tucker, "Christmas, South, 1865," in *Poems* (New York, 1867), 205–207.

their work on their wartime experiences. The study found three peak eras of publication: (1) the first two years after the war; (2) the early 1890s, with a resurgence beginning in the mid-1880s; and (3) the first decade of the twentieth century—the most popular period—with the peak year being 1903. These novelists used ten broad themes: sentimental reactions to the war; the Negro; persecuted Unionists; sectional reconciliation, with particular emphasis on intersectional marriages; romanticized adventures; justification of the southern cause; divided kinsmen or neighbors; Copperheads; nonplantation southern life; and combat. The author concluded that more southern writers came from the Upper South than from the Lower South.[60]

Most Confederate fiction writers in the North, seven of whom appear in the study from the 1950s, fit the generalized picture presented there. They published most of their work from the mid-1880s to about 1905, when public demand produced a torrent of historical romances "from every half-trained pen in the land." No Confederate carpetbagger published fiction in the first few years after the war, but several short-story writers swung into action before the 1860s had ended, and by the 1870s, a slack period for longer works, George Eggleston, Allen Redwood, Sherwood Bonner, Constance Harrison, and many others were hard at work writing short stories. Confederates in the North ignored some of the ten themes listed above. None wanted to write about persecuted Unionists, Copperheads, or nonplantation southern life. Only Irwin Russell and Sherwood Bonner treated black southerners realistically, and no one dealt convincingly with slavery as a cause of the war. Nine of fifteen writers came from the Upper South (including Virginia, North Carolina, Missouri, Tennessee, Maryland, and Kentucky), and seven of those people hailed from Virginia or Maryland. If one adds poets to this group, however, only nine of nineteen hailed from the Upper South.[61]

The writers of nonfiction published the bulk of their work after 1885, when a period of blossoming sectional reconciliation inspired exhaustive treatment of the war years. Thirty-three of fifty writers discuss military events to some extent. Twelve writers harken back to antebellum days, thirteen touch on postwar experiences in the North, and

60. Robert A. Lively, *Fiction Fights the Civil War: An Unfinished Chapter in the Literary History of the American People* (Chapel Hill, 1957), 21–23, 42–64. Sheldon Van Auken, "The Southern Historical Novel in the Early Twentieth Century," *Journal of Southern History,* XIV (1948), 157–91, reaches similar conclusions.

61. Lively, *Fiction Fights the Civil War,* 23, n. 9.

eight dwell on civilian aspects of the war. Thirty writers had ties to the Upper South; twenty-two of them came from Virginia or Maryland. Many more writers than one might expect criticized some feature of the Confederate effort, which fictional writers rarely did. A fair number of writers, including Noel, Pollard, and Smith, laid defeat at the door of Jefferson Davis, and most people had unkind words for at least one Confederate general or leader (sometimes a personal rival). They did not try to mask defeat behind shortages of supplies, men, or money, although they recognized these as legitimate factors. Nor did they often seek defeat in the guise of divine intervention, as did far too many writers who remained in the South.

Another characteristic of Confederate writing observed by some scholars is the shift in emphasis over time from vindication of southern life and the Lost Cause to a glorification of the war and the Confederate veteran. The change is usually identified as occurring in the early to mid-1880s. It is evident in both the fiction and nonfiction of Confederate carpetbaggers. Certainly works written after 1890 wrap a glamorous facade around the war and obscure the suffering and poignancy of many earlier writings.[62]

Walt Whitman once claimed that "the real war will never get in the books." He meant that no writer, whether of fiction or nonfiction, would ever be able to convey the brutality or drama of the war as experienced by the people who lived through it. He was substantially correct, not only about his own generation of writers but about all future generations. The war generation, too intimately and emotionally involved in the contest, lacked the perspective necessary to treat events dispassionately. Moreover, "spiritual censorship" prohibited the war generation from publicly discussing unpleasant aspects of the war— disease, drunkenness, crime, lice, and obscenity—necessarily attendant to all armed conflict. Later generations, however, lacked the intimacy and passion necessary to give the war the "epic treatment" it deserved. This is not to say that the war has not worked a profound influence on American literature. Writers as diverse as Robert Penn Warren and Margaret Mitchell, William Faulkner and H. L. Mencken, Michael Shaara and Ellen Glasgow, not to forget scores of historians, have grappled with

---

62. Freeman, *The South to Posterity,* 172; Susan Speare Durant, "The Gently Furled Banner: The Development of the Myth of the Lost Cause, 1865–1900" (Ph.D. dissertation, University of North Carolina at Chapel Hill, 1972); Foster, *Ghosts of the Confederacy,* 87–95.

the war—its causes, meaning, and effects. Probably no single event in American history has produced so many tons of printed pages, so many gallons of printer's ink, so many catalog entries at local libraries. Yet none of the writers who produced these millions of pages has been completely satisfying or convincing. Instead, writers of all generations, of all literary classifications, have draped the war in myths and symbols. They have used the war for their own purposes, frequently with little concern for the men and women who fought the war or their real reasons for committing fratricide.[63]

Logically, believes one scholar, the "ideal author" of the unwritten Civil War masterpiece, be it fictional or not, should have been a Confederate male loyal to the cause but not so parochial as to accept unquestioningly all southern racial and political assumptions. He should have been an "insider" familiar with both Confederate military and political operations. He should have been a humorist and an ironist, a "student of behavior," who understood that the Confederacy really consisted of eleven separate countries, each with its own heroes, traditions, and history. Finally, he should have possessed the grace, wit, and skill to transfer his observations and emotions to the printed page in a language that would capture the rage of war from both sides and, from the Confederate side, record with "Chekhovian nostalgia the passing of a way of life."[64]

Had such a man lived, he probably would have been a Confederate carpetbagger, one of the people best able to detach themselves from the Confederacy and render the balanced yet impassioned story required. Alas, the writings of Confederate carpetbaggers differed little from those of Confederates who remained in the South. Both sets wrote defensively. Both sets eulogized the Lost Cause and its heroes. Although few southerners in the North wrote their reminiscences for at least a decade after Appomattox, they never relinquished entirely the partisanship they had felt during the war. None seemed to understand the meaning of the war. Few depicted graphic battlefield scenes. All were, to a certain extent, self-serving, blind, biased, or myopic in their views. This summation is not intended as an indictment. It would be exceedingly unfair to single out Confederate carpetbaggers for failing where no one else succeeded. It is intended only to point out their tendency to

63. Daniel Aaron, *The Unwritten War: American Writers and the Civil War* (New York, 1973), xiv–xix.
64. *Ibid.*, 227–28.

produce a literature not strikingly different from the work of other southern writers in their generation.

One of the most popular characters of postwar southern fiction is Colonel George Fairfax Carter of Carter Hall, Cartersville, Virginia, a creation of F. Hopkinson Smith. Colonel Carter is about fifty years old, tall, slightly bald, with twinkling eyes, goatee and drooping mustaches, and iron-gray hair. Colonel Carter goes north after the war to raise money for a railroad scheme. He knows nothing about railroads and very little about banks and commerce. He does know a good deal about honor and the code of the gentleman. For Colonel Carter is a vestige of the Old South. He is chivalrous, charming, generous, tender, "of good birth, fair education, and limited knowledge of the world and of men, proud of his ancestry, proud of his State, and proud of himself; believing in states' rights, slavery, and the Confederacy." The "reconstruction" of any such rebel must prove hopeless. Yet Colonel Carter symbolized "something irresistible" for hundreds of thousands of Americans in 1891, when he came to life. He represented a South that, if still defiant, bared the teeth of an old, worn lion that yawned more often than it roared. Colonel Carter represented a South that had slipped into a romantic identity seldom wholly true but accepted increasingly by both northerners and southerners as a genuine representation of antebellum southern life. His acceptance in the North as the new southern stereotype, a replacement for the ferocious fire-eaters and malevolent slaveowners of earlier days, permitted a much ballyhooed "sectional reconciliation" in the last two decades of the nineteenth century. Confederate carpetbaggers had something to do with that reconciliation.[65]

65. F. Hopkinson Smith, *Colonel Carter of Cartersville* (Boston, 1891), 10; Weaver, *Southern Tradition at Bay*, 331–33.

8

The Rocky Road to Reunion

As Burton and Constance Harrison assumed north-
ern identities and settled into northern ways, a vague uneasiness, an
uncertainty, haunted them. The Harrisons presumed to know something about the war. They had lived at the very heart of Confederate
political, military, and social life. Yet as the twentieth century slipped up
on them, they occasionally felt as though the war they thought had
ended in 1865 was still being fought. A spirit of distrust, even hatred,
between North and South persisted. The Harrisons had expected passions to remain high for awhile, perhaps even a few years, but to hear the
epithet "Rebel" and to see the bloody shirt waving high atop Republican
flagpoles thirty, even forty, years after the war saddened them. True,
many northerners and southerners, for a variety of honorable and dis-
honorable reasons, soon embraced national unity; but to determine
precisely when and to what extent the majority of Americans adopted
this generous spirit could befuddle the most perceptive observer.

Some people blamed continuing sectional bitterness on political rhetoric and the vehemence of a minority. Had it not been in the interest of
politicians and their journalist allies to keep war fires burning, complained observers, "the people" of North and South would have ended
the dispute swiftly and so avoided the demoralizing, self-destructive
rigors of prolonged fraternal strife. "I hardly know what to think about
public affairs," admitted a strong Unionist from Philadelphia in the
summer of 1866. "They look alarming enough if one judges by what the
papers say." The Philadelphian liked to think that both northerners and
southerners were "too prosperous & anxious for peace & quiet" to
allow "demagogues" to direct the national will. "But who can tell?" he

sighed. "It is the aggressive & violent few, not the passive many, that causes trouble."[1]

Other observers, probably more realistically, knew that it took more than rhetoric to create either division or sectional reconciliation. Reconciliation first became a serious national political theme in the election of 1872. Horace Greeley, candidate of the renegade Liberal Republican party, tried to use the issue as a means of solidifying northern and southern opposition to President Ulysses S. Grant. He failed. "To talk of reconciliation through the election of a particular man, without reference to the state of public sentiment," wrote Greeley foe Edwin L. Godkin in his analysis of the election, "is absurd." Reunion, he explained, required "mutual determination" to forget the past. Without such agreement between North and South, no single person, no political party, could accomplish the deed. Thus even when southerners completely recaptured political control of the South in the late 1870s, the nation had achieved only a point of departure for a more comprehensive restoration of sectional goodwill. The people, being wise and forgiving, had said let there be peace; but the people are inconsistent, not to say fickle. Whatever progress reconciliation made after 1877, the nation witnessed occasional rancorous, sometimes bitter, sectional disputes well into the new century.[2]

Small wonder the Harrisons remained puzzled. They lived in confusing times. Quickly announcing himself "reconstructed" and "harmonized," Burton Harrison saw no reason why he should not be accepted by his northern neighbors. The war, he sincerely believed, had reunited the country, making it "much more powerful, far more imposing than ever before." "I know," Burton prophesized more in hope than certainty, "that individuals among Southern men have a much wider field for energy and influence than they had before or than they could have had in a Southern Confederacy. . . . I know that in a very few years the Southern people as a community will have a very loud voice in the conduct of this 'huge Democracy.'" If Harrison learned anything from the fall of the Confederacy—and he learned much—it was the need for southerners to act nationally. "And whereas, Southern men were in old times necessarily partizans of the interests of a Section," he explained further,

1. Sidney G. Fisher to Elizabeth Fisher, August 8, 1866, in Sidney George Fisher Collection, HSP.

2. [E. L. Godkin], "Lessons of the Campaign," *Nation*, XV, October 17, 1872, p. 244.

"they can now, with all manhood and righteousness, be spokesmen for the whole country." Burton could even tease a northern friend soon after the war about the tendency of Yankees to treat July 4 as "their" holiday. "I am altogether too well 'reconstructed,' too melodiously 'harmonized,'" he explained with cheek betraying only a slight bulge from the pressure of his tongue, "to agree with the sentiments of your Independence Day harangue."[3]

No one was more ready for peace than Harrison, but his good intentions did not spare him and his family occasional abuse. The Harrisons' eldest child, Fairfax, engaged in a number of schoolboy fistfights in defense of southern honor. Just a few weeks into a new school term, Fairfax entered the lists four times, suffered two "bluddy noses," and inflicted one bloody nose and a black eye. Fairfax did not specify the cause of all these encounters, but judging from other episodes in his youth, unflattering remarks about "rebels" may have stirred his southern passion. At play, when impersonating heroic warriors of the past, Fairfax frequently chose the part of Titus Labienus, the Roman general who betrayed Julius Caesar. It was an interesting choice for a young Confederate and one that brought double-edged taunts of "traitor" from his playmates.[4]

As late as 1875, Burton confessed that he still had a hard time helping fellow southerners find jobs in the city. "Of course I shall gladly do whatever I can to advance Young's interests," he told his old friend James Chesnut of South Carolina, "'tho the mere fact that he is known to be a Southerner may be an obstacle to me." At the time, Burton worked as private secretary to Mayor William H. Wickham, and Chesnut's request for assistance evidently involved a patronage post in city government. This led Burton to complain about northern misconceptions, nay, ignorance, of the full evil of carpetbagger rule in the South. Northerners, he said, either did not care or did not appreciate how Republican control of states such as South Carolina virtually drove ambitious young southerners out of the South. "I am frequently met in my efforts here for old friends," Burton explained to Chesnut, "with the

3. Burton N. Harrison to Constance Cary, July 13, 1866, in Burton Norvell Harrison Family Papers, LC; Fairfax Harrison (ed.), *Aris Sonis Focisque: Being a Memoir of an American Family, the Harrisons of Skimino* (New York, 1910), 207–208.
4. Fairfax Harrison to Constance Harrison, October 23, 1878, to Frank F. Abbott, November 13, 1917, both in Francis Burton Harrison (ed.), *A Selection of the Letters of Fairfax Harrison* (Charlottesville, 1944), 6, 72.

reminder that no immigrants (except those from Erin!) are necessary when it comes to questions of public moneys."[5]

The burden of Confederate identity weighed particularly heavy on Burton at this juncture in his career. Just a fortnight earlier, he had been shocked to learn that the admissions committee of the Century Club had rejected his nomination to membership. The club, founded in 1847 for "gentlemen engaged in or interested in letters or the fine arts," included many of Burton's friends, among them William H. Aspinwell, Joseph H. Choate, John J. Cisco, William M. Evarts, Manton Marble, Charles O'Conor, Frederick Law Olmsted, Augustus Schell, Samuel J. Tilden, and William C. Whitney, but no former Confederates. The committee on admissions, not populated by prosouthern friends, wanted to keep it that way. It based its rejection not just on Burton's Confederate past but, more particularly, on his close association with Jefferson Davis.[6]

Some of Burton's friends sensed that the committee's action smacked of partisan politics, which frequently lurked in the background of sectional divisions. Burton's recent appointment as Mayor Wickham's private secretary galled some people, as did Wickham's appointment of former Union general Fitz-John Porter as commissioner of public works. Many northerners considered Porter a coward and traitor because of his actions at Second Manassas. Wickham's appointment of Harrison and the general to plum patronage posts (a five-thousand-dollar annual salary for Burton) raised the ire of important Century Club members against the "swallow-tale," "silk-stocking" pedigree of Wickham's friends. The new mayor seemed to be controlled by the upstart Manhattan Club, the Democrats' answer to the Republicans' Union Club, and a clique that already included several former Confederates.[7]

Harrison would not be admitted to the Century Club until 1891, and yet his earlier rejection remained something of an abberration in the Harrisons' generally kind treatment by the community. Thinking back on those early, unpredictable years in Yankeedom, Constance recalled, "We now found ourselves in a circle of acquaintances, alien in political

5. Burton N. Harrison to James Chesnut, April 2, 1875, in Williams-Chesnut-Manning Family Papers, SCL.

6. Francis Gerry Fairfield, *The Clubs of New York: With an Account of the Origins, Progress, Present Condition and Membership of the Leading Clubs* (New York, 1873), 31–54, 139–66; New York *Times*, January 1, 1875, p. 8.

7. Allan Nevins and Milton Halsey Thomas (eds.), *The Diary of George Templeton Strong* (4 vols.; New York, 1952), IV, 553–54, entry of March 19, 1875; Fairfield, *Clubs of New York,* 161–66.

creed, with a few exceptions among the Southerners already established in New York, but most kind and considerate always, and every year the number grew and firmer friendships were cemented." No one makes firm friendships without effort. Burton and Constance owed their popularity not to chance or any universal spirit of forgiveness in the North but to their own straightforward, candid desire to accept the brute facts of history.[8]

The past is now the past, all is now the future; Burton's words remained their credo. They taught their sons the same lesson. "Certainly they scrupulously avoided any tinge to their conversation which might prejudice us children," remembered Francis Harrison. "We were meant to share as fully as any member of the community in the opportunities of the day." Francis recalled the family's excitement during the presidential campaign of 1884. "My father," he revealed, "with tears streaming down his face, marched in a pre-election parade of ten thousand business and professional men of both parties." Grover Cleveland, who won the election, became the first Democrat in a quarter century to reside in the White House. Burton and many others saw his election as the end of the war, the end of partisan feeling. They were wrong. It was another decade, for example, before Congress lifted political sanctions against all former Confederate officers, including Burton's brother-in-law Clarence Cary. Disappointed but not discouraged, the Harrisons continued working hard to demolish northern prejudices. They succeeded to a remarkable degree. They became Confederate ambassadors of goodwill and proved to some very dubious northerners that Confederates could be gracious, intelligent, and charming.[9]

George Templeton Strong, New York lawyer and diarist, referred to southerners as traitors, ruffians, and bullies in the summer of 1865. "Parts of Secessia may have to pass through a period of absolute anarchy and barbarism," predicted Strong, "longer or shorter, before they become Christianized and civilized." Two years later, in 1867, as the Reconstruction Acts began knocking the South into a satisfactory image of northern decency and respectability, Strong still railed against "arrogant" southerners, filled with "inveterate obstinacy of pride and bad temper," who opposed northern political will. A year later, he vented his spleen against southern clergymen touring the North asking alms for

8. Mrs. Burton Harrison, *Recollections Grave and Gay* (New York, 1911), 284.
9. Francis B. Harrison, "About It and About" (Typescript in Francis Burton Harrison Papers, UV), 25, 33.

southern famine relief. The clergymen, Strong decided, represented "one of the class that ministered to the blind fury of the people in 1860 and 1861, and did more than any other class except the politicians and the women to bring on the most causeless of civil wars." Strong wondered that such men had "the cheek to come begging of Philadelphia and New York." Confederates in New York would do well to stay out of Strong's way.[10]

Soon, however, Strong found it impossible to avoid all the "paroled pauper rebel colonels and captains" surging through New York streets. Upon closer inspection, these mendicant rebels did not look so exotic or dangerous as he had imagined. Clarence Cary was one of the first Confederates Strong met. The lawyer inspected Cary as skeptically as he would banknotes from a known counterfeiter. Cary, after all, was descended from "the high and mighty F.F.V. Fairfaxes." Yet Strong soon learned, after an evening of conversation with Clarence, that, despite his handicaps of birth and breeding, this particular Confederate was "quiet, refined, and gentlemanlike!"—everything a Confederate ought not to be. A few months later, having been introduced to Clarence's sister and brother-in-law, Strong approached the gates of conversion. He did not much care for Burton's Chief, "that pagan full of pride," but Burton seemed a different sort, more like his brother-in-law. Constance, of course, bewitched him. How could she fail? Strong saw not a hardened traitor but a "nice looking blonde, cultivated, pleasant mannered, and with the most honest, earnest feeling for the best music." Strong was particular about music. He found Richard Wagner incomprehensible, and even less esoteric "moderns" disturbed his eighteenth-century sense of order. Imagine his delight to learn that Constance spurned Verdi and adored Haydn. Such a woman, even though southern, Strong admitted, "enslaves me at once." Besides, Constance came well recommended, the sister of his "nice young friend," Clarence.[11]

Over the next few years, Strong and the Harrisons crossed paths frequently and always congenially. Constance sang with Strong in the Church Music Association choir, and the duly impressed New Yorker noted that she attended its rehearsals "with laudable punctuality." Strong and the Harrisons mixed socially, and the urbane New Yorker included the Harrison household on his New Year's Day progress. He

10. Nevins and Thomas (eds.), *Diary of George Templeton Strong,* IV, 8, 158, 228–29, entries of June 13, 1865, October 30, 1867, October 25, 1868.

11. *Ibid.,* IV, 250, 265, entries of August 1, December 20, 1869.

even deigned to record in his diary the birth of the Harrisons' first child, with hopes that the tiny rebel might "thrive and prosper." When Burton encountered trouble with his Century Club nomination, Strong supported him. When he had only a few months left to live, Strong took a considerably kindlier view of ruffians such as Harrison. Chagrined over Burton's trouble with the Century Club, Strong reasoned: "But Harrison merely went with his people, wrongly enough, of course. He has lived here as a loyal and reconstructed citizen for ten years and, I believe, voted and worked for Grant in 1872." In the last remark about the war, Confederates, or the South in his famous diary, Strong wrote of Burton's pending nomination, "Is the day of forgiveness never to come?"[12]

The Harrisons were not the only Confederate carpetbaggers to inspire kindly feelings among their former foes. Perhaps the most lasting legacy of former Confederates in the North is their contribution to sectional reconciliation. They did not accomplish the feat alone; they may not even have been the most important contributors to reunion; but they were among the earliest. Cynics might smirk and say they had to be first. Confederates in the North found themselves in a ticklish spot, rather like the Six Hundred at Balaklava, and most of them plunged into the Valley of Death several years prematurely. The dove of peace remained an endangered species through the 1860s and 1870s. Reunion did not gain the ascendancy until the 1880s and 1890s, and even then there was much vacillation and backsliding. Some northerners were in no mood to be conciliatory in 1865 or even in 1895. Confederate carpetbaggers, then, whatever the motives, deserve some credit for marching in the reconciliation vanguard.

Not many Confederate carpetbaggers came north intending to inspire national unity. They did not see themselves as revivalist preachers destined to deliver inspirational messages of national goodwill to mass audiences of cantankerous Yankees. Oratory would play an important part in healing sectional wounds, but most of the southern orators—such men as Henry Watterson, Henry W. Grady, John B. Gordon, and Lucius Q. C. Lamar—made their forays into the North while residing in the South. Among Confederates resident in the North, only Roger A. Pryor earned a national reputation as a reconciliation orator. Most Confederate carpetbaggers operated as lonely friars, roaming the countryside, settling in cities, towns, and villages, scattering their seeds of

12. *Ibid.*, IV, 265, 339, 547, 553–54, entries of December 20, 1869, January 3, 1871, January 11, March 19, 1875.

peace. They helped to heal the nation's sectional wounds in the slowest, most laborious manner possible: through individual ministerings and personal friendships. They taught northerners with whom they lived and worked to distinguish between the South as a region and southerners as people. The South had stood as a threat to the republic. With the end of the war, northerners demanded a "New South" and a "New South creed" to reassure themselves that the sinful South—tainted by slavery, secession, and war—had been converted to "American" ways. But as more northerners met and lived alongside southerners, especially former Confederates, they conceived of sectional ills in personal terms. The South might be a tainted land, but southerners, as individuals, were usually worthy of forgiveness.[13]

Northerners settling in the South faced a similar situation. Current historical wisdom tells us that before passage of the Reconstruction Acts and congressional control of southern government in the spring of 1867, Yankees and rebels in the South did their best to live in harmony. Southerners who recognized the need to attract northern capital and labor tried to coexist with Yankees, so long as the newcomers did not claim victory in the war as justification for sneering at southerners or their Lost Cause. Many northerners moved south with no other intention than to live peacefully with their old enemies. Unfortunately, hard economic times, aggravated by a succession of crop failures in 1866–1867, destroyed much of the initial goodwill. The carpetbaggers' takeover of southern politics demolished most of what remained. Many economic and political adventurers returned north, but well-intentioned folk who stayed learned how to disarm prejudiced minds through personal friendships and soft words. Reporting the dedication of a Confederate memorial in Georgia, the Atlanta *Constitution* commented on the large number of northerners in attendance. This "gratifying and cheering" event convinced the reporter that "not quite all is dark, that not quite all is selfish and vindictive in the human heart." Many southerners welcomed demonstrations of friendliness by Yankees in their midst. One southerner cheered the "cordiality" of northern visitors in 1869 as

13. Huber Winton Ellingsworth, "Southern Reconciliation Orators in the North, 1868–1899" (Ph.D. dissertation, Florida State University, 1955), 279–81; Waldo W. Braden, "Repining over an Irrevocable Past: The Ceremonial Orator in a Defeated Society, 1865–1900," W. Stuart Towns, "Ceremonial Orators and National Reconciliation," and Howard Dorgan, "Rhetoric of the United Confederate Veterans: A Lost Cause Mythology in the Making," all in Waldo W. Braden (ed.), *Oratory in the New South* (Baton Rouge, 1979), 8–37, 117–42, 143–73.

a sign of lessening northern fanaticism. "The constant visitations of thoughtful persons to our cities and State," he observed, "is visibly removing the hard crust of prejudice, and acting on both sides, the generous part of peace-makers."[14]

Some northerners who remained at home never required conversion either. "The feelings of the people, with some exceptions, were most cordial and friendly towards us," observed a South Carolinian recently returned from a trip through the Northeast, "and the bonds of Union were being rapidly woven into an indestructible woof." "Barring the fact that there is no chance of getting employment for a Southerner or Rebel in New York," reported a Marylander, "there is little else left to show that a war existed for four years. It is already a thing of the past, and these people, whose impressions last but a day, have already forgotten it." Only the "newspaper scribblers and pot house politicians," he insisted, preached a gospel of revenge. "Gen. [Joseph B.] Kershaw says much sympathy was expressed in Boston as well as New York for the South," recorded a North Carolina woman, "which many considered has been very hardly dealt with."[15]

As impressive and hopeful as these remarks seem, judging prevailing northern sentiment at any moment, particularly in the first few years after the war, proves difficult. Abraham Lincoln's assassination and the outbreak of southern racial conflict in the summer of 1866, for example, made the sincerity of southern professions of peace seem questionable. Fluctuating northern attitudes, in turn, confused southerners. One Georgian, newly arrived in New York in the summer of 1865, encountered "entire respect and polite consideration." A southerner, he insisted, could move about the city "with even more ease than in his own subjugated country." By November, the situation had changed. The Georgian felt trapped in a "cold selfish . . . bad and corrupt world." Former northern acquaintances seemed to hold him personally respon-

14. Lawrence N. Powell, *New Masters: Northern Planters During the Civil War and Reconstruction* (New Haven, 1980), 56–57, 64–69, 144–45, 149–50; Atlanta *Constitution*, May 5, 1872, p. 1; "The North in the South," *XIX Century*, I (June, 1869), 30–31.

15. Paul H. Buck, *The Road to Reunion, 1865–1900* (Boston, 1937), 115–16; John Hammond Moore (ed.), *The Juhl Letters to the Charleston Courier: A View of the South, 1865–1871* (Athens, Ga., 1974), 40, letter of September 4, 1865; Bayly Ellen Marks and Mark Norton Schatz (eds.), *Between North and South: A Maryland Journalist Views the Civil War, The Narrative of William Wilkins Glenn, 1861–1869* (Rutherford, N.J., 1976), 215, entry of May 16, 1865; John F. Marszalek (ed.), *The Diary of Miss Emma Holmes, 1861–1866* (Baton Rouge, 1979), 470, entry of August 25, 1865.

sible for Andersonville and the death of Lincoln. New York newspapers told him about "what horrid creatures" lived in the South. "Do they live near you, my darling," the Georgian factitiously asked his sweetheart, trying to keep up his spirits. "You have never mentioned them in your letters—are they like cows, or horses? How odd they must be indeed!"[16]

The optimism of some hopeful new arrivals soured when they learned of the experiences of friends and relatives who had preceded them, especially the trials of southerners who had been abused by Yankees during the war. "Uncle Jim has suffered so terribly on account of the South," reported a Virginian in New York, "that his hatred and abhorrence of Yankees amounts to a monomania. I can not in a letter convey to you the remotest idea of the fierce condition of his emotions." "The half of Sister's troubles with Yankees during the war was not told us," a Texan discovered upon arriving at the North. "There was none of the reserve & restraint of sentiment which Pa & all of us had supposed." His sister had lost all of her earlier admiration for Yankees. "She has had a bitter time here with them I tell you, & her dislike of and contempt for them is stronger and deeper than ours in Texas." She remained in the North only because of her husband's business interests. The brother, reacting to her attitude, decided the North would not suit him.[17]

Tension hung heavily, almost visibly, in the northern air. Confederate general Samuel G. French, visiting Philadelphia shortly after the war, sensed that northern residents were "distrustful of each other, as though under surveillance." Old friends invited him to their houses only after dark, or they arranged to meet in out-of-the-way places. His friends feared "their loyalty being challenged if seen with a so-called 'Rebel.'" Northerners also questioned the motives of southerners who seemed too eager to take the loyalty oath. They refused to believe that former rebels could so quickly cleanse their foul minds and purify their treacherous hearts. They could not understand, complained a Virginian, "how sharp was our need to have formalities of submission over and done with."[18]

As late as 1873, a young southern woman attending school in Phila-

16. Elizabeth Fisher to Sidney G. Fisher, July 23, 1865, in Fisher Collection; John F. King to Lin Caperton, July 17, November 17, 21, 1865, all in Thomas Butler King Papers, SHC.

17. L. Minor Blackford, *Mine Eyes Have Seen the Glory: The Story of a Virginia Lady, Mary Berkeley Minor Blackford, 1802–1896* (Cambridge, Mass., 1954), 241; Gideon J. Buck to Mollie Buck, April 29, 1868, in William C. Buck Family Letters, LSU.

18. Samuel G. French, *Two Wars: an Autobiography of General Samuel G. French* (Nashville, 1901), 324–35; Ellingsworth, "Southern Reconciliation Orators," 221–25, 228–30, 233–37; Myrta Lockett Avary, *Dixie After the War* (Boston, 1937), 128–29.

delphia found a yawning gap separating her from northern students. She expressed shock at the frivolity of her northern classmates. Not having experienced personally the chaos and destruction of war, they seemed to have no conception of privation or suffering; they had "no idea of the earnestness of life." Sometimes the young woman blamed herself for not trying harder to cultivate northern friendships, for not striving "to influence them for good." She admitted that many northerners had "admirable qualities"; yet she could not bring herself to be openly cordial. She sensed a "barrier" between herself and her Yankee class-mates, created by "Northern and Southern feeling." A year after her arrival, she lived on "pleasant terms" with most of the students but still felt uneasy. She was "not at all sure" that she had been "right" in her cordiality.[19]

Other southerners, like the young woman in Philadelphia, failed to take full advantage of opportunities to make northern friends. It is hard to say why. Most likely, they were too quick to find in northern society the insult and arrogance they expected to find, even if they had to look very hard for it. They went north with a mingled sense of shame and injured pride. They were extremely defensive, ready to bristle at the slightest hint of disrespect. Sometimes these martyrs made individual exceptions to their general rule, but they never relaxed their guard. Euphania Ellis, a charming woman but deficient in sporting blood, hated Chicago and its inhabitants more passionately with every passing day. "While individual exceptions have multiplied," reported her hus-band, "her feelings towards the aggregate are those of a Modoc." A Missourian in Iowa admitted meeting some "noble and big hearted men," but they had little influence on "public sentiment." "Even a stronger mental organization than mine," he complained, "would be contaminated and weakened by the ignorance and fanaticism both po-litical and religious which prevail here."[20]

Even businessmen, generally among the earliest advocates of reunion, sometimes consented to wear happy faces only under duress. Some Alabama and Georgia merchants visiting New York seemed mildly shocked at the kindness they encountered, even feeling a little disap-pointed "at not finding the Yankees all eager to drink their blood for

19. Minnie Adger to Jane Smyth, December 26, 1872, January 1, June 1, 1873, all in Adger-Smyth-Flynn Family Papers, SCL.
20. Thomas H. Ellis to George W. Munford, July 4, 1873, in Munford-Ellis Family Papers, DU; S. Christy to John F. Snyder, October 14, 1866, February 3, 1867, both in John F. Snyder Papers, IHL.

desert after dinner." Instead of following the lead of these friendly acquaintances, they complained about the few Yankees who still considered them rebels. They resented friendly Yankees. They did not trust them, or, if trusting them, they loathed their condescension. As one observer commented incisively, the Confederates' "utter impotence" served "to increase their malice." A young Mississippian staying with friends near Boston hoped to return home as soon as possible. The northerners he met were "kind and attentive," but living in the heart of abolitionist territory made him nervous. "I cannot rest easy in Massachusetts," he confessed; "I cannot stand the general pressure."[21]

Intersectional marriages became a much-touted symbol of reconciliation, but evidence of their contributions to peace is mixed. There must have been something in the air, and it was not tension. Southern girls seemed to drop like flies at the feet of dashing federal officers stationed in the South, and southerners in the North, both male and female, thought it great sport to flirt with Yankees. So long as palpitations remained unconsummated, no harm was done; but calamity often befell families when fluttering eyelashes and heavy sighs led to courtship and marriage. Seventy-two percent (113 persons) of the core group who married after moving north married northerners, and a few people had married northerners before moving north. These intersectional marriages could throw friends and relatives across the South into convulsions. "I cannot for the life of me sit down to write her a letter of congratulations," confessed a North Carolinian at the impending marriage of an old friend to a federal naval officer; "my heart turns in disgust from the unnatural union." Most of the friends and relatives of a former North Carolina governor refused to attend the marriage of his daughter to a Yankee colonel. Some people spat on their invitations. A Mississippian tried twice to kill the Yankee who married his fair sister. A South Carolinian even forbade his sister to serve as bridesmaid in a "mixed" marriage.[22]

21. Whitelaw Reid, *After the War: A Southern Tour, May 1, 1865, to May 1, 1866* (New York, 1866), 361–62; Enose Farrar to Alexander K. Farrar, July 9, 1865, in Alexander K. Farrar Papers, LSU.

22. Francis Butler Simkins and James Welch Patton, *The Women of the Confederacy* (Richmond, 1936), 61–62; Louis H. DeRosset to sister, September 9, 1865, in DeRosset Family Papers, SHC; Clement Eaton, *The Waning of the Old South Civilization, 1860–1880s* (Athens, Ga., 1968), 117–18; Blanche Butler Ames (comp.), *Chronicles from the Nineteenth Century: Family Letters of Blanche Butler and Adelbert Ames* (2 vols.; Clinton, Mass., 1957), I, 315–16; Nathaniel R. Middleton, Jr., to Alicia Middleton, March 9, 1869, in Middleton Family Papers, SCL.

Yankees seemed less horrified by the possibility of rebel blood infect-
ing their lineage. Perhaps they approached intersectional unions with
more of a missionary spirit; the marriages afforded them opportunities
to convert the heathen. George T. Strong called one such marriage "an
encouraging event." "Oh what a nice wedding it was," commented a
Philadelphia matron on the physical union of Pennsylvania and South
Carolina, "everything just as it should have been." It is difficult, of
course, to judge the lasting effect of these marriages. Matrimony often
goes wrong, and one could antagonize a spouse by unpleasant reminders of the war. One Mississippi woman yelled at her husband
during quarrels, "You dirty, nasty Yankee you. I wish you were dead." A
Massachusetts woman advised a northern friend to carry his southern
bride "away from rebeldom." If he remained in the South, she reasoned,
his in-laws, "who put politics above religion," would "cause him trouble or annoy his wife to death."[23]

Some southerners, aware that they must contain their emotions and
hide their opinions in the North, displayed enormous restraint. A southern woman in Massachusetts did her best, as did most northerners she
met, to avoid mentioning the war. Every now and then a Yankee would
touch on the subject and rile her, but she tried to smile and remain silent.
"My lips are sealed," she pledged, "tho, I should burst in the effort to say
nothing." The tension proved especially hard when dealing with relatives or friends loyal to the other section. A South Carolinian staying at
the home of New England relatives observed, "I think Aunt Maria has
been rather more attentive to Mamma—but I dont think there is any
real change of feeling." Her Yankee aunts happened to be devout Roman
Catholics, an unfortunate combination, thought the young lady, for she
supposed Catholics to be notoriously intolerant of people who opposed
their beliefs. "I could not help thinking," she mused to a friend, "if that
is the religion of our poor aunts what can we expect." "William is
natural," reported a Georgian of an antebellum business acquaintance,
"has not said a word on politics to me, and so long as he is reasonable I
shall be friendly with him."[24]

23. Nevins and Thomas (eds.), *Diary of George Templeton Strong*, IV, 130, entry of
April 8, 1867; Katherine Johnstone (Brinley) Wharton Diaries, February 10, 1872 (MS in
Katherine Johnstone (Brinley) Wharton Papers, HSP); Ames (comp.), *Chronicles from the
Nineteenth Century*, I, 410–11.

24. Ann E. Lane to Sarah L. Glasgow, [*c.* 1870], in William Carr Lane Papers, MOHS;
Lottie Middleton to Nathaniel R. Middleton, October 8, 1866, in Middleton Family
Papers; Davis H. Bryant to Octavia Stephens, January 26, 1866, in Stephens Collection, UF.

Other people, moving north with the best intentions, broke under the strain. Some young Confederates, less willing than their elders to tolerate Yankee slights, defended southern honor, as had Fairfax Harrison, in schoolyard fisticuffs. A former Confederate drummer boy earned such a pugnacious reputation at a New York boarding school that his parents felt obliged to send him to Germany. Older people, too, took a stand when adequately provoked. One lady attending a northern ball suddenly spotted, gleaming on the bosom of a northern lady, a brooch stolen from her by Yankee soldiers during the war. The southerner walked straight up to the northerner and, with a full measure of rightful indignation, demanded, "Madam, give me that brooch. It is mine." The northerner, obviously stunned by the sudden confrontation, hesitated a moment, but, fearful of an unpleasant scene, surrendered the sacred object. A former Confederate soldier named Frank B. Mason lived unobtrusively in Brooklyn until roused by a case of mistaken identity. Another Frank B. Mason, a Union veteran, had applied for a job at the New York custom house. Custom-house officials sent an apologetic rejection to the federal Mason, but through some error the Confederate Mason received the letter. Confederate Mason fired back an indignant missive to the custom house, saying that he had applied for no Yankee-Republican favors, that he did not ever intend to apply for such favors, and that even if they were offered to him he would reject them as beneath the dignity of a loyal Democrat and unreconstructed rebel.[25]

One Virginian gave a detailed account of his churning emotions as he sought work in the North. He had gone north in the summer of 1870 armed with letters of introduction to the head of an insurance agency. The letters had little good effect. The agency head was either unable or unwilling to help him. "I do not see the smallest chance of getting anything to do here," he informed friends in Virginia, "except to kick my heels in the air & have my dandor raised by looking at the airs of the snobs & cod fish aristocracy." He then revealed one reason why his prospective employer had seemed so cool. "I thought it but fair," he admitted, "to tell Mr. H. that I was a *rebel* (God save the mark) believed I was right *then*, & had seen no reason since to change my belief and that I so little repented of what I had done, that I should do precisely the same, if all were to be done over again." This self-confessed "hothead"

25. Marjory Stoneman Douglas, *Adventures in a Green World—Story of David Fairchild and Barbour Lathrop* (Miami, 1973), 3–4; David Macrae, *The Americans at Home* (New York, 1952), 148–49; New York *Times*, August 12, 1879, p. 8.

believed he had shown marvelous restraint in performing this courtesy. He had not, after all, given a detailed justification of southern secession or lectured Mr. H. on the causes of the war. Nor had he aired dirty Confederate linen by stating his unflattering opinion of the Confederacy's political leadership. No need, he thought, to give the Yankee that satisfaction. He also held in check the traitorous thoughts with which he concluded his letter home: "We have suffered & must continue to suffer; but there will come a day—not in your time or mine,—when the South will sweep the North with a fury broom & leave nothing behind. Slavery is dead, but vengeance lives and will yet slake her thirst—else there is no such thing as Retribution." Not surprisingly, this Confederate returned south.[26]

Former Confederates were not unwilling to respond to northern overtures, and sometimes the most trifling events might awaken kindly feelings. A Tennessee veteran resident in Boston experienced little overt northern sympathy during his first six months in the North. Even though he became fairly active in the community by attending night school and church functions, he made few friends, certainly no close ones. Early in 1866, however, he attended a lecture given by Henry Ward Beecher and J. G. Holland on the issue of Reconstruction. Both men impressed him as fair-minded. Holland, in particular, captured his attention. "He paid several compliments to·Southern *manhood*," noted the Tennessean in his diary, "which is the first, I may say, true manly avowal that there was such a thing as manhood in the South that I have seen or heard." Most lecturers and newspapers, he complained, still espoused partisan northern doctrines and enumerated "*their own* glorious deeds." Holland did criticize the South for slavery, but he also suggested that "wrong opinions . . . were entertained both North & South." Near the end of the year, the Tennessean attended a lecture by Frederick Douglass. He could not agree with the black abolitionist's attack on Andrew Johnson's southern policy, but he admitted to being "agreeably surprised" by the black man's dignity, language ("entirely free from the negro dialect"), and refinement. Following Douglass' speech, one of John Brown's sons appeared on the platform to lead the audience in singing the "John Brown Song." The Tennessean remained

26. C. H. Kennedy to Matthew F. Maury, June 27, 1870, in Matthew Fontaine Maury Papers, LC.

mute during the vocalizing, but he noted later, "As much as I condemn the course of John Brown I could not but feel a sympathy for his son."[27]

Perceptive southerners in the North learned the wisdom of Henry Fielding's advice to readers of *Tom Jones:* "It is not enough that your designs, nay that your actions, are intrinsically good, you must take care they shall appear so." However sincerely southerners desired peace and reconciliation, they had to prove their willingness to live harmoniously in action, deed, and word. Proper demeanor could be a positive force. What northerner would not be impressed by the Georgian in New Jersey who declared, "I am one of those who will not brood over the past. I have commenced life anew." The most loyal Unionists gave in to the natural grace of people such as Confederate general Richard Taylor. A New York lady recorded Taylor's presence at "a very pleasant dinner" attended by, among others, Albert Bierstadt, the painter. Bierstadt behaved a little stiffly with "the *rebel*" at first, but Taylor, the soul of knightly chivalry, "won upon him by the charm of his manner and conversation." "I was pleased with the rebel relations," reported a Philadelphian not always so pleased with former Confederates, relatives or no; "their tone was so natural and quiet." Quiet tones often turned the trick. The Philadelphian believed Union victory in the war had been "absolutely necessary," but she sympathized with her relations when they told her of federal military raids against southern civilians. Her husband, another strong Unionist, reported from Richfield, New York, "The Southern men here seem to me, good Union men compared to our copperheads."[28]

A vivacious lady from South Carolina made her northern dentist a special target for conversion. The man was a hard case who sorely tested her patience and resolve. "He tells me that Abram Lincoln is the greatest man that ever lived," she marveled to a friend. She withstood his appraisal without a murmur, partly, no doubt, because of her vulnerable position in the dentist's chair. "Then I hear a great deal of the harmony of the Universe—and Eternal Laws—and the progress of perfection,"

27. James M. Morey Diary, January 16, February 23, December 25, 1866 (MS in James Marsh Morey Papers, TL).

28. James L. Paterson to Alexander H. Stephens, August 15, 1865, in Alexander H. Stephens Papers, Series I, EU; Harold Earl Hammond (ed.), *Diary of a Union Lady, 1861–1865* (New York, 1962), 372–73, entry of November 17, 1865; Elizabeth Fisher to Sidney G. Fisher, August 11, 1865, Sidney G. Fisher to Elizabeth Fisher, July 29, 1865, both in Fisher Collection.

she continued in reporting the rather one-sided conversation, "perfection being N. England Republicanism." "Whenever Mama sees him," she reported further, "she rakes him with broadsides." The daughter had a "far more feline" approach. She wanted her teeth repaired so that she might "gnash them whenever I think of the Yankees." Until then, she would purr like a kitten to disarm the Yankee. "He is the blackest kind of Republican," she concluded, "but I think under the hands of Alice Mary Cheves & myself is getting a little milder."[29]

Other young Confederates pursued the challenge of conversion among their peers. A North Carolinian attending college in upstate New York experienced trouble with some of his classmates. Rather than resort to pugilism, he simply ignored "mean-spirited" fellows. When, in response, classmates called him "conceited" and ridiculed his false "Southern pride," he smiled. Still trying to draw the Carolinian into an argument, they called him "dull" and "uncultivated," but he went on reading. "Ah!" he rejoiced, "but I like to show these Yankees what a 'Reb' can do on the foot-ball field. I, made desperate by their ways, made frequent alarming charges, and their cries of 'Good enough' kind of soothe my feelings." Still, whatever personal respect his athletic prowess brought him, he continued to feel exasperated by how little his northern classmates knew about the South. He took it upon himself to correct their erroneous assumptions. Concerning his closest friend and roommate, he announced, "Old Guion is a Yankee, and when we are not disputing about any thing else, I am engaged in getting some of those outrageous lies out of his head, such as bringing slaves to market in chains! If he was not so bigoted, I could make something out of him."[30]

Other Confederates set off for school with specific reminders about their heritage and the need to correct erroneous Yankee notions about southern behavior and habits. "When you see what *enemies we have*," a South Carolinian reminded her college-bound son, "and how *our fair name* is trying to be *clouded* by *some*—let it be a stimulant to you to defy them! and show by your *honorable career,* that no blood flows in your veins, but that of a *noble brave man!*" She urged him to be ambitious, to strive for excellence, but never to "degrade" himself by an ungallant or ignoble act. Periodic reminders of his duty arrived by mail

29. Harriott Middleton to Susan Middleton, July 15, 1866, in Cheves-Middleton Papers, SCHS.

30. Richard A. Meares to Katherine Meares, September 18, October 12, 1873, both in Meares and DeRosset Family Papers, SHC.

through his college days. "One man can give a character—a name to his state of high tone," his mother told him, "or can diminish its honor." We may assume the young man followed his mother's advice; all appearances suggest that he did. Certainly the advice never faltered. The week of graduation, mother urged him to devote his last few days to visiting northern friends. "Go to see every body! who has been kind to you—tell even the servants good bye. . . . Leave pleasant memories behind you. Show you have been *well bred*."[31]

John Wellborn Root, a young Georgian destined for architectural greatness, won northern understanding if not acceptance of Confederate views while attending New York University. Root rarely talked about the war, but from time to time he made his feelings known. On one memorable occasion, Root, a gifted musician, accompanied some classmates on the chapel organ while they all sang favorite college songs. At one point, when a lull enveloped jollity, Root—often overwhelmed by impish impulses—broke into a rousing rendition of "Dixie" on the organ. "We were hushed, touched, thrilled by the soul that rose like a lark from its nest," recalled one of Root's classmates. "We did not speak when the song ended, but we knew ever after that there were two hearts of equal love that suffered in the lost cause." The Georgian, without speaking a word, had found a sure-fire way to "conquer prejudice, disarm opponents," and promote "fraternity and justice."[32]

A hardworking if perpetually unlucky South Carolinian did his best to represent the South, and with some success. Lewis M. Grimball served the Confederacy as both private soldier and surgeon. After the war, he settled with his new bride at Frog Level, South Carolina, where he practiced medicine and shared the operation of a drugstore. When the store and his practice failed to prosper, Grimball moved to Philadelphia. As in many such cases, this particular southerner had friends in the North, a well-placed aunt who, in turn, had friends among Philadelphia businessmen. "You know he will have to take anything," she informed her sister, Grimball's mother, "and rise by his own exertions, only let him come to me, and I will see what can be done. In the mean time he will have a comfortable home here with me." But Grimball did not prosper in Philadelphia, and his dependent position made him irritable.

31. Mary Jane McMaster to James McMaster, November 19, 1877, January 3, 1878, June 9, 1880, all in Fitz William McMaster and Mary Jane Macfie Papers, SCL.

32. Harriet Monroe, *John Wellborn Root: A Study of His Life and Work* (Boston, 1896), 15–16.

Tension grew between family members; Grimball could not find a house of his own; his practice did not pay. He moved to suburban Shoemaker-town, but financial success eluded him. His health began to suffer. "I am of nervo:Billious temperament," he explained to his father in May, 1870, three years after leaving South Carolina, "nerves predominantly, which makes my system so excitable . . . & whenever there is the tension there is always a corresponding depression." He inquired elsewhere about the prospects of a practice, determined "to take advantage of any opportunity which offers."[33]

A brief return to Philadelphia proved fruitless, so Grimball abandoned medicine to work at a woolens mill in Bristol, Pennsylvania, where he rose rapidly. Starting as a bagger, he soon won promotion to paymaster, entrusted with a payroll of two thousand dollars for nearly two hundred employees. He even found opportunity to practice medicine at the mill by attending to the workers' injuries and ailments. Life improved dramatically for Grimball; to know perfect bliss, he lacked only the presence of his wife and son, who had returned to live with relatives in South Carolina in hopes of relieving his financial burden. His family was about to rejoin him when bad luck struck again. Grimball lost his job, the result of a disagreement with the mill superintendent's brother. He returned to South Carolina hoping to buy a farm, but closer inspection proved he could not afford the venture. "I might live here & perhaps eke out an existence," he reasoned from South Carolina, "but I have decided that it would not pay. A man seeks contentment & a little happiness in this world & he must seek it." He decided to return north.[34]

Grimball and his family headed for Philadelphia but stayed only a week before moving to Vineland, New Jersey, encouraged by a plea from local residents for his services as physician and druggist. Grimball arrived at Vineland to discover five physicians and two druggists already established. He tried Philadelphia once more, and this time, after a year of hard work, achieved modest success. Still dissatisfied, he talked of moving to Colorado. His family urged him to return south, where he could live among his "own people." He took their advice and spent the

33. Gabriella Butler to Meta Grimball, October 29, 1866, Arthur Grimball to John B. Grimball, October 18, 1867, Lewis M. Grimball to John B. Grimball, May 28, 1870, all in Grimball Family Papers, SHC.

34. Lewis M. Grimball to John B. Grimball, March 5, August 23, 1871, in Grimball Family Papers, SHC; Berkley Grimball to John Grimball, February 19, 1871, in Grimball Family Papers, SCHS.

remainder of his days in South Carolina, practicing medicine and managing one of the family plantations. Sadly, Grimball's story holds one more unhappy chapter. When he returned south for the final time, his wife remained in Philadelphia with their child. She promised to join him soon, but she never did. She had grown tired of the constant movement and failure. Their penny-scraping style of life had "soured" her as early as the first unsuccessful venture in Philadelphia, six years previous. She supported herself and the child by keeping a small school for "children of respectable position." Four years later, Clementine Grimball divorced Lewis Grimball.[35]

The importance of Lewis Grimball's story is not its sad ending—such tales were common enough among southern emigrants—but his response to the tribulations of northern residence. Lewis did not stomp and curse his ill-fortune; he did not blame his disappointments on Yankee prejudices. From all outward appearances, Lewis Grimball remained cheerful and confident of the future. Everyone liked him. He forged strong friendships and nourished good feeling wherever he went. The good people of Shoemakertown expressed "sorrow and regret" when he abandoned his practice there. As one shopkeeper expressed it, "He was very much liked." During one of his stints in Philadelphia, Grimball announced he was "gaining friends." He won praise for his dedicated attention to the victims of a smallpox epidemic in Philadelphia. When his old patients in Shoemakertown appealed for his help during the epidemic, he visited them, too. "I found warm friends," he reported from Shoemakertown, "& I have the promise of much practice at the old stand." The owner of the Bristol woolens mill expressed "much regret" at losing Grimball from his employ. Admittedly, Grimball's popularity reflected his kindly nature more than any conscious attempt to promote sectional reconciliation, but the effect could be the same.[36]

Potentially, John C. Pemberton had an even tougher row to hoe than Lewis Grimball. Pemberton was one of those northerners who fought for the Confederacy and then returned north after the war. Such people

35. John B. Grimball to Lewis Grimball, February 7, 1873, Lewis M. Grimball to Mrs. Legge, July 26, 1873, both in Grimball Family Papers, SHC; John B. Grimball to John Grimball, January 3, February 26, 1873, both in Grimball Family Papers, SCHS; John B. Grimball Diaries, October 15, November 10, 1877 (MS in Grimball Family Papers, SHC).

36. Lewis M. Grimball to John B. Grimball, May 28, 1870, Meta Grimball to Berkley Grimball, October 18, 1870, December 8, 1871, all in Grimball Family Papers, SHC; Grimball Diaries, May 25, 1871.

sometimes felt unwanted in both regions. Pemberton, a West Pointer from Pennsylvania, married a Virginian before the war and rose to lieutenant general in Confederate service. He enjoyed the challenge of high command, but too often responsibility is rewarded by blame. Southerners blamed Pemberton for losing Vicksburg, just as they blamed two other northerners, Mansfield Lovell and Franklin Gardner, for losing New Orleans and Port Hudson. "It is a singular fact," observed a former Confederate general in summarizing the failure of these three Yankee rebels, "that the Southern men in the Federal service were remarkably successful, while the Northern men in our service, though brave and true, brought disaster to our arms." Pemberton's mother loved him, however, and bought him a farm near Warrenton, Virginia, after the war. Isolated and lost in the glories of bucolic life, Pemberton contented himself with being a farmer. He spread manure, cleared brush, built a large shed for eighteen head of cattle, and did all the things farmers are supposed to do. Latin translation became his chief recreation. He read the newspapers to keep tabs on the "malignant unprincipled set of villains" who led the congressional Radicals, but he said nothing publicly about political events. His chief ambition, he insisted, was "to increase the value of my farm as a something to leave to my wife & children."[37]

Pemberton did not return to the North until Christmas 1871, when he and his wife visited relatives in Philadelphia. He enjoyed the trip, perhaps too much. On his return to Virginia, rural life seemed less satisfying. He visited in town and called on distant neighbors more often. By 1873, his farm showed more "wear and tear" than improvement. He tried to sell the farm for six thousand dollars, enough money to establish himself in the North. Two sons had already drifted northward, one to Pittsburgh, with both eventually settling in Philadelphia. A third son pleaded to join his older brothers. By 1875, the time seemed right to move. Thinking originally of settling in Philadelphia, where he had not only family and friends but real estate investments, Pemberton finally selected Allentown, Pennsylvania, as his new home, for reasons of economy.[38]

37. Daniel H. Hill, "Address Before the Mecklenburg (N.C.) Historical Society," *Southern Historical Society Papers*, I (1876), 394; John C. Pemberton to Israel Pemberton, January 6, April 12, 1868, December 9, 1866, all in Pemberton Family Papers, HSP.

38. John C. Pemberton to Israel Pemberton, December 30, 1871, May 27, 1872, February 13, April 27, 1873, June 12, 1874, Janaury 18, 1875, all in Pemberton Family Papers; John C. Pemberton, *Pemberton: Defender of Vicksburg* (Chapel Hill, 1942), 274–77.

"The people here from the beginning," Pemberton wrote from Allentown, "[have] been very polite to me, and several of the best families have called on Pattie & some young girls on Anna." "Altogether," he added, "we shall have as much & probably more society than we will care for." Still, Pemberton had to convince some of these friendly folk that a rebel general rated kind treatment. Most often, he succeeded. One former Union soldier from Allentown testified that Pemberton "was always well dressed, carried himself well and was what I call mighty 'spunky.'" "There were a lot of us soldiers around here then," he recalled, "and many of us young fellows were ready to start an argument, but he always had good answers, took the teasing good-natured but didn't back up an inch." This veteran remembered the fun of having "a real live Rebel general . . . to tease and pick at," but he also recalled what "a 'good sport'" Pemberton had been and how difficult it had been to be angry with him.[39]

Military service frequently provided the necessary ingredient for harmonious relations. Former northern soldiers, like Pemberton's neighbor, often admired the courage of postwar Confederate invaders. There were inevitable exceptions. The Grand Army of the Republic acted as a principal agent in maintaining sectional passions through the 1890s. Many individual Union veterans likewise never buried the hatchet. Other Union and Confederate veterans, however, welcomed and encouraged peaceful reunion. Joint encampments of northern and southern veterans' groups inspired the earliest public optimism about reconciliation in the 1870s. By the 1890s, joint parades and battlefield reunions had become the rage. Perhaps the mutual respect, forged, tempered, and tested in four years of combat, created the bond. Perhaps the weariness of the long struggle, the shared experience of "seeing the elephant," as soldiers called participation in battle, put them beyond petty civilian political considerations. Whatever the reason, common membership in the "bloodied fraternity" produced a core of dedicated reconciliation advocates in the North.[40]

39. John C. Pemberton to Israel Pemberton, January 18, 1875, in Pemberton Family Papers; Pemberton, *Pemberton*, 276–77.

40. Mary R. Dearing, *Veterans in Politics: The Story of the G.A.R.* (Baton Rouge, 1952), vii–viii; Cruce Stark, "Brothers at/in War: One Phase of the Post–Civil-War Reconciliation," *Canadian Review of American Studies*, VI (1975), 174–81; Daniel Aaron, *The Unwritten War: American Writers and the Civil War* (New York, 1973), 189–91. Gaines M. Foster, *Ghosts of the Confederacy: Defeat, the Lost Cause, and the Emergence of the New South, 1865 to 1913* (New York, 1987), 66–67, believes that a rosy recollection of battle rather than the genuine experience of combat best explains this spirit. It certainly must be counted as one factor.

Virginius Dabney, a hardened and shameless optimist, nonetheless nourished the usual apprehensions about forsaking his native Virginia for the cold weather and colder hearts of New Jersey. His fears, if not dissolving, at least shrank soon after he joined the faculty of the Princeton Preparatory School. Among his associates, he encountered a former federal cavalry officer. Expecting a rough time from his new colleague, Dabney marveled at the Yankee's kindly nature. The federal, who bore the scars of more than one Confederate bullet, held "the warmest possible feeling for Southerners & especially Southern soldiers." The two men spent many congenial hours reminiscing about the perils of combat and the discomforts of camp life. When Dabney later moved to New York, he harbored fewer fears about his reception.[41]

General Lew Wallace became one of Private Maurice Thompson's closest friends in Crawfordsville, Indiana. Both men practiced law in Indiana's courts, but their friendship more likely developed over common interests in literature, sports, and the out-of-doors. Their love of sport involved the two men and four other Union and Confederate veterans in one of the most memorable events in Crawfordville's history. Thompson and several of his Confederate friends in town were avid archers. Aware that Wallace and local federal veterans preferred rifles, Thompson and two other Confederate bowmen challenged the general and the two best marksmen he could muster to a shooting match, bows versus rifles. To their delight, and to the amazement of the riflemen, the archers won. No one spoke of the event as a contest between North and South, Yankees and rebels; all contestants enjoyed the match as "a day's excellent sport."[42]

Bushrod Johnson inspired "resentment and animosity" when he settled on a farm near Brighton, Illinois, in early 1875. Johnson's Ohio birth only aggravated his identification as a "rebel general" among the patriotic citizens of Macoupin County. Most of his neighbors gradually accepted Johnson, some because they pitied his son's mental imbalance, others because they disapproved of the way his tenant farmer cheated Johnson. Still, Johnson, who never knowingly insulted or offended any-

41. Virginius Dabney to John H. Chamberlayne, February 25, July 9, 1874, November 14, 1875, all in Chamberlayne Family Papers, VHS.

42. Robert E. Morsberger and Katherine M. Morsberger, *Lew Wallace: Militant Romantic* (New York, 1980), 218; Otis B. Wheeler, *The Literary Career of Maurice Thompson* (Baton Rouge, 1965), 24; James Maurice Thompson, "Merry Days with Bow and Quiver," *Scribner's Monthly,* XVI (May, 1878), 3–4.

one, made few friends. A neighboring youth became devoted to him, largely because the general opened his library to the lad and tutored him in history, mathematics, science, and engineering. Johnson's closest adult friends were two federal veterans, one a colonel, the other a general. Their mutually high ranks may have partly inspired the friendships; in addition, both federal officers had been born in the South. They appreciated Johnson's decision to fight for the Confederacy and understood his delicate position in returning to the North. Whatever the personal bonds, the three men set an example for the town. By the time Johnson died, nearly six years later, he had won the affection of most of the community. People remembered him as being "reticent in all matters that would stir bad blood." One local newspaper attributed Johnson's "quietude" to his desire to "cover up what of the past could not be atoned for," but it also admitted that "many friends" would grieve for the general.[43]

Roger and Sarah Pryor faced every possible provocation when they settled in Brooklyn, yet they, perhaps better than any other two people, symbolize Confederate reconciliation efforts in the North. "The great difficulty in my way," Roger told Sarah in explaining his slow progress in establishing a law practice, "is the prejudice against 'rebels'; and that I am sorry to see is not diminishing." The press mercilessly harassed the distressed general. One scornful reference to his activities appeared in the Boston *Post:* "The Rebel Pryor has opened an office in New York for the practice of Law, but he has not yet had a *rap.*" Pryor regarded the pun on his initials (R. A. P.) "trifling and flippant," but he admitted that some jibes "cut . . . to the heart." Compounding his melancholy situation, many southerners "misunderstood" his reasons for going north. Yankees called him "Rebel," and former Confederates labeled him "Radical."[44]

Sarah, who moved north only because of her grievous heartache at being separated from her partner in joy and sorrow, courageously ignored snide remarks about the family. "We had made no friends among our neighbors," she recalled of their first few months in Brooklyn, "to whom, of course, we had made no advances." A "sickening sense of loneliness" haunted the Pryor household. "All seemed so desolate, so

43. Charles M. Cummings, *Yankee Quaker Confederate General: The Curious Career of Bushrod Rust Johnson* (Rutherford, N.J., 1971), 368–71; *Republican Examiner* (Jerseyville, Ill.), September 17, 1880.

44. Mrs. Roger A. Pryor, *My Day: Reminiscences of a Long Life* (New York, 1909), 284, 286, 325–26.

hopeless," she remembered. "We knew ourselves not only strangers but aliens, outcasts." Not even the children escaped the taunts. One of her sons told Sarah they must change the name of the family dog from "Rebel" to "Prince" because neighborhood boys threatened to stone the dog if it continued to bear the offensive name. On another occasion, one of Sarah's daughters reported that neighborhood children had called them "Rebels, and slave-drivers, and *awful* people!" and had threatened to drive them out of the city. "These painful incidents," lamented their mother, "were of everyday occurrence."[45]

Most families would have kept well below the parapets, but not the Pryors. The children, as might be expected, possessed the amazing resiliency of youth. "My own little brood positively refused to be miserable," observed their proud mother. Taunts, jeers, rebuffs, and black eyes were all part of growing up, and all the little Pryors survived. Sarah gradually won friends through her energetic charitable work, reputation as a gracious hostess, and literary accomplishments. A revealing and somewhat comical episode, occurring nearly a quarter century after her move north, summarizes her rite of passage. In 1891, Sarah found herself unwittingly enmeshed in a struggle for control of New York's chapter of the Daughters of the American Revolution. It was an awesome contest. An insurgent wing of the chapter, seeking to seize power from the original regents—which included Mrs. Pryor—attacked Sarah for not being a "representative New-York woman." Did they call her "Virginian," or "Rebel," or "carpetbagger"? No. They accused her of being a "Brooklynite" who had only recently moved to Manhattan. Sarah was experienced at this game. She tendered her resignation as regent and retained her post only after a large delegation of ladies swooped down upon the Pryor home to woo her back. Sarah shot off a letter to the New York *Times* to protest its insinuation that in challenging the attacks of the insurgents she had tried to disassociate herself from Brooklyn. She was proud of Brooklyn, she told the *Times*. Brooklyn had been her home for fifteen happy years, endeared to her, she insisted, "by the friendships of the noblest men and women I ever knew."[46]

Unlike the Harrison family, however, where the wife accepted the public lead in converting northern opinions, Roger became the most visible Pryor. During his earliest, bleakest days in the North, Roger vowed to reconstruct himself and northern opinions of the South. In

45. *Ibid.*, 316, 331–32.
46. *Ibid.*, 332–33; New York *Times*, June 11, 1891, p. 8, June 14, 1891, p. 20.

December, 1865, even as he complained about Yankee prejudice against rebels, he promised "to wear it away after a while." "It is my last cast," he said of his desperate gamble in coming north, "and I am resolved to succeed or perish in the attempt." He tried to make light of the intolerance that threatened, menaced, hung over him like the blade of a guillotine. " 'The Rebel Pryor' has had 'a *rap*' at last," he informed Sarah early in 1866; "I have had a call from a *bona fide* client!" But it would require years of patience and frequent public recantations by Pryor, the most visible leader of the secession movement to move north, before he won forgiveness. Not that he calculated his pleas for reconciliation to reap legal profits or to deliver him from Yankee persecution. The knees of Roger Pryor's trousers had never shown signs of groveling. His call for sectional peace came as a challenge, not a concession.[47]

Pryor's challenge rang sharp and clear as the crack of a rifle in the brisk autumn air. Even before moving north, he had told Virginians in remarks widely copied in northern newspapers, "We have been fairly whipped. . . . For myself, I yield that the cause is hopeless . . . I will go back to the plough and my duty as a loyal citizen." He aimed his first public northern statement about reconciliation at fellow southerners, too. Responding to criticism of his move north published in the Richmond *Whig,* Pryor insisted that he had renounced all political activities and ambitions with the collapse of the Confederacy. He desired only to support his family and pursue his profession. "When I renewed my oath of allegiance to the Union," he elaborated, "I did so in good faith and without reservation; and as I understand that oath, it not only restrains me from acts of positive hostility to the government, but pledges me to my utmost for its welfare and stability." Pryor loved the South, but northerners and southerners, he insisted, must learn to think nationally and to foster their love for the whole nation rather than its separate parts. "Hence," Pryor stressed, "while I am more immediately concerned to see the South restored to its former prosperity, I am anxious that the whole country, and all classes, may be reunited on the basis of common interest and fraternal regard."[48]

Pryor also advised fellow southerners about how to defuse sectional tensions. Southerners must "accept the situation" and "adjust their

47. Pryor, *My Day,* 284, 292.
48. New York *Times,* May 21, 1865, p. 4; Robert S. Holzman, *Adapt or Perish: The Life of General Roger A. Pryor, C.S.A.* (Hamden, Conn., 1976), 88–89; Pryor, *My Day,* 326.

ideas to the altered state of affairs." Specifically, they must treat Negroes fairly, cease "profitless" political agitation, and devote themselves to the financial and physical recovery of the South. Small wonder some southerners called Pryor a Radical, but the general spoke from entirely different motives than Thaddeus Stevens. Pryor would not take sides in Pollard's war of ideas. He knew the cost of taking sides. The "wasted fields and desolated farms" of the South, the eclipse of southern liberties, and the "sinister aspect of the future" convinced Pryor of the need for reconciliation. He would cast aside his Rhett and his Yancey for his Blackstone and his Bible, the latter two assuring him that peacemakers are among the blessed. The "chief obstacle to a complete and cordial" sectional reunion, insisted Pryor, might be traced to the "suspicion and resentment" each section harbored against the other. He would assure northerners that the South reentered the Union in good faith and convince southerners that the majority of Yankees had the kindest thoughts and intentions for the South.[49]

In his usual eloquent fashion, Pryor had laid the groundwork for the reconciliation debate to follow. His letter to the *Whig* contained all the right catchwords, to be heard time and again over the next several decades: good faith, restored, reunited, fraternal, confidence, goodwill, kindness, compassion, reunion, moderation, magnanimity, peace, forbearance, and good feeling. He was slower to advertise his views to northerners. Political passions ran too high against him. His opinion on reconciliation would have been no more welcomed in the North than his earlier treasonous advocacy of secession. Yankees would suspect his motives. "Would a frank, full utterance of my opinions on reconstruction, be tolerated?" he asked in response to an invitation to speak in New England. "Am I not so obnoxious in Boston as to repel all the sympathies of the audience?" "The truth is," he explained as lightly as his spirits would permit, "all my political convictions have been modified, by recent events, almost to the point of revolution." For the moment he would decline all requests from sharp-eyed promoters who knew that controversy produced dollars and would work unobtrusively on the South's behalf. Indeed, Pryor may have been unsure of his emotions at this stage of his life. Sometime around 1869 he scribbled the following verse on a scrap of paper:

49. Pryor, *My Day,* 327–29.

Our loyalty is still the same
Whether we lose or win the game
True as the dial to the sun
Although it not be shone upon

The question is, which loyalties did he have in mind?[50]

Pryor kept his nose in a law book for several years, quietly winning and influencing northern friends as occasion presented. Not until 1872 did he address a northern audience on the subject of reconciliation. No less august a body than the Grand Army of the Republic asked Pryor to participate in its Decoration Day program at Brooklyn's Academy of Music. Not all the veterans wanted Pryor to speak, and their criticism of him led the general momentarily to withdraw his initial agreement to appear. Cooler heads prevailed, and Pryor responded with the best-reasoned, least passionate public statement on reconciliation yet given by a southerner in the North. One can imagine Pryor—tall, thin, raw-boned, back crooked, hands clasped together before him—standing at the rostrum until the echoes of polite applause that greeted his appearance in the red, white, and blue draped hall had faded away. He immediately turned the tables on the veterans who had opposed his presence there. He knew, he told them, that he had been asked to speak not as a compliment to him or to his rebel past. Rather, the invitation represented "an overture of reconciliation" by the GAR. He praised the organization's magnanimity. He enthusiastically endorsed its noble desire for "peace and fraternal feeling between the lately belligerent sections." He thanked its members for their vision and compassion. Some members of the audience squirmed. Pryor had them.[51]

Pryor's speech exonerated the fighting men on both sides for responsibility in causing the war. The "bloody business of secession" could be blamed on northern and southern politicians, he said, following an already familiar theme. The common soldiers of both sections had cared nothing for constitutional arguments and had fought, each in his own light, from "genuine patriotism." They contested with their lives what

50. Roger A. Pryor to James Redpath, June 29, 1869, poem fragment, n.d., both in Roger Atkinson Pryor Papers, DU.

51. Pryor, *My Day,* 367–70; Holzman, *Adapt or Perish,* 105–107; James Herbert Morse Diaries, June 5, 1887 (MS in NYHS); New York *Times,* May 31, 1877, p. 8, June 7, 1877, p. 5; Roger A. Pryor, *The Union: A Plea for Reconstruction, Being an Address by Hon. Roger A. Pryor* (Brooklyn, 1877), 3.

orators had wrought with words. Most southerners, he maintained, viewed the fall of the Confederacy as a blessing, ordained by Providence. They felt the same way about the destruction of slavery. In any case, Pryor insisted, slavery had been but the "occasion" for the war, not its cause. The clash between state sovereignty and federal supremacy had unleashed the dogs of war. Now that southerners had accepted the victorious principles of federal rule, nothing need further retard national unity. It was right, Pryor concluded, that Decoration Day, representing as it did the "common glory" of North and South, be used to symbolize national reunification. "Thus, even in the tomb," he argued, "the Federal and the Confederate soldier will prove the friends of peace; and their blended memories serve as a safeguard of the Union." Prolonged waves of applause washed over the speaker. Northern and southern newspapers praised him for his patriotism and good sense. The demand for copies of his speech became such that the Brooklyn *Eagle* published it as a pamphlet, earnestly entitled *The Union: A Plea for Reconstruction.*[52]

Surely the most curious development in Pryor's growing reputation as a peacemaker was his legal defense of Adelbert Ames, Mississippi's carpetbag governor, against bribery charges. Pryor's decision to defend a New England Republican in the general's own home state of Mississippi must rank as one of the more startling episodes of Reconstruction. A deliciously savory twist to the story is that Pryor's services were obtained by Benjamin F. Butler, the "Beast" who had terrorized wartime New Orleans during federal occupation. Butler was Ames's father-in-law, and he asked Pryor to join a three-man defense team in hopes that the Confederate might dissuade Mississippi Democrats from their determination to impeach Ames. Butler's selection of Pryor was wise, if unexpected. Butler knew Pryor to be an able lawyer who threw every ounce of energy into a client's case. "You will like him immensely," Butler assured his skeptical son-in-law. "He will do you good service and if any man can save you he will." Pryor traveled to Mississippi optimistic that the evidence would be insufficient to convict Ames. Once in Jackson, however, he saw the lay of the land. Evidence would have little to do with the case. Ames would be convicted and dismissed from office whatever the proof of his misconduct. Pryor immediately busied himself with negotiations behind the scenes. He struck a deal. Ames would resign from office if not prosecuted. "The settlement finally effected is infinitely more

52. Pryor, *Union*, 4–7, 18–20, 23–24.

satisfactory than I conceived possible on my arrival at Jackson," Pryor informed Butler. "His enemies there consider he retired unscathed and with all the honours of war."[53]

Butler had met Pryor in legal circles before the Ames episode, and their relationship grew afterward. Whatever his military failings, Butler was an astute criminal lawyer who had given Pryor sound advice on occasion and had engaged him as a special assistant for particular pieces of litigation. During the early 1880s, they also began to consult each other on political matters. In 1880, Pryor convinced Butler to support Winfield Scott Hancock's presidential bid. Pryor called Butler, who had shifted his political allegiance to the Republican party in 1865, "an incorrigible Democrat," who ought to rejoin his old friends. "Your great abilities and vast influence are needed," Pryor insisted, "and they should not be withheld any longer." In 1882, when Butler ran successfully for the governorship of Massachusetts, he asked Pryor to campaign for him. "I want you to play a role nobody can play so effectively as yourself," Butler told him plainly, "that of a thoroughly reconstructed union loving rebel." In 1884, after Butler had been defeated for reelection, Pryor urged him to seek the Democratic presidential nomination and promised to work on his behalf in New York. After losing the nomination to Grover Cleveland, Butler ungraciously refused to support the Democratic ticket. His desertion did not sit well with Pryor, and the two men soon drifted apart. They corresponded only occasionally thereafter and only on legal matters. Their relationship had been a curious one from the start, based more on the prospects of mutual gain than on solid friendship. Yet it broadened Pryor's reputation, at least in the North, as a sincere Unionist. A Confederate who liked the Beast could embrace any Yankee.[54]

With Roger Pryor, as with nearly every other Confederate who promoted sectional reconciliation in the North, personality governed ac-

---

53. Benjamin F. Butler to Adelbert Ames, March 25, 1876, Thomas J. Durant to Benjamin F. Butler, April 3, 1876, Roger A. Pryor to Benjamin F. Butler, April 3, 1876, all in Benjamin F. Butler Papers, LC. Blanche Ames, Adelbert's wife, insisted privately that she had suggested the idea of a compromise with Mississippi Democrats and that Pryor had not acknowledged her contribution. See Ames (comp.), *Chronicles from the Nineteenth Century,* II, 355.

54. Hans L. Trefousse, *Ben Butler: The South Called Him BEAST!* (New York, 1957), 243, 250–53; Holzman, *Adapt or Perish,* 100–101; Benjamin F. Butler to Roger A. Pryor, October 31, 1875, October 13, 1882, Roger A. Pryor to Benjamin F. Butler, July 22, 1880, November 22, 1883, March 17, July 21, 1884, all in Butler Papers.

tion. One is hard-pressed to define that personality or to dissect it and lay out its component parts. It would most likely be described as tolerant. Certainly Roger Pryor could be called a tolerant man, at least after the war and partly as a result of the war. One Sunday evening in 1890, Pryor wrote a letter to an old Virginia friend, George Bagby, "the only person," claimed Pryor, "to whom I speak confidentially." As he wrote, Pryor smoked a cigar. As he smoked, his brain cells responding to the cigar's bouquet, Pryor's mind wandered back in time. He thought of the good times; he thought of the bad times. He had shared both with Bagby. Pryor unburdened himself to Bagby in his nostalgic mood. "It makes me smile now," he confessed, "to remember how infallible I used to consider myself, but, alas! how differently things look when the mists of passion and prejudices have passed away and we see with clearer eyes!"[55]

Writing at another time to Bagby, Pryor defended his adopted northern home as stoutly as he had once defended the South. "I regret to see how eagerly anything tending to degrade the great metropolis of our country is read and believed without the slightest inquiry or examination," he lamented. "Did I not know better, I would be inclined to think that it is because people love to believe ill of those they do not like." His thoughts racing to a loftier level of contemplation, Pryor added, "My experience in life has taught me that it is much safer—not to say more magnanimous—to readily believe the good and with suspicion hear the ill that is spoken of others."[56]

Newspaper obituaries and public testimonials tend to exaggerate the accomplishments and virtues of their subjects. Still, a community's public estimate of its citizens is not usually so divorced from reality that it may be cavalierly dismissed as fiction. If one accepts even as half-truths the laudatory comments heaped upon many Confederate carpetbaggers by Yankee neighbors, the respect and affection remain impressive. Daniel Britton, former lieutenant in Company A, 61st Tennessee Infantry, became "one of the live and wide-awake business men" of Williamsburg, Indiana. Following the death of Edward Colston, the Virginia cavalryman's fellow lawyers in Cincinnati remembered him as "a man of rare attainment and insight . . . a man of warm and generous heart and of the most affectionate nature." Colonel D. L. Hardesty of Kentucky impressed

55. Roger A. Pryor to George W. Bagby, September 14, [1890], in Bagby Family Papers, VHS.

56. *Ibid.*, June 5, [1891].

his Madison County, Indiana, neighbors as a "whole-souled southern gentleman, generous and warm hearted." Residents held Hardesty in the "highest esteem." The good people of Evansville, Indiana, remembered Lee Howell, late of the 4th Alabama Cavalry, as "a loyal, public spirited citizen" whose "genial disposition and kindly ways endeared him to all with whom he came in contact." Mr. and Mrs. George K. Leonard, both Virginians, made "a wide circle of friends" in Columbus, Ohio, where they occupied "a very enviable position in a society where true worth and intelligence" served as their passports to community acceptance.[57]

Some Yankees, loath to admit that southern neighbors had ever donned Confederate gray, made excuses for their wicked pasts. Understanding citizens in Alexander County, Illinois, reasoned that O. P. Storm necessarily found his "sympathies" with the South once the war began, but they emphasized that he had steadfastly opposed secession. M. W. Suter's neighbors in Licking County, Ohio, decided it was only "natural" that the "highly esteemed" doctor, "a representative of an old southern family," should have followed the fortunes of his native Virginia. Residents of Johnson County, Illinois, insisted that David Y. Bridges' fatherless childhood (he was a "headstrong boy") explained his Confederate service. Besides, they added for good measure, "whatever were his sentiments" at the start of the war, community pressure in Missouri, not rebel sympathies, had forced young Bridges to join the Confederate army. Brazil, Indiana, citizens avoided possible mortification over Edward W. Smith's Civil War record by referring only to his dedicated "service" during the war. They could not bring themselves to say his service came as captain in a North Carolina regiment. J. D. Pool's Jackson County, Iowa, friends claimed that he had joined the 51st Virginia Infantry to avoid the embarrassment of inevitable conscription. "Throughout the struggle," said Pool's neighbors, "he felt that the south was in the wrong, but he also felt that he would be a traitor to his home if he went to the northern side, and now there is no man more loyal to the Union than Mr. Pool."[58]

57. *History of Johnson County, Indiana* (Chicago, 1888), 745–46; *Memorial Adopted by the Lawyers' Club of Cincinnati upon the Death of Edward Colston* (Pamphlet in Colston Family Papers, CS), 8–9; *Portrait and Biographical Record of Madison and Hamilton Counties, Indiana* (Chicago, 1893), 842–43; Evansville *Courier*, January 4, 1918, p. 3; *A Centennial Biographical History of the City of Columbus and Franklin County, Ohio* (Chicago, 1901), 194–95.
58. William Henry Perrin (ed.), *History of Alexander, Union and Pulaski Counties, Illinois* (Chicago, 1883), 114; *Memorial Record of Licking County, Ohio* (Chicago,

Colonel William H. Fulkerson received the ultimate and, so far as is known, singular honor of receiving an official testimonial from a local Grand Army of the Republic post. Fulkerson, an errant East Tennessean who wound up commanding the Confederacy's 63rd Tennessee Regiment, moved to Jerseyville, Illinois, in 1866, where his wife had inherited some land. The Fulkersons were "land poor" at first, but within a few years, the colonel built a beautiful brick mansion and developed a magnificent stock farm, Hazel Dell. Shorthorn cattle and wise business investments made Fulkerson a wealthy man. During his fifty-three years in Jerseyville, he received many honors from his former foes. He served a term as judge of the county court, two terms as president of the state board of agriculture, and several terms on the board of trustees for the University of Illinois. Despite these and many other public acknowledgments of his ability and integrity, Fulkerson's most satisfying honor must have been the GAR testimonial. At a special meeting, held May 10, 1898, local Union veterans endorsed Fulkerson as "a proper person" to raise a regiment of Illinois volunteers for service in the war with Spain. As evidence of his fitness for this task, the veterans swore the following: "Whereas, Col. William H. Fulkerson served in the Confederate army, during the Civil War, as Lieutenant, Captain and Colonel, and whereas record shows that he rendered good and efficient service and who has lived a citizen of Jersey Co. for more than twenty-five years, known to be a man of unimpeachable character and great integrity, progressive in his business relations and highly respected by all who know him, regardless of political affiliation."[59]

Varina Davis, widow of the Confederate president, deserves credit as the ultimate sectional peacemaker. Although appearing late on the scene, Mrs. Davis eagerly pursued reconciliation in the North through personal conversion. Following the death of her husband, Mrs. Davis believed she had inherited a mission to maintain the dignity and honor of the Lost Cause. She resided in New York City for the last fifteen years of her life, and she spent most of those years writing and talking about

1894), 191; *Portrait and Biographical Review of Johnson, Massac, Pope, and Hardin Counties, Illinois* (Chicago, 1893), 178; Charles Blanchard (ed.), *Counties of Clay and Owen, Indiana: Historical and Biographical* (Chicago, 1884), 386; James W. Ellis, *History of Jackson County, Iowa* (2 vols.; Chicago, 1910), II, 447–48.

59. Oscar B. Hamilton (ed.), *History of Jersey County, Illinois* (Chicago, 1919), 560–61; Grand Army of the Republic testimonial, in possession of William H. Fulkerson, Jerseyville, Illinois.

the Confederacy. She always arrayed herself quietly, like Queen Victoria, in black and enthusiastically welcomed every opportunity to justify or explain southern actions, praise Confederate courage, eulogize her gallant husband, and correct erroneous notions about Confederate history. Her zealous defense of the South produced frequent "covert little smiles" on the faces of northerners. Yet she behaved so openly, radiated such a kindly nature, and strove so earnestly to win friends for the South that she won the admiration of all.[60]

Mrs. Davis represented a widespread Confederate attitude in the North. Most former Confederates, whatever new northern identities they assumed, remained proud of the South and their roles in seeking southern independence. Loyalty to the Lost Cause, no less than service in the Confederacy, remained a matter of honor for southerners, and honor had always been a potent force in southern character. Yet pride in their section and their heritage did not diminish their willingness to subordinate old loyalties to future good. "Sectional pride is the proper thing," explained one Confederate carpetbagger, "sectional prejudice is the silly one." Unfortunately, this was the very point that northerners misunderstood most often about the attitudes of their former enemies. Conversely, southerners too often failed to see that continuing northern resentment of the South stemmed from this same misunderstanding. Appreciating the difference between pride and prejudice became the single biggest obstacle for Confederate carpetbaggers to overcome before they proceeded with their lives. It required that they take special pains to declare the subordination of old loyalties to new.[61]

Surely without this Confederate element in the North, national reconciliation might have been retarded many more years. Continued residence in the South, amid the rubble of war and chaos of Reconstruction, may have hardened the hearts of Confederate emigrants against Yankees. Their honey-dewed words of friendship and gallant gestures of acceptance would have been far fewer and much delayed. Burton Harrison accepted the results of the 1876 presidential election without rancor. What might his reaction have been as a New Orleans lawyer? Indeed, would Louisiana's electoral votes have been "disputed" had

60. Eron Rowland, *Varina Howell: Wife of Jefferson Davis* (2 vols.; New York, 1927–31), II, 541–42, 547.
61. Bertram Wyatt-Brown, *Southern Honor: Ethics and Behavior in the Old South* (New York, 1982), xviii; Thomas C. DeLeon, *Belles, Beaux and Brains of the Sixties* (New York, 1907), 459.

Harrison and the several thousand other energetic Louisianians who moved north during the 1860s and 1870s remained in the South? No answer to that question is possible, but one conclusion seems inescapable. The presence of Confederate carpetbaggers in the North speeded and ensured the quickest possible movement toward peace. The road to reunion had been soggy with blood for four years; it remained rocky and treacherous for the next thirty-five years, but determined, adventurous souls traveled it more in hope than in despair.

9

The Feathered Sword

No Confederate in the North was more hopeful of sectional peace than Constance Harrison; none was so deft at skirting boulders and stepping lightly over chasms along the road to reunion. She had handled George Templeton Strong superbly, and she appreciated the need to continue winning individual converts with honest convictions, gracious manners, and a charming personality. But Constance and other "writers in exile" also recognized the need for mass conversions. As authors, they knew that sensitive southerners with facile pens might combine a talent for reminiscence with their desire for sectional peace. The magic wands they used to conjure up loving images of a vanished past might also serve as mighty weapons to cleave the dragon of sectional animosity. The best writers might even convince some northerners that the Old South had not been such an evil place after all, that Confederates had gone to war from motives as pure and noble as those of any New England Congregationalist abolitionist, and that postwar southerners were anxious to forge a harmonious and mutually prosperous future for North and South.

Despite the opportunities for literary and journalistic careers in the postwar North, serious obstacles confronted southern writers in Yankeedom. Although a few writers with antebellum reputations to recommend them found publishers in the North, northern prejudices against the South stymied the majority. Even writers who enjoyed "cordial business and personal relations" with northern editors and publishers often had trouble publishing their work in the first few years after the war. New northern periodicals, such as *Scribner's Magazine*, *Lippincott's Magazine*, the *Galaxy*, the *Round Table*, and *Appleton's Journal*, published the work of unknown southerners, either from political sympathy or in hopes of increasing their circulation, but more influential journals, such as *Harper's Monthly* and the *Atlantic Monthly,* were less receptive. Getting a book published proved equally difficult. Some demand existed for biographies and histories of the war, but few southerners published novels in the North before 1880. The earliest publisher to favor southerners was D. Appleton and Company, which sponsored John Esten Cooke's biographies of Robert E. Lee and Stonewall Jackson in 1866 and 1870. Between 1868 and 1871, G. W. Carleton and Company published four novels by Cooke, and Charles Scribner and Company published works by Cooke and Edward Pollard in the late 1860s. Both men, however, had long-standing literary reputations, and Pollard's history was extremely critical of Jefferson Davis. As late as 1879, Sidney Lanier believed the best solution was to have his brother join him in the North so that they might establish their own publishing firm.[1]

In all fairness, it should be pointed out that often the southern writers who complained most vociferously about northern literary prejudices could explain their piles of rejection slips on circumstances other than flaming northern fanaticism. Some of the rejected work, even by established writers, simply was not very good. Southern editors rejected bad poetry and poorly written stories, too. William Hand Browne, editor of the *Southern Review* in Baltimore, complained about the difficulty of getting high-quality contributions. People with something to say, he lamented, did not know how to say it, and writers with attractive styles produced nothing worth reading. Alabama poet Samuel M. Peck learned, to his dismay, that having work accepted and receiving good reviews often depended on one's social and business connections. He acknowledged that sectional prejudices sometimes influenced editors and reviewers, but more often it was simply a question of "literary 'log rolling.' "[2]

1. Paul H. Buck, *The Road to Reunion, 1865–1900* (Boston, 1937), 220–35; Arthur John, *The Best Years of the "Century": Richard Watson Gilder, "Scribner's Monthly," and the "Century Magazine," 1870–1909* (Urbana, 1981), ix–x; Jay B. Hubbell, *The South in American Literature, 1607–1900* (Durham, 1954), 701–702, 726–27; Frank Luther Mott, *A History of American Magazines* (5 vols.; Cambridge, Mass., 1938–68), III, 48–49; Laura Newell Young, "Southern Literary Magazines, 1865–1887: With Special Reference to Literary Criticism" (M.A. thesis, Duke University, 1940), 23–24; Rayburn S. Moore, "Southern Writers and Northern Literary Magazines, 1865–1890" (Ph.D. dissertation, Duke University, 1956), 2–12; Sidney Lanier to Clifford A. Lanier, June 8, 1879, in Charles R. Anderson *et al.* (eds.), *The Centennial Edition of the Works of Sidney Lanier* (10 vols.; Baltimore, 1945), X, 121.

2. William H. Browne to Thomas J. Hand, August 12,1867, in Kane and Hand Family Papers, CU; Samuel M. Peck to James M. Thompson, November 26, 1887, in James Maurice Thompson Papers, EU.

More to the point, much early postwar southern writing—be it fiction, history, or poetry—was too self-consciously Confederate to win northern acceptance. Northerners, the bulk of the reading public, wanted to read about the war. War themes, even those of reconciliation, enjoyed wide popularity through the 1860s. Most of the successful authors, however, were northerners writing from a northern perspective. The northern public, understandably, was in no mood to read southern justifications of the war. Very soon after the war it became permissible to draw nostalgic pictures of the Old South, but southern writers had to make sure their rosy portrayals of plantation life did not degenerate into apologies for slavery and secession. The war and its causes had to be treated gingerly when addressing northern readers. Successful Confederate literary aspirants learned to temper their own sectional prejudices and to integrate their praise of the Old South with appeals for sectional peace.[3]

Constance Harrison's postwar fictional and nonfictional reminiscences clearly paid homage to the Old South, even the Confederacy, yet she enjoyed a successful northern literary career for two reasons. First, she always restrained her praise of the Confederacy. She never trampled on northern sensibilities by portraying Yankees as fiendish fanatics or by bestowing a monopoly of wisdom, virtue, or courage on southerners. Second, Constance benefited from good timing. She did not begin her postwar literary career until 1876, and she did not make it a full-time avocation until the mid-1880s. By that time, the most zealous northern resistance to southern writers had long since passed. In fact, by the 1890s, writings about the South enjoyed a new vogue, following a decline in popularity in the 1870s. As American literature entered an age of realism and regionalism, the South exercised an irresistible, almost exotic, hold on northern readers. In the hands of a skillful writer, the South's colorful cast of genteel aristocrats, coquettish belles, devoted mammies, and rumptious hill folk could be enchanting. By the mid-1880s, a former Yankee carpetbagger asserted that American literature had become "not only Southern in type, but distinctly Confederate in sympathy." He exaggerated somewhat, but certainly southern writers found it easier than twenty years earlier to express their devotion to the Old South and the Lost Cause. It would have been "a miracle of

3. Buck, *Road to Reunion*, 196–235; Robert A. Lively, *Fiction Fights the Civil War: An Unfinished Chapter in the Literary History of the American People* (Chapel Hill, 1957), 77–78; Joyce Appleby, "Reconciliation and the Northern Novelist, 1865–1880," *Civil War History*, X (1964), 117–29.

Stupidity," noted an observer in the mid-1890s, "if in the . . . heyday of provincial literature," southerners had not reaped golden rewards.[4]

Constance reaped the benefits of much spadework, but her own contributions, if usually belated, cannot be ignored. If not an early literary leader in reunion, she did join the ranks of the reconciliation army when a few skirmishes, at least, remained to be won. She pursued the theme in various ways. Some of her short stories showed how North and South might forget sectional differences by dwelling on common interests. In "Golden-Rod," the finest of northern and southern postwar aristocracy hobnob at an elegant New York banquet. Both sets ignore "their mutual slight unpleasantness of a few years gone by" to savor a shared sense of "superiority" over the "mass of Americans not endowed like themselves with *sangre azul.*" In another story, "Cherrycote," a family divided by the war seeks to reunite itself. The hero, Lancelot Barksdale, is educated in the North following the death of his northern mother. When the war comes, Lance's "Northern training and sympathies" cause a family rupture. Lance returns to the North and stays there for ten years. He fancies during those years that he has outgrown his sentimental attachment to the South, but when he at last returns to the old plantation, he feels a lump rising in his throat, a flush coming to his cheek. He is still a southerner, and he and surviving family members soon forgive and forget the past. Lance's fiancée, who had renounced him when he went north, is again his for the asking.[5]

Constance sought always to convince both North and South that neither side should shoulder all the blame for the war. The war had been a tragic blunder, a conflict no one wanted, yet sectional loyalties and honor had produced inevitable divisions. Who, now, she asked, would be so foolish as to say which side had been more honorable, more virtuous, more devoted to its convictions? True, convention required southern writers to admit that the Union was worth preserving and to rejoice that the Confederacy, after all, had fallen. Some Confederates found it impossible to utter or write such words. These diehards circumvented the difficulty by declaring that Union victory had been God's

4. Sheddon Van Auken, "The Southern Historical Novel in the Early Twentieth Century," *Journal of Southern History*, XIV (1948), 162–63; Francis Pendleton Gaines, *The Southern Plantation: A Study in the Development and the Accuracy of a Tradition* (New York, 1924), 62–64, 89; Lively, *Fiction Fights the Civil War*, 22–23; Hubbell, *South in American Literature*, 701–702; Buck, *Road to Reunion*, 197.

5. Both stories appear in Mrs. Burton Harrison, *An Idelweiss of the Sierras: Golden-Rod and Other Tales* (New York, 1892), 72, 147–59.

will. This approach allowed them to accept defeat graciously without suggesting that their cause had been totally lacking in idealism or nobility. Constance herself frequently stressed how reluctantly Virginians had seceded, resisting leaving the Union until northern aggression demanded the defense of southern soil. Colonel Throckmorton, in *Flower De Hundred,* pronounced secession unthinkable. A similar character, in "Crow's Nest," exclaims, " 'Egad, sir, . . . it's arrant nonsense. Talk about breaking up the Union. . . . It can't be done, sir. Of one thing you may be certain—Virginia, Mother of Presidents, will stand firm, sir.' "[6]

Constance obscured, indeed, very nearly obliterated, slavery as a cause of the war. In her stories, no southerner ever went to war to preserve slavery. Likewise, no northerner ever fought to liberate the slaves. Defense of southern rights and preservation of the Union became the predominant justifications of her characters. Colonel Lancelot Carlyle, one of Harrison's heroes in *The Carlyles,* returns to Virginia after the war with "hope for the future." "In his heart," explains Constance, "there was left no enmity. The constitutional theory of the right of secession having been fought out, there assuredly remained to him the right to snatch his salvation from the wreck." Lancelot's chief rival for the hand of Monimia Carlyle is a federal soldier, Donald Lyndsay. Though only a private, Lyndsay is a Yale graduate who has thought long and hard about secession. "With all the strength that was in him," Harrison assures readers, "he believed the North to be in the right." Yet Lyndsay had "no particular feeling in the matter of slavery." In *Flower De Hundred,* as young men of both sections march off to the front, they represent "soldiers of a caliber no other nation's history has surpassed." They were idealistic, dedicated, and totally committed to their respective views of government and nationhood. Colonel Throckmorton, who had always lamented that he had not "been born free of the responsibility of slaves," saw the war not as a contest to defend slavery but a means of shedding that terrible burden. The gentle colonel ordered his overseers "to make no effort to restrain those who showed any desire to go."[7]

Northern and southern characters respect each other in Constance's stories, and no one anticipates major problems of readjustment when

6. Mrs. Burton Harrison, *Crow's Nest and Belhaven Tales* (New York, 1892), 131.

7. Mrs. Burton Harrison, *The Carlyles: A Story of the Fall of the Confederacy* (New York, 1905), 36–37, 78, *Flower De Hundred: The Story of a Virginia Plantation* (New York, 1890), 186, 200–201.

the war ends. Lancelot Carlyle, in charting his postwar course, "felt sure that the problem not only of existence, but of success, would soon be solved for him." He had survived the storm; he was young and strong. Although rivals for the same belle, Lancelot and Lyndsay respect each other. Monimia and Lyndsay, headed pell mell toward one of those reconciliation marriages, find not only personal love for each other but love for the opposite section. Monimia learns that Yankees, too, "had been fighting for a principle." She becomes convinced, like her lover, "that all the glory and power of the future of their land was to be maintained, as it had been won, only by a united nation." " 'If all the *other side* were like him, papa,' " she gushes upon realizing her affection for the Union private, " 'I think it would not be long before the breach was healed.' " The heroine in "A Daughter of the South," Berthe de Lagastine, a Mississippi belle, cannot understand how the chief rivals for her hand, again a federal and a Confederate soldier, can be on such "amiable terms." Gradually, Berthe sees the light. She melts before the Yankee colonel's charm and admits, " 'I am afraid I am getting to like him.' " The Yankee wins the heroine yet again, although this time with a clever twist. " 'The only thing I fear,' " insists Berthe to her fiancé, " 'is that people will say I have done this to avenge history.' " [8]

Constance expressed those thoughts in the 1890s, and she wrote *The Carlyles* in the early 1900s. Despite all the reassuring talk about national unity, she still felt obliged, forty years after the war, to persuade readers that northerners and southerners were friends. True, Constance also recognized the popularity of reconciliation themes and Civil War literature generally during the 1890s. The genre reached one of its periodic peaks of popularity in the decade, an indication that Americans craved further assurance about the unity of their nation. Constance knew how to pander to public demand and popular trends; yet she was not a literary hack. She never wrote insincerely about the South or the Confederacy. The reconciliation theme remained popular because it seemed timely, and Constance wrote because she wanted to feed the reconciliation spirit.

Long before Constance Harrison approached being reconstructed, Charles Force Deems embarked upon one of the earliest campaigns for sectional peace. A Marylander by birth and a North Carolinian by residence, Deems opposed secession but worked unceasingly for the

8. Harrison, *The Carlyles*, 36–37, 82–83, 114–15, 196, *A Daughter of the South and Shorter Tales* (New York, 1892), 34–55, 64, 111.

Confederate cause. He raised money to care for the state's homeless, destitute, and bereaved. He labored to establish a college for the orphans of southern soldiers. He operated a military academy, started just before the war, until most of his young cadets had been called into the ranks. Notwithstanding his tireless efforts and fervent Confederate prayers, Deems rejoiced when the war ended. The carnage of war had touched him deeply; his own eldest son had died at Gettysburg. Although convinced of the constitutionality of secession, Deems loved the Union and believed that the nation, to be great, must be reunited. In August, 1865, Deems traveled to New York "to look at things." "I'm clean for a man's adapting himself to his altered condition," Deems confided to a friend before going north. After a short visit, he decided to move his family to Gotham, where he could provide for them while working to nourish a spirit of amenity and forgiveness between North and South. The entire family arrived on a dreary December night to try its luck.[9]

Deems's vehicle for promoting "the timely and supremely important mission" of sectional peace became a weekly newspaper entitled the *Watchman*. As founder, publisher, and editor of the *Watchman*, Deems promised his readers intelligent, fair-minded articles and commentary on politics, finance, commerce, foreign affairs, religion, popular culture, sociology, history, agriculture, and literature, as well as original fiction and poems. Deems lifted much of his material from other American and British periodicals, but most of his original contributions came from southern authors, including Essie Cheesborough and Augustus J. Requier. Deems assumed that the largest portion of his early audience would be southern. If he was a "Watchman," reporting the "signs of the times" to all citizens, he would be particularly mindful that southerners knew "the movement of events." The South, he knew, must lead the way in reconciliation; it must set the tone of moderation. "We want," Deems declared bluntly, "the South to do right."[10]

Deems acknowledged the difficulties of addressing North and South on such a delicate issue so soon after the war. Yet not to speak, he

9. Daniel E. Sutherland, "Charles Force Deems and the *Watchman:* An Early Attempt at Post–Civil War Sectional Reconciliation," *North Carolina Historical Review*, LVII (1980), 410–12; Charles F. Deems to Zebulon B. Vance, August 23, 1865, in Zebulon B. Vance Papers, NCA; Charles Force Deems, *Autobiography of Charles Force Deems and Memoir by His Sons, Rev. Edward M. Deems and Francis M. Deems* (New York, 1897), 170–71.

10. *Watchman*, January 13, 1866, p. 4, October 10, 1866, p. 324.

asserted, would be "cowardly," "selfish," and "mean." Admitting that
he found many northern principles "odious," Deems insisted that he
had never hated the northern people. The South had faults, too, he
believed; not all southerners were paragons of virtue. The important
thing to recognize, he stressed, was that neither section should be
blamed for the war and that neither side should suffer alone the burden
of peace. "Is forgiveness never to come?" he pleaded. "Is wrath to be
nursed forever?" Deems continued to beseech and prod North and
South to join his crusade. He sometimes allowed southern sympathies to
cloud his interpretation of events, as demonstrated by his editorials
against the protective tariff, Freedmen's Bureau Bill, and Fourteenth
Amendment. More often, Deems appealed by humble petition to Americans to forget past disagreements and to rejoice in their common
heritage and government. Temper justice with mercy, he advised northern readers. Allow the South to recoup its losses so that southerners
might contribute, as they wished to do, to a strong, robust United States.
He advised southerners in a similar manner. "There is much magnanimity, much moderation, much forbearance at the North," he informed
southerners. "Let us not hold a large portion of the people of our
common country responsible for the sayings of a few of the specially
irritable. God be thanked that all the Northern people are not Sumners
and Stevenses."[11]

Deems's plea caught public attention. Several journals in both sections reprinted his opening editorial on reconciliation. Many Americans doubtless applauded his observations on the national situation.
Like many observers, Deems blamed the nation's political leaders for
fomenting unnecessary sectional discord. What made the politicians
especially dangerous, he submitted, was the political apathy that had
infested the country since the war. Lack of public interest had allowed
"unprincipled men" to assume control of the nation. Deems urged people to be active and independent in politics. People must vote, and they
must vote for the best men, not for old party labels that had become
"hollow and false." Americans must employ their voting power in the
same fashion that Deems wielded his editorial pen: as a righteous weapon with which to smite political Philistines. As Deems stepped up his
rhetoric, his paper's circulation increased. Readers wrote letters to the
editor praising his crusade. "I am a Northern man," confessed one

11. *Ibid.*, January 27, 1866, p. 20, February 3, 1866, p. 28, June 16, 1866, p. 180,
August 4, 1866, p. 236.

correspondent, "and, of course, can not agree with you in all respects; but I do not hesitate to say that yours is the best paper of the kind published in New York. You have certainly deserved success, and I hope and trust you may obtain it."[12]

And yet the *Watchman* failed. Despite last-minute efforts by a number of northern and southern businessmen in New York to save the financially distraught journal, Deems issued his last number on January 1, 1867. Numerous reasons explain the journal's untimely demise. Deems's amateur business practices, his failure to reach a wider audience, and his southern background may have contributed, but the biggest single explanation was poor timing. In 1866, the nation was not ready for sectional reconciliation. The war had left too many loose ends, political, social, and economic, for northerners and southerners to be entirely at ease with one another. Most Americans probably wanted to move on, but they did not want to march ahead too quickly. Deems, who suffered an "almost deadly blow" when the *Watchman* failed, recognized this fact belatedly. "Prejudices naturally engendered" by the war, he admitted in the mid-1870s, had scuttled a noble project. Radicals of both sections and of both political parties kept their constituents in doubt as to the wisdom of rapid reunion. Everyone agreed that reunion must come, but important political, financial, and humanitarian interests must be protected in the process. As Henry Watterson later observed, a policy of reconciliation would have deprived political extremists of "their best card." "South no less than North, 'the bloody shirt' was trumps."[13]

Deems was not the only Confederate to establish a reconciliation paper in New York. Sumner A. Cunningham, born and raised on a Tennessee farm and a veteran of the 41st Tennessee Regiment, engaged in a variety of mercantile and journalistic pursuits in Tennessee and Georgia after the war. About 1880, Cunningham decided to try his luck in New York City, where he lived for about four years and published a monthly newspaper entitled *Our Day*. A curious New Yorker who purchased the first issue of *Our Day* would have discovered that Cunningham, like Reverend Deems, intended his journal to serve multiple

12. *Ibid.*, February 24, 1866, p. 52, July 21, 1866, p. 220.

13. Sutherland, "Charles Force Deems and the *Watchman*," 422–25; Charles F. Deems to Daniel L. Swain, January 24, 1867, in David Lowry Swain Papers, SHC; Deems, *Autobiography,* 259–60; Henry Watterson, *"Marse Henry": An Autobiography* (2 vols.; New York, 1919), I, 184–85.

purposes. The paper, Cunningham insisted, would be nonpartisan and would seek sectional reconciliation, but it would do so by vindicating the South ("subjected to so much calumny for a score of years by designing politicians") and explaining the southern perspective to unenlightened northerners. Cunningham also planned that his paper should provide a registry and directory for southerners in New York, so that friends might locate one another. He intended *Our Day* to be a guide for southerners visiting the city, providing information on entertainment, hotels, and local customs. Finally, he would give his paper a literary flavor by filling it with fiction, poetry, biographical sketches, political commentary, humor, and essays on southern life.[14]

Some people predicted a great future for *Our Day*. Andrew H. H. Dawson, a Confederate resident of Gotham, prophesied success based on "a proclivity to clangishness" in the human race. With fifty thousand southerners in New York, he reasoned, the project could not fail. "The mission of *Our Day*," he advised, "should be to unite all Southern exiles on Northern soil in the strongest bonds of social sympathy, without meddling directly or indirectly with politics, or seeking to excite the remotest shadow of prejudice against any other section or race." A Virginian sent Cunningham one dollar for a year's subscription. She believed the editor would give the southern people "an impartial hearing." "The South," she lamented, "is more a *terra incognita* to the world than Africa or China."[15]

Cunningham's newspaper survived about a year and a half. It might have lasted longer, but Cunningham's tone became increasingly sectional and partisan. In fact, he became openly Confederate in his sympathies, encouraging Confederate reunions and raising funds to build a home for disabled Confederates. Cunningham could be a cantankerous fellow under the best of circumstances, blunt in his opinions even with fellow southerners. When he began preaching the virtues of the Confederacy in his gospel of reunion, it became too much for northern readers, even in the 1880s. They stiffened when he complained about the prejudices of northern journals against southern writers. They grew angry when he blamed continuing sectional antagonism on the northern press and politicians. However correct he may have been in his accusations and however sincere in his desire to "refute the slanders" against the

14. *Our Day*, I (January, 1883), 1–2; Reda C. Goff, "The Confederate Veteran Magazine," *Tennessee Historical Quarterly*, XXXI (1972), 45–60.
15. *Our Day*, I (May, 1883), 118, 125.

South, Cunningham seemed equally guilty of inflaming public opinion. Still mumbling about Yankee villainy, he returned south and, in 1893, started a new monthly magazine, the *Confederate Veteran*.[16]

George Cary Eggleston promoted reconciliation in both his private life and his writing, but he took his lead from a Yankee. Eggleston received his first northern job, as a reporter on the Brooklyn *Daily Union,* through the influence of his antislavery, Unionist brother Edward. The former Confederate cavalryman began work with some misgivings, for he expected a rough time from the newspaper's staunch Republican editor, Theodore Tilton. "I have often wondered over his attitude towards me," Eggleston recalled of Tilton. "I was an ex-rebel soldier, and in 1870 he was still mercilessly at war with Southern men and Southern ideas. My opinions on many subjects were the exact opposite of his own, and I was young enough to be insistent in the expression of my opinion, especially in conversation with one to whom I knew my views to be *Anathema Marantha*." Yet Tilton did not react hostilely. Perhaps his wife's confession of her adulterous affair with Henry Ward Beecher a few weeks before Eggleston arrived in Brooklyn distracted Tilton. Perhaps Tilton's recent defection from Republican radicalism and his drift toward Liberal Republicanism made him more sympathetic toward southern rebels. Whatever the reason, from their first meeting, marveled Eggleston, Tilton proved "courteous and genial," and he later became positively "cordial and even enthusiastic in his friendship." Within a matter of weeks, Tilton promoted Eggleston from reporter to editorial writer. The friendship endured, and a few years later, when the Tiltons and Beecher became tangled in their unsavory litigation, Eggleston aided Tilton in behind-the-scenes negotiations that possibly saved all the principals from donning prison clothes.[17]

Eggleston's experience with Tilton holds an important lesson. Tilton directed whatever antisouthern feelings he harbored against southern "ideas" rather than against southerners. When confronted with a real Confederate, human elements came into play that could confuse and

16. *Ibid.,* I (May, 1883), 125, I (July, 1883), 184, II (October, 1883), 49, II (December, 1883), 65–66, II (March–April, 1884), 125, II (June, 1884), 142–46; Gaines M. Foster, *Ghosts of the Confederacy: Defeat, the Lost Cause, and the Emergence of the New South, 1865 to 1913* (New York, 1987), 106, 110.

17. George Cary Eggleston, *Recollections of a Varied Life* (New York, 1910), 109, 116–17, 129; Altina L. Walker, *Reverend Beecher and Mrs. Tilton: Sex and Class in Victorian America* (Amherst, 1982), 8, 84; James Herbert Morse Diaries, April 21, 1910 (MS in NYHS).

sometimes explode ideological prejudices. Time and again personal acquaintance proved the key to alleviating tensions and inspiring a spirit of reconciliation between northerners and southerners. In this instance, Tilton, the northerner, initiated the truce, but Confederates just as often took the lead. Eggleston quickly learned the lesson and sallied forth from the office of the *Daily Union* a loyal disciple of sectional harmony. During the next forty-odd years, he won enduring northern friendships with his forthright yet modest personality. Eggleston possessed what one Yankee called "a free social lovableness," so that even though he wore his southern loyalties conspicuously on a broad Confederate sleeve, he never betrayed any bitterness or boisterousness that would have soured northern acquaintances.[18]

Eggleston's conciliatory efforts attracted national attention in 1874 with serial publication of his wartime reminiscences in the prestigious, antisouthern *Atlantic Monthly.* John Esten Cooke called the Boston-based journal "a New England coterie affair altogether," and few southerners, not even men with national literary reputations, like Cooke, found their names among its contributors before the 1880s. But William Dean Howells, editor of the *Atlantic* and leader of the northeastern literary establishment, had met Eggleston and liked him. He believed Eggleston was just the right person to write a lively yet dispassionate account of a rebel soldier's role in the rebellion. Eggleston hesitated, recognizing the delicacy of the task. The "passions aroused by the war . . . had scarcely begun to cool," and Eggleston feared that the least slip of his pen would exacerbate northern prejudices. He finally accepted the task because, as he explained to his friend Cooke, "the opportunity is a good one for running in bits of fact which may change some people's views of the South and Southerners, for both are sadly misunderstood."[19]

Publication of the first installment of "A Rebel's Recollections" brought "a hornet's nest" upon Howells, not so much for what Eggleston said as because he said it in the *Atlantic.* Howells, to his credit, stood by his Confederate protégé. As the next six installments appeared, swarming hornets gave way to sweet "psalms," as both public and critics

18. Evelyn M. Craig to Harold F. Brigham, August 31, 1960, in Edward Eggleston Papers, ISL; Morse Diaries, March 25, 1884.

19. John E. Cooke to William C. Church, March 26, 1866, in William Conant Church Papers, NYPL; Eggleston, *Recollections of a Varied Life,* 147–49; George C. Eggleston to John E. Cooke, April 26, 1874, in John Esten Cooke Papers, DU.

praised Eggleston's "spirit and temper" in handling such a "sensitive subject." Northern reviewers agreed that his humorous, honest, and gracious rendition of the war from the view of a private soldier contained "nothing at which the most captious could take offence." Eggleston became the toast of northern literary circles, fêted by former abolitionists and Unionists at an endless string of receptions and banquets. His series, dubbed by one modern historian "an early Civil War classic," set the tone for much of the reconciliation literature to follow.[20]

Eggleston's other creative work, both fiction and nonfiction, repeated the tone. His favorite topics were the South and the war; his favorite themes were southern greatness and sectional harmony. For Eggleston, the two themes were never at odds; they flowed imperceptively together. Typical of his nonfiction is *The History of the Confederate War*. Despite its partisan title, Eggleston's history is one of the first balanced accounts of the war written by a Confederate. "The American people are again completely one," Eggleston concludes in his history; "the bitterness and resentment to which the fierce struggle gave birth have been displaced by kindlier thoughts in all but the narrowest and most ungenerous minds." His own efforts to tell the story of the war "with the utmost impartiality and the most scrupulous regard for truth" represented, he suggested, a new nationalism. Admittedly, by the time he published his history, in 1910, the bitterness of a half century earlier should have receded. Yet the book reflected Eggleston's philosophy since 1870; it represented the culmination of his postwar work.[21]

Less formally, Eggleston published a volume of brief episodes recounting his military experiences as a private soldier. *Southern Soldier Stories* combines fictional sketches with firsthand observations of the war. Through the entire work, Eggleston sprinkles reminders that northern and southern soldiers were much alike, all Americans. "There were two instances of supreme heroism in the Civil War," he maintains in one story—Pickett's charge at Gettysburg and the federal assault on Marye's Heights at Fredericksburg. One represented an act of southern heroism, the other a display of northern courage. Other stories suggest

20. Eggleston, *Recollections of a Varied Life*, 149–50; George Cary Eggleston, *A Rebel's Recollections*, ed. David H. Donald (1875; rpr. Bloomington, 1959), 16; Thomas L. Connelly, *The Marble Man: Robert E. Lee and His Image in American Society* (1977; rpr. Baton Rouge, 1978), 71, 107.

21. Daniel Aaron, *The Unwritten War: American Writers and the Civil War* (New York, 1973), 314; George Cary Eggleston, *History of the Confederate War, Its Causes and Its Conduct: A Narrative and Critical History* (2 vols.; New York, 1910), II, 350.

similar contrasts. For the benefit of southern readers, Eggleston even excuses the wanton destruction of southern property by Yankee armies during the war. He compares the careers of two federal officers, one a low scoundrel who destroyed for pleasure, the other an absolute gentleman who protected southern property. Such contrasts must be expected in wartime, Eggleston maintains. No nation can vouch for the personality or character of every man in uniform.[22]

The same spirit prevailed in Eggleston's fiction. His novels, already cited for their sympathetic and nostalgic glimpses of southern life, also promoted the cause of sectional harmony. Eggleston's first novel, *A Man of Honor,* does not give heavy-handed treatment to the theme, yet any story about North and South that concludes with the marriage of a northern man and a southern woman, even if they are distant cousins, has made its point. More than thirty years later, in *A Daughter of the South,* Eggleston enthusiastically argued the same issue. This novel portrays the rightness and wrongness of the war on both sides: the South ought not to have seceded; the North ought not to have waged war on her sister states. Eggleston depicts the honor and courage of both northern and southern soldiers, and he reminds readers of a dilemma faced by many Americans during the war. "I have near friends in the Northern army and other near friends in the Southern," reasons the story's hero. "I cannot regard any of them as enemies."[23]

Eggleston's balanced perspective owed little to his northern birth, for that had been neutralized by his ancestry, his years in Virginia, and his service in Lee's army. It came, rather, from his postwar residence. Living among northerners, asserted an observer, enabled Eggleston "to treat the scenes of his youth in a broadly national spirit." "He is without partisanship," this commentator continued, "his Southern sympathies live, but they have been mellowed and nationalized by the varied experiences of middle and later years." Eggleston had close Confederate friends in the North, including Roger Pryor, and he was among the earliest members of the New York Southern Society and the Confederate Veteran Camp of New York. Yet, throughout his literary and journalistic careers, Eggleston secured warm northern friends, too. His profession, like those of so many other Confederate carpetbaggers, served

22. George Cary Eggleston, *Southern Soldier Stories* (New York, 1898), 22, 206–209, 215–19.

23. Eggleston, *Recollections of a Varied Life,* 1515–53; George Cary Eggleston, *A Man of Honor* (New York, 1873), 221–22, *A Daughter of the South: A War's-End Romance* (New York, 1905), 6–9, 384–86.

as his bridge to northern acceptance, respectability, and security. Indeed, he became far more active as a member and officer in the Authors Club, which included such folk as Richard Henry Stoddard, Edmund Clarence Stedman, Richard Watson Gilder, and Brander Matthews, than in the Southern Society. By 1880, he was firmly entrenched in the northern literary world, and by 1892 he could speak to a northern friend about "our New York." Not by chance—and probably with a shrewd eye to effect—did Eggleston sign the preface to his fourth edition of *A Rebel's Recollections,* in 1905, from the Authors Club.[24]

Other southerners believed, like Eggleston, that the printed page held vast possibilities for defusing northern prejudices. Sidney Lanier understood the necessity of heeding northern opinions, allaying northern suspicions, and diminishing northern prejudices if the South was ever again to prosper. "Our people have failed to perceive the deeper movements under-running the time," he complained to his brother; "they lie wholly off, out of the stream of thought, and whirl their poor dead leaves of recollections round and round, in a piteous eddy that has all the wear and tear of motion without any of the rewards of progress." Lanier could be arrogant and sectional. He once confessed to his wife, "The more I am thrown against these people here, and the more reverses I suffer at their hands, the more confident I am of beating them finally." Yet Lanier hastened to add that he felt no hatred for the Yankees. "I do not mean, by 'beating,'" he explained, "that I am in opposition to them, or that I hate them, or feel aggrieved with them: no, they know no better, and they act up to their lights with wonderful energy and consistency: I only mean that I am sure of being able, some day, to teach them better things and nobler modes of thought and conduct." Lanier was condescending, perhaps, but not irredeemably so.[25]

Like his private thoughts, Lanier's published work, both prose and poetry, varies widely in tone and purpose. He was capable of writing biting denunciations of northern political actions. On occasion, as in "Corn," the first poem to win him national attention, Lanier could

24. John Calvin Metcalf, "George Cary Eggleston," in Edwin Anderson Alderman and Joel Chandler Harris (eds.), *Library of Southern Literature* (17 vols.; Atlanta, 1909), IV, 1530; Allan Nevins, *The Evening Post: A Century of Journalism* (New York, 1922), 412–14; Morse Diaries, January 30, 1883, April 21, 1910; George C. Eggleston to Edmund C. Stedman, December 1, 1877, November 19, 1880, September 13, 1892, all in Edward Clarence Stedman Papers, CU; Eggleston, *Rebel's Recollections,* 24.

25. Sidney Lanier to Clifford A. Lanier, June 8, 1879, to Mary D. Lanier, September 24, 1874, both in Anderson *et al.* (eds.), *Works of Sidney Lanier,* X, 123, IX, 88.

criticize his own section and people. But several of his most widely circulated poems, albeit not always his best ones, pursued the reconciliation theme.

Tiger-Lilies is Lanier's only novel. He began writing it during the war, completed it early in 1867, and published it, largely at his own expense, later that year. *Tiger-Lilies* is a confusing, almost plotless story seldom read today, which is unfortunate, for Lanier provides realistic scenes of soldier life in camp, on the march, in battle, and in prison. Lanier dwells, too, on the trials of wartime civilian life, particularly among the hill folk he knew so well. *Tiger-Lilies* is one of the earliest southern war novels to view the war through the eyes of nonslaveholding southerners. Indeed, one of Lanier's characters complains about being snared in "'a rich man's war an' a poor man's fight.'" Most important, however, is Lanier's nonpartisan tone, the book's lack of "sectional rancor." Even most northern reviewers admitted this point, with not a little surprise.[26]

But Lanier conceived and consummated *Tiger-Lilies* long before he thought of moving north. Although the book suggests that the Georgian could view the war in a way that would ensure his welcome in Yankeedom, it reflects nothing of his northern experience. That could not be said of two important poems, "The Centennial Meditation of Columbia" and "Psalm of the West," Lanier wrote on commission for the nation's centennial celebration. It is possible to overdramatize the centennial as a turning point toward national unity. In 1876 federal troops still supported Republican political regimes in Florida, Louisiana, and South Carolina; most of the South had yet to feast at the "Great Barbecue" that had produced economic prosperity and a Gilded Age elsewhere in the country. Still, many northerners and southerners used the symbol of national birth as a means of reducing sectional passions, and with some success. The selection of reconciliation as a theme for the celebration showed progress and indicated that political prejudices were losing their stranglehold on the national conscience. The festivities of that year inspired an avalanche of orations and publications that demonstrated the importance of the issue in public opinion.[27]

Lanier penned his "Centennial Meditation," adjoined to music by Dudley Buck, as a cantata for the opening ceremonies of the Centennial

26. Jack DeBellis, *Sidney Lanier* (New York, 1972), 23–31; Anderson *et al.* (eds.), *Works of Sidney Lanier,* V, vii–xxix.

27. Buck, *Road to Reunion,* 134–40; Huber Winton Ellingsworth, "Southern Reconciliation Orators in the North, 1868–1899" (Ph.D. dissertation, Florida State University, 1955), 52–53.

Exposition at Philadelphia. The Centennial Commission had already asked John Greenleaf Whittier to contribute a hymn for the ceremonies when Lanier's friend Bayard Taylor suggested that a non–New Englander write the cantata. The commission outdid itself in selecting a former Confederate soldier. Few could miss the symbolic juxtaposition of abolitionist and rebel as authors of the hymn and cantata. "The Southern people make a great deal more of my appointment to write the cantata-poem than I ever expected," admitted a surprised Lanier, "and it really seems to be regarded as one of the most substantial tokens of reconciliation yet evinced by that vague *tertium quid* which they are accustomed to represent to themselves under the general term of 'The North.'"[28]

Lanier became infected by the spirit. He wanted to write "a poem of reconciliation" that would celebrate a united American republic, a nation that had survived the most malevolent forces of man and nature. Winds, seas, droughts, famines, and wars had whispered menacingly to Americans through the decades, *"It shall not be,"* but all obstacles had been scaled, all evils had been conquered. The republic had survived for a hundred years because its people were united in their determination that it should survive:

> Toil through the stertorous death of the Night,
> Toil when wild brothers—wars new—dark the Light,
> Toil, and forgive, and kiss o'er, and replight.

Later, an angel of the Lord assures Columbia:

> Long as thine Eagle harms no Dove,
> Long as thy Law by law shall grow,
> Long as thy God is God above,
> Thy brother every man below,
> So long, dear Land of all my love,
> Thy name shall shine, thy fame shall glow![29]

Lanier's cantata received a tepid critical reception, but that had nothing to do with the sentiments it expressed. Critics railed, rather, against the ambiguity of its imagery and the utter impossibility of singing it with

---

28. Aubrey Harrison Starke, *Sidney Lanier: A Biographical and Critical Study* (New York, 1964), 235; Sidney Lanier to Mary D. Lanier, January 8, 1876, to Gibson Peacock, April 27, 1876, both in Anderson *et al.* (eds.), *Works of Sidney Lanier*, IX, 293–94, 359–60.

29. Sidney Lanier to Dudley Buck, January 29, 1876, to Bayard Taylor, April 8, 1876, Sidney Lanier, "The Centennial Meditation of Columbia," all in Anderson *et al.* (eds.), *Works of Sidney Lanier*, IX, 310, 352, I, 60–62.

any degree of clarity. "He has written a beautiful poem," decided the New York *Herald,* "but it is obscure to the eye and must be unintelligible to the ear." Reconciliation unheard is reconciliation unappreciated. In the end, the poem produced hard feelings by causing southern critics to snipe at northern critics who sniped at Lanier. Southerners did not like the poem any better than northerners, but they resented hearing Lanier's well-intended efforts criticized in unsympathetic tones by Yankee know-it-alls.[30]

Lippincott's Magazine commissioned Lanier's second reconciliation poem, "Psalm of the West." *Lippincott's* had from its inception in 1868 been on friendly terms with the South and southern writers. More to the point, Lanier had always been treated kindly by its editors, who had published "Corn" after both *Scribner's* and the *Atlantic* had rejected it. Now *Lippincott's* offered Lanier three thousand dollars for a poem to be published in the July, 1876, issue. "Psalm of the West" does not preach reconciliation quite so self-consciously as does "Centennial Meditation," but it certainly overflows with patriotic fervor. Lanier had originally entitled the poem "To the United States of America." Writing it became an emotional experience for him, and the critics received it far more appreciatively than they did his cantata. Lanier's poem portrays America as "the West," a new land, filled with hope for all mankind:

> Land of the willful gospel, thou worst and thou best;
> Tall Adam of lands, new-made of the dust of the West;
> Thou wroughtest alone in the Garden of God,
> Till he fashioned lithe Freedom to lie for thine Eve on thy breast.

Only near the end does he stress the sectional antagonism that had nearly wrecked the garden. When he does, Lanier sings hopefully of the future:

> Thy Past sings ever Freedom's song,
> Thy Future's voice sounds wondrous free;
> And Freedom is more large than Crime,
> And Error is more small than Time.[31]

James Maurice Thompson may have produced even more solid contributions to sectional peace than Lanier. Thompson did not care much

30. Anderson *et al.* (eds.), *Works of Sidney Lanier,* IX, 360–68; Jane S. Gabin, *A Living Minstrelsy: The Poetry and Music of Sidney Lanier* (Macon, Ga., 1985), 89–104.

31. Anderson *et al.* (eds.), *Works of Sidney Lanier,* I, xxxviii–xlix; Sidney Lanier, "Psalm of the West," in Anderson *et al.* (eds.), *Works of Sidney Lanier,* I, 62, 82.

for Lanier's poetry. "Psalm of the West," he conceded, possessed a degree of "power" and "much originality," but the poem, he contended, was "too often bizarre, strained." "He cares for nothing but notoriety," Thompson decided somewhat unfairly, having never met Lanier. "He is not in love with pure Art. He is a poetical mountebank, a rhyming gymnast, a versifying acrobat, a grand and lofty tumbler in the garden of the Gods." Significantly, however, Thompson, who made his caustic evaluation privately and to a fellow southerner, recognized a kindred spirit in Lanier. "He is young," conceded Thompson (two years Lanier's junior), "and I hope good things may yet come of him. I should not thus attack his poetry publicly. I would help him rather than hinder him." Then, getting to the crux of the matter, Thompson declared, "I admire him for his high aim."[32]

By aim, Thompson referred, in part, to Lanier's *avant-garde* symbolism and style, but he also meant Lanier's desire to be a national, rather than a southern, poet. Thompson would gently admonish even men he deeply admired, such as Paul H. Hayne, if he detected an excessive Confederate or parochial tone in their published work. Writing to Hayne, Thompson told the aging poet that northerners admired much of his art, but that he must beware not to destroy his hard-earned success with "any more bitter war poems." Such poems could only "retard and hinder" Hayne's reputation as "a *National* poet." "You must not permit yourself to become *sectional* or *local,*" Thompson warned. Look ahead, not back, he urged. "Forget, as a poet," Thompson advised, "that there ever was a so-called Confederacy. A poet must have wide visions, and you have."[33]

So did Thompson. He seems to have made few northern enemies in private life. One of his closest friends was former Union general Lew Wallace, himself an avid supporter of sectional peace. Admittedly, Thompson found it easier than did Hayne to adopt a broad view. South Carolinian Hayne, aristocratic, aging, and set in his ways, belonged to a different generation and entertained a different social perspective than the Indiana-born, Georgia-raised adventurer. Thompson could write movingly of the South, even of the Confederacy, but he always did so within prescribed limits of northern approval. "I must, for all my haste," wrote southern renegade George Washington Cable to *Century* editor

32. James M. Thompson to Paul H. Hayne, [1876], December 8, 1876, both in Paul Hamilton Hayne Papers, DU.
33. *Ibid.,* March 15, 1883.

Richard Watson Gilder, "take time to tell you how I have been stirred by Maurice Thompson's Song of a Mockingbird. To hear the patriotic note in American verse once more!" Cable had read the poem to New Englanders Sarah Orne Jewett and Mrs. James T. Fields, "to their great delight & admiration." Thompson himself wrote to Gilder a few weeks later, "I assure you that I want no sectionalism East, West, North or South."[34]

Although Thompson is best known as a poet, his verse may not be the best expression of his patriotism. Most of his poetry deals not with politics or history—the implicit subjects of reconciliation—but with nature and outdoor life. He entitled his first volume of poetry, published in 1883, *Songs of Fair Weather,* and his finest poetical efforts thereafter conjure up images of fields, flowers, streams, and fleecy clouds. One catches occasional glimpses of reconciliation in poems like his heartfelt tribute to Abraham Lincoln, but Thompson's nonnature poetry more often waxes nostalgic over the magic of the Old South and the glories of the Lost Cause. He wrote most of his patriotic verse in the 1890s, much of it inspired by the war with Spain. His short stories hit a bit closer to the mark. Many of them deal with slavery, the war, emancipation, and Reconstruction; but most of the stories, like the poetry, are so pro-southern that northern editors rejected them when they were first written in the 1870s. Not until Thompson resubmitted the stories twenty years later, during the sectional honeymoon of the 1890s, did they see the light of day. Thus Thompson's novels best express his views on reconciliation. Three novels, in particular, published between 1881 and 1886, are worth considering.[35]

The earliest of the three, *A Tallahassee Girl,* is the least successful. The plot focuses on a love triangle: a southern woman and her two suitors, one northern, one southern. Both men are veterans of the war. Unlike most reconciliation novels, the northern suitor, Lawrence Cawthorne, loses the girl, Lucie LaRue. All three characters make gestures toward reconciliation, however, and both North and South are portrayed sympathetically. In a letter to Paul Hayne, Thompson described the period of

34. Otis B. Wheeler, *The Literary Career of Maurice Thompson* (Baton Rouge, 1965), 24; Robert E. Morsberger and Katherine M. Morsberger, *Lew Wallace: Militant Romantic* (New York, 1980), 218; George W. Cable to Richard W. Gilder, October 2, 1886, in Thompson Papers, EU; James M. Thompson to Richard W. Gilder, November 25, 1886, in James Maurice Thompson Papers, NYPL.

35. Wheeler, *Literary Career of Maurice Thompson,* 93, 96–97; Maurice Thompson, *Stories of the Cherokee Hills* (Boston, 1898), 5–6.

the story, the 1870s, as "the *Transition period*" in southern history, a time of readjustment between the Old South and the emerging New South. His southern hero, Arthur Vance, although formerly a colonel under Stonewall Jackson, was not blind to postwar change. Lucie, only a schoolgirl during the war, lacks the deep prejudices against Yankees held by her parents' generation. Both Arthur and Lucie are young enough to feel the pulse of change generated by the 1870s. Both characters react, Thompson explains, to "the mighty ground swell of energy the young south has recently caught from the North."[36]

Thompson provides a more powerful statement of the reunion theme in *His Second Campaign,* published in 1883. The story contains the same principal ingredients as *A Tallahassee Girl*—a southern belle with northern and southern suitors—but this time the Yankee wins the love contest. The potential conflict is more intense, too. Tallahassee did not suffer destruction by federal armies during the war. Georgia and South Carolina, the settings of *His Second Campaign,* did; Georgians and Carolinians had genuine cause for hating Yankees. The northern hero in *A Tallahassee Girl* is a wishy-washy newspaper reporter from New York; the hero in *His Second Campaign* is an energetic Chicago businessman, again a veteran, who delivers political speeches for the Republican party. The book's title focuses attention on this Yankee, Edgar Julian, as the forceful principal character. The heroine, a Georgian named Rosalie Chenier, is, like Lucie LaRue, a schoolgirl during the war. The book actually has two southern heroes. One, Frank Ellis, is something of a renegade, the most outspoken former Confederate in the story and a man who fought as a guerrilla during the war. The other southerner, dignified and handsome Colonel Warren Talbot, is more respectable than Ellis but only slightly less outspoken.

Thompson begins and develops his story by emphasizing the many differences between North and South. The women are different, the ways of farming are different, the cities are different, the very atmospheres are different. Thompson and his characters believe that the physical differences between the sections will never change—"a millennium could not affect the arrangement." Yet despite the intransigent disparities, despite the bitter feelings inspired by war, Thompson's fictional Yankees and rebels are more American than northern or southern. The Yankee hero, who had rampaged with Sherman through Geor-

36. Wheeler, *Literary Career of Maurice Thompson,* 125–26; James M. Thompson to Paul H. Hayne, May 1, 1882, in Hayne Papers.

gia, admits, "Yes . . . we were a sad lot, and I was as bad as any. But it's all over now and the hatchet's buried.' " " 'I am a Southerner sir,' " rejoins Rosalie's father, " 'but I hope I am no fanatic. Why should I object to you on the ground that you were on the other side? The war is over, and that issue is settled forever.' " But wait. In the sort of coincidence permitted only in fiction, Julian confesses to Rosalie's father that it was he who had set torch to the Chenier house and stabbed Rosalie's older sister during Sherman's romp across the countryside. Here, indeed, was a test of sectional and personal forgiveness, but the Cheniers pass with honors. Rosalie marries Julian. Symbolically, they divide each year between homes in Chicago and Savannah. "Julian has not become altogether a Southern man," concludes narrator Thompson, "and Rosalie cannot quite agree to the Northern winters, which would seem to be about all that is left to quarrel about between the sections."[37]

Thompson delivers a more subtle plea for reconciliation in *A Banker of Bankersville*. He does not allude to buried hatchets, bloody chasms, or any of the other accepted symbols of sectional division and peace. He seems more concerned with attacking Social Darwinism and deflating midwestern, small-town pretensions to moral purity. Yet an underlying theme, hammered at time and again, is the unwarranted antagonism faced by reconstructed Confederates in the North. Parts of the story are autobiographical. Thompson's southern hero, Louis Milford, moves from Georgia to the Indiana town of Bankersville, where he establishes a law practice. Perhaps Thompson suffered the same verbal abuse as Milford about his "rebel record." Many "good people" in Bankersville deem it "a bit of brazen impudence for an unrepentant rebel to come into the North and complacently open an office, with a view to competing with loyal men." Thompson goes on to tell the old story of personal acquaintance versus philosophical isolation. Milford and his new neighbors discover, like many real-life Confederate carpetbaggers and Yankees, that personal acquaintance frequently softens sectional animosity and inspires "great kindness." Only people "who knew little of him" continued to glare at Milford.[38]

Thompson heightens the effect of Bankersville's prejudices by making Milford a gentle person. Milford suffered a terrible struggle with his conscience while in Confederate service. His southern birth required

37. Maurice Thompson, *His Second Campaign* (Boston, 1883), 66–67, 83, 101, 166–67, 190, 260–61, 273, 322, 341.
38. Maurice Thompson, *A Banker of Bankersville: A Novel* (1886; rpr. New York, 1890), 24, 88–92, 134–39.

that he defend his homeland, yet he believed it wrong to fight a war to perpetuate human bondage. Milford's repugnance toward slavery eventually triumphed over his sectional instinct and he deserted the army. Very few Confederate authors created such conscientious heroes. Milford is also a tranquil, dreamy poet. Yet Milford, dubbed a "rhyming rowdy from rebeldom," must withstand snide remarks about his poetry when it is published—for the sole purpose of ridicule—in the local newspaper, the *Scar*. Milford is made of stern stuff, however. He marries a beautiful northern girl and quits his law practice to write poetry. "Milford's 'record' does not trouble him much now," reports Thompson in conclusion. "Once in a while, when news items are scarce and the *Scar* editor is suffering from an unusually stubborn attack of malaria, there appears in his journal a grave warning to the people against harboring ex-rebels," but most citizens of Bankersville, as well as Thompson's readers, laugh at the editor's misplaced fears.[39]

Katherine Sherwood Bonner was five years younger than Maurice Thompson, but she lived eighteen fewer summers. Dr. Charles Bonner, a planter-physician who moved his family from their Mississippi plantation to the nearby town of Holly Springs when Kate was eight, instilled an unquenchable love of literature in the eldest of his four children. The seed of that love took root during Kate's formal education at a local female academy and a fashionable boarding school in Alabama. It blossomed during the war years, when Kate first turned her hand to poetry and fiction. She kept a diary during the war, too, recording each *"Glorious"* Confederate triumph. After the war, literature still the dominant force in her life, she joined the local literary society. Three years later, in 1869, she published her first story, "Laura Capello." This bit of romantic froth appeared under a male pseudonym in the *Massachusetts Ploughman*. A romantic, and consequently tragic, aura would hover over Kate Bonner for the rest of her life.[40]

A "beautiful, wayward, gifted girl" is how one friend described Kate. She might have added coquettish and resolute, for all those qualities shaped Kate's adult life. She married handsome, romantic, unlucky Edward McDowell in 1871. This unfortunate union produced one child

39. *Ibid.*, 321–23.
40. The two most useful biographies of Bonner are William L. Frank, *Sherwood Bonner* (Boston, 1976), and Hubert Horton McAlexander, *The Prodigal Daughter: A Biography of Sherwood Bonner* (Baton Rouge, 1981). See also Daniel E. Sutherland, "Some Thoughts Concerning the Love Life of Sherwood Bonner," *Southern Studies*, XXVI (1987).

and lasted, in practice, two years, although Kate lived apart from Edward for the better part of ten years before seeking a divorce. She left Edward when he failed to provide adequate support for herself and their daughter Lilian. Kate then left the child in the care of her family while she went to Boston, where she intended to support Lilian with her pen. With the help of Naphum Capen, editor of the *Massachusetts Ploughman* and the only person she knew in all New England, Kate prospered. Capen became a lifelong friend and introduced her to other Massachusetts literary lights and reformers; but Kate took the most important, not to say audacious, step in securing a northern literary livelihood. In December, 1873, she wrote a note to Henry Wadsworth Longfellow requesting an interview. "I am a Southern girl away from my home and friends," she admitted. "I have come here for mental discipline and study—and to try to find out the meaning and use of my life." The directness and innocence of her request captivated the old poet. So did Kate's beauty, youth, and brains when she visited his large, rambling yellow house in Cambridge. Longfellow employed her as a private secretary for several years, and he became a devoted friend and confidant who, until his death in 1882, opened many social and literary doors for the Mississippi belle.[41]

Bonner's friendship with Longfellow also produced her first novel, *Like Unto Like*. Longfellow encouraged her to write the book and used his influence with Harper Brothers to have it published. Kate, using the pen name Sherwood Bonner, repaid Longfellow's many kindnesses by dedicating the book to him. Published in 1878, *Like Unto Like* includes large chunks of autobiography. More important, it is one of the first novels of sectional reconciliation published by a Confederate carpetbagger. Bonner shows clearly through her heroine, Blythe Herndon, an abiding love for the South, but, having come under strong northern intellectual influences, she is able to see both northern and southern perspectives on the war more clearly from Beacon Street than she had from Holly Springs. As the Civil War ends, Blythe announces her hope that fellow residents in Yariba will open their doors to the occupying Union army that has invaded their town. " 'I have no doubt there are gentlemen among the Yankees just as good as there are anywhere,' " she confidently tells her friends; " 'and I should like every house in town to open to them.' " Later, she explains even more emphatically, " 'The war is ended; and besides, the soldiers are not to blame. They only did their

41. Sophie Kirk, "Preface," in Sherwood Bonner, *Suwanee River Tales* (Boston, 1884).

duty.'" Teased by friends about the possibility that her sentiments might lead her to marry a Yankee, Blythe shoots back, "'I would marry any man I loved—were he Jew, Roman Catholic, Yankee, or Fiji Islander!'"[42]

That is reconciliation with a vengeance, and soon most of Yariba catches the spirit. Yariba's young ladies fairly line up to marry dashing federal officers. Blythe becomes betrothed to a Yankee carpetbagger, Roger Ellis, who has come south to help the Negro and mobilize Republican political efforts, but she eventually breaks her engagement, and for a most revealing reason. She rejects Ellis not because he is a Yankee, not even because he is a Radical Republican, but because he is too cold, too unsympathetic, too intolerant. During their courtship, Ellis ignores the little courtesies of love that young ladies so much appreciate. He is occasionally condescending to Blythe's sex, an attitude her budding feminism resents. Most important, Roger Ellis does not sympathize with the southern people; he is no fit partner in reconciliation. Thus, when Blythe's family breathes a sigh of relief over her broken engagement and gently teases her about their narrow escape from having a "black radical" in the family, she lashes out, "'I am a radical myself! . . . And I don't want you ever to hint that I gave him up because of his politics, or because of his being a Northern man. It is simply that we don't suit each other.'"[43]

Still, the romance with Ellis serves as a convenient way for Blythe (and Kate Bonner) to express her views about the South and the war. For instance, no truly reconstructed rebel could justify slavery after 1865. Blythe goes a step further by telling Ellis she has *always* opposed slavery. Blythe insists that she, like many other southerners, had supported the Confederacy on the issue of states' rights, not human bondage. On the other hand, Blythe shows that even reconstructed rebels could maintain a sentimental attachment to the Lost Cause. Having listened to an emotional recitation of Father Ryan's "The Conquered Banner," she whispers, "It will be long before a Southern audience can hear that poem without the accompaniment of tears."[44]

Kate Bonner could also view postwar political events with a sober eye. While poets such as Lanier burst into song celebrating the nation's

42. McAlexander, *Prodigal Daughter*, 126–29; Sherwood Bonner, *Like Unto Like: A Novel* (New York, 1878), 13.

43. Bonner, *Like Unto Like*, 164–65.

44. *Ibid.*, 67–68, 90–92.

centennial, Bonner, in *Like Unto Like,* observes that most southerners reacted less enthusiastically than northerners to the festivities. "It dawned in the North," she observed of the centennial year, "with the ringing of bells summoning all nations to witness America's prosperity." In the South, however, 1876 represented not so much a national celebration as a very important presidential election year, in which Democrats and the South lost their bid to recapture Congress and the White House. Bonner, like so many other commentators, blamed scheming politicians for deliberately inflaming sectional passions. Even Roger Ellis admits the truth of this assertion. " 'The South, in the mind of Northern thinkers,' " he explains to Blythe, " 'means not the Southern people, but the leaders and exponents of feudal as distinguished from popular or republican theories of government.' " No northern politician, he implies, could rest until all exponents of southern feudalism had surrendered.[45]

One of the most interesting chapters in Bonner's novel is a political dialogue in which Kate, seeking a "political creed," asks the men around her to explain their beliefs and the differences between Republicans and Democrats. The resulting dialogue between three northerners—a radical (Ellis), a liberal, and a conservative—and a moderate southerner drives Blythe to distraction. Three of the men speak in platitudes that tell her nothing. The fourth, the northern liberal, is a brash federal officer who describes America's political system as "ins and outs," "we-uns and you-uns," "office-seekers" and "office-holders." What was his political creed? " 'To go for good men, snap your fingers at parties, and hurrah for the side that is up. It's all the same, you know. It's a game of see-saw.' " Blythe senses that the young officer is right, but she wants something more definite. Driven to despair, she records in her diary: "I am getting to have a sort of—of—disdain of people who have opinions. I can't find anything to put in the place that I emptied of my prejudices." Many of her readers must have known the feeling.[46]

Other Confederate carpetbaggers, not so well remembered as Eggleston, Lanier, Thompson, and Bonner, contributed to reconciliation literature. Emma Connelly, of Kentucky, developed a unique reconciliation plot in *Tilting at Windmills.* The novel's hero, George Allerton, of Boston, saves the life of a wounded Confederate soldier during the war. In 1872, the Confederate dies, but, remembering the kindness of his

45. *Ibid.,* 142, 151.
46. *Ibid.,* 146–55.

former enemy, he bequeaths him a six-hundred-acre plantation in Kentucky. The only stipulation for receiving the property is that Allerton live on it for ten years. "I remember now," recalls Allerton as he speaks of his benefactor, "that he said what the North and South needed was to know each other. He thought there ought to be two continuous processions; the North going southward, the South going northward." The departed rebel had forced Allerton to join the southward procession. The result, after some twistings of plot, is a triumph of sectional friendship. Connelly provides not one but two intersectional marriages. Allerton marries a Kentucky belle, and his sister marries a Confederate rival for that same maiden.[47]

Poets, of course, had a field day. Subjects like patriotism, national harmony, and brotherhood lend themselves to the measured, emotional punches of verse. Mary E. Tucker, of Alabama and Georgia, was one who knew the secret of her muse. Her long narrative poem *Loew's Bridge: A Broadway Idyl* expresses a southerner's impressions as she strolls through the heart of Manhattan. On every side she sees northerners and southerners treating each other as friends; around every corner she finds hope for the future of a united nation. She spies a one-armed, legless Union veteran grinding out "Dixie" on his organ. Into his cup, a Confederate veteran drops what small alms he can spare. Both men had fought for causes they believed to be right. Now they live, once again, under a common flag. More the pity that

> . . . its folds are dyed with the blood
> Of the murdered martyrs, the brave, the true,
> Who wore the GREY, and who wore the BLUE![48]

Rosa Vertner Jeffrey, born in Mississippi and raised in Kentucky, rarely minced words. She got right to the point in "Reconciled":

> Northmen, we have met each other
> In a fierce and deadly strife;
> Brother fighting brother,

---

47. Frances E. Willard and Mary A. Livermore (eds.), *American Women: A Comprehensive Encyclopedia of the Lives and Achievements of American Women During the Nineteenth Century* (2 vols.; New York, 1897), I, 199; John W. Leonard (ed.), *Who's Who in New York City and State* (3rd ed.; New York, 1907), 321; Emma M. Connelly, *Tilting at Windmills: A Story of the Blue Grass Country* (Boston, 1888), 13–15.

48. James Grant Wilson and John Fiske (eds.), *Appleton's Cyclopedia of American Biography* (6 vols.; New York, 1891–93), VI, 173–74; Mary Eliza Tucker, *Loew's Bridge: A Broadway Idyl* (New York, 1867), 20–22, 52.

> Blood for blood and life for life.
> Striving for the rights we cherished,
> Both were brave and one was strong;
> All our bonds of Union perished,
> Right led madly on to wrong.

Both North and South suffered in the madness, Jeffrey goes on to say; both must recognize the need to lay aside bitterness. The South cannot live in the past, she asserts, and both North and South must forgive and forget if the nation is to wax healthy and prosperous. She offers a prayer of hope for the nation's future:

> Ere the new year's snow-wreaths shelter
> Northern hills from leafless gloom,
> Ere its springs of sunlight filter
> Into seas of southern bloom,
> By the fire of tribulation,
> Or through joy,—if not too late,—
> God of mercy, cleanse this nation
> From its leprosy of hate![49]

Jeffrey tried her hand at a "Centennial Hymn," too. It is neither more nor less successful than other centennial hymns, but that, in itself, is significant. That Jeffrey, a southern partisan, should attempt such a tribute, that she felt the need to express her sense of national pride, lends her otherwise pedestrian verses a measure of poignancy:

> Hundred years of a nation's life,
> Stirred with glory, marred with strife,
> Scarred with bullet and the knife,
> With eager pulsing fervor rife,
> Strong in the newness of its life,
> Weak in its elements of strife.
> > Stand firm, ye patriots and seers,
> > Or Freedom's star will set in tears
> > Before another hundred years.[50]

We have no way to measure the effectiveness of these poets and writers in nudging fellow citizens toward sectional peace. The regular appearance of their writings in the nation's most popular magazines and

---

49. Daniel E. Sutherland, "The Kentuckians in New York," *Filson Club History Quarterly*, LVII (1983), 361–63; Rosa Vertner Jeffrey, "Reconciled," in *The Crimson Hand, and Other Poems* (Philadelphia, 1881), 154–57.

50. Rosa Vertner Jeffrey, "Centennial Hymn," in *Crimson Hand*, 105–107.

their distribution by the nation's largest publishers suggest that they struck a responsive chord with the reading public. The writers managed to earn livings with their feathered swords, and reviewers generally received their work—or at least its spirit—kindly, sometimes enthusiastically. Yet no one can say whether they helped to create a mood of national harmony or merely profited from a national predisposition in that direction. The earliest writers surely helped to set the mood, but even those who joined in during the 1880s and 1890s helped to solidify earlier gains. If nothing else, perhaps these writers embarrassed some readers. Surely some people sensed the absurdity of these continued appeals for sectional peace thirty years after the war. But maybe not. Scholars frequently cite *Century Magazine*'s "Battles and Leaders of the Civil War" series, launched in 1884, as a literary turning point on the road to reunion. Yet *Century*'s own editors also recognized the "commercial appeal" of such a series. The notion of sectional reconciliation had already been made palatable by 1884. The genuine pioneers of literary reconciliation had been at work for at least a decade.[51]

The reconciliation theme these pioneers preached should not, however, be identified too closely with the much ballyhooed New South movement of the 1870s and 1880s. New South writers advocated reconciliation as part of their campaign to attract northern capital and industrial expertise with which to modernize the South and spur southern economic revival. Many Confederate carpetbaggers balked at this campaign. They remained attached to the Old South, the South of their memories, and objected to some bastardized version of Yankee progress. They sometimes found themselves identified as New South advocates, for their contemporaries were not so prone as latter-day historians to probe, dissect, and categorize the various branches of southern literature. They also approved of this hybrid territory as a meeting place for suspicious folk in both sections, a place where northern ideas and ingenuity became flavored with just enough old southern virtue, honor, and romance to make reconciliation acceptable. But their interest in reconciliation remained personal and emotional, not a blueprint for industrialization or commercialization of the South.

In one sense only might all reconciliation writers be lumped together. Some scholars see a chronological division in the New South catechism. Early New South writers, they believe, sought to convince southerners

51. Stephen Davis, "'A Matter of Sensational Interest': The *Century* 'Battles and Leaders' Series," *Civil War History*, XXVII (1981), 338–39.

and northern friends that a rejuvenated southern economy was possible. Only James D. B. DeBow and Edwin DeLeon among Confederate carpetbagger writers joined in this early phase, although many financiers— Inman, Wilson, and the rest—worked toward the same end. By the late 1880s, however, much of the New South economic program had become reality. The purpose of New South propagandists thus shifted to praise the economic transformation and link southern social and racial advances to the same spirit. Propagandists insisted that these sweeping reforms proved the South had cast off any objectionable traditions that, in the past, may have impeded northern acceptance of the South as a genuine part of American intellectual, social, political, and economic advancement. This aspect of the New South movement, praise of southern progress, most certainly found its way into the thinking and writing of Confederate carpetbaggers. Today's scholars accept the notion that most New South spokesmen tried to balance their enthusiasm for a new economic order with respect for the best of the Old South. This could be a tricky proposition, and most Confederates in the North found themselves more inclined to glorify the old traditions than praise the new. Yet they, like the more legitimate, more conscious messengers of a New South creed, wanted to obliterate lingering suspicions about southern patriotism and destroy all remaining sectional dissension.[52]

52. Paul M. Gaston, *The New South Creed: A Study in Southern Mythmaking* (New York, 1970), 6–7, 32–33, 83–86, 153–55; Wayne Mixon, *Southern Writers and the New South Movement, 1865–1913* (Chapel Hill, 1980), 3–10.

10

Legacy: Not Dying

For several years before 1904, Burton Harrison's failing heart had forced him to spend winters in Washington, D.C. By March, in his sixty-seventh year, the end seemed near. Constance summoned her sons to be with their beloved father, "the most stimulating and the most agreeable man they had ever known." All three boys had followed their father's path to Yale and the New York bar. Francis, now Congressman Harrison of New York's 13th District, arrived first at his father's bedside. Christened Francis Brand Harrison, he had changed his name while a schoolboy to Francis Burton Harrison, in honor of his father. Fairfax, now a railroad executive, and Archibald, a financier, rushed south by train from New York. Who can tell Burton's thoughts as he lay in the house on N Street, his eyes and mind slowly dimming. Constance sat beside his bed. As he looked at her, Burton may have heard Tennyson whispering to him across the years:

> To love one maiden only, cleave to her,
> And worship her by years of noble deeds.[1]

His sons carried Burton's lifeless form across the river to Alexandria on the day preceding Good Friday. Burton had been in the habit of returning to New York about this time each year, but the South had always been his real home; he could not conceive of being buried anywhere else, not even among his fellow carpetbaggers in the hundred

---

1. Fairfax Harrison (ed.), *Aris Sonis Focisque: Being a Memoir of an American Family, the Harrisons of Skimino* (New York, 1910), 220; Francis B. Harrison, "About It and About" (Typescript in Francis Burton Harrison Papers, UV), 3; Alfred, Lord Tennyson, "Guinevere," in *The Poems and Dramatic Works of Alfred, Lord Tennyson* (Boston, 1898), 440.

square feet of Confederate soil at Mount Hope Cemetery. They bore him
from Christ Church, where both George Washington and Robert E. Lee
had worshiped, along King Street to the green, shaded seclusion of Ivy
Hill Cemetery. That was the proper place for Carys, Fairfaxes, and
Harrisons. Burton's infant daughter, Ethel, had been waiting patiently
for thirty years for someone to join her in the family plot. Now, together
again, father and daughter could rest. Constance knew she would rest
there in the end. Perhaps even the sons, still in the summer of life, sensed
that they, too, must return:

> Yet waft me from the harbor mouth:
> Wild wind! I see a warmer sky,
> And I will see before I die
> The palms and temples of the South.[2]

It was too bad Burton did not survive one year more, to enjoy one
more Broadway season. George M. Cohan's *Little Johnny Jones* opened
at New York's Liberty Theatre in November. Cohan's jocular brand of
patriotism might have mildly shocked Burton. Burton's generation took
a more sober view of patriotism. Yet two of Cohan's show-stopping
songs, "Give My Regards to Broadway" and "Yankee Doodle Boy,"
would have been perfect tributes to Burton's final months in New York,
and a third song, "Life's a Funny Proposition After All," may have
produced a pleasantly bemused smile. "Did you ever sit and ponder, sit
and wonder, sit and think," asked Cohan, "why we're here and what
this life is all about?" Then, adding a slight chill to his ruminations:

> Ev'rybody's fighting, as we wend our way along,
> Ev'ry fellow claims the other fellow's in the wrong;
> Hurried and worried, until we're buried and there's no curtain call;
> Life's a very funny proposition after all.[3]

Burton had been thinking about life—about the old days—in the
weeks preceding his death. He and Constance had visited the old army
arsenal, scene of the ordeal that, more than any other single event in his
life, had weakened Burton's heart. Nothing looked the same. The army
had begun constructing its new war college on the site of the old prison.
Even the soldiers looked different. They wore olive drab instead of

2. Alexandria (Va.) *Gazette*, March 30, 1904, p. 2, March 31, 1904, p. 3; Tennyson,
"On a Mourner," in *Poems and Dramatic Works*, 60.
3. John McCabe, *George M. Cohan: The Man Who Owned Broadway* (New York,
1973), 59–64.

Yankee blue. And more than the army had changed. When Burton first arrived in New York, street railways had not yet started operation. As he lay dying, the city's subway was beginning service. The country had horseless carriages and motion pictures, telephones and electric lights; only three months earlier, the Wright brothers had first flown their airplane. Nine different men, most of them Republicans, had occupied the White House since 1867. Burton liked the latest president. Theodore Roosevelt, born of a southern mother, had supported Burton's second nomination to the Century Club thirteen years earlier. Still, Burton preferred the old ways and familiar faces: "So sad, so fresh, the days that are no more."[4]

Perhaps, in those final days and hours, Burton weighed his life since the war. Had he done right in going north? Had he been a good husband and father? Had he been successful in life? Had he spent his years wisely? He must have, in all humility, answered yes to those questions. Burton and Constance Harrison had forged a happy, contented life in Yankeedom. They enjoyed modest wealth and some fame. They raised intelligent children who, in turn, made their marks in the world. Not all Confederate carpetbaggers could say as much. Essie Cheesborough and Carlie Oakley, Lewis Grimball and Thomas Ellis, come to mind as hardworking people with more desire than luck. Not a few people, even successful people, like Charles C. Jones, Jr., returned south frustrated and discouraged. Many who stayed in the North only survived. "Perhaps you know," Sidney Lanier informed a northern friend, "that with us of the younger generation in the South since the War, pretty much the whole of life has been merely not-dying." Most Confederate carpetbaggers avoided premature death, even in the figurative sense. Indeed, an impressive number thrived in the North. They became pioneers and leaders in nearly every walk of life, contributing to progress in business, literature, science, medicine, politics, law, education, and art. Perhaps these people would have been just as successful in the South. Then again, maybe the advantages of northern residence tipped the scales from anonymity toward immortality.[5]

If Burton brooded very long on the subject of success, he need only have thought back to the annual banquets of the New York Southern

4. Mrs. Burton Harrison, *Recollections Grave and Gay* (New York, 1911), 228, 237; Tennyson, "The Princess," in *Poems and Dramatic Works,* 134.

5. Sidney Lanier to Bayard Taylor, August 7, 1875, in Charles R. Anderson *et al.* (eds.), *The Centennial Edition of the Works of Sidney Lanier* (10 vols.; Baltimore, 1945), IX, 230.

Society for reassurance. Scores of rich, powerful, and famous Confederates had occupied the banquet tables. Burton missed those February celebrations of southern prosperity once he started spending his winters in Washington. Despite the frosty weather, the banquet hall had always radiated a warm, cozy feeling. Southern palms, flowers, ferns, and moss gave even the most stark hall a romantic lushness and lent even the most garish setting a serene quietude. Southern state flags and emblems, displayed like heraldric banners and shields, reminded banqueters of their chivalric heritage. Talk and laughter gradually swelled until they all but obliterated the orchestra's sentimental renditions of traditional southern melodies. From time to time, a particular favorite, like "My Old Kentucky Home" or "Old Folks at Home," caught the ear of some amateur baritone who led the multitude in a spirited sing-along. More lively tunes, like "I'm Gwine Back to Dixie" or "Dixie," produced even livelier hand-clapping, foot-stomping ensembles. Parts of the evening, between the eating and the formal speeches, bordered on chaos. No one cared. Banqueters drank more wine and laughed all the louder. Wives and female guests filled a gallery of boxes above the main floor. Varina and Winnie Davis attended whenever possible, and they always received a rousing ovation. The ladies, too, enjoyed the evening as they chattered, laughed, and pointed to the festivities below.[6]

Burton could not have imagined anything like it twenty years before the first banquet in 1887. Perhaps, in 1904, he recalled the admiring words heaped upon the society by speakers at the annual celebration. "It is gratifying to find you all doing so well in your efforts to soften the rigors of exile," William L. Trenholm had joked at the inaugural banquet. "It speaks well, gentlemen," Trenholm continued, "for the stuff of which you are made, and it speaks well for the place you have chosen for your residence." Senator M. C. Butler of South Carolina had kidded "this likely set of carpet-baggers" along the same lines. "They are certainly the most thrifty, the most prosperous looking carpet-baggers that I have ever seen," he vouchsafed to mingled laughter and applause. It was true. Some of the banqueters, including Burton, had waged uphill battles, but the survivors could be proud of their achievements.[7]

Likely no one felt more pride in their accomplishments than the society's millionaire financiers and businessmen. They dominated the

6. New York *Times,* February 23, 1889, p. 5, February 22, 1891, p. 8.
7. *Account of the Proceedings at the First Annual Banquet of the New York Southern Society* (New York, 1887), 23–24, 39–40.

scene. Richard T. Wilson, Charles B. Rouss, John H. Inman, Thomas F. Ryan, Charles H. Bosher, John C. Latham, John C. Maben, Joseph L. Robertson, James H. Parker, and John C. Calhoun, Jr., were only the most recognizable names of the many members to compile impressive financial credentials in the North. "The aggregate wealth of Southerners in Wall Street," Marion J. Verdery, Georgia-born son-in-law of Charles Force Deems, told the third annual banquet, in 1889, "is over $100,000,000, and the great bulk of that vast amount has been accumulated within the last 20 years," an average of four million dollars a year since the war. These financial wizards, above all others, would nod agreement with the speaker who told 1891 banqueters that southerners in North and South had at last "come out from under the midnight shadow of reconstruction" to witness the "dawning of a day of unimaginable splendor." The society's financiers had reaped large profits from that new day. Several of them, innovative as well as bold, far-sighted as well as lucky, had created its splendor.[8]

Across the room from Burton at the 1891 banquet, Charles B. Rouss and Richard T. Wilson sat cheek by jowl. The former Confederate major and private probably said little to each other, but their difference in rank did not limit the conversation. Wilson simply preferred to chatter and joke with the newspaper reporter seated on his opposite flank. That was Wilson's style, to make sure his name appeared in the next day's papers. Rouss had become increasingly crotchety and withdrawn as his eyesight faded. The growing darkness preyed on his mind. He had spent huge sums of money on doctors and medical treatment hoping to save his eyes, but to no avail. "What good this vast fortune," he rhetorically asked friends, "with the melancholy, the blindness, and old age?" Rouss rarely attended the society's regular meetings and seldom entered the clubhouse on 25th Street, but he never missed the annual banquet. As he smoothed his dapper little mustache, Charles Broadway Rouss, the "Napoleon of Gotham," could savor the South's triumph in the North, much as Bonaparte—Charley's principal hero—would have enjoyed a triumphal dinner at Versailles.[9]

Rouss had always lived by simple but very effective rules in the busi-

8. New York *Times*, February 23, 1889, p. 5, February 22, 1891, p. 8.

9. Cornelius Vanderbilt, Jr., *Queen of the Golden Age: The Fabulous Story of Grace Wilson Vanderbilt* (New York, 1956), 25–28; *Fifth Annual Report of the New York Southern Society* (New York, 1891), 20–23; Charles B. Rouss to Frederick W. M. Holliday, November 24, 1896, in Frederick William Mackey Holliday Papers, DU.

ness world: Never sell on credit, sell for a modest profit (5 percent), advertise, and work harder than your competitors. Rouss certainly worked hard. Sixteen-hour days were his regular routine. He had even slept in his store during the early years, so as not to waste time walking to and from work. He advertised nationally in his *Monthly Auction Trade Journal,* first published in 1876. Beginning as a one-page sheet, the *Journal* became a sixty-page directory for Rouss's forty thousand retail outlets. Rouss did not own most of the outlets, but they all carried and advertised his stock and adopted his business rules. Rouss became a pioneer in developing the chain store. Montgomery Ward and Company, founded four years before Rouss started to rebuild his postwar fortune in the mid-1870s, did not reach a million dollars in annual sales until 1888. By the mid-1890s, Rouss earned twelve million dollars annually, whereas Richard Warren Sears, in business for a decade, could gross only half a million. Rouss held the advantage over these two merchants by procuring the least expensive stock available and selling a staggering variety of goods. He acquired his stock directly from the factory, at auction, and from bankrupt houses forced to liquidate. By tacking on only 5 percent to his already low costs, Rouss could undersell anyone in the country.[10]

Rouss's unique journal not only listed and illustrated hundreds of items, from trouser suspenders and perfumed soaps to kitchen utensils and carpenter tools, it espoused his personal philosophy. Alongside the latest price listings ran editorials that justified Rouss's business methods and explained his unorthodox views. Rouss peppered his editorials with the maxims of Napoleon, Nathan Bedford Forrest, and Stonewall Jackson, most often to emphasize the need for aggressive action in business. He drew on his own observations about the war to attack his *bête noire:* the credit system. "The private soldier who sped the bullet that stilled the great heart of Albert Sydney Johnston, the immortal Jackson and the chivalrous Stuart," Rouss insisted, "did greater service to the Federal arms than either Grant, Sheridan, or Pope." Young, unknown merchants, Rouss argued, could play just as dramatic a role in the business world. By forsaking "the luckless road to credit" in favor of the broad highway to success and "solid cash," merchants could reap larger profits

10. Larry A. Mullin, *The Napoleon of Gotham: A Study of the Life of Charles Broadway Rouss* (Winchester, Va., 1974), 21–23, 87–89; *Monthly Auction Trade Journal,* December, 1879, p. 1, November, 1899, p. 2.

and do more service for their communities than opportunistic men who speculated and gambled with society's wealth.[11]

Several innovative financiers who approved of Rouss's philosophy sat at an adjoining table. Everyone knew John H. Inman and James Swann, longtime partners in a cotton commission firm. Silent John, as people called Inman, cultivated the mystique of an international tycoon. He enjoyed life, made lots of money, and said very little. But Inman could be eloquent when it suited him. He once dazzled a group of Liverpool cotton men with a speech delivered in England. Blessed with a finely honed sense of humor and a hearty laugh, Inman rarely lost his temper; he was "gentle as a girl," people said. He never relished the life of a "club man," either. He could be sociable and friendly, but he did not belong to many clubs and did not frequent the ones he joined. Yet, like Rouss, Inman always attended the Southern Society banquet.[12]

By 1891, John Inman ranked as the "foremost Southerner in New York," or in the North, for that matter. Certainly he ranked as the richest. He owned one of the world's largest cotton houses. As leader of a group of "militant southerners" in the North that included Richard T. Wilson, Inman reshaped and rehabilitated the antebellum cotton trade. Inman quickly seized the postwar cotton market by the throat and never let go. He refused at first to speculate, that is, to deal in "futures." He gained control of the market by developing his own system for buying and storing huge quantities of cotton and then selling on time. Inman possessed an uncanny feel for the market, making more money and losing less than any other broker of his era. His system earned him a reputation for sound credit and dependability. He helped establish the New York Cotton Exchange in 1870, the first such exchange in the United States, and used the exchange to govern the rapidly growing cotton trade with fixed rules and regulations. The exchange personified Inman's business methods of deliberate dealing and sound calculation. His active business years became known as the "reign of John H. Inman."[13]

11. *Monthly Auction Trade Journal*, February, 1880, p. 1, November, 1899, pp. 1–2.

12. James Harle and S. T. Hubbard interviews, in Arthur C. Inman Notebooks (Typescripts in AHS).

13. Henry Hall (ed.), *America's Successful Men of Affairs: An Encyclopedia of Contemporaneous Biography* (2 vols.; New York, 1895), I, 345–46; Ethel Armes, *The Story of Coal and Iron in Alabama* (Birmingham, 1910), 383; *Confederate Veteran*, IV (December, 1896), 418; Isaac F. Marcosson, "The Perilous Game of Cornering a Crop, IV—Famous Corners in Cotton," *Munsey's Magazine*, XLII (November, 1909), 236–39.

Thomas F. Ryan sat at the other end of Inman's table. There was no mistaking Ryan, even in a crowded banquet room. His broad shoulders, erect carriage, and charismatic presence made the Virginian stand out. If Inman headed the list of rich southerners in the North, Ryan ran a close second, and, at just forty years of age in 1891, he seemed destined to surpass Inman. By the early twentieth century, Ryan amassed an incredible $125 million, and his political power in Tammany Hall and the national Democratic party was just as impressive as his bank balance. Ryan became so influential that he had publicly to justify nearly every business transaction he made; when he spoke, Wall Street listened. Mayors served as his messenger boys; governors jumped to please him. He helped to form the first holding company in United States history, the Metropolitan Traction Company, in 1886. Critics of the robber barons and their new corporate system abused Ryan and his associates, especially William C. Whitney, mercilessly. If the genius of Whitney had conceived this "monument to infamous graft," jeered one critic of the Metropolitan, than "the skill and unscrupulousness of Thomas F. Ryan" made it a functional success.[14]

Whatever one's opinion of Ryan's business practices, he unquestionably ranked as the premier railroad executive and corporate financier of his day. He influenced the boards of over a dozen banks, railroads, insurance companies, and related interests. Ryan took it all in stride. His success was a question of timing, he explained. The American economy was primed and ready to explode when Ryan began his rise to power in the late 1870s. The country was expanding; new industries were emerging; corporate structures were evolving. When audacious men with vision and grit developed the opportunities presented by these trends, growth doubled, quadrupled, and accelerated. No man, claimed Ryan, could control such an avalanche of opportunity and prosperity. What was more, he declared emphatically, no one in his financial circle would use his wealth and power to the detriment of the nation.[15]

Confederate physicians, "full of phrase and fame," formed an equally

14. Mark D. Hirsch, *William C. Whitney: Modern Warwick* (New York, 1948), 223–24; Alfred Henry Lewis, "Owners of America: II. Thomas F. Ryan," *Cosmopolitan,* XLV (July, 1908), 141; W. N. Amory, *The Truth About Metropolitan* (2nd ed.; New York, 1906), 3.

15. Hall (ed.), *America's Successful Men of Affairs,* I, 561–62; John W. Leonard (ed.), *Who's Who in New York City and State* (3rd ed.; New York, 1907), 1138–39; Lewis, "Owners of America," 141; Thomas Fortune Ryan, "Why I Bought the Equitable," *North American Review,* CXCVIII (August, 1913), 175–77.

impressive group at the banquet. No fewer than seven nationally re-nowned doctors enjoyed the festivities of 1891, and four of these men had international reputations. One other man, the son of J. Marion Sims, dean of nineteenth-century southern physicians, reminded ban-queters of the high standards southern physicians in the North must maintain. Sims had died three years before the Southern Society had been formed. Known as "the Father of American Gynecology," the South Carolinian had moved north for his health before the war. His articles on trismus nascentium and vesicovaginal fistulas established him as an authority in the field by the 1850s. In 1855, he founded Women's Hospital in New York City. In Europe when the Civil War started, Sims did not return to the United States until 1865. Poor health prohibited him from joining the Confederate forces or living in the South, but he refused to live in the North while war raged. Sims received honors and decorations from seven foreign countries during his il-lustrious medical career. As the 1891 banqueters met, a movement had been initiated by Dr. Sims's friends to erect a statue to his memory. When the lifelike bronze effigy was unveiled in New York's Bryant Park in 1894, it became the first monument dedicated to a southerner in the North since the war.[16]

Only one man present at the banquet might have questioned Sims's reputation. Dr. Nathan Bozeman, an Alabama veteran of Confederate service, claimed that he, not Sims, had perfected treatment for ves-icovaginal and rectovaginal fistulas. It was a moot point. Actually, Bozeman had perfected Sims's method for suturing fistulas between the bladder and vagina. The two men shared equally in reducing the suffer-ing of childbearing women. Both earned international reputations in obstetrics and gynecology. Bozeman, a good friend and partner of Sims when the two lived in Alabama, opened a private hospital for women in New Orleans on the eve of the war. He opened a similar hospital in New York after moving there in 1866, and for ten years, 1878 to 1888, he served as attending physician at Sims's hospital. Bozeman penned nearly forty medical monographs and contributed frequently to medical jour-

16. Howard A. Kelly and Walter L. Burrage, *Dictionary of American Medical Biogra-phy* (New York, 1928), 1114–17; J. Marion Sims, *The Story of My Life* (New York, 1884), 365–66, 453–65; Seale Harris, *Woman's Surgeon: The Life Story of J. Marion Sims* (New York, 1950). Edwin S. Gaillard, a Confederate surgeon nearly as famous as Sims, moved to New York in 1879, but he died in 1885. See Emmet Field Horine, "A Forgotten Medical Editor," *Annals of Medical History,* n.s., II (1940), 375–82. Josiah Clark Nott had died in 1873.

nals. He also invented a self-retaining vaginal speculum and a portable operating chair that permitted a knee-chest operating position for treatment of vesicovaginal fistulas.[17]

John A. Wyeth forged a more personal link to Sims by marrying his daughter, Florence Nightingale Sims. Wyeth did not follow his father-in-law's specialty of gynecology. He was a pathologist, who, after a decade of study in New York and Europe, won national attention in 1882 by helping to establish the New York Polyclinic Medical School and Hospital. The polyclinic was the first postgraduate medical school in the United States, and Wyeth served as its chief professor of surgery until 1922. He served the polyclinic as president, too, an office he also held at one time or another in most of the nation's leading medical societies, including the American Medical Association. Wyeth wrote extensively about surgical techniques and authored a textbook on surgery used in United States medical schools for a quarter century. Wyeth accomplished the first known cure for tumors caused by streptococcus infection and introduced a method for treating inoperable tumors by injecting them with boiling water. He discovered a bloodless method of amputation at the shoulder and hip joints, known thereafter as "Wyeth's method." He pioneered an operation for correcting deformity of nose, lip, and palate. He stood, without doubt, as one of the most esteemed surgeons of his time.[18]

Dr. W. Gill Wylie followed Wyeth in the alphabetical listing of Southern Society members, and he ranked not far behind in medical reputation. Like Dr. Sims, Wylie hailed from South Carolina and chose obstetrics and gynecology as two of his medical specialties, another one being abdominal surgery. Wylie also came directly under Sims's influence when he worked at Women's Hospital following an internship at Bellevue Hospital. Wylie traveled to Europe in 1873, where he studied English and Continental nursing systems and methods of hospital construction. Florence Nightingale, with whom he corresponded, shaped many of Wylie's ideas about nurses' training. When he returned to the United States, he helped establish a nurses' training school at Bellevue, one of the first such schools in the country. Wylie then concentrated on

17. Kelly and Burrage, *American Medical Biography,* 135–36; *Dictionary of American Biography* (26 vols. and index; New York, 1928–80), II, 538–39.

18. Kelly and Burrage, *American Medical Biography,* 1339–40; *Dictionary of American Biography,* XX, 576; John Allan Wyeth, *With Sabre and Scalpel: The Autobiography of a Soldier and Surgeon* (New York, 1914), 349ff.

private practice for nearly a decade, but in 1882 he assisted Wyeth in establishing the polyclinic, where he became a professor of gynecology. He also served on the gynecology staff at Bellevue for more than a quarter century. Wylie contributed frequently to medical literature on hospital administration, gynecology, and surgical techniques. His most important contributions to medicine, which garnered him international acclaim, were his remarkably successful methods of abdominal surgery and operations for salpingitis.[19]

George T. Harrison, Richard C. M. Page, Seneca D. Powell, and Prince A. Morrow rounded out the Southern Society's medical elite. Harrison and Page, both Virginians and protégés of Sims, worked together at Women's Hospital in their early careers. Harrison specialized in gynecology and obstetrics. He won praise and numerous awards from medical societies in both the United States and England. A man of broad learning, Harrison also sparkled as a wit and raconteur in New York social circles. Page joined the staff of the polyclinic in the 1880s as professor of general medicine and of diseases of the chest. He became a charter member and first vice-president of the New York Academy of Medicine in 1889. Page achieved his widest acclaim for a much-praised textbook on general medicine. Powell's chief fame derived from his stimulating classes on minor surgery at Bellevue and other New York medical schools, but he was also a medical pioneer. He introduced the carbolic acid treatment of leg ulcers and a new surgical technique for treating cerebral disease. Additionally, he helped establish the *Post-Graduate Medical Journal* and served as its coeditor for eighteen years, until 1905.[20]

Prince A. Morrow, of Christian County, Kentucky, began his northern medical career in 1874, following study in Europe and private practice in Kentucky. He soon became a leading authority on venereal diseases and a driving force in the campaign to increase public awareness of their causes. Additionally, Morrow became one of the first American physicians to demand a new candidness about the culpability of men for spreading the dread infections. He complained in the press and on the platform that women suffered unjustly from a double standard that

19. Kelly and Burrage, *American Medical Biography,* 1340–41; *National Cyclopaedia of American Biography* (59 vols. and index; New York, 1898–1980), XXXVII, 88.

20. *National Cyclopaedia of American Biography,* XXII, 159; Kelly and Burrage, *American Medical Biography,* 534, 986; Daniel Van Pelt (comp.), *Leslie's History of the Greater New York* (3 vols.; New York, 1898), III, 423–25, 496–97; Lyon Gardiner Tyler, *Encyclopedia of Virginia Biography* (5 vols.; New York, 1915), II, 335.

placed the burden of blame for venereal disease on "fallen women." He also earned a national reputation as an expert on skin diseases, particularly leprosy, and genitourinary infections. He penned important works on all these subjects and held a professorship at Bellevue. He helped found and, for sixteen years, edit the *Journal of Cutaneous Diseases*.[21]

Representatives of a dozen other professions attended the Southern Society banquet, but the society could not claim to be the sacred preserve of Confederate success in the North; nor is New York the United States. Wall Street and the polyclinic may have monopolized the best-known financiers and physicians, but the Confederate carpetbagger legacy extended from Maine to Iowa.

Among the many southern writers and poets to move north—often but not always to New York—Virginius Dabney, George Cary Eggleston, and F. Hopkinson Smith stand out among the Southern Society's members. If members' wives are considered, Constance Harrison and Sarah Pryor must be added. All five achieved contemporary literary fame and made comfortable livings with their pens, as did James Maurice Thompson, living "out West" in Indiana. That became the norm for Confederate writers in the North, including the many other minor authors and poets mentioned in earlier chapters. Very few achieved the sunny uplands of genuine greatness. They were all competent, but very few grew in their art or contributed anything of striking originality.

Among authentic Confederate carpetbaggers, only Katherine Sherwood Bonner and Sidney Lanier erected artistic legacies that extended beyond their lifetimes. Mark Twain and George Washington Cable might be mentioned as honorary members of this select group, but both men were flawed Confederates. Twain stands head and shoulders above all others, but his Confederate service was meager at best. Cable served in Confederate ranks, but he did not move north until 1884, and, by that time, he had become more a critic than an advocate of the Confederacy. Bonner and Lanier, however, merit attention. Part of their legacy—a double one, actually—relates to their advocacy of sectional reconciliation. Yet they also made lasting contributions to American letters.

Kate Bonner's one completed novel, one novella, and nearly forty short stories helped launch the local-color school that pushed American

21. Kelly and Burrage, *American Medical Biography,* 873–74; Charles W. Eliot, "The Pioneer Qualities of Dr. Morrow as a Social Reformer," *American Social Hygiene Association Publication,* No. 58 (New York, 1916), 15–19.

literature toward realism in the 1860s and 1870s. Bonner lacked an original mind. Realism at first repelled her. She began writing as a Romantic, and tinges of her lineage clung to her work thereafter. She sometimes pirated plots, settings, and chapters from other, more genuinely original, writers. For instance, when Mary Noailles Murfree demonstrated the popularity of genre stories set in the Cumberland Mountains, Bonner produced her own stories about white mountain folk. Yet even as a reflection of genuine brilliance, Bonner's writing contains a fresh style, some original plots, and sprightly dialogue. She used Negro dialect several years before Irwin Russell and Joel Chandler Harris gained national attention for their deft handling of black idiom. Many of her characters, both black and white, strike modern readers as dated stereotypes. Her black characters are too often comic; nearly all are childlike. Her mountain tales helped to create the stereotype of the sexually promiscuous poor-white girl. Yet her characters inhabit such compelling stories that one can easily accept them on Bonner's own terms.[22]

Lanier's literary reputation is even more secure than Bonner's. Examples of his poetry appear in every anthology of southern literature and most anthologies of American literature. After Walt Whitman and Emily Dickinson, Lanier ranks as the most important American poet in the second half of the nineteenth century. His realism may not have been ideal. Like Bonner—indeed, like nearly every postwar southern literary figure—Lanier would have been happier in an earlier, more romantic age. He railed, as did such lesser writers as Essie Cheesborough, against editors and publishers (mostly northern) who seemed more concerned with "the *forms*" of literature than with the heartfelt emotions of the poet. Lanier believed that art, whatever its form, whatever the age, should express passion. In music and literature, he scorned popular tastes that seemed rooted in old or new prejudices. "A great Artist," he declared, describing a combination of virtues that would occur only to a dedicated Confederate, "should have the sensibility and expressive genius of Schumann, the calm grandeur of Lee, and the human breadth of Shakespeare, all in one." He accepted as "inevitable" his early failure to win acclaim from a public that valued "cleverness" above "Art." Lanier was young and, therefore, impatient. Envisioning a literature beyond the slowly evolving realism of his day, he was fated never fully to understand

22. Hubert Horton McAlexander, *The Prodigal Daughter: A Biography of Sherwood Bonner* (Baton Rouge, 1981), 72–74, 126–29, 182–95.

or to articulate his vision. Like Bonner, he died too soon, unaware of the legacy he left behind.[23]

The northern climate nourished Confederate painters and sculptors, too. Sculptors James W. A. MacDonald and William R. O'Donovan, close personal friends, earned reputations not yet obliterated from the pages of history. Of course, the big advantage enjoyed by sculptors, especially monumental sculptors like MacDonald and O'Donovan, is that their work—even the bad pieces—is so hard to ignore. Like the poor, it is with us always, staring down from pedestals in parks and courthouse squares generation after generation. It is less trouble to tolerate it than to haul it down. This is not to suggest that anyone would want to haul down the work of MacDonald and O'Donovan. Quite the contrary; both men excelled as sculptors, able to arouse even Yankee souls by tender strokes of art. They rank a distinct notch below Augustus Saint-Gaudens and John Q. A. Ward (O'Donovan's old nemesis), but most of their work, tarnished and ill kept as much of it is, still pleases the eye.

Certainly during their lifetimes MacDonald and O'Donovan enjoyed no end of distinguished patrons and subjects. As little as six years after the war, MacDonald had commissions amounting to over a hundred thousand dollars. He produced portrait busts of Charles O'Conor (on commission from the New York Bar Association and still a guardian of the Appellate Court Building in New York City), Thurlow Weed, and William Cullen Bryant. His heroic bust of Winfield Scott Hancock still surveys Hancock Square in New York, just as his seated statue of Fitz-Greene Halleck oversees Central Park. Visitors to Forest Park, St. Louis, may still gaze up at his giant tribute to Edward Bates. One commission, however, MacDonald desired above all others. Very soon after Jefferson Davis' release from prison, MacDonald sought an introduction to the former president through Charles O'Conor, Davis' attorney. He wanted to produce a heroic bronze statue of Davis, and he believed his own

23. Jay B. Hubbell, *The South in American Literature, 1607–1900* (Durham, 1954), 758–77; Jack DeBellis, *Sidney Lanier* (New York, 1972), 146–50; Aubrey Harrison Starke, *Sidney Lanier: A Biographical and Critical Study* (New York, 1964), 170–71; Sidney Lanier to Mary D. Lanier, October 18, 1874, October 23, 1874, both in Anderson *et al.* (eds.), *Works of Sidney Lanier*, IX, 102–103, 105–106; Louis D. Rubin, Jr., "The Passion of Sidney Lanier," in *William Elliott Shoots a Bear: Essays on the Southern Literary Imagination* (Baton Rouge, 1975), 107–44. For Lanier's influence on American music, see Jane S. Gabin, *A Living Minstrelsy: The Poetry and Music of Sidney Lanier* (Macon, Ga., 1985), 47–63.

"fidelity and sacrifice to the cause of independence" qualified him for the project. MacDonald never received that most cherished assignment.[24]

O'Donovan, twenty years younger than MacDonald, did not make his mark as quickly as his friend, but he eventually enjoyed an even broader reputation. Ten years after moving north, O'Donovan still survived largely on "great expectations," but some people had begun to recognize him as a rising star. In 1878, the prestigious *Art Journal* devoted an article to O'Donovan, even though his only important work at that time was a "colossal statue" of Father Matthew. Not long after the *Art Journal* article, O'Donovan produced portrait busts of painters Winslow Homer, Thomas Eakins, and William Page (all three his personal friends), Walt Whitman, Theodore Tilton (for whom he rooted during the Beecher trial), Edmund C. Stedman, and former Union general Daniel E. Sickles. He exhibited work at the National Academy of Design and the National Gallery of Art. He collaborated with Thomas Eakins to model life-size equestrian reliefs of Abraham Lincoln and Ulysses S. Grant as parts of the celebrated Soldiers' and Sailors' Memorial Arch in Prospect Park, Brooklyn. O'Donovan twice sculpted statues of George Washington, one for delivery to Caracas, Venezuela, the other to crown the Battle Monument at Trenton, New Jersey.[25]

In his own gentle way, painter Robert L. Newman proved every bit as successful as the flamboyant O'Donovan. Newman had never wanted to be anything more than a painter. As a boy, he devoured every art book he could acquire. As a teenager, he instructed himself in painting. As a young man, he traveled twice to Europe, where French painters Thomas Couture and Jean François Millet nurtured and shaped his as yet unformed Romantic inclinations. Newman had only begun to master his art when the Civil War began. He immediately offered his services to the Confederacy as a draftsman, a capacity he filled until mustered into the 16th Virginia Regiment during the final year of fighting. He resumed his artistic career after the war, first spending a year in Baltimore painting political banners, then moving to New York to design stained glass. Recognition, however, came slowly, and so discouraged did Newman

24. William R. O'Donovan to Mary Bright O'Donovan, July 21, 1871, in William Rudolf O'Donovan Correspondence, HSP; *Dictionary of American Biography*, XII, 16; James W. MacDonald to Charles O'Conor, May 14, 1867, in Jefferson Davis Papers, AA.

25. William R. O'Donovan to Mary Bright O'Donovan, December 15, 1876, in O'Donovan Correspondence; "A Sculptor's Method of Work," *Art Journal*, n.s., IV (1878), 62–63; *Dictionary of American Biography*, XIII, 627.

become that in the early 1870s he sought work in Tennessee as a newspaper editor and teacher.[26]

Newman returned to New York after a few years, but by then he was nearly fifty and lacked much of his youthful vigor. Rather than seek power, fortune, and fame, Newman became something of a recluse. He resided in New York's Bohemian district, but his aging body and spirit drew no energy from the sophomoric intellectual repartee that characterized O'Donovan's circle. A beguiling character at this stage in life, with "an appealing sensitive poet's face," Newman allowed his hair and beard to grow unchecked for several years, so that he looked like Walt Whitman in old age. Newman had few southern acquaintances in the North, but he attracted a following of influential northern friends, including Robert Underwood Johnson, Wyatt Eaton, Francis Lathrop, Richard Watson Gilder, William Merritt Chase, and Stanford White. His northern friends, who thought him "irresponsible as a child in all practical matters," outfitted the artist with clothes and paid his passage to Europe on two occasions. They also arranged Newman's admission, in his declining years, to a respectable "home" for the elderly, although the painter deserted the place after a single night to resume "his own ways" in shabby but familiar lodgings.[27]

Not until the 1890s did Newman's paintings, shown infrequently in public galleries, catch the attention of collectors and connoisseurs. Northern friends arranged the only two major exhibitions of his work during Newman's lifetime, one in New York, the other in Boston. Even then, Newman's admirers showed an *avant-garde* appreciation of an artist more widely hailed after death than during life. His best-known paintings, such as *The Good Samaritan* and *The Fortune Teller,* draw on religious and secular literature. They possess a misty, mystical quality distinguished by brilliant color and, in his mature work, modest abstraction. One critic found "the poetry of color and of life" in Newman's work and considered him "a greater artist" than some of his contemporaries who were "unquestionably superior painters." His art radiated imperfect beauty; it embodied an elusive charm. By the late 1930s, a

26. *Dictionary of American Biography,* XIII, 465–66; Marchal E. Landgren, "Robert Loftin Newman," in *A Memorial Exhibition of the Works of Robert Loftin Newman, Virginia-Born Master* (Richmond, 1942), 21–25.

27. Landgren, "Robert Loftin Newman," 25–28; *National Cyclopaedia of American Biography,* XIII, 179; Frederic Fairchild Sherman, "Robert Loftin Newman: An American Colorist," *Art in America,* IV (1916), 183; Marchal E. Landgren, "Robert Loftin Newman," *American Magazine of Art,* XXVIII (1935), 134–40.

quarter century after his death, critics compared Newman to Albert Pinkham Ryder. Some rated him above Ryder and hailed Newman as "one of the greatest" American painters. In the 1950s, art historians compared him with Eastman Johnson and William Morris Hunt—not bad company for a worn-out rebel.[28]

Two other painters, Thomas Satterswhite Noble and James Reeve Stuart, earned the praise of peers and patrons, even though neither man fulfilled his potential. Noble, a Kentuckian, studied painting in New York and Paris before the war. Service as a captain in the Confederate army occupied his time from 1861 to 1865, but after the war he returned to New York. By 1867, he had earned associate membership in the National Academy. Two years later, he accepted an appointment as professor of art at McMicken University, Cincinnati, where he lived most of his remaining thirty-eight years. His legacy thus rested on his popularity as a teacher. Interestingly, Noble's best paintings depict the evils of slavery, particularly his *The Slave Mart in the Republic of America* and *The Price of Blood, a Planter Selling His Son.*[29]

South Carolinian Stuart attended the University of Virginia and Harvard, but he devoted most of his youthful intellectual curiosity to studying art in Boston and Europe. He returned to South Carolina when Fort Sumter fell and served in the Confederate artillery. The war ruined the Stuarts financially, so James wandered westward seeking employment. He lived briefly in Georgia, Tennessee, Missouri, and Iowa. Finally, in 1873, he settled in Wisconsin, where he spent the remaining forty-two years of his life. Like Noble, Stuart taught art for awhile, first at Milwaukee College, later at the University of Wisconsin. Unlike the Kentuckian, Stuart preferred painting to the classroom. Scores of his portraits, mostly of midwestern political and social leaders, hang in Wisconsin museums and public buildings. His portraits lack the psy-

28. Landgren, "Robert Loftin Newman," in *Memorial Exhibition*, 25–28; *National Cyclopaedia of American Biography*, XIII, 179; Sherman, "Robert Loftin Newman," 183; Landgren, "Robert Loftin Newman," *American Magazine of Art*, 134–40; Margaret Breuning, "Ryder and Newman," *American Magazine of Art*, XXXII (1937), 714–16; James W. Lane, "A View of Two Native Romantics, Newman and Ryder: Recluses of the Brown Decades in America," *Art News*, XXXVIII (November 11, 1939), 9; Virgil Barker, *American Painting: History and Interpretation* (New York, 1950), 609, 614, 617.

29. George C. Groce and David H. Wallace, *The New-York Historical Society's Dictionary of Artists in America, 1564–1860* (New Haven, 1957), 473; Charles Theodore Greve, *Centennial History of Cincinnati and Representative Citizens* (2 vols.; Chicago, 1904), II, 534–35.

chological insight necessary for great portraiture, but his immense technical skill secured him a broad regional reputation.[30]

But painters come and painters go. Today few people know Newman, Noble, or Stuart by name. The same could be said of at least half a dozen other Confederate painters and illustrators. Conrad W. Chapman, John L. Chapman, John D. Perry, David E. Henderson, Allen C. Redwood, and William L. Sheppard come most readily to mind. Architects are a different matter. Their work, like that of monumental sculptors, is hard to ignore. We cannot shut it up in a storage bin or a closet so easily as we can an outdated canvas; but then no one ever dreamed of treating the work of Henry Hobson Richardson or John Wellborn Root in so cavalier a fashion. Both men lived on the fringes of the Confederacy; neither served in the military. Richardson remained in Paris, studying at the Ecole des Beaux Arts, for most of the war. He had graduated from Harvard before going to France in 1859, and his New England fiancée lived in Boston. Duty and family drew him to Louisiana; a sweetheart's tears entreated him to remain safe in the North. He visited Boston following the capture of his native New Orleans in 1862, but he refused to take the loyalty oath and soon returned to Paris, at least partly at the urging of his mother and brother. Root, only eleven when the shooting started, spent most of the war in Atlanta. When the city fell to William T. Sherman, his blockade-running father sent him to school in England under the escort of family friend Richard T. Wilson.[31]

Richardson returned to the United States in October, 1865. He had struggled with his conscience during his last months in Paris. His sweetheart and influential Yankee friends beckoned him back to Boston; his family urged him southward. Southern friends and relatives predicted great opportunities for him in Louisiana, just as Burton Harrison's friends predicted a thriving law practice on Canal Street. Like Harrison, Richardson divined wider opportunity in the North. An architect requires patrons, even more than a painter or sculptor, and Richardson knew that the largest and most numerous commissions must come from Boston and New York, rather than New Orleans and Atlanta. Northern in-laws and Harvard connections arranged for Richardson's early com-

30. James Reeve Stuart, "Autobiography" (MS in HSW), 20–27; Madison (Wisc.) *Democrat,* December 24, 1915; Porter Butts, *Art in Wisconsin* (Madison, 1936), 116–19.

31. Mrs. Schuyler Van Rensselaer, *Henry Hobson Richardson and His Works* (Boston, 1888), 4–17; Henry-Russell Hitchcock, Jr., *The Architecture of H. H. Richardson and His Times* (New York, 1936), 42; Harriet Monroe, *John Wellborn Root: A Study of His Life and Work* (Boston, 1896), 7–9.

missions. By 1870, Richardson's reputation as an architectural genius brought him all the work he needed. Almost single-handedly, he revived interest in Romanesque design, newly christened "Richardsonian" and characterized by the "Richardson arch." By 1880, the world knew him as America's greatest architect, and his designs dominated America's architectural landscape until the gleaming "White City" of Chicago's 1893 world's fair announced a new era of Classical and Renaissance revival.[32]

But Richardson's legacy was secure by 1893, seven years after his death. Among American architects, only Louis Sullivan and Frank Lloyd Wright offer worthy standards by which to measure his genius. Not only did Richardson establish the dominance of his personal style, he rescued American architecture from the "slough" into which it had sunk during the 1860s. Richardson, with his irrepressible jollity, yellow waistcoats, and appreciation of good wine and cheese, rekindled American enthusiasm, ingenuity, and dedication to architectural art. He and a few other reformers reversed an alarming trend toward shoddy construction, both in workmanship and materials, that characterized much American architecture, even in the 1870s. Unfortunately, the strength of Richardson's example and style waned with his death. No one of his students or protégés (including, briefly, Louis Sullivan) had his artistic gifts or the formidable personality necessary to continue the tradition. No one could match his Trinity Church, his Marshall Field Building, his libraries and railroad stations in Massachusetts, his private residences in Chicago, his jail in Pittsburgh, or his state capitol in Albany. Still, even jaded, modern architectural critics, a century after Richardson's death, recognize his claim to the title "master."[33]

John Root, like most architects of his generation, felt Richardson's influence. The Roots moved to New York after the war. Sidney Root, unlike his friend Dick Wilson, quickly squandered the fortune he had accumulated during the war. His son John did considerably better. He entered the architectural office of James Renwick, Jr., after graduating

32. Van Rensselaer, *Henry Hobson Richardson,* 16–17; William Richardson to Henry H. Richardson, July 5, 1865, in Papers of Henry Hobson Richardson, AAA; Hitchcock, *Architecture of Richardson,* 53–54, 70–82.

33. Henry-Russell Hitchcock, Jr., *Richardson as a Victorian Architect* (Baltimore, 1966), 48; Hitchcock, *Architecture of Richardson,* 11–12, 265, 290–300; *Houston Chronicle,* November 16, 1982, Sec. 4, p. 5. The most recent study of Richardson, which I did not have time to consult, is James F. O'Gorman, *H. H. Richardson: Architectural Forms for an American Society* (Chicago, 1987).

with honors in civil engineering from New York University. Two years later, in 1871, John Root moved to Chicago, where he shortly entered a partnership with Daniel H. Burnham, a native New Yorker. Few collaborations, regardless of field, have ever been so fruitful. Burnham and Root literally changed the face of Chicago following the disastrous fire of 1871. They brought the Richardson look to Chicago, but with their own touch of genius. Root, in particular, appreciated the need to make architecture fit the purposes of its environment. He believed, like his contemporary Louis Sullivan and Sullivan's student Frank Lloyd Wright, that form follows function. The modern office building, the "skyscraper," became the heritage of that dictum. Though not the first architect to experiment with steel and glass construction, Root helped lead the way in Chicago. The Grannis Block and Montauk Block, built in the early 1880s, heralded the new style; the Rookery, constructed between 1885 and 1888, ensured Root's immortality, with many triumphs still to come.[34]

All this national acclaim for former Confederates is most impressive, but it represents only the peak of the proverbial iceberg if one is seeking to understand the Confederate carpetbagger legacy. Few people, even very successful people, ever earn national attention. In the nineteenth century, most "famous" people rated only as local or county celebrities, perhaps with some recognition in their states. If this standard is used to identify people who made their marks on northern society, scores of Confederates fit the description. Former rebels helped shape their adopted communities and states as politicians, farmers, merchants, financiers, and professional people. Preceding chapters are filled with examples of Confederates who wielded influence and earned the respect of their neighbors, but perhaps a few random additional cases might win the point.

Some people may have recognized John F. Snyder as a national figure. He won a place in the *Dictionary of American Biography.* Nonetheless, Snyder's fame as a physician, anthropologist, and geologist existed largely in Illinois. As a colonel of Confederate cavalry, Snyder fought at Wilson's Creek, Pea Ridge, Helena, and Corinth. Captured in 1863, he was released on parole in November. Snyder hesitated in accepting the parole; he preferred at first to wait for a prisoner exchange, but by the end of 1863, he had pretty much decided that the Confederacy "was

34. Monroe, *John Wellborn Root,* 13–14; Donald Hoffman, *The Architecture of John Wellborn Root* (Baltimore, 1973), 2–12, 19–27, 65–83, 246–47.

about collapsed." Not only that, he found himself "financially and otherwise completely 'chawed up and spit out.'" He tried earning a living as a lawyer in southwest Missouri but gave it up after a year. While in New Mexico on a legal errand in 1864, he inspected the Southwest with an eye to emigration. He finally decided to settle with his wife and children in Illinois. He arrived at the village of Virginia in late 1864, aged thirty-four, "afoot and absolutely penniless."[35]

Snyder had acquired professional training as both doctor and lawyer before the war, and he decided that medicine would pay better in Illinois. Not that a physician in the rural, nineteenth-century Middle West ever got rich. Sparsely settled countryside and poor roads made Snyder's job less attractive and more arduous than John Wyeth's New York practice. In wet weather, when Illinois roads looked more like swamps than highways, Snyder walked miles to attend patients. Walking simply proved faster than riding a horse through two feet of mud. Snyder tried his hand at politics, too, but the Illinois legislature frustrated him. The tall, full-bearded, dark-visaged Snyder could be as gentle as Jesus when treating a patient, as jolly as Saint Nicholas with friends, but he also possessed an irascible temper. He was quick to anger and slow to forgive, blunt in speech and obstinate in his views, not ideal traits for an aspiring politician. Nearly from the day he arrived in Illinois, Snyder became embroiled in political arguments, not just with Republicans but with fellow Democrats. When the time came for his election bid, some Democrats looked skeptically on their "very jovial . . . but somewhat odd" candidate. Almost inevitably, his victory produced cries of chicanery from unsuccessful candidates. Equally predictable was Snyder's determination to resign his newly won legislative seat rather than suffer unjust abuse. Friends convinced him to weather the storm, but, once in the legislature, Snyder became so "thoroughly disgusted with politics" that he refused to seek another term.[36]

But Snyder's real interests lay outside medicine and politics. His first

35. *Dictionary of American Biography*, XVII, 389; John F. Snyder to Dr. Whelpley, February 9, 1910, in Medical Papers, MOHS.

36. A. R. Lyles, "Dr. John Francis Snyder, 1830–1921," *Journal of the Illinois State Historical Society*, XIV (1921), 241; Phyllis E. Connolly, "Biographical Essay," in *John Francis Snyder: Selected Writings*, ed. Clyde C. Walton (Springfield, Ill., 1962), 6–7; Carl E. Black, "A Country Doctor, John Francis Snyder, M.D." (Typescript in John F. Snyder Papers, IHL), 1–4, 10, 14; Menard County (Ill.) *Axis*, February 15, 1868; St. Louis *Globe*, October 10, 1879; Edward Channing to John F. Snyder, November 20, 1878, in Snyder Papers.

love was geology, followed closely by anthropology and archaeology. He found more fascination digging for buried bones than healing broken ones. His expertise made him the "ranking pioneer" of archaeology in Illinois. He conducted research for the Smithsonian Institution, excavated Indian mounds, and authored numerous articles and volumes on prehistoric American Indian tribes, archaeological methods, and the geology of the Middle West. He wrote history, too, and helped establish the Illinois State Historical Society. Self-taught in all these fields, Snyder never hesitated to challenge professional authorities. When the Missouri Historical Society published a pamphlet on the battle of Wilson's Creek, Snyder took the editor to task for the pamphlet's pro-Union view and its "guesses and surmises." When the newly founded Illinois State Historical Society failed to win political autonomy from the Illinois State Library, Snyder resigned from the society. The society had failed to meet his expectations of scholarly activity, and he refused to belong to an organization that had "no power to accomplish anything but the getting up of annual entertainments for the ladies and school children of Springfield." "From any point of view one might take," summarized a friend, Snyder was "a 'Character,' " but he left his mark on Illinois.[37]

Illinois attracted other Confederates destined for local accolades. William H. Phillips left Virginia for southern Illinois after the war. This nineteen-year-old former captain of Confederate infantry, worn in health and wasted in worldly goods, moved from place to place and tried his hand at a variety of trades before settling at Marion, Illinois. There, Captain Billy, as he was known, operated an extensive hardware business, sat on the town council, and directed local Masonic affairs. H. L. Hunt, a Georgian, worked his way to prominence in Fayette County, Illinois, after service in the 37th Arkansas Regiment. While helping to support his mother, sister, and two brothers, he labored for local farmers in hopes of saving enough money to buy his own stock farm. Industry produced success. He bought his farm, married a local girl, allied himself with the Republican party, and joined a number of fraternal orders, including the Masons and Odd Fellows. Hunt's crowning achievement came when he won election as county sheriff. A former rebel thus gained responsibility for guarding the lives and property of many former enemies. Elliot W. Mudge, one of eleven Mudge children to grow up in

37. Lyles, "John Francis Snyder," 239–40; *Dictionary of American Biography,* XVII, 389; Connolly, "Biographical Essay," 6–7; John F. Snyder to Oscar W. Collect, January 8, 1883, to Mrs. S. P. Wheeler, March 12, 1906, both in Snyder Papers; Black, "Country Doctor," 2, 9–10, 14.

Madison County, Illinois, had a northern father and a Louisiana mother. His father died shortly before the war, so Elliot left school in New York to join his mother and younger siblings at New Orleans in 1861. He enlisted in the Crescent Regiment and fought through the war, the last two years in Nathan Bedford Forrest's cavalry. Mudge wandered back to Madison County by way of St. Louis after the war, settled on the old homestead, leased sixteen hundred acres, made his fortune, and, like so many other young Confederate veterans in the North, married a Yankee. In addition to his extensive farming interests, Mudge established the first electric light plant at Edwardsville. He held a number of political posts, including township supervisor and county deputy clerk. His congenial manner, benevolence, and sincerity made him one of the county's "most popular citizens."[38]

Evansville, Indiana, boasted one of six northern camps of the United Confederate Veterans. Most members had been drawn to Evansville by the town's growing postwar importance as a river port and railroad terminal. Typical of Evansville Confederates was Alabama cavalryman Lee Howell, who became a successful investor and railroad director. Howell first arrived at Evansville as a contracting agent for the Louisville and Nashville Railroad. He eventually won promotion to general freight agent; but Howell, not content to make other men's fortunes, wanted his own railroad. In combination with other progressive entrepreneurs, he organized the Evansville, Newburgh and Suburban Railway, the Evansville Cross Tie Company, and the Evansville, Ohio, and Green River Transportation Company. Evansville neighbors respected Howell for his aggressive yet congenial nature, for his candor, sagacity, and public spirit. He contributed significantly to the sleepy river town's postwar growth and prosperity.[39]

William Field, a Kentuckian, settled in Evansville, too. Field's father, a prominent Kentucky lawyer, moved his family to Missouri when William was a lad. The son moved farther west as a young man but returned to Missouri from Colorado when the war started to serve in the 10th Missouri Regiment. Captain Field entered the grain business at his

38. George Washington Smith, *A History of Southern Illinois* (3 vols.; Chicago, 1912), II, 619–21, 680–81; Robert W. Ross and John J. Bullington (eds.), *Portrait and Biographical Record of Madison County, Illinois* (Chicago, 1894), 156–57; *Historical Encyclopedia of Illinois and History of Fayette County* (2 vols.; Chicago, 1910), II, 762.

39. Joseph P. Elliott, *A History of Evansville and Vanderburgh County, Indiana* (Evansville, 1897), 450–52; *History of Vanderburgh County, Indiana* (Madison, Wisc., 1889), 405–406.

native Louisville after the war. Successful there, he moved to Evansville in 1868, where he took an Indiana bride, expanded his grain business, and amassed extensive property holdings. Field became known as "one of the most honest and conscientious business men along the Ohio River."[40]

The Midwest also profited from the invasion of the George Taylor family, from Virginia. Service as a Confederate surgeon ruined Dr. Taylor's health, and Philip Sheridan's troops ruined his Shenandoah Valley home. So in 1865, the good doctor, accompanied by his wife and three sons, moved to Illinois. Taylor slowly recovered his health and began a medical practice at Rosetta, Illinois, where Mrs. Taylor bore a daughter. Mrs. Taylor, the former Mary Jane Lynn, enjoyed a modest reputation as poet and novelist. Following the birth of her daughter, she added to her accomplishments by earning a degree from a homeopathic medical college in Cincinnati. She maintained an active practice for the next twenty-five years, much of it spent in rural countryside that required lonely night visitations to remote parts of the county. Friends urged her to carry a pistol on these night rides, but the spunky little woman replied scornfully, "For an ordinary criminal? I should be ashamed of myself if I could not outwit three or four of them." Two Taylor sons became physicians, both eventually settling in Crawfordsville, Indiana. The third son became a Chicago lawyer. George and Mary Taylor followed their physician sons to Indiana in the 1870s and eventually settled at Greencastle. Their daughter, Minerva, grew up to become a nationally known club woman, linguist, lecturer, and author.[41]

Residents of Licking County, Ohio, enjoyed the medical services of M. W. Suter. The war disrupted Suter's medical studies in Virginia. He laid down his books to bear both rifle and saber for Virginia infantry and cavalry regiments. Twice he fell captive to the Yankees; twice he found himself incarcerated at Camp Chase, Ohio. After witnessing Lee's surrender at Appomattox, Suter entered medical school in Philadelphia. Following graduation in 1867, he wandered west to Ohio, where he tended the ills and fevers of former foes in several places before settling at Newark. In addition to a thriving medical practice, Suter participated in local historical and agricultural societies. He helped to establish the first daily newspaper in Newark, and he served as a corre-

40. Evansville *Courier*, July 28, 1907, pp. 1–2.
41. Jessee W. Weik, *Weik's History of Putnam County, Indiana* (Indianapolis, 1910), 435–41.

spondent to leading Ohio newspapers. Suter and his wife also enjoyed a "highly esteemed" position in Licking County's leading social circles.[42]

Some Confederate success stories seem straight from Horatio Alger, who, incidentally, published his first rags-to-riches tales two years after the Civil War. One example is William M. Tugman, respected member of the Cincinnati bar. Tugman began life in the mountains of North Carolina. Financial reverses during the war forced his father to sell the family farm. His mother died midway through the war, and the son, in his early teens, had to look after his younger siblings while their father served in the Confederate ranks. The postwar years became a time of pilgrimage through North Carolina, Kentucky, and Ohio in search of work. Largely self-educated, young Tugman labored as a farmhand while acquiring a formal education in Adams County, Ohio. He soon earned a teaching certificate, which enabled him to work his way through Ohio University and to study law. Tugman passed the state bar examination in 1879 and opened a practice in Cincinnati two years later. Shortly thereafter, he married a New Englander, who bore him three sons. Tugman's social status, based on his reputation as a Freemason and clubman, reinforced his high professional standing. "He has justly earned the proud American title of a self-made man," claimed one admirer. Another friend, less gracefully, echoed the sentiment: "It is safe to say not many would have undertaken what Mr. Tugman did and succeed in."[43]

And not all the success stories involved professional and business people. Virginia-born Philip L. Stickley had never been anything but a farmer. When the war came, Stickley propped his hoe against a fence post on his father's Shenandoah Valley farm and went off to become an artillerist in Turner Ashby's brigade. He earned sergeant's stripes and suffered severe wounds before returning home in 1865. Hard times drove Stickley to Ohio in 1868. He labored four years as a hired hand in Champaign County, long enough to save some money and buy his own land. Stickley eventually owned three hundred acres. Marriage to a daughter of one of the county's pioneers advanced his social and political fortunes. He joined the Masons and Knights of Pythias and served two terms as township treasurer. Neighbors hailed Stickley as a "repre-

---

42. *Memorial Record of Licking County, Ohio* (Chicago, 1894), 190–91.
43. *Cincinnati: The Queen City* (3 vols.; Chicago, 1912), III, 228–30; Nelson W. Evans and Emmons B. Stivers, *A History of Adams County, Ohio* (West Union, Ohio, 1900), 889–91.

sentative farmer," a "self-made man" of whom the county could be justly proud.[44]

Still, success did not always bring happiness. Not a few Confederates who earned enviable reputations in northern communities returned south. Andrew E. Cafee, of Alabama, moved to New York after service in the Confederate artillery. He clerked in Gotham for two years before moving to Indianapolis, where he had attended college before the war. He built a praiseworthy career as a journalist in Indiana and Iowa before returning to Alabama in 1878 to enjoy life as a prominent planter, editor, sheriff, probate judge, state senator, and railroad commissioner. Christopher W. Robertson hailed from Tennessee and rode with Nathan Bedford Forrest. After the war, he knocked around New York and Pennsylvania in "various callings," including laborer in a brick yard, salesman, drugstore clerk, and canal boatman. In 1873, he took a degree from Bellevue Hospital Medical College, but two years later he returned to Tennessee, where he served as the mayor and public health officer in his town and headed the local bank.[45]

Daniel A. Tompkins ranks as the most successful Confederate carpetbagger to return home. Born on a cotton plantation in South Carolina, Tompkins described himself as "a child of the Old South," yet his northern training and experiences made him one of the creators of a New South. He entered South Carolina College after the war, but Tompkins, who wanted to be a mechanical engineer, transferred, in 1869, to Rensselaer Polytechnic Institute, at Troy, New York. He earned a "B+" record at Rensselaer and, in his junior year, won election as "Grand Marshall" (president) of the student body. Unfortunately, Rensselaer did not supplement its classroom courses in engineering with practical experience in laboratories and shops. While still a student, Tompkins entered a Troy steel plant to learn steelmaking from the bottom up. His experience and friendships in the mill won him a job in Brooklyn designing steel plants, including the mighty Bethlehem Iron Works, in Pennsylvania. In 1874, Tompkins took a job at the newly constructed Bethlehem plant designing machinery for the country's foremost iron master, John Fritz. Tompkins worked in Fritz's drafting rooms for three years, but he missed life in the shop. He wanted to make steel, not draw

44. *A Centennial Biographical History of Champaign County, Ohio* (New York, 1902), 392–95.

45. Thomas McAdory Owen, *History of Alabama and Dictionary of Alabama Biography* (4 vols.; Chicago, 1921), III, 279–80; Christopher W. Robertson, in Civil War Veterans Questionnaires (Confederate), TL.

pictures. He badgered Fritz relentlessly, seeking a transfer. Fritz, unwilling to lose such a talented draftsman, consistently refused his requests. Not until 1878 did Tompkins enter the machine shop.[46]

Tompkins believed his real career in the iron industry began the day he entered Bethlehem's machine shop. He had to take a reduction in pay, but he gained invaluable experience, not to mention satisfaction. He worked at a roll lathe, which pressed hot iron sheets into railroad rails. At the same time, his growing experience in steelmaking increased his dissatisfaction with life in Pennsylvania. He wanted to go home to the South. He had developed and maintained business connections in South Carolina during his years at Bethlehem, and in 1878, he began probing for industrial opportunities there and in Kansas, Missouri, Tennessee, and Georgia. In 1881, he left Bethlehem for Crystal City, Missouri, to superintend the machine shop of a plate glass company. A year later, he accepted a job as sales representative in the Carolinas for the Westinghouse Machine Company of Pittsburgh. Tompkins had been studying industrial conditions in the South and southern industrial history. He became convinced that the South of seventy years earlier had enjoyed the same potential for industrial expansion as the North but had wasted its opportunities and resources by turning to staple agriculture and slave labor. Settling in Charlotte, North Carolina, Tompkins saw an opportunity to help the South regain lost ground and time.[47]

Tompkins became an industrial missionary and apostle of the New South. Southerners ignored him at first. Talk of building textile mills and cottonseed oil factories roused little enthusiasm; but Tompkins' position with Westinghouse and his fast-growing reputation as a machinist and designer gave him the leverage he needed. Steadily he publicized his message. He wrote extensively about southern industrial capabilities, even going so far as to purchase the Charlotte *Observer* to broadcast his views. People began to listen. Two years before returning to the South, Tompkins had explained his vision to his northern fiancée: "But as its soil and climate made a race of men proud of it as a birthplace in the past, so I believe [the South] will be again in the future and it is not only

46. George Tayloe Winston, *A Builder of the New South, Being the Story of the Life of Daniel Augustus Tompkins* (Garden City, N.Y., 1920), 3, 23–30, 33, 75–76; Howard Bunyan Clay, "Daniel Augustus Tompkins: An American Bourbon" (Ph.D. dissertation, University of North Carolina, 1950), 6–9, 13–15.

47. Clay, "Daniel Augustus Tompkins," 15, 19–20, 22–24; Winston, *Builder of the New South*, 68–72.

my immediate interest but these general impressions as well that lead me [on]."[48]

The stories of Caffee, Robertson, and Tompkins raise important questions about Confederate carpetbaggers: Would the many southerners who made their marks in the North, whether as local bankers, state politicians, or nationally acclaimed artists, have been equally successful in the South? Why did they succeed? Why them and not some other southerners? Why not equally capable northerners with whom they contended? What accounts for their success—their own perseverance, talent, and ambition, or northern opportunities for education, investment, patrons, and employment? Maybe it was simply luck. These are difficult questions to answer. Perhaps they do not require answers. Perhaps it is enough that the questions be asked and that we understand their imponderable nature. Most Confederates, after all, remained in the South; many of them became as famous and successful as their comrades who moved north. Yet emigrants continued to pour across the Ohio River because they saw no hope for success or happiness in the South. Had they misjudged conditions? Did they lack patience? They certainly did not lack courage. Maybe they were just restless. Americans are a mobile people. Sixty-four percent of the Confederates studied here crossed state boundaries at least one other time during their lives, either before or after moving north. One-third moved at least two other times during their lives, and that does not include temporary sojourns for education, business, or pleasure.

Perhaps the question is so futile because "success" escapes not only universal definition but definitive formula. In the end, perspective defines success. Was William R. O'Donovan more successful than sculptor Edward V. Valentine, who remained in Virginia? Valentine earned more honors and fame in the South, but O'Donovan enjoyed a broader national reputation and wider influence on contemporary trends and standards. He, not Valentine, won election to the National Academy. Would Valentine, who remained in Europe during the war and who lacked O'Donovan's aggressiveness, have survived in New York's cutthroat art world? Would O'Donovan, who lacked Valentine's family position and opportunity to study in Europe, have fared as well in the more parochial atmosphere of postwar Richmond? And what if we compare O'Donovan and Valentine to Moses J. Ezekiel, the greatest southern sculptor of

48. Winston, *Builder of the New South*, 78–79, 83–84; Daniel A. Tompkins to Harriet Brigham, December 28, 1880, in Daniel Augustus Tompkins Papers, DU.

his generation? After a brief postwar residence in Cincinnati, Ezekiel spent most of the rest of his life in Europe. How would he have fared had he stayed in the North or had he never left Virginia?

On the subject of artists, consider again the checkered career of James R. Stuart. As Stuart trudged home through Georgia and South Carolina following his surrender with Joseph Johnston's army, he saw nothing but desolation. He tried to establish a country school in Georgia but failed. He next opened a studio, and, although ("queer enough") he made fifteen hundred dollars in six months, "everything was going to confusion and ruin." Stuart returned to South Carolina, but "the place swarmed with carpetbaggers and negroes." Total strangers occupied his family's confiscated house. He obtained work in Beaufort plotting and drawing survey maps, but the job soon ended. A cousin secured work for him in Memphis, so he hurried there. In a short time, the ruined Tennessee economy ended his position. He set up another art studio but attracted few patrons. He moved to St. Louis and opened a third studio. He found work and Confederate friends in St. Louis, but the city was "the most uncomfortable place" he had ever lived, combining the worst of cold northern winters with the least desirable features of hot midwestern summers. He stayed in St. Louis five years but always with an eye to someplace better. He spent one summer in Iowa City, another in Lexington, Kentucky, a third in Madison, Wisconsin. Not until he sampled life in Madison, seven years after the war, did he sense the possibilities of success and happiness. Not until then did his life and career fall into place. Why not in Beaufort, or Memphis, or St. Louis? No single reason explains his earlier failures; no single ingredient can explain his ultimate triumph.[49]

Among writers, George Cary Eggleston and Constance Harrison have recently been "rediscovered" as important exemplars of the Old South and as pioneers in the postwar romanticization of antebellum Virginia, but their reputations have not worn as well as those of three other Virginia writers: John Esten Cooke, George W. Bagby, and Thomas Nelson Page. That may be partly prejudice, reflecting a belief that Eggleston and Harrison "abandoned" the South, but, again, perspective is important. Cooke and Bagby thought about moving to New York, and Bagby lived there for a few months in 1865. Page, who was just twelve years old when the war ended, became successful only after attracting the attention of northern publishers and after others such as

49. Stuart, "Autobiography," 24–26.

Eggleston and Harrison had established the popularity of the sort of fiction that made Page famous. What was more, Confederate carpetbagger Sophie Bledsoe Herrick, as an editor for *Century Magazine,* helped Page get his early writings published and improved his prose style. The principal difference between Eggleston and Harrison and their southern counterparts is subject matter. Cooke, Bagby, and Page are associated almost exclusively with Virginia, whereas Eggleston and Harrison are equally famous for their writings on other subjects. Northern residence gave them the opportunity and experience necessary to write on a broader range of topics. Eggleston might never have become an author had he not moved north and received encouragement from such men as Howells and Bryant. Harrison probably would have been an author regardless of where she lived, but she never would have penned those pungent satires on northern society had she remained in Virginia.

Could Sidney Lanier have blossomed as a major American poet in rural Georgia? Would he have attracted anyone's attention? Or was he a person—confident, ambitious, impatient—destined to make his own breaks wherever he lived? On more than one occasion, Lanier said that an artist could not grow or develop in the South. He, like many southern writers and artists, had gone north seeking wider exposure and more intense intellectual stimulation. One literary scholar insists that life in the South stunted Lanier's imagination and technical writing skill. Not until his late poetry, just before his premature death, judges this scholar, did Lanier begin to realize his potential.[50]

The northern influence on Lanier is unmistakable. He certainly expressed no southern experience when he wrote in "The Symphony":

> We weave in the mills and heave in the kilns,
> We sieve mine-meshes under the hills,
> And thieve much gold from the Devil's bank tills,
> To relieve, O God, what manner of ill?—
> The beasts, they hunger, and eat and die;
> And so do we, and the world's a sty;
> Hush, fellow-swine: why nuzzle and cry?

This robust attack on industry, trade, and big business is not one of Lanier's best poems, but it is one of the most famous, and it grew from outrage at what he saw during his northern residence. Lanier's decision to be a poet rather than a musician also sprang from his northern

---

50. Rubin, "The Passion of Sidney Lanier," 140–42.

residence. Shortly before writing "The Symphony," Lanier received a rejection notice for another poem. He retreated in despair to his boardinghouse room. Perched high above the streets of Brooklyn, he gazed upon the teeming masses, "and there," he recalled, "during a day whose intensity was of that sort that one only attempts to communicate to one's God," Lanier meditated. "And when evening came," he confessed to a friend, "I found myself full of the ineffable contents of certainty and of perfect knowledge and of decision. I had become aware . . . that my business in life was to make poems." Without that decision and the literary friends he made during his northern residence, Lanier would not have received commissions for "The Centennial Meditation of Columbia" or "Psalm of the West."[51]

How might southern financial and political history have been redirected had all former Confederates remained in the South? Is it possible that the loss of so many thousands of energetic, ambitious, and capable people gave an edge to the postwar army of northern political and economic opportunists that invaded the South? Some contemporaries criticized emigrants harshly, accusing them of deserting the South in its hour of greatest need. Did they? Could they have helped the South more by staying at home? Were they smart enough, able enough, to outwit Yankee carpetbaggers and their scalawag neighbors? Could they have halted the political and social revolution wrought by Reconstruction? Probably not. White southerners in the South could not have been any more united against Yankee carpetbaggers and freedmen. On the other hand, Confederate carpetbaggers might have sensed more accurately than Confederates who stayed behind the need to adapt to inevitable change; they might have better channeled southern energy in the era of a "New South."

Had John Inman remained at his uncle's bank in Georgia, or had William H. Inman and Alfred Austell not established a New York office and sent young Inman north to learn the cotton trade, he might have become just another southern banker, a very wealthy banker, no doubt, but one among many. The cotton trade would not have suffered; northern investors would have established the cotton exchange without Inman's aid. One wonders, however, what portion of Inman's investments in southern railroads and industry northern investors would have hazarded. Could Richard T. Wilson, Thomas F. Ryan, or John C. Latham

51. Sidney Lanier, "The Symphony," Sidney Lanier to Edmund Spencer, April 1, 1875, both in Anderson *et al.* (eds.), *Works of Sidney Lanier,* I, 47, IX, 187.

have succeeded so spectacularly in the South? Would they have been able
to invest so lavishly in the South? If Charles Rouss had not seen his
southern mercantile career destroyed by the war, would he have been
fired by the desire to move north? Had he not moved north, would he
have established his massive fortune? Had he returned to Virginia, discouraged after his first failure in New York, how might mercantile
history have been changed? Probably not at all; Ward and Sears were
already on the scene. But who would have built the Battle Abbey?

Could southern politicians in the North have used their energies more
effectively in the South? In some ways, they may have been more useful
in the North, spies and provocateurs, as it were, in the enemy camp; but
at least one northern Democrat thought otherwise. Abram S. Hewitt,
former congressman and mayor of New York, praised members of the
New York Southern Society, at their annual banquet in 1894, for their
impressive leadership in the community. "It has been to the great and
lasting benefit of this metropolis," admitted Hewitt, "that you have
come among us. But," he continued, "it seems that what has been our
gain has been the loss of the South. . . . Where are her sons today to
compare with the giants whom she was wont to send to the national
Capitol?" Where were the Washingtons, Jeffersons, Calhouns, Clays,
and Jacksons? Where the southern giants who dominated the nation's
affairs before the war? Hewitt's remarks caused a furor in the South.
"The Southern men of brains who have gone North," contended an
indignant Georgia congressman, "are few and far between. . . . The
Southern people do not want to go North. They have no business there,
unless they go to gamble in stocks and bonds and join the robber band."
Both Hewitt and the congressman exaggerated their points, but the issue
was valid and emotional. No one in 1894 could know who was more
correct. Neither can we.[52]

What about voters? Did enough Confederates go north to prolong
Republican rule unnecessarily? The numbers say no. Certainly the loss
of one thousand Floridians to the North between 1860 and 1880 did not
affect that state's political fortunes; nor would Mississippi's political
fate have been altered if its two thousand expatriates had stayed home.
Among the nine southern states to suffer Republican rule for as long as
five years, Georgia lost the most people to northern emigration between
1860 and 1870 with 2,345—hardly enough to help the Democrats.
Some states, such as North Carolina and South Carolina, actually had

52. New York *Times,* December 23, 1894, p. 1, February 24, 1894, p. 1.

fewer native sons and daughters living in the North in 1870 than in 1860. Emigration to the West may have hurt the South, but even that is doubtful. Only Texas gained an advantage from these population shifts. Its southern-born population grew by 33,000 between 1860 and 1870, with an additional 192,000 arriving by 1880. Yet Texas could not oust the Republicans before 1873.

Whatever losses the South incurred must be measured qualitatively, not quantitatively, and even the qualitative losses may have been a good investment. The money Confederate carpetbaggers pumped into the South, the connections they afforded business associates and friends in the South, and the happy effect they had on sectional reconciliation at least equal the good they might have accomplished at home. As for the wisdom of their decisions to move north, results must decide. People who made decent livings and found happiness probably made wise decisions. Those who found only loneliness and misery in the North probably—though not necessarily—made the wrong choice. It is sure, however, that enough people succeeded in their aims for Yankeedom to maintain its fascination and allure for future generations of ambitious and desperate southerners.

Epilogue

Strange Faces, Other Minds

Constance Harrison lacked the heart to stay in New York after Burton died. She felt restless and depressed staying anywhere very long. She and Burton had traveled abroad during the last decade of his life—to Britain, Scandinavia, Europe, the Holy Land, Russia— seeking temporary respites from "hard-and-fast New York." Now, with her trooper gone, Constance returned most often to France and Italy, generally to escape American winters. In summer she divided her time between Bar Harbor and her eldest son's home in Virginia. The family still owned Sea Urchins, but Constance did not spend as much time there as she would have liked. The cottage held too many memories. It was "too large and too lonely," she said with regret.[1]

Constance moved to Washington, D.C., in 1907, where she continued to write, though less often, and to enjoy society, though less frequently. She most enjoyed introducing favored young debutantes into Washington society. "I am at present engaged in conducting through one of the gayest weeks of the Season, one of the prettiest girls I have ever seen in many a long summer's day," she confided to a brother. People asked where she found her seemingly inexhaustible supply of pretty protégées. Constance laughed; her eyes twinkled. What debutante would not swoon at the chance to be sponsored by one of the most storied southern belles of the last half century! Constance escorted her chosen ones to luncheons, musicales, teas, and evening parties. She loved it; she sparkled like a dew-dropped last rose of summer. Yet, at nearly seventy years of age, Constance felt herself slowing down just a tad. "It is well for me

---

1. Mrs. Burton Harrison, *Recollections Grave and Gay* (New York, 1911), 361–70; Constance Harrison to Wilson M. Cary, April 2, 1911, in Wilson Miles Cary Collection, UV.

this week will end my night duty," she confessed of her escort duties, "as I could not stand it long."[2]

In 1910, Constance completed her most memorable piece of writing, *Recollections Grave and Gay.* Public response to her life's story, first published serially in *Scribner's Magazine,* warmed the heart of an aging Confederate. "It has been very exciting getting the letters about the Recollections [from] all over this country & Europe," she admitted privately, "but more to me is that I have been able to tell and publish the truth about the South, and to have it recognized as undisputed history which could never have been before! I thank God for that!" She was still trying to tell about the South, still hoping to win sympathy for the Lost Cause. If only Burton could have shared her triumph. She missed him. Her joy was dampened, too, by the death of Clarence Cary shortly after the reminiscences appeared in print. When, responding to overwhelming public demand, Scribner hurriedly published the articles in book form, Constance used the opportunity to dedicate this, her last volume, to the memory of a beloved brother.[3]

Constance began writing a second volume of memoirs, but she never completed it. Paralysis struck in 1916, sharply restricting her activities. By the end of summer, 1920, doctors ordered her confined to bed. Constance died in her apartment at 1302 18th Street on a chilly Sunday in November. She joined Burton and Clarence in the still cooler earth of Ivy Hill two days before Thanksgiving. Her sons laid Constance's coffin beside Burton's. A single stone slab covered them both. Reading the inscription carefully, a mourner would realize that Constance had rejoined her husband three days before their fifty-fourth wedding anniversary, fifty-four years after embarking on their northern adventure.[4]

A good many other Confederates had fallen victim to the ravages of time by 1920. Varina Davis had died in 1906. Katherine Bonner, Essie Cheesborough, Virginius Dabney, Charles Force Deems, Edwin De-Leon, George Cary Eggleston, Thomas and Euphania Ellis, John R. Fellows, Lewis M. Grimball, John H. Inman, Sidney Lanier, John C.

2. Constance Harrison to Wilson M. Cary, January 2, 1910, in Cary Collection.

3. Mrs. Burton Harrison, "Recollections Grave and Gay," *Scribner's Magazine,* XLIX (March, 1911), 315–26, XLIX (April, 1911), 456–68, XLIX (May, 1911), 556–68, XLIX (June, 1911), 727–41, L (July, 1911), 109–21; Constance Harrison to Wilson M. Cary, April 2, 19, 1911, both in Cary Collection.

4. Fairfax Harrison to Constance Harrison, September 4, 1916, in Francis Burton Harrison (ed.), *A Selection of the Letters of Fairfax Harrison* (Charlottesville, 1944), 67–68; Alexandria *Gazette,* November 22, 1920, p. 1, November 23, 1920, p. 1.

Latham, James W. A. MacDonald, Robert L. Newman, Theophilus Noel, Josiah Clark Nott, Carlie Oakley, William R. O'Donovan, John C. Pemberton, Allen C. Redwood, Charles Broadway Rouss, Roger and Sarah Pryor, George and Josie Rozet, John F. Snyder, Maurice Thompson, Richard and Melissa Wilson, and many hundreds of other carpetbaggers were all gone. United Confederate Veterans' camps were being superseded by the Sons of Confederate Veterans. Confederate survivors began falling at an accelerated pace. The last Confederate in New England, Nathaniel Poynitz, died in 1928. The last rebel veteran in the Midwest, G. A. Frazier, died in 1933. Edwin Selvage, New York's last Confederate, a veteran of thirty battles, suffered a premature death in 1930 when struck down by a taxicab on Flatbush Avenue.[5]

As old veterans began to cross over the river, Confederates and their children continued to arrive in the North. New arrivals resembled carpetbaggers of the 1860s and 1870s in many ways, and yet, somehow, they were different. Veterans arriving after 1880 were not as young, as scared, or as hungry, not so near the ragged edge of life as their predecessors. Businessmen and financiers such as John C. Calhoun, Jr., James P. Litton, James H. Parker, Robert McCulloch, John W. Frazer, and Philander P. Pease had already made comfortable fortunes in the South when they arrived in Yankeeland. Writers and poets James Lane Allen, Mary F. Childs, Susan B. Elder, Sarah B. Elliott, Ruth McEnery Stuart, and George Washington Cable had already published popular works. Lawyers Jacob M. Dickinson, Carroll Spriggs, Julius A. Coleman, and Hugh R. Garden; scholars such as Thomas R. Price; and physicians such as Benno A. Hollenberg and Richard K. Taylor had attended southern schools and earned respectable professional positions before moving north. Artists John G. Chapman and Cowles M. Collier knew they would earn northern commissions. Politicians James R. Sneed, Hugh S. Thompson, William L. Trenholm, John S. Wise, and Thomas P. Ochiltree sought semiretirement. Clergymen G. A. Frazier (the "Boy Preacher of the South"), Joseph D. Pickett, and Robert A. Gibson accepted invitations to tend existing northern congregations, not forge them, as had Reverend Deems.

5. *Confederate Veteran*, XXXVII (February, 1929), 67; Tuscola (Ill.) *Journal*, May 4, 1933, p. 1; New York *Times*, October 16, 1930, p. 25; *Confederate Veteran*, XXXVIII (December, 1930), 456–57. For an interesting account of the last surviving Confederate veterans in North and South, see Jay S. Hoar, *The South's Last Boys in Grey: An Epic Prose Elegy* (Bowling Green, Ohio, 1986).

Increasing numbers of latecomers, particularly among the younger generation, shared new ideas about the war and the South with the children of emigrants from the 1860s and 1870s. *Confederate* emigration gave way to a resumption of *southern* emigration. The Confederate era, fast coming to a close, gave way to a triumphant New South, even a new America, in which the nostalgic glow of sectional reconciliation masked, even if it did not cleanse, the blood and horror of recent memory. Children born of Confederate parents and raised on southern traditions, whether living in North or South, grew up in an atmosphere that invited—and sometimes demanded—compromise with northern values and beliefs. The new perspective signified more than a generation gap; it hinted at reevaluation of an entire way of life.

Constance had seen change coming. "What am I to do?" she asked a northern friend only half in jest. "My boy came back from Yale the other day and said, 'Mother, that was a beautiful system you had in the South, but on the Constitutional question you were all wrong!' " Confederates back home would have smiled smugly at Constance. What had she expected her sons to learn at an abolitionist college? Did she think New Englanders would teach them the fine points of John C. Calhoun's nullification theory? Had not the diehards predicted all along that if sons and daughters went north to live and be educated they would come back—if they came back at all—Yankeeized? The diehards may have exaggerated. Certainly no one could say the Harrison boys grew up to be Yankees. They loved the South. Yet they understood, perhaps better than their parents, the cruel posture in which the war—their parents' war—had placed the South. They felt a burden, different from that of their parents, in being southern.[6]

Fairfax Harrison, eldest son, corporate lawyer, and railroad executive, expressed the confusion of the Harrison boys. "I was born both too late and too soon and belong to the end of an era," he brooded, a southern echo of Henry Adams. "I find many of my friends in the same predicament, arguing for the old order with the old arguments which convinced men a generation ago, but, though they are still listened to respectfully, they are not heeded." The golden stain of time colored Fairfax's vision of the Old South. He believed that the Old South represented "the most agreeable phase of civilization" the country had ever known. "It bred generous instincts and a broader education in the true

6. Robert Underwood Johnson, *Remembered Yesterdays* (Boston, 1929), 208.

sense," he insisted in 1911, "than is possible in our present intense industrial life, stimulating as it is to every man of energy." As late as 1916, Fairfax considered his northern birth "one of the atrocities of the reconstruction period." Yet Fairfax knew that beyond the romance and glamour of his mother's novels, the Old South had been politically rebellious and economically "wasteful." As a college student, he had caused his mother distress by questioning the legitimacy of secession. He approved of the New South; he applauded "progressive" political policies; he endorsed a strong central government to direct the nation's economy; and he disapproved of sectional politics. The South, even if it wished otherwise, declared Fairfax, must function as part of the nation.[7]

Brother Francis agreed. Having served New York as a congressman for ten years and the Philippine Islands as governor-general for eight years, Francis possessed a genuinely national spirit. Yet his broad view of life had not come easily. As late as 1946, he still seethed to think how, during his childhood, the Grand Army of the Republic had claimed "a complete monopoly of public virtue and of public office." The GAR's ignoble arrogance and "lack of tolerance for a beaten foe," Francis insisted, "still stings like a whip across my memory." "If common sense had not triumphed in me," he confessed further, "I should have become a belated but 'unreconstructed' rebel in consequence. At best I could never forget that they destroyed a civilization in the South which had held much of the best culture our country ever had." But common sense *had* triumphed, thanks in no small measure to the teachings of his parents. Burton and Constance would have been terribly disappointed had their sons not shaken free of Confederate partisanship. To love the South was one thing, but to have seen their sons continuing to pay homage to a cause that, even in 1867, they knew must be buried, would have pained them.[8]

Yet the more things changed the more they stayed the same. One unchanging southern tradition particularly bothered Fairfax. When, in 1907, Fairfax moved to Virginia, he soon realized, in acute despair, that Virginia had progressed very little since the war. The population of

7. Fairfax Harrison to H. S. Haines, April 24, 1911, to Francis B. Harrison, July 24, 1912, to Key Compton, October 7, 1912, to Franklin K. Lane, November 21, 1912, all in Harrison (ed.), *Letters of Fairfax Harrison*, 35–36, 44, 46, 48–49; Fairfax Harrison to William G. McCabe, June 17, 1916, in William Gordon McCabe Papers, UV.

8. *National Cyclopaedia of American Biography* (59 vols. and index; New York, 1898–1980), XLVI, 24; Francis B. Harrison, "About It and About" (Typescript in Francis Burton Harrison Papers, UV), 33–34.

Fauquier County in 1917 was no larger than it had been in 1830. The reason was "lack of economic opportunity at home." Thousands of young Virginians continued to seek their fortunes and reputations outside the South. "I meet them and hear of them everywhere in the bustle of the world," he complained. "The loss of their driving energy bleeds white our poor old patient fertile Virginia." Even more disheartening came the realization, shortly after his mother's death, of the terrible psychological burden the war had placed on his generation. If the war had freed the Negro, he said, it had enslaved white southerners. It had tied them to dead memories that had steadily become living prejudices—racial, sectional, and political. C. Vann Woodward would call it the "burden of Southern history." Fairfax Harrison saw it as a burden of conscience that barred southern access to "the free congresses of the soul."[9]

"The free congresses of the soul" is a good phrase. It could have many meanings. But southerners who moved north from Fauquier County and elsewhere after 1880, particularly those born after 1860, understood what Harrison meant. Confederate carpetbaggers had left the South under abnormal conditions and, like Micawber, had contented themselves with living one day at a time. Preoccupied with the challenge of settling into Yankee ways, they had no definite expectations and few grand designs for the future. Their children and later emigrants could not be so patient. They must plan ahead, and they must live according to new political and economic rules. Ending Reconstruction and establishing a New South had been the political and economic themes of postwar southern life. With Reconstruction over and the New South established, southerners reached a juncture that presented certain points of interest. How would they respond to the need for further political and social change? How could they maintain the South's economic vitality? As the Confederate emigration reverted to a southern emigration, a new breed of southern emigrant reexamined the South's place in the nation.[10]

George Washington Cable was the first Confederate veteran in the

9. Fairfax Harrison to Earl G. Swen, March 26, 1917, to John Stewart Bryan, November 15, 1923, both in Harrison (ed.), *Letters of Fairfax Harrison*, 70–71, 97–98.

10. Historians and sociologists have devoted little attention to the twentieth-century emigration of white southerners to the North. Particularly mysterious is the period 1900–1920. See Jack Temple Kirby, "The Southern Exodus, 1910–1960: A Primer for Historians," *Journal of Southern History*, XLIX (1983), 585–600; Neil Fligstein, *Going North: Migration of Blacks and Whites from the South, 1900–1950* (New York, 1981), 69–70, 112.

North to understand the need for further change. Cable moved to Massachusetts in 1885, eighteen years after Louisiana-born Burton Harrison settled in New York. Those additional eighteen years on the Gulf Coast made Cable an authority on shifting tides. Cable moved north under a cloud, virtually hissed and booed out of his native New Orleans. Part of the uproar stemmed from his portrayals of Creole life in such novels as *The Grandissimes* and short stories collected in *Old Creole Days*. No less an authority than Creole historian Charles Gayarré accused Cable of being "completely ignorant" of Creole culture. But the real charge against Cable, and the real cause of Gayarré's accusation, had little to do with Creoles. Rather, it centered on Cable's statements about Negroes.[11]

In January, 1885, *Century Magazine* published Cable's essay "The Freedman's Case in Equity." This essay was nothing less than an attack on the white South for its treatment of the black South. Cable had not intended it as an attack. He had hoped only to arouse the South's conscience, to encourage white southerners to treat their black neighbors more kindly, more equitably. It was a sound, reasonable analysis of what had become known as the "negro problem." Cable carefully emphasized that he advocated not social integration but political and legal fairness. Still, most white southerners interpreted his remarks as a betrayal of his section and his people. His references to the South's "habit of oppression" in its treatment of the black race, his reminder that the South had relinquished slavery—an "extinct and . . . universally execrated institution" in "the rest of the civilized world"—only after a bloody civil war, angered whites.[12]

Printed criticism and verbal abuse rained down from all directions. No less a personage than Henry W. Grady, the very embodiment of the modern, advancing South, wrote the "official" southern response to Cable's blasphemy, published in *Century*'s April issue. Cable published his response to Grady's rejoinder in the September issue. Cable reiterated his loyalty to the South. He repeated his belief—stated in the original essay but ignored by most readers—that both North and South shared the blame of slavery and its resulting race problems. Yet he stood by his insistence that the white South must change its attitudes and behavior toward blacks. Cable denied that the criticism drove him

11. Arlin Turner, *George W. Cable: A Biography* (1956; rpr. Baton Rouge, 1966), 199–203.

12. *Ibid.*, 194–97, 214–16; George W. Cable, "The Freedman's Case in Equity," *Century Magazine*, XXIX (January, 1885), 409–18.

northward. He claimed to have moved to improve his wife's health, benefit his daughters' education, and place himself in closer proximity to northeastern publishers. Yet Cable had been hurt by the attacks on him in the southern press, and he would have been positively sick had he read some of the private comments. Paul H. Hayne called him a "mongrel cur."[13]

In 1889, Cable wrote but never published a brief intellectual autobiography entitled "My Politics" to justify his position. The essay explains not only Cable's rite of passage but the creed of many younger southerners who joined him in the North. Cable had opposed secession in 1861, but, being a devout advocate of "Slavery and a White Man's Government," he served the Stars and Bars faithfully through the war. He returned to New Orleans after the war and remained for some time an unreconstructed rebel. Soon, however, Cable began to study the doctrines he had fought to defend. He eventually declared secession an unreasonable doctrine, but slavery eluded fast and easy evaluation. Slavery "seemed" wrong, admitted Cable, yet he remained convinced for many years that blacks were unfit for freedom. More disturbing to him at first was the philosophy of the southern Democratic party. Its leaders seemed bent on restoring the old order of "rule by race and class." Cable sensed that this could never work; it seemed "hopelessly at variance with the national scheme." Yet Cable "shuddered" to think of the alternative: Republican rule. Consequently, he said nothing.[14]

Not until publication of *The Grandissimes* in 1879 did Cable make a public political statement. His friends disapproved of the novel, which mildly condemns slavery, southern indolence, and the closed southern mind. "But I did not intend to offend," Cable responded. "I wrote as near to truth and justice as I knew how, upon questions that I saw must be settled by calm debate . . . questions that will have to be settled thus by the southern white man in his own conscience before ever the north and south can finally settle it between them." Cable himself had not yet entirely come to grips with the "riddle" of the "Southern question," but his writings and speeches on racial issues became increasingly bold over the next five years. "The Freedman's Case in Equity" represents his final solution of the problem. Cable hoped that southerners would work "to

13. Turner, *George W. Cable,* 214–16; Lucy Leffingwell Cable Bikle, *George W. Cable: His Life and Letters* (New York, 1928), 122–23; Daniel Aaron, *The Unwritten War: American Writers and the Civil War* (New York, 1973), 272–73.

14. George W. Cable, "My Politics" (MS in George Washington Cable Papers, TU), 2–18.

establish true and lasting national peace, fellowship and wealth" on the basis of "equal justice and equal liberty to all the people."[15]

Cable considered himself a loyal southerner; he never publicly repented of his role in the war. Like many pre-1880 Confederate emigrants to the North, he spoke passionately about the need for sectional reconciliation and a New South; but Cable's vision of national harmony differed sharply from that of his predecessors. One cannot imagine Constance Harrison, or Sidney Lanier, or George Eggleston, or any other pre-1880 emigrant seeking reunion on the terms offered by Cable. Many of those earlier carpetbaggers condemned slavery after the war. Many of them believed the Negro deserved benevolent treatment; but none of them considered blacks worthy of full political or social rights. None of them ever admitted that slavery had anything to do with southern secession.

What was it Burton Harrison had read in Tennyson?

> You ask me, why, though ill at ease,
> Within this region I subsist,
> Whose spirits falter in their mist,
> And languish for the purple seas.
> It is the land that freemen till,
> That sober-suited Freedom chose,
> The land where girt with friends or foes
> A man may speak the thing he will.

Those lines had an entirely new, and much sadder, meaning for southerners like Cable. Burton Harrison's generation of Confederate carpetbaggers, with obvious irony, saw the North as a place where it might express itself, free from the restrictions of northern military and political rule in the South. Many post-1880 emigrants ran north to escape the censorship of their own people. Only after fleeing to abolitionist Massachusetts did Cable feel free to tell about the South, to explain it to northerners, and, he hoped, to convince southerners of the need for social change. Cable had come north to escape the South, "to escape the clutches of tradition." He, surely, traveled a new road northward.[16]

Cable was a rare bird, indeed, among the Confederate generation, but his views on the South and the war proved to be typical of younger

15. *Ibid.*, 23–25, 43; Fred Hobson, *Tell About the South: The Southern Rage to Explain* (Baton Rouge, 1983), 110–20.

16. Hobson, *Tell About the South*, 118–21; Alfred, Lord Tennyson, "On a Mourner," in *The Poems and Dramatic Works of Alfred, Lord Tennyson* (Boston, 1898), 60.

emigrants. Walter Hines Page, born in 1855, had been too young to participate in the war. His father, in any case, had been an antisecessionist Whig. After a brief northern residence in 1881–1883, Page went north to stay in 1885. Like Confederate Cable, southerner Page criticized the South because he loved it and wanted it to do right. Good sense proved to be the biggest difference between Page and Cable. Page waited until he arrived in New York before leveling his most severe criticisms at the South. Then, too, this future ambassador to the Court of St. James used more moderate language, with only occasional lapses, than the Louisianian. Arousing the South became an obsession with Cable. Page, by 1890, only occasionally expressed public embarrassment at southern antics. Page also avoided the issue of race; his main concern became the educational and economic backwardness of the white South. Compared to Cable, Page remained more expatriate than exile.[17]

That is not to discount Page once he warmed to his subject. His famous "Mummy letter," published in the Raleigh (N.C.) *State Chronicle* a year after his return to New York, marked Page as a man who saw things differently from the Confederate emigrants. The "mummies" he abused so mercilessly were southern reactionaries who opposed any new idea, any new solution, any social or economic innovation that had not been accepted before 1861. They were the old politicians, the Confederates, who had a vested interest in maintaining the old order. Page, no less than the old Confederate heroes, was dedicated to the South, but his South bore a later date of issue: April, 1865. He wanted a "new" South in every sense of the word: politically, educationally, economically, one might almost add emotionally.[18]

Page produced his most telling criticism of the South and, as one scholar has put it, the "clearest exploration of his identity as Southerner," in a semiautobiographical novel, *The Southerner: A Novel; Being the Autobiography of Nicholas Worth*. First published serially in the *Atlantic Monthly* in 1906, the book appeared, with some revision, in 1909. Page took aim, once again, at the Old Confederate leadership. Speaking as a southerner of the postwar generation, Page blamed the war generation for placing terrible economic and moral burdens on the

17. Hobson, *Tell About the South*, 157–64, 178–79; John Milton Cooper, Jr., *Walter Hines Page: The Southerner as American, 1855–1918* (Chapel Hill, 1977), 52–81.

18. Hobson, *Tell About the South*, 164–67; Cooper, *Walter Hines Page*, 77–79; Burton J. Hendrick, *The Training of an American: The Earlier Life and Letters of Walter H. Page, 1855–1913* (Boston, 1928), 29.

postwar South. The younger generation had been "disinherited," made to "suffer the consequences of both slavery and the war." This is what Fairfax Harrison, far more politely, had meant when he lamented southern access to the free congresses of the soul. The heaviest burden bequeathed by the war generation, asserted Page, was sectional consciousness. Left on his own, Page, speaking through Nicholas Worth, felt no sectional passion, certainly no sectional hatred or suspicion. "It is the community that will not let me lose it," Worth complains, "the present community, the past, and the shadows of the past, the whole combination of forces that we mean when we speak of 'The South.'" Sectional self-consciousness, he decided, had stifled southern creativity.[19]

One alternative for sensitive southerners was to go north, as did Page and Nicholas Worth. Both of them went north to escape the burden of being southerners in the South. Something of a reversion had occurred. Post-1880 emigrants, both fictional and real, sound like antebellum emigrants who claimed to be escaping the moral and economic lethargy of slavery. "Now a Southerner is a proper and proud thing to be," explains Worth, "but (here comes the sorrowful paradox) I cannot be the Southerner that I should like to be, because of the presence of this must-be 'Southerner'—this self-conscious 'Southerner' that is thrust upon one." A southerner living in the South had to conform to an established definition, an antebellum definition, of southernism. Only in the North could young men and women escape being Confederate southerners. "I was now at home at Harvard," confesses Worth; "free, too, as I had not before been. Could I ever be free in the South?"[20]

Page understood why the war generation behaved as it did. The war had provided Confederates with "the intensest experience" of their lives. "Thus it stopped the thought of most of them as an earthquake stops a clock. The fierce blow of battle paralyzed the mind. Their speech was in a vocabulary of war; their loyalties were loyalties, not to living ideas, but to old commanders and to distorted traditions." Again, the mummies. They were "dead men, most of them, moving among the living ghosts." Page sympathized with them, but he refused to be haunted by their specter. He honored the Confederate generation, but he pitied it more.

19. Hobson, *Tell About the South*, 171–78; Cooper, *Walter Hines Page*, 198–202; Walter Hines Page, *The Southerner: A Novel; Being the Autobiography of Nicholas Worth* (New York, 1909), 74–75, 389–90.

20. Page, *The Southerner*, 106, 389–90.

The Confederates had been noble and brave; they had stood by their convictions. But their convictions, like themselves, must be buried if the South was to live. They *must* be buried, insists Nicholas Worth, for "we did not become ourselves till they were buried, if indeed we are become ourselves yet." Without the bitterness of war to leaven their experience, Page's generation of southern emigrants blamed the South more often than the North for southern social, economic, and intellectual retardation. They turned against a generation that, as they interpreted southern history, had outlived its usefulness. Even if the war for southern independence had been a just war—and many of the younger generation still held it to be so—their parents had erred in not fully accepting the defeat of ideas, traditions, and principles that had sparked the uprising. The new breed of southern emigrant would honor the Confederate past only as the past, not as a living presence.[21]

Page joined Ellen Glasgow and preceded Thomas Wolfe, William Faulkner, Flannery O'Connor, and a host of other twentieth-century southern fiction writers in using images of exile and exodus, restlessness and wanderlust, isolation and alienation to symbolize escape from an economically stagnant and intellectually provincial South. Novelists of the war generation, including Constance Harrison, George Eggleston, Katherine Bonner, Maurice Thompson, and Virginius Dabney, had sent fictional southerners—usually Confederates—northward, too. So had northern contemporaries, like Henry Adams and Henry James. But nearly all pre-1890 fictional carpetbaggers went north to flee the effects of the war and the consequences of Yankee rule in the South. Rebellious Blythe Herndon, in *Like Unto Like*, may have been the only exception. " 'I cannot tell you how I long for life, movement, action,' " Blythe sighs. " 'I am so tired of this place!—the quiet streets, the hills and the streams, and the moss eternally waving. I want to get away from it all.' " Not Yankees but the dead South's want of opportunity and adventure threatened to chase Blythe away. Her lament reverberated as an echo of voices to come.[22]

" 'If you stay here long enough, the broomsedge claims you,' " warns one of Ellen Glasgow's characters seeking to escape the South's barren

21. *Ibid.*, 46–47.
22. Louis D. Rubin, Jr., *George W. Cable: The Life and Times of a Southern Heretic* (New York, 1969), 212–38; C. Vann Woodward, *The Burden of Southern History* (Baton Rouge, 1960), 109–40; Sherwood Bonner, *Like Unto Like: A Novel* (New York, 1878), 99.

ground; " 'there's failure in the air.' " " 'But there's no opportunity in a place like this,' " complains another of Glasgow's restless spirits. " 'All the young men are going away.' " Old people who had lived through the war and Reconstruction continued to blame the Yankees for this exodus. One of Faulkner's withered Mississippi matrons resents the desertion of bright young southerners to the North because, she claims, the " 'Northern people have already seen to it that there is little left in the South for a young man.' " But most fictional characters no longer held Yankees directly accountable for the South's miseries. "Even as a child," explains Thomas Wolfe, "George Webber realized that in a general way it was better to be more North than South." Webber leaves the South as a young man with an almost orgasmic thrill, "For he had dreamed and hungered for the proud unknown North with that wild ecstasy, that intolerable and wordless joy of longing and desire, which only a Southerner can feel." Wolfe insisted that "there in the dark South, there on the Piedmont, in the hills, there by the slow, dark rivers, there in coastal plains, something was always burning in their hearts at night—the image of the shining city at the North." Even when the shining city turned out to be a damp, lonely tenement, smelling of garbage and urine, twentieth-century fictional southerners preferred the excitement and stimulation of northern life. When one of Flannery O'Connor's characters visits her son's wretched New York apartment, she mutters in shocked disbelief, " 'You wouldn't live like this at home.' " "No!' " the son rejoins in ironic ecstasy, " 'it wouldn't be possible!' "[23]

Walter Hines Page first met Thomas Woodrow Wilson, another ardent young southerner wearied by southern veneration of the Old South, in 1882. By rights, Wilson, a year younger than Page, should have been more loyal to the Lost Cause. His father, although born in Ohio, had defended slavery and secession. Yet by 1880, as a law student at the University of Virginia, Wilson declared himself glad that the Confederacy had failed. By the 1890s, as the author of *Division and Reunion*, the first scholarly synthesis of the period between 1828 and 1876, Wilson could condemn secession as a "*morally* wrong" and specious doctrine. He considered himself part of a "younger generation of

23. Ellen Glasgow, *Barren Ground* (1902; rpr. New York, 1957), 88, *The Sheltered Life* (Garden City, N.Y., 1932), 294; William Faulkner, *Absalom, Absalom!* (1936; rpr. New York, 1972), 9–10; Thomas Wolfe, *Of Time and the River: A Legend of a Man's Hunger in His Youth* (1935; rpr. Garden City, N.Y., 1944), 23–24, *The Web and the Rock* (1937; rpr. Garden City, N.Y., 1940), 15, 246–47; Flannery O'Connor, "The Enduring Chill," in *Everything That Rises Must Converge* (New York, 1965), 89.

Southern men" eager to promote "agreement and harmony" between North and South. But Wilson did differ from earlier promoters of sectional reconciliation by criticizing the South's maudlin concern with the Lost Cause. He even disapproved of Confederate Decoration Day: "I think that anything that tends to revive or perpetuate the bitter memories of the war is wicked folly." Wilson believed that Confederate graves deserved to be "kept in order with all loving care" but condemned the attendant hoopla, parades, and sentimental speeches. Such demonstrations of Confederate fervor, he submitted, were "exceedingly unwise."[24]

Like many other southern gadflies, particularly those who criticized from the North, Wilson sometimes felt guilty about attacking his people and his section. He admitted on one occasion that an "intensely Southern" cousin made him feel uneasy and aroused in him "rather mixed feelings" about his southern identity. Had he been "Northernized," Wilson asked himself, by his association with Yankees? He shuddered to think so. He finally decided that his cousin's provincialism, rather than his "*Southern* traits," had caused the distress. Yet, in describing his emotional travail to Mrs. Wilson, he could not help but appeal to her: "Darling, *I love the South*—don't you believe that I do?" The Virginian, perhaps, doth protest too much. His loving wife, Ellen, reassured him. She called him the South's "*greatest* son" in his generation, "an American citizen—of Southern birth," "free from 'provincialisms' of *any* sort," free from all southern "prejudices."[25]

Ellen Wilson had put the case in a nutshell. Woodrow *was* largely free of southern provincialism and prejudice, but exactly here he became part of the new breed. The greatest southern prejudice for a generation had been the Lost Cause. By rejecting that, regardless of how often he ate corn bread, whistled "Dixie," or voted Democratic, Wilson would not be—could not be—part of the Confederate migration. He could criticize the Confederacy, pillory Jefferson Davis, question Robert E. Lee's tactics at Gettysburg, denounce slavery, even suggest that Confederate defeat, after all, may have been best for the nation. Many loyal Confederates had done as much. But Wilson lost his Confederate credentials

24. Arthur S. Link, *Wilson: The Road to the White House* (Princeton, 1947), 1–8; Arthur S. Link (ed.), *The Papers of Woodrow Wilson* (47 vols.; Princeton, 1966–84), II, 48, 64, VIII, 148, 205–207.

25. Arthur S. Link, "Woodrow Wilson: The American as Southerner," *Journal of Southern History,* XXXVI (1970), 3–17; Woodrow Wilson to Ellen Axson Wilson, May 16, 1886, Ellen Axson Wilson to Woodrow Wilson, May 22, 1886, both in Link (ed.), *Papers of Woodrow Wilson,* V, 232–33, 250–55.

once he rejected the notion of publicly honoring the Confederate dead and declared secession a legal impossibility and a moral wrong.

But if the younger generation remained confused and defensive, Confederates remained the sadder generation. Their children may have been denied the free congresses of the soul, but the parents often felt that their souls had been lost altogether. "Though my father seldom spoke of his younger days to me," revealed Francis Harrison, "and never in complaint, I know that he carried with him to the end his sorrow for the 'Lost Cause.'" Burton Harrison's melancholy eyes betrayed his sorrow. His brain functioned, his heart beat, but he, like Sidney Lanier and most other Confederate carpetbaggers, knew the difference between living and not dying.[26]

"The men of my father's race whom I remember," recalled Francis Harrison shortly after World War II, "were as unlike the New Yorkers and New Englanders of my day as, say, a Frenchman is from a German. My father was not sectional, his four years at Yale and the many Northern friends he made while there and held throughout his life, gave him a broad enough vision. He was simply different." So were they all, all those adventurous souls who moved north after the war. The amazing thing is that they did not consider themselves to be different. They did only what they thought needed to be done. Few Confederates moved north enthusiastically; most would have preferred to stay at home. Yet their decisions to settle in the North when they did showed them to be made of sterner stuff than both the antebellum southerners who preceded them and the new breed of southerner that followed. Whether all Confederate carpetbaggers were as nonsectional as Burton Harrison may be doubted. Probably not even Burton was as pure as his son supposed him to be. Few Confederate carpetbaggers ever forgot that once upon a time, in their fiery, impetuous youth, they had loved a cause enought to fight, bleed, and suffer for it. Most of them continued to bear a tender regard for a cause that, even if lost, even if better lost, had, after all, been their cause.[27]

Clarence Cary knew all about lost causes, but he had come to terms with his own. He regretted neither his years as a rebel nor his ultimate identity as one of his sister's Good Americans. He saw no contradiction between the two, and yet he recognized that Confederates were a breed apart—different from both their old Yankee foes and their southern

---

26. Harrison, "About It and About," 40a.
27. *Ibid.*, 40b.

descendants. Cary expressed his sense of pride and distinctiveness in a two-hundred-line poem entitled "Johnny Reb," composed for his comrades in the Confederate Veteran Camp of New York. The poem, meant to celebrate the eighty-ninth anniversary of Robert E. Lee's birth, in 1896, describes the course of the war in Virginia, the trials of combat, and the relief of the bivouac. It closes with thoughts similar to those that must have passed through the minds of most old Confederate veterans as they neared the end of life's campaign:

> Well-ole cumrads! soon a signal, will soun' out toe you, en me,
> Fur to strike our tents, below hyar, en onct mo' to camp with Lee.
> His ole sojers wont much worrit, 'bout whar 'tis, nur how, nur w'en,
> Knowin well, thet ole Marse Robbut gwine tek' c'yar o' all his men.
> . . . .
> Yes! yo' bet thet som' whar yander, up in goddlemitey's blue,
> Our Mass Bob waits at the picket, fur toe pass all we-uns thru.[28]

It was sentimental poetry for a sentimental occasion, military poetry for military men, Confederate poetry for a Confederate era. Other men in other times would be sentimental; military men would always have their place in the way of the world; but time was running out for the Confederates. Cary's children, like his sister's children, would not fully understand the feelings of his generation, particularly not the feelings of those who had been lured northward. They could not be expected to understand. Clarence Cary, in his spare time, liked to translate Latin poets, but perhaps his reading strayed occasionally to Tennyson. If so, he would be familiar with lines that Burton Harrison had known well:

> The days darken round me, and the years,
> Among new men, strange faces, other minds.[29]

---

28. Clarence Cary, "Johnny Reb" (Booklet in Wilson Miles Cary Collection, UV).
29. Tennyson, "The Passing of Arthur," in *Poems and Dramatic Works*, 449.

Appendix

TABLE 1 Characteristics of the Core Group*

Characteristic	Number
AGE AT ARRIVAL	
Under 20 years	52
20–25 years	152
26–30 years	104
31–35 years	61
36–40 years	68
41–45 years	41
46–50 years	19
51–55 years	12
56–60 years	12
61–65 years	5
Over 65 years	6
Unknown	39
Total	571
ANTEBELLUM EDUCATION	
Southern precollege	419
Southern college	186
Northern precollege	55
Northern college	75
Northern and southern schools	66
European study or travel	50
MARITAL STATUS AT ARRIVAL	
Single	283
Married	130
Married with children	90
Widowed or divorced	10
Widowed or divorced with children	19
Unknown	39
Total	571
NORTHERN ASSOCIATIONS	
Antebellum northern college	75
Antebellum northern residence	97
Friends or relatives in North	167
No northern associations	36

*Totals are not given for Antebellum Education and Northern Associations because many people fall into more than one category.

TABLE 2 Confederate Service

MILITARY SERVICE	NUMBER
Infantry	112
Cavalry	94
Artillery	28
Staff	27
Medical	22
Chaplain	5
Secret Service	4
Engineer	2
Navy	2
Unknown	77
Total	373
MILITARY RANK	
Enlisted	113
Officers below major	59
Officers above captain	80
Physicians	22
Chaplains	5
Unknown	94
Total	373
NONMILITARY SERVICE	
Civilian	178
Government	20
Total	198

TABLE 3   Sources of Emigration

Place	Parents' Birth	Carpetbaggers' Birth	Point of Departure
Alabama	14	43	47
Arkansas	0	6	20
Florida	1	2	3
Georgia	26	33	43
Kentucky	42	56	67
Louisiana	5	11	33
Maryland	21	24	20
Mississippi	8	21	22
Missouri	1	9	25
North Carolina	44	40	32
South Carolina	41	43	36
Tennessee	44	62	68
Texas	0	0	7
Virginia	133	136	134
North or D.C.	84	60	0
Outside U.S.	41	19	1
Unknown	637	6	13
Total	1,142	571	571

TABLE 4   Destinations in North*

PLACE	NUMBER
New York	322
Illinois	164
Indiana	82
Ohio	75
Pennsylvania	68
Massachusetts	21
Iowa	19
New Jersey	14
Michigan	8
Delaware	6
Connecticut	3
Minnesota	2
New Hampshire	1
Wisconsin	1
YEAR OF ARRIVAL	
1861–1864	24
1865–1866	240
1867–1868	99
1869–1870	69
1871–1872	26
1873–1874	30
1875–1876	27
1877–1878	21
1879–1880	24
Unknown	11
Total	571
LENGTH OF NORTHERN RESIDENCE	
1 year or less	36
2 years	36
3 years	12
4 years	16
5–10 years	38
11–15 years	16
16–20 years	9
21–25 years	7
Over 25 years	21
Remainder of life	360
Unknown	20
Total	571

*The number of places selected as northern destinations exceeds the number in the core group because many people lived in more than one place, and the first place they arrived was not always the place where they stayed the longest.

TABLE 5   Principal Occupations

	Before War	In North
CARPETBAGGERS' OCCUPATIONS		
Merchant/businessman	65	93
Physician	37	71
Farmer/planter	63	66
Journalist/literary person	37	58
Lawyer/jurist	28	48
Banker/financier	6	31
Student	179	29
Artist	16	21
Clergyman	12	19
Wife/mother	15	16
Educator	20	14
Bookkeeper/clerk	10	12
Manufacturer or representative	0	10
Real estate/insurance	3	10
Railroad official	0	9
Salesman	0	8
Civil engineer	4	3
Actor/actress	0	3
Miscellaneous white collar	17	18
Miscellaneous craftsman	19	11
Miscellaneous manual labor	6	1
None	0	11
Unknown	34	9
Total	571	571
FATHERS' OCCUPATIONS		
Farmer	105	
Planter	79	
Merchant/businessman	58	
Physician	32	
Clergyman	20	
Lawyer/jurist	17	
Journalist/literary person	9	
Public official	6	
Educator	5	
Military	5	
Banker/financier	3	
Artist	3	
Miscellaneous craftsman	18	
Miscellaneous white collar	6	
Unknown	205	
Total	571	

Bibliographical Note

This book's footnotes serve as its most comprehensive guide to sources. I will add here only a few remarks about the value of certain sources and a complete alphabetical listing of manuscript collections.

My reading in secondary literature on the Civil War, Reconstruction, migration theory, art, economics, finance, transportation, medicine, politics, American and southern literature, Confederate emigration abroad, and a dozen other topics was extensive. But because biography is the bedrock of the Confederate carpetbagger story, I found the most important secondary sources to be biographies of individuals. A surprising number of carpetbaggers have merited their own biographies, either in the form of books or of magazine and journal articles. I consulted some eighty such biographies.

Equally important were the hundreds of biographical sketches, varying in length from a paragraph to several pages, appearing in a variety of biographical directories, dictionaries, and encyclopedias. Formal entries by historians and biographers in standard national biographical reference works such as the *Dictionary of American Biography* proved helpful, as did numerous professional encyclopedias for groups such as doctors, lawyers, and authors. Regional, state, county, and city histories and biographical directories, most of them published between 1875 and 1910, were even more useful, primarily because the information they contain usually came from the subjects themselves and because the subjects are frequently ordinary folk otherwise unknown to history. I concentrated my reading of local histories on the principal northern towns and cities (New York, Chicago, Philadelphia, Boston, Cincinnati, Indianapolis, Pittsburgh, Columbus, and Evansville) and on the states of Illinois, Indiana, Iowa, Ohio, and Pennsylvania. The most important repositories for the histories of these cities and states are the Illinois State Historical Library, Indiana State Library, Iowa State Historical Library, Ohio Historical Society, and Pennsylvania State Library. Finally, obituaries in local newspapers and serial publications such as the *Confederate Veteran* provided valuable, if sometimes limited, information about otherwise obscure people. As mentioned in my Acknowledgments, information provided by descendants of Confederate carpetbaggers via correspondence, telephone conversations, and personal interviews shed light on the lives of their kin.

Most valuable of all were the many forms of autobiographical information, particularly as found in personal and business correspondence, diaries, memoirs, and reminiscences. These included both manuscript and printed sources, although I used manuscripts more extensively. These firsthand testimonials include the reflections of both Confederate carpetbaggers and the people who knew them, both southern friends and the northerners among whom they settled. I also found the fiction, poetry, and nonfiction of Confederate carpetbaggers enlightening. The fiction and poetry must be used with particular care; yet so many novels, short stories, and poems contain verifiable autobiographical elements that it would be foolish to ignore them. Even if not telling us anything about the personal experiences of the writer, these works frequently provide a sense of the time and insights into the mind of the Confederate carpetbagger.

Listed below are the manuscript collections I found most useful. The depositories are designated by the same abbreviations used in the footnotes. Collections preceded by an asterisk contain correspondence, diaries, and memoirs written by Confederate carpetbaggers. One collection, the Civil War Veterans Questionnaires, has recently been published in Gustavus W. Dyer and John Trotwood Moore (comps.), *The Tennessee Civil War Veterans Questionnaires,* ed. Colleen Morse Elliott and Louise Armstrong Moxley (5 vols.; Easley, S.C., 1985).

* Adger-Smyth-Flynn Family Papers, SCL
Thomas Affleck Papers, LSU
* Edwin A. Alderman Papers, UV
* James Blythe Anderson Papers, UK
* Anderson Family Papers, UV
Archer Family Letters, MHS

William G. Armstrong Diaries, HSP
Arnold and Appleton Family Papers, SHC
Arnold and Screven Family Papers, SHC
Alfred Austell Correspondence, AHS

* Bagby Family Papers, VHS
John Lancaster Bailey Papers,
    SHC
William Pitt Ballinger Papers, UT
Barnsley Family Papers, TL
Robert Battey Papers, EU
Battle Family Papers, SHC
Thomas F. Bayard Papers, LC
Alva (Smith) Vanderbilt Belmont
    Scrapbook, AA
* Eleanor Robson Belmont Papers,
    CU
Judah Philip Benjamin
    Collection, LC
Park Benjamin Papers, CU
Milledge Luke Bonham Papers,
    SCL
* Alexander Robinson Boteler
    Papers, DU
* Breckinridge Family Papers, LC
* William Phineas Browne Papers,
    AA
* Thomas Barbour Bryan
    Collection, CHS
Bryan Family Papers, VL
* Bryant-Godwin Collection,
    NYPL
William C. Buck Family Letters,
    LSU
* Armistead Burt Correspondence,
    DU
* Benjamin F. Butler Papers, LC
George Washington Cable
    Manuscripts, CU
George Washington Cable
    Papers, CU
George Washington Cable
    Papers, TU
* Cadwalder Collection–Judge
    John Cadwalder
    Correspondence, HSP

* Cadwalder Collection–J. Francis
    Fisher Section, HSP
Cadwalder Collection–McCall
    Correspondence, HSP
Eli J. Capell Papers, LSU
* Isaac Howell Carrington Papers,
    DU
* Cora Watson Carey Papers, MSA
Anna Ella Carroll Papers, MHS
* Wilson Miles Cary Collection,
    UV
* Chamberlayne Family Papers,
    VHS
* Conrad Wise Chapman Papers,
    VHS
* Conrad Wise Chapman Papers,
    VM
* Esther B. Cheesborough Letter,
    SCL
* Esther B. Cheesborough
    Manuscripts, SCL
John Cheesborough Papers, SHC
* Cheves-Middleton Papers, SCHS
Christian County Folder, FC
* William Conant Church Papers,
    NYPL
Civil War Papers, MOHS
* Civil War Veterans
    Questionnaires, TL
* Henry Whitney Cleveland
    Papers, NYHS
Clubs and Societies Papers,
    MOHS
* Howell Cobb Papers, UG
* Colston Family Papers, CS
* Raleigh Edward Colston Papers,
    SHC
* Mary E. Compton and Family
    Papers, LSU
Confederate Miscellany, EU
John Esten Cooke Papers, DU

Francis P. Corbin Papers, NYPL
Crutchfield-Fearn-Steele Papers,
  MSA
* Telamon Cuyler Collection, UG
* Richard Heath Dabney Papers,
  UV
Mary (Brand) Dall Papers, DU
* James Wood Davidson Letters,
  SCL
Jefferson Davis Papers, AA
* Mary Roselle Davis Diary, UT
Robert Means Davis Papers, SCL
* James D. B. DeBow Papers, DU
* James D. B. DeBow Papers, UT
* Charles Force Manning Deems
  Papers, DU
* Felix G. DeFontaine Letter, SCL
* Edwin DeLeon Papers, SCL
* Thomas Cooper DeLeon Papers,
  SCL
* DeRosset Family Papers, SHC
* DeRosset Family Papers, II, SHC
* Jeannie A. Dickson
  Correspondence, DU
John S. Dobbins Papers, EU
John W. DuBose Papers, AA
Stephan Duncan
  Correspondence, LSU
Jubal A. Early Papers, LC
George Bibb Edmondson
  Papers–Porter Family
  Correspondence, AA
* Presley Judson Edward
  Autobiography, CHS
* Edward Eggleston Papers, ISL
* George Cary Eggleston
  Correspondence, ISL
* Ellis Family Papers, VHS
* James Taylor Ellyson Papers, UV
John Williams Elwood Papers,
  EU

Benjamin Holland Epperson
  Papers, UT
* Moses Jacob Ezekiel Memoirs,
  AAA
* Charles S. Fairchild Papers,
  NYHS
* Fergusson Family Papers, TL
* William Hawkins Ferris Papers,
  CU
Joshua Francis Fisher Papers,
  HSP
Sidney George Fisher Collection,
  HSP
* Henry Delaware Flood Papers,
  LC
Fordyce Collection, MOHS
* Sydney Howard Gay Papers, CU
Robert Wilson Gibbes, Jr.,
  Letter, SCL
Ellen Shackelford Gift Papers,
  SHC
Glasgow Family Papers, MOHS
* Glenn Family Papers, MHS
* Gordon Family Papers, GHS
* Gordon Family Papers, SHC
* Armistead C. Gordon Papers,
  VHS
Robert Newman Gourdin
  Papers, EU
* Graves Family Papers, SHC
Charles Iverson Graves Papers,
  SHC
* Horace Greeley Papers, LC
Horace Greeley Papers, NYPL
Green Collection, WK
Edwin Luther Green Papers, SCL
* Gregorie and Elliott Family
  Papers, SHC
Grigsby Family Papers, FC
* Grimball Family Papers, SCHS
* Grimball Family Papers, SHC

*John Grimball Papers, SCL
John Berkley Grimball Diaries, SHC
*John Berkley Grimball Papers, DU
*John Berkley Grimball Papers, SCL
Gunter and Poellnitz Family Papers, SHC
*Edward Jones Hale Papers, NCA
*Edward Joseph Hale Papers, SHC
Hall-Stakely Family Papers, KPL
James Pinkney Hambleton Papers, EU
*Hammond, Bryan, and Cumming Families Papers, SCL
Hampton Family Papers, SCL
Harrison Family Papers, UV
*Harrison Family Papers— Additional, UV
*Burton Norvell Harrison Family Papers, LC
Francis Burton Harrison Papers, UV
*Robert Lewis Harrison Papers, UV
*Harrold Brothers Papers, EU
Frances Harvey Papers, UT
*Francis Lester Hawks Papers, SHC
Barrie Hayne, "Confederate Exiles in Canada West, 1865– 1868" (Typescript), VHS
*Paul Hamilton Hayne Papers, DU
William J. Hinchey Diary, MOHS
Thomas H. Hines Papers, UK
*James Ripley Wellman Hitchcock Papers, CU

Hobson Family Papers, VHS
*Frederick William Mackey Holliday Papers, DU
Humphrey H. Hood Correspondence, IHL
Hunt-Morgan Family Papers, UK
Eliza Horn Diary, UF
James V. Hutton, "The Barefoot Boy of Apple Pie Ridge: Life of Charles Broadway Rouss" (MS), VHS
*John Daniel Imboden Papers, UV
Inman Biographical and Genealogical Folders, AHS
Arthur C. Inman Notebooks, AHS
James Family Papers, OHS
*Jay Family Papers, CU
Jeffrey Family Papers, UK
D. Jennings and Company Papers, SCHS
Jones Family Papers, GHS
*Charles Colcock Jones, Jr., Collection, UG
*Charles Colcock Jones, Jr., Papers, DU
*Thomas Jordan Papers, DU
Kane and Hand Family Papers, CU
*Keeler Collection, HL
Ellison Summerfield Keitt Papers, SCL
John McIntosh Kell Papers, DU
Julia Louisa (Hentz) Keyes Diary, AA
Joseph Buckner Killebrew Papers, TL
*Thomas Butler King Papers, SHC
*King-Wilder Papers, GHS
Kollock Family Papers, EU
Kollock Family Papers, GHS

* Gazaway Bugg Lamar Papers, UG
* William Carr Lane Papers, MOHS

Alice and Rita Lawrence Papers, CU

Lawrence Family Papers, TL
* Robert E. Lee Papers, VHS

Burwell B. Lewis Papers, DU

Liddell Family Papers, LSU
* Little-Mordecai Collection, NCA
* William Wing Loring Papers, UF
* Seth Low Papers, CU

Lowe Family Papers, MHS
* William Gordon McCabe Papers, UV
* William H. McCardle Papers, MSA
* McClung Family Papers, KPL
* McCue Family Papers, UV
* Charles McClung McGhee Papers, KPL

Robert McKee Papers, AA
* William B. McKoy Papers, SHC

Fitz William McMaster and Mary Jane Macfie Papers, SCL

William B. McPheeters Papers, MOHS

William H. McRaven Papers, TL
* William Mahone Papers, DU
* Peter Mallett Papers, SHC
* Henry D. Mandeville and Family Papers, LSU
* Matthew Fontaine Maury Papers, LC
* Meares and DeRosset Family Papers, SHC
* Medical Papers, MOHS
* Middleton Family Papers, SCL
* William Middleton Papers, SCL

* Nathaniel Russell Middleton Collection, SCHS

William Porcher Miles Papers, SHC

Thomas Overton Moore Papers, LSU
* James Marsh Morey Papers, TL

James Herbert Morse Diaries, NYHS
* Mullanphy Family Collection, MOHS
* Munford-Ellis Family Papers, DU

Charles Torrence Nesbitt Papers, DU

Robert Loftin Newman Papers, TL

New York and Texas Land Company Papers, UT

James Nicholson Papers, UT
* Meredith Nicholson Papers, ISL

Northcott Collection, WK
* William Rudolf O'Donovan Correspondence, HSP

William O'Driscoll Papers, GHS
* Thomas Nelson Page Papers, DU

Palmes Papers, GHS
* William J. Pattison Papers, SHC

Sarah P. Payne Correspondence, VHS
* Pemberton Family Papers, HSP
* John C. Pemberton Papers, MSA

W. N. Pendleton Correspondence, NYHS

John Perkins Papers, SHC

Preston Family Papers–Davie Collection, FC

Preston Family Papers–Joyes Collection, FC
* Roger Atkinson Pryor Papers, DU

W. W. Pugh and Family Papers,
LSU
* Pulitzer Papers, CU
* William Greene Raoul Papers,
EU
Henry Hunter Raymond Papers,
SCL
Manley A. Raymond Family
Papers, EU
Keith Read Collection–Gourdin
and Young Papers, GHS
* Henry Lee Reynolds Papers, SHC
Thomas C. Reynolds Papers,
MOHS
* Henry Hobson Richardson
Papers, AAA
* Papers of Henry Hobson
Richardson, AAA
* Ridley Family Papers, VHS
* William James Rivers Papers,
SCL
Rives Family Papers, UV
* Rouss Collection, WHS
* Charles Broadway Rouss Papers,
NYHS
* Papers of George N. Sanders, LC
William Rutherford Savage
Papers, SHC
Robert K. Scott Papers, OHS
Henry Churchill Semple Papers,
AA
* Edward Morse Shepard Papers,
CU
* William Ludwell Sheppard
Diaries, VL
James Marion Sims Papers, AA
Slack Family Papers, SHC
Francis Hopkinson Smith
Collection, MHS
* Thomas L. Snead Papers, MOHS

* John F. Snyder Papers, IHL
* John F. Snyder Papers, MOHS
Henderson Middleton Somerville
Papers, AA
Southern Famine Relief
Commission Papers, NYHS
* James Southgate
Correspondence, DU
* Cornelia Phillips Spencer Papers,
NCA
* Cornelia Phillips Spencer Papers,
SHC
* Ephraim George Squier Papers,
LC
* Edmund Clarence Stedman
Papers, CU
* Stephens Collection, UF
Alexander H. Stephens Papers,
DU
Alexander H. Stephens Papers,
EU
Walter B. Stevens Scrapbooks,
MOHS
* Stuart Family Papers, VHS
* James Reeve Stuart
Autobiography, HSW
Oscar J. E. Stuart and Family
Papers, MSA
* David Lowry Swain Papers,
SHC
Miles Taylor and Family Papers,
LSU
Edward Smith Tennent Papers,
SCL
Tennessee Society in New York
Papers, TL
Lewis Texada and Family Papers,
LSU
Alfred Wordsworth Thompson
Papers, NYHS

* John Reuben Thompson Papers, UV
* James Maurice Thompson Letters, HU
* James Maurice Thompson Letters, VU
* James Maurice Thompson Letters, YU
* James Maurice Thompson Papers, EU
* James Maurice Thompson Papers, ISL
* James Maurice Thompson Papers, NYPL
* Daniel Augustus Tompkins Papers, DU
* Daniel Augustus Tompkins Papers, SHC
Robert Augustus Toombs Letter, UG
* John Allen Trimble Family Papers, OHS
United Confederate Veterans Association Records, LSU
* Zebulon B. Vance Papers, NCA
* Arnold Vander Horst Papers, SCHS

* Thomas S. Waring Papers, SCL
* Henry Watson, Jr., Papers, DU
David Weeks and Family Papers, LSU
* Susan Archer Talley Weiss Correspondence, VM
Edward Clifton Wharton and Family Papers, LSU
Katherine Johnstone (Brinley) Wharton Papers, HSP
* Joseph G. Wheeler Papers, AA
* Whitner Family Papers, SCL
Louis T. Wigfall Papers, UT
Wildman Family Papers, OHS
Micajah Wilkinson Papers, LSU
* John Skelton Williams Papers, UV
Williams-Chesnut-Manning Family Papers, SCL
* Michael Leonard Woods Papers, AA
Josepha Wright Papers, UT
Wynne Family Papers, TL
Yeatman-Polk Collection, TL
* Maltilda Young Papers, DU

Index